WEiRD U.S.

WEiRD U.S.

Your Travel Guide to America's Local Legends and Best Kept Secrets

MARK MORAN

MARK SCEURMAN

STERLING

New York / London
www.sterlingpublishing.com

WEiRD U.S.

STERLING and the distinctive Sterling logo are registered trademarks of Sterling Publishing Co., Inc.

Library of Congress Cataloging-in-Publication Data Available

10 9 8 7 6 5 4

Published by Sterling Publishing Co., Inc.
387 Park Avenue South, New York, NY 10016
© 2005 Mark Sceurman and Mark Moran
Distributed in Canada by Sterling Publishing
c/o Canadian Manda Group, 165 Dufferin Street,
Toronto, Ontario, Canada M6K 3H6
Distributed in the United Kingdom by GMC Distribution Services,
Castle Place, 166 High Street, Lewes, East Sussex, England BN7 1XU
Distributed in Australia by Capricorn Link (Australia) Pty. Ltd.
P.O. Box 704, Windsor, NSW 2756, Australia

Printed in China

Sterling ISBN 978-0-7607-5043-8 (hardcover)

Sterling ISBN 978-1-4027-6688-6 (paperback)

Photography and illustration credits are found on page 351 and constitute an extension of this copyright page.

For information about custom editions, special sales, premium and corporate purchases, please contact Sterling Special Sales Department at 800-805-5489 or specialsales@sterlingpublishing.com.

Design: Richard J. Berenson
 Berenson Design & Books, LLC, New York, NY

Weird U.S. is intended as entertainment to present a historical record of local legends, folklore, and sites throughout the United States. Many of these legends and stories cannot be independently confirmed or corroborated and the authors and publisher make no representation as to their factual accuracy. The reader should be advised that many of the sites described in *Weird U.S.* are located on private property and such sites should not be visited or you may face prosecution for trespassing.

Contents

DEDICATION

This book would not have been possible without the invaluable assistance of a great team of collaborators and cohorts who helped us bring it all together. We'd like to thank our co-authors Troy Taylor and Chris Gethard, editor Matt Lake, art director Richard Berenson, and publisher Barbara Morgan for their generous contributions. Our greatest appreciation also goes out to all the writers, artists, and photographers whose work is featured within these pages. And to the thousands of folks who have written to us over the years, sharing a story or lead, or just offering us encouragement in our quest, we thank you most of all. Yours is the voice of America's modern folklore, which we have sought to document in this work. Whether your story is featured in this book or not, we're glad you all came along on our weird ride!

Last but not least, we'd like to dedicate this book to our families and friends, whose infinite patience with this all-consuming hobby of ours has allowed us to explore so many roads less traveled for so long now.
–Mark and Mark

Introduction

t all started a long, long time ago in a land called New Jersey. Once a year or so we'd compile a homespun newsletter, called *Weird N. J.,* to hand out to our friends. The pamphlet was a collection of odd news clippings, bizarre facts, little-known historical anecdotes, and anomalous encounters from our home state. The newsletter also focused on the kind of localized legends that were often whispered around a particular town but seldom heard outside the boundaries of the community where they first originated.

Something about *Weird N. J.* seemed to strike a nerve with the folks of the Garden State. Our little "zine" was getting passed around and finding its way into the hands of people we had never even met. And then a funny thing happened: All the people that read it seemed to have their own weird tale to tell and wanted to share it with us! So with each new issue of the newsletter, we'd publish stories by our readers, incredible firsthand tales of cursed roads and ghostly visitations. By and large these stories had never before been documented in print— or anywhere else for that matter.

By the seventh issue of *Weird N. J.* we started to realize that our little hobby had taken on a life of its own, and there seemed to be no end in sight to the amount of material that was out there waiting to be uncovered. We had started the pub-

lication with the simple theory that every town in the state had at least one good tale to tell. We were beginning to find out that this was a gross underestimation. Great stories were flowing into our post office box daily from all over the state—places we'd never even heard of! The more that *Weird N. J.* got passed around, the more these never before heard tales would come in from all corners of the state.

By the eighth issue of what was now becoming a full-fledged magazine, we had made the decision to actually do our own investigating and see if we couldn't discover where all these seemingly unbelievable stories were coming from. Was there, we wondered, any factual basis for these fantastic local legends that people were telling us? Armed with not much more than a camera and notepad, we set off on a mystical journey of discovery. Much to our surprise and amazement a lot of what we had initially presumed to be just urban legend turned out to be real, or at least contained a grain of truth.

Reporting about unique and mysterious sites and people, such as reclusive colonies of albinos and evil cult sacrifices in the woods, soon became an all-consuming preoccupation for us. So much so that after about a dozen years of doing it, we were asked to write a book about our adventures. After *Weird N. J.:*

Your Travel Guide to New Jersey's Local Legends and Best Kept Secrets was published in 2003, another funny thing happened—people from all over the country began writing to us, telling us strange tales from their home states. As it turns out, what we had first perceived to be a very local interest genre was actually just a small part of a much larger phenomenon. People throughout the United States had strange tales to tell. They believed them to be true, and they wanted somebody to tell them to. That's how *Weird U. S.* came to be.

So how do we decipher fact from fiction? How do

we separate the history from the mystery? We don't. What we do is listen to what people tell us is weird about their own hometown. We collect these stories and try, wherever possible, to corroborate these seemingly fantastic tales with actual events and historical data. Sometimes we are successful and manage to uncover a little-known tidbit of historical validity, and sometimes we don't. If we find that a local legend is patently untrue, do we refrain from publishing it? Absolutely NOT—not if it's a great story!

So how will you, the reader, know which stories are real and which are imagined and where to draw the line between fact and fantasy? That's all up to you. We merely present these local legends in the most unadulterated form possible. We document them because we believe that they are an important and intrinsic part of our modern American culture and worthy of recognition as such. One thing we will tell you, though: None of the stories in this book are fiction—some might not be completely true, but none were made up solely for the purpose of entertainment.

All the tales contained here reflect actual people or events, or recount an existing legend of a site-specific nature. What does this mean to you? It means that you can actually GO there and see for yourself where these stories took place and, in some cases, are still taking place! That is the most important distinction between *Weird U. S.* and your run-of-the-mill collection of tired old urban legends—this book is a travel guide! Now, having said that, we must point out that just because you can go to all the places featured in these pages, that doesn't necessarily mean that you should. Some of the sites are located on private property, and we do not in any way recommend or condone trespassing or breaking any laws to visit them. Please leave that up to

us—we're professionals. Other sites, such as abandoned buildings, can be extremely dangerous and are probably better left to the imagination. For this reason we often refer to our journal as a "travel guide of the mind." We present many of the sites featured here not as destinations to be explored, but rather as the catalysts of local mythology.

With that in mind we now present for your consideration this collection of the shared repartee that makes up the *Weird U.S.* voice. One can only imagine the countless tales out there across the country yet to be told. Even after years of traveling, we know that we've only just begun to scratch the surface. In this respect *Weird U. S.* is a lot like life; it's the journey itself, not the destination that is really important. So come take a ride with us now as we hit the roads less traveled throughout America to see just what a weird, weird place it really is.—*Mark and Mark*

SHOW US YOUR WEIRD!

Do you know of a weird site found somewhere in the United States, or can you tell us about a strange experience you've had? If so, we'd like to hear about it! We believe that every town has at least one great tale to tell, and we're listening. It could be a cursed road, haunted abandoned site, odd local character, or bizarre historic event. In most cases these tales are told only in the towns in which they originated. But why keep them to yourself when you could share them with all of America? So come on and fill us in on all the weirdness that's lurking in your backyard!

You can e-mail us at: Editor@WeirdUS.com, or write to us at:
Weird U.S., P.O. Box 1346, Bloomfield, NJ 07003.
www.weirdus.com

Local Legends
Tales of Suburban Youth

*"The myth comes from the imagination, and it leads back to it.
The society teaches you what the myths are, and then it disengages you so
that in your meditations you can follow the path right in."*
—Joseph Campbell, *The Power of Myth*

There are *sites* throughout the U.S. that attain legendary status, even though the location consists of nothing more than an old railroad bridge or a fallow patch of earth. The stories that have grown out of these humble landmarks, though, are the stuff of nightmares. Are these stories merely the products of overactive imaginations, or is there more to it than that?

Whether they like to admit it or not, people need mythology in their lives. Most folks still want to believe that somewhere there are still places of mystery and wonder, even in our technologically advanced society. Sites such as the Devil's Tramping Ground and Crybaby Bridge are the physical manifestations of our own mythological nature. They are like springboards for our collective unconscious and serve to fuel the dark side of our imagination. Most people just love a good scary story, and visiting a location associated with the fable simply adds to the thrill.

It is said that most legends have their basis in fact. Sometimes it is possible to uncover the historical origins of these terrifying tales; in other instances it is a little less clear how the story came to be. What's really important, though, is the unique and site-specific nature of these legends.

Almost everyone has heard of urban legends. Tellers of these tall tales claim the events happened to a friend of a friend or swear that they heard the story from a legitimate news source. Unbeknownst to them, year after year, hundreds of well-documented, tried-and-untrue urban legends circulate around the country with only slight variations. The primary differences are the location where the incident supposedly took place and the names of the principal characters involved.

We often see examples of these urban legends incorporated into the local tales that we document, as in the case of the many Crybaby Bridges found throughout the country. But most of these legends are very site-specific and unique to a particular location. For example, there is just one Bunnyman Bridge, and it can be found only in Virginia.

Folktales have always been passed down to us as part of an oral tradition, and these local legends are no different. This is the modern folklore of our nation, the kind that you will not find mentioned in your town's public library. But how do these dark and disturbing legends start, and why do they continue to be told from one generation to the next? The answer might lie in the need for people to prove themselves to their peer group and to themselves.

Every culture has its own rites of passage for its young adults. Some primitive tribes practice scarification, circumcision, or even knock out the teeth of their young. Joseph Campbell, a preeminent scholar of mythology said, "The rituals of primitive initiation ceremonies are all mythologically grounded and have to do with killing the infantile ego and bringing forth an adult." After undergoing the ordeal, the young man or woman is changed forever and emerges as a full-fledged member of the tribe, ready to take his or her place in the society.

In modern Western culture we have, for the most part, done away with such painful and traumatic practices, marking the passage into adulthood with the more genteel (though sometimes still harrowing) traditions of bar mitzvahs and confirmation ceremonies. But are these rituals really enough to usher in manhood and womanhood? Sometimes it takes a little more than facing a banquet hall full of your relatives to test one's mettle. Sometimes a late-night ride to come face-to-face with the devil himself is what is really needed to separate the men from the boys.

The Damned Village of Dudleytown

Can a family be so cursed that they carry their dark fortunes across an ocean to an entirely different continent? And can the place they settle in absorb so much of their bad blood that it forever affects the fates of those who live there—even when they flee the place forever? Some swear that this can happen—and that such a place actually exists.

In the woods of northwestern Connecticut there lies a remote community where unexplained orbs of light swirl around in the dark forest, where residents go mad or succumb to violent and unnatural deaths, and where even the local wildlife dares not go. This is the story of Dudleytown—Village of the Damned.

Dudleytown—A Real New England Ghost Town

The remains of Dudleytown, a small hamlet filled with ghostly tales, demons, unexplained events, and curses can be found in the otherwise picturesque town of Cornwall, Connecticut.

Today the Dudleytown area looks much like it did when it was first settled 250 years ago—a very thick forest and incredibly rocky terrain in the shadow of three mountains: Bald Mountain, Woodbury Mountain, and the Coltsfoot Triplets. The dense tall forest, which was given the ominous name of Dark Entry Forest, and the shadows of the mountains ensured that the village received little sunlight.

All that remains of the hamlet that once stood there are cellar holes and a few foundations. The roads have become forest trails. Many people claim that the woods are strangely silent—the birds and bugs that sing and call during a hike up to Dudleytown don't follow into the village.

The Curse

The legend of the Dudleytown curse begins in England in the year 1510, when King Henry VIII ordered Edmund Dudley to be beheaded. The legend goes that at the time of the beheading, all of Dudley's descendants were cursed for his crimes. And one of those descendants was William Dudley, born on June 8, 1639, aboard a ship headed for America. William's son, Joseph, was born in Saybrook, Connecticut, on September 14, 1674.

In 1745 a man named Thomas Griffis settled in the area that eventually was named Dudleytown. In 1748 Gideon Dudley bought some land from Griffis to start a small farm. By 1753 Gideon's two brothers, Barzillai and Abiel had also purchased land nearby. The three Dudley brothers gave the place its name—and its curse.

The noted demonologist, author, and ghost hunter Ed Warren picks up the story.

"The curse in Dudleytown started after the village became a thriving town. People went mad and reported seeing monstrosities in the forest—things that were unnatural. Everyone left the town."

The Troubles Begin

By 1759 Abiel Dudley, old "Biel," had lost his mind and become a ward of the village. Nathaniel Carter bought

Dudley's house, but within four years he abandoned the hard living in Dudleytown and took his wife and four of his children to nearby Binghamton, New York. Shortly after settling in their new home, the Carters were attacked by Indians. Mr. and Mrs. Carter were tomahawked, and their infant was smashed against the wall. Their cabin was burned, and the Indians took the rest of the Carter children, Sarah, Elizabeth, and Nathaniel junior, hostage and brought them to Canada. There, the daughters would be ransomed to the British army — a common practice and lucrative business for the Indians at the time.

The rest of the Carters of Dudleytown — Nathaniel's brother Adoniram and his family — were struck by a cholera epidemic in August of 1774 that wiped out the entire family.

One of Cornwall's most famous residents, General Heman Swift, who served under George Washington in the Revolutionary War, also suffered a tragedy at Dudleytown. In April of 1804 his wife, Sarah Faye, was struck by lightning on their front porch and killed instantly. Shortly after his wife's death General Swift was reported to have become "slightly demented."

Over the next hundred years Dudleytown's population dwindled. Children who grew up there married and moved away. In 1901 tragedy struck one of its last residents, John Patrick Brophy. Brophy's wife died of consumption, and shortly afterward his two children mysteriously disappeared in the woods, possibly on the lam because they had been stealing sleigh robes in the area. They were never heard from again. Then Brophy's home burned to the ground, perhaps at his own hand, distraught as he was over the loss of his wife and the disgrace of his children. Brophy walked away from Dudleytown, never to be seen again.

Soon Dudleytown was deserted. The forest continued to reclaim the land, but not for long.

Dudleytown Is Reborn

In 1903 Dr. William Clarke, a cancer specialist from New York City, came to Cornwall. He fell in love with the surroundings, bought some land off Dark Entry Road, and built a cabin there where he and his wife, Harriet Banks Clarke, spent many weekends.

During 1917 Harriet Clarke was diagnosed with a chronic illness. Dudleytown folklore says that while her husband was in New York she was attacked by a specter in the woods and went mad. In 1918 she took her own life in their New York City home.

Dr. Clarke continued his love affair with Dudleytown. He would often bring his friends and associates on his weekend getaways, and others also became enamored with the solitude of the Dudleytown forest. In December 1924, together with some of his friends, Dr. Clarke formed the Dark Entry Forest Association (DEF). "The Dark Entry Forest Association was formed as a nature preserve," explains Dr. John F. Leich, former president and current shareholder of the DEF. The charter stated the land would remain "forever wild," a nature preserve for its members to enjoy.

Paranormal Accounts

Whether Dudleytown was cursed or is cursed now, many stories circulate about covens of witches, cultists, and satanists. Many people believe the area is haunted.

Steve Firth, an off-road motorcycle enthusiast encountered something strange on his first motorcycle trip through Dudleytown. "I rode through Dudleytown on three occasions, and something unusual happened each time."

On one of Firth's rides with some friends through the area, he encountered a horrific scene: "In a foundation, we found the carcass of a horse—pretty rotten. If someone had been riding and the horse fell into the hole and broke a leg, maybe there was no way to get it out. We didn't get too close because of the smell. One friend commented that something didn't seem to want us there. I've read about the quiet in the woods and the lack of birds and animals and can only say that my friends and I have experienced this. You have to go there to feel it."

But not everyone agrees.

"There never was a curse," said the Reverend Gary Dudley, a Dudley family genealogist and author of the book *The Legend of Dudleytown* (Heritage Books, 2001). According to the reverend, the first published mention of any curse associated with the Dudley name or with Dudleytown is in the book *They Found a Way* (Stephen Daye Press, 1938). "I have never read anything before that time. There was never an article before 1938," Dudley said.

Nancy Zeigler, a paranormal investigator from Watervliet, New York, and a Dudleytown regular, says, "The people living in the Dark Entry Forest have a vested interest in saying there is nothing up there. Well, if there's nothing up there, then why do we get strange things on our photographs? I've been slapped across the face and scratched with no one standing there."

Some researchers have theorized that the troubles in Dudleytown may have their origins in chemicals, not curses. They point out the high lead content in the area's rocks. If that heavy metal was present in the village's drinking water as well, it may have contributed to collective madness in the local population.—*Jeff Belanger*

Dudleytown Today

The Dark Entry Forest Association still owns most of the land on which Dudleytown once stood. And since 2000 the DEF has no longer allowed hikers to go onto their land. Yet many ghost seekers still sneak in, trying to see what may lie in the shadow of the mountains.

Dudleytown is located just south of Coltsfoot Mountain. Dark Entry Road is found off Route 7 about two miles south of Cornwall Bridge.

Camping in the Shadows of Dudleytown

I am twenty-one and have lived my entire life in Cornwall, CT. When my friends and I were about eighteen, we planned to camp out overnight beside the foundations of the homes of the allegedly "cursed" former residents of Dudleytown. We got a late start, and we were all on edge by the time darkness fell. After about an hour of cursing the damp kindling and rotten firewood, we finally got a campfire started. It was early autumn, and as night fell, the temperature dropped considerably. We all huddled around the small fire and passed around bags of chips.

It was then that I realized that aside from the crackle of our little fire and the rustle of the snack bags there was no other sound in the forest. There were no crickets or frogs or anything, just dead silence. One of my friends said that it was just too late in the year for crickets, though he seemed to be trying to convince himself of this as much as us.

As dark as Dudleytown may be in the day, it is nothing compared to the night. If there was a moon in the sky that night, it could not be seen in the hollow where we were camped. The light from our feeble fire didn't extend far and seemed to be absorbed by the blackness that had closed in all around us.

Then all of a sudden we heard a noise, and we all jumped up. It was a low muffled tone coming from somewhere off in blackness.

"Owl," someone said. "It's just an owl! That's all it is."

We all stood with our backs to the flames, staring off into the woods and listening. Suddenly a breeze kicked up that gave the dwindling fire new life. Now our shadows seemed to take on a life of their own and danced across the rock walls of the foundation and in and out of the cellar pits. It was the eeriest thing I had ever seen. I was just about to say something about it when the owl sound shattered the silence once again, only this time it was so loud and close it sounded like a shriek, and we all let out startled screams simultaneously.

At just that moment the fire suddenly went out. It was as if somebody flicked a light switch off and extinguished it, leaving us standing there in the absolute blackness. I swear, I felt as if I'd just gone blind—I couldn't see my hand right in front of my face!

We all stood there for one long moment, breathing heavily and not saying a word. All of a sudden the forest was not so quiet anymore. The owl (or whatever it was) was sounding off repeatedly and at close range, and there seemed to be a rustling in the leaves all around us. I definitely felt a presence of some kind out there in the darkness, and it was everywhere!

"That's it," someone finally spoke up, "I'm outta here!"

We scrambled to gather up any belongings we could find, threw our packs on our backs, and started walking away—fast! The forest seemed to be alive with sounds now as we trampled through the dry leaves, tripping over rocks and branches all the way. We all just stared down at the dim flashlight beams before us as we beat a hasty retreat out of the Dark Entry Forest. We walked faster and faster and tripped and fell time and time again. It was every man for himself as we raced down the rocky trail. We all just wanted to get the hell out of Dudleytown.

It was about midnight when we emerged from the woods, and life was going on in Cornwall just as normal. People wandered in and out of convenience stores and bars, and cars were gassing up at the all-night service station. It all seemed strange to me that everything was so business-as-usual here in town. It was almost as if Cornwall existed in a different reality, the modern-day world, while off in the woods outside of town there was something much older, darker, and weirder.

We returned from our foray with about half of our equipment, but we brought back a strange and unexplainable feeling with us. Perhaps we were just scared by our own shadows, but that's not how it felt. Though no one said it, we all knew that none of us would be going back to retrieve our abandoned gear anytime soon. As far as I know (or care), it is still there to this day.

—Ryan M.

Demonic Encounter on Dudleytown Trail

In July of 1998 my fiancé and I and two other friends went to check out the so-called curse. We pulled up to Bald Mountain Road around eleven thirty p.m. and parked next to the entrance to one of the trails leading into Dudleytown. We grabbed flashlights and cameras and started walking toward the trail entrance. We heard nothing. No wind, no animals . . . nothing. We walked only a few feet before we heard a noise. The sound is difficult to describe, but it sounded like a huge metal dumpster dragging against asphalt. We were freaking out, but we kept going.

When we got to the entrance, we started reading the sign, and all of a sudden I took the flashlight and shone it at the ground where we just walked, and we saw the words in huge letters NEVER RETURN. . . . SATAN."—*Sarah, Torrington, CT*

A Bunny Not for Cuddling

Sometimes the most outwardly nonthreatening things are the most frightening. We cannot grasp the idea of something cute and cuddly being evil underneath. But who (aside from Jimmy Carter) could be afraid of a bunny rabbit? Generations of folks in the Fairfax County, Virginia, area, that's who. Like an evil killer clown, the axe-wielding maniac dressed head to toe in a fuzzy rabbit costume and known as the Bunnyman is downright disturbing.

Tales of the Bunnyman

In Reston, Virginia, there used to be a dirt road leading off Sunset Hills Road, just before it intersected with Reston Avenue. All the kids knew that the road led to the Bunnyman's house. Supposedly, one Halloween night he dressed up in a bunny costume, shot his wife and kids, then opened the door to trick-or-treaters all night with the corpses of his family still in the house. I've talked to a few other northern Virginians lately, and everyone has a different variation of what it was the Bunnyman did. The only things the stories have in common are that he kills people, preferably children, he wears either a bunny suit or rabbit skins, and he scares little kids. There's been a lot of development in the area, so the site may be gone. Too bad—it was a pretty freaky local legend.—*Ali Davis*

Escaped from Asylum, Bunnyman Lives to Kill Again

I have heard through numerous sources that the Bunnyman was a town hermit who lived up the long dirt driveway off to the right of the bridge back in the '40s. He dressed in a bunny costume every Halloween. From what I understand, years before he had escaped from a mental institution and apparently suffered from schizophrenia—why no one was able to find him is unclear. He often lured young children into his cabin to play with him. Eventually he snapped and murdered the children. The next morning they were found hanging from the big tree in the wooded fenced-off field to the left of the bridge. He was sent to the state prison for twenty or so years, and after being released, he disappeared. From then until 1985 strange things happened in the area, such as unexplained murders of young teens.—*Vivisect*

A Real-Life Rabbit Tale

They say that behind every good story there's a kernel of truth. As it turns out, the Bunnyman tale hopped into the collective conscience of the people of Fairfax County because of a very real (and really bizarre) case.

Brian Conley, a researcher at the Fairfax County Public Library, began tracking the Bunnyman's roots at the Maryland Folklore Archive. There, he found research by University of Maryland student Patricia Johnson that recorded the earliest reports of the Bunnyman around Halloween of 1970. Conley researched newspaper archives of the time and located a *Washington Post* article that may just uncover the origins of the cotton-tailed terrorist.

"Fairfax County police said yesterday they are looking for a man who likes to wear a 'white bunny rabbit costume' and throw hatchets through car windows," the article stated. "Air Force Academy Cadet Robert Bennett told police that shortly after midnight last Sunday he and his fiancée were sitting in a car in the 5400 block of Guinea Road when a man 'dressed in a white suit with long bunny ears' ran from the nearby bushes and shouted 'You're on private property and I have your tag number.' The 'rabbit' threw a wooden handled hatchet through the right front car window, the first year cadet told police. As soon as he threw the hatchet, the 'rabbit' skipped off into the night. Police have the hatchet, but no other clues in the case."

The police speculated that the Bunnyman was a local resident who resented the explosion of development in the Fairfax County area. This theory was validated two weeks later, when the *Washington Post* detailed another sighting of the Bunnyman in an article entitled "The Rabbit Reappears."

"A man wearing a furry suit with two long ears appeared again on Guinea Road in Fairfax County Thursday night, police reported, this time wielding an ax and chopping away at a roof support on a new house.

"Paul Phillips, a private security guard for a construction company, said he saw the 'rabbit' standing on the front porch of a new, but unoccupied house.

" 'I started talking to him,' Phillips said, 'and that's when he started chopping.'

" 'All you people trespass around here,' the Rabbit told him as he whacked eight gashes in a pole. 'If you don't get out of here, I'm going to bust you on the head.' The Rabbit, carrying the long-handled ax, ran off into the woods."

Fondly Remembers Bunnyman

I lived in Annandale back in the early '70s. Every Halloween we were warned to watch out for the Bunnyman. Supposedly, he dressed up in a bunny costume and terrorized little kids, and also possibly exposed himself. What great times those were!

—Kathy

Echoes of the Bunnyman

I'm from Falls Church, Virginia, and we had a Bunnyman story too. It's about a guy in a bunny costume standing at the bottom of a hill, in the middle of a road that turned sharply to the right. Apparently, as people drove down the hill, he would throw an axe at the car. When I was a kid, I was always on the lookout for the Bunnyman at that curve of the road.*—Katie Roberts*

The Bunnyman Has His Own Bridge

I first heard about the Bunnyman Bridge from my high school track coach about five or six years ago. There are two main versions of the legend. One involves a teenager who killed his family one Easter and then hanged himself from the bridge while wearing a bunny costume. This version seems less likely than one about a mental patient who escaped from a bus that was transporting patients. He hid out in the woods, and people started finding the carcasses of rabbits around the bridge. When some teenagers were found gutted, hanging from the bridge, the local authorities put out a manhunt for the "Bunnyman." Eventually they caught up with him, but just as they were about to apprehend him, he jumped in front of a train.

Since then, it is said that the Bunnyman's spirit haunts the bridge that bears his name and that on Halloween at midnight his spirit becomes visible right over the structure. You will usually find a good group at the base of the bridge at midnight on Halloween, waiting to see if the spirit of Bunnyman will appear.

The bridge is located about twenty-five miles from Washington, DC, in the middle of nowhere. It is on Colchester Road and is painted bright white. Because of all the kids that flock there, there is a sign posted on the bridge that states that the area is under video surveillance, but so far I've never had any run-ins with the local police. So if you ever find yourself in northern Virginia, go ahead and check out one of our most famous local legends at Bunnyman Bridge. *–Brad Byrnes*

This Bridge Was Made for Hanging

I heard that between 1920 and 1930 two prisoners escaped from jail. Search parties found only half-eaten bunny corpses and soon found one of the prisoners hung at one end of Bunnyman Bridge. They assumed the other prisoner had killed him. I think it was in the 1960s that three teens, two boys and a girl, went to Bunnyman Bridge. The next morning they were found hanged, the two boys at one end and the girl at the other end. After that, teens kept coming to the tunnel to spray-paint the walls, so they put a video camera in the tunnel to catch teens and maybe a glimpse of the Bunnyman. *–XF Chic*

Bunnyman Claims Ten to Fifteen Confirmed Kills

This is how I understand the Bunnyman Bridge legend. There was an insane asylum in Lorton, Virginia, in the early 1900s, and around 1920 the asylum's members were shuttled on buses to a new location farther south. The story says that the bus crashed on this trip, and several of the inmates escaped. All but two were found shortly thereafter. The local police searched for months but found only bunny carcasses near an old train bridge in the woods. Then one day one of the men was discovered hanging from the bridge, gutted, with a rustic knife-tool near his feet. The other man was never found.

There are actually about ten to fifteen documented murders at that site since the 1920s, most of them occurring before 1950, although the most recent was in the early 1980s. There are lots of legends about the place now—like if you go at midnight on Halloween, there will be a flash of a bright light, and then you will end up hanging, throat slit, from the bridge's edge. It's pretty creepy and definitely worth going if you have the time! Just make sure not to turn your car ignition off once you're under the bridge, because the car won't start again.*–KS*

Camera-Shy Bunnyman Kills Documentarian

There was a show on TV about the Bunnyman Bridge. Some college students decided to go there at midnight with a camera and film what really happens. It was pitch-black, and there was a lot of screaming. They got through the tunnel and realized one of their friends was missing. The next day they came back and found their friend hanged from the bridge. I don't know if this is true, but it sure scared me!*–Eggen*

The Legend of Crybaby Bridge

The Crybaby Bridge is a familiar legend all over the United States. The basic story runs like this: A young woman gets pregnant and delivers a baby she cannot keep, so she decides to get rid of the infant. The mother takes the helpless newborn to a remote bridge over a stream and throws the baby into the water, killing it. In some versions of the story the mother does herself in as well. If you go to the bridge late at night and sit very quietly, you will hear the faint sobbing of the doomed infant from beneath the bridge.

Because of the widespread proliferation of this myth and the bridges that feature in it (there are Crybaby Bridges in Maryland, New Jersey, and Ohio), this tale would seem to be a simple urban legend—or would it? The Crybaby Bridge in Upper Marlboro, Maryland, has made bridge believers out of several skeptics. Unlike many alleged sites, this bridge seems to really deliver the goods!

To make the trip even more thrilling, while you are parked on the lonely bridge late at night listening to the baby, there just might be a half-goat, half-man creature lurking in the dark woods nearby listening to you!

I've Heard the Baby Cry!

There is a legend in our part of Maryland about Lottsford Vista Road, a country road between Bowie and Upper Marlboro. Actually, there are two legends. The first is the Church of the Upside-Down Crosses, which supposedly hosts devil-worship. The second is Crybaby Bridge.

Some of my friends and I piled in the car twenty years ago and drove over there. Down the unlit, spooky road, you come to the church first. We all got out and looked around, but I wasn't impressed. The upside-down crosses in the stained glass windows appeared to be just part of the leading holding the glass together. Then we got back in the car and headed up the road to Crybaby Bridge.

The legend has it that a long time ago a woman had a baby out of wedlock, and rather than face her family, she went out to the bridge in the dead of night and threw the baby off it. Supposedly, if you went there late at night and sat still, you could hear the baby cry.

We got to the bridge and killed the engine and sat there for about fifteen minutes. I remember thinking, This is so lame; then all of a sudden we all heard it, clear as day. There was no question that it was a baby crying, and it sounded like it was coming from under the bridge! We were all freaked and got out of there as fast as we could. I never went back. *–LH*

Orphans, Ghosts, and Gore

The legend of the Gore Orphanage near Vermilion, Lorain County, Ohio, is the stuff of nightmares. Imagine the scene: As fire engulfs an old wood-framed building, the agonized cries of small children trapped inside pierce the night air. Horrified onlookers stand by, unable to help. The hellish inferno continues for over an hour, until finally the screams fall silent and the only sounds that linger are the roar of the flames and the cracking of timbers. Before long the building is reduced to a pile of glowing embers and a few stone foundation pillars.

As red-hot sparks trail off into the black sky, suspicions focus on Old Man Gore, the man in charge of the institution. His cruel and sadistic treatment of those in his care had long been the subject of hushed gossip around the shores of Lake Erie. Could he have set the fire himself?

Many in the greater Cleveland area have reported strange occurrences in the woods near the site of that fateful fire. It is said that the screams of the trapped and dying children can still be heard there to this day. Many believe it to be one of the most haunted locations in all of Ohio.

But although Gore Orphanage Road does exist, no one with the name Gore has ever lived there. Bill Ellis, associate professor, English and American Studies, Highacres, Penn State Hazleton, has another explanation for the road's name.

"The road was originally laid out along the boundary line dividing Lorain County from its western neighbor, Huron County," he explained. "When a surveying error was discovered, a thin strip of land resembling the gore of a dress had to be annexed to Lorain. The route then became known as Gore Road."

In 1902 a Lutheran minister, the Reverend John Sprunger, established an orphanage nearby known as the Light of Hope. As people associated the road with the institution, the street came to be known as Gore Orphanage Road. However, the site that most people associate with legends of the Gore Orphanage is not where the Light of Hope Orphanage stood. Instead, most visitors go to a

deep ravine nearby known as Swift's Hollow. Although the orphanage did buy the land, it never put the magnificent Greek Revival house that once stood there to practical use.

Known as the Swift mansion, the house, once owned by a successful farmer named Joseph Smith, has its own weird legends. Though only the foundations of the house remain, in its glory the house had elaborate furnishings, ornate window frames, marble columns, and other lavish decorations. The first weird stories to come out of the hollow appeared in the early 1900s, when Swift sold his home to Nicholas Wilber, a renowned spiritualist. Rumors spread of the rituals and séances that Wilber regularly held in the house.

The tales of dead children in the Gore Orphanage legend may have their origins in some real tragedies at the mansion. According to the book *Aliens, Ghosts, and Cults: Legends We Live,* by Bill Ellis (University Press of Mississippi/Jackson, 2001):

"The Wilbers were in the habit of calling the spirits of small children back to earth during their séances. Nicholas Wilber's son, Miller, had four children, aged two to eleven, who died during the course of seven days at the height of a diphtheria epidemic. Residents insist that they died at the Swift mansion and were buried there. The tragic deaths of these four children were vividly remembered by this tight-knit farming community."

When the home was abandoned in 1901, it became a mecca for late-night vandals and teenagers visiting it on a dare. It is presumed that one of them was responsible for burning the house down in late 1923.

The legend of Gore Orphanage also owes much to a historically documented disaster that took place forty miles away in the town of Collinwood. In 1908, 176 elementary school students there died in a fire at their school, either from the fire or from being trampled to death in the stampede to escape it. This historical event has many uncanny similarities to the Gore Orphanage legend, so the details may very well have migrated from the school to the already legendary site at Swift's Hollow.

Ghostly Handprints at the Gore Orphanage

I have been to the Gore Orphanage only once. It turned out to be a pretty frightening night.

Apparently, in the early 1900s one of the orphans was walking to the outhouse with a lantern. He tripped and fell, igniting a huge fire. The steps leading from the top floor to the bottom collapsed almost immediately. Townsfolk from Vermilion gathered, but all they could do was stand and watch as the hundreds of orphans many floors above them met their collective doom. They say that it was so gruesome that people safe on the ground died just from the shock of seeing those kids burning in the inferno.

Ever since then, people have said that the ghosts of these orphans haunt the spot on which the orphanage used to stand. Kids from my school said that they had heard strange sounds in the woods, like kids crying and doors slamming shut, even though there are no buildings close by. Some kids even said they actually saw some orphan ghosts, but I never believed them.

When my friends and I went there, I was a bit creeped out by the road leading up to the place. It's really dark because of the overhanging trees, and there's a messed up–looking wooden bridge you cross over. When we arrived at the site where the orphanage had once stood, I did hear some strange creaking noises, but I'm pretty sure it was just the trees rubbing together in the night breeze. What happened when we made our way back to the car, however, would change my tune.

As we got close to the car, my friend Jake noticed that all the windows were fogged up. There wasn't another human being in sight, it was a cool night, and there was no explanation as to why the windows were fogged up. Then my other friend, Shawn, saw the back window. There, on the misty glass, were the faint impressions of little handprints. We all freaked out instantly.

Trying to calm down my friends, I pointed out that Jake had a little brother who is only four years old, and the marks had surely been made by him. Secretly though, I was just as freaked as anyone else there. I was just trying to convince myself that there was a rational explanation for them—which there was not. If those handprints had belonged to Jake's little brother, how is it that nobody noticed them on the way up there that night?–*Victor E.*

La Llorona and the Bloody Box

When I was growing up in the dusty desert city of El Paso, Texas, right near the Mexican border, I heard many fascinating legends, ghost stories, and superstitions. The area is rich with folklore and a bloody history that lends itself to all kinds of interesting tales. This one is probably my favorite—the story of La Llorona (pronounced la yo-ro-na). Just saying the name gives me chills. La Llorona means "The Crier," and she is part sorrowful banshee, part angry spirit, part cursed creature.

I was told that long ago, a widow with two small children lived in the poorest section of Juarez, the town across the border from El Paso. She began a relationship with a wealthy man and wanted to marry him, but the man did not want to marry her, because she had children. So in the dead of night she took them down to the Rio Grande, stabbed them both, and threw them into the river. Then she slipped through the night to her lover's house. When the man saw her blood-streaked white gown, he was horrified and immediately rejected her. This drove her mad, and she ran back to the river, screaming and tearing at her hair, trying in vain to find her poor children. But it was too late.

The story varies here. Some people say she stabbed and drowned herself. Others insist that she was caught by an angry mob of people and killed for her crimes. Either way, she died, and that's when the creepiness begins.

Soon people started to report hearing a horrible wailing from the river's banks. Then the sightings began. People related tales of seeing an apparition wandering the riverbanks at night—something with the body of a woman and the head of a horse. The creature, who wore a long white, bloody nightgown, was wailing as it searched the waters. The locals said that it was the spirit of the woman, cursed to wander the banks of the Rio Grande for all eternity, wearing a horse's head as punishment for her awful sins. To this day, whenever someone is found drowned in the Rio Grande (which happens constantly), people whisper that La Llorona is still lonely and looking for company.

I had a very freaky, mysterious experience out there once. We drove over a bridge across the river to the darker, scarier side and got out to look around a little bit. One friend yelled out like he was startled. We saw him hurl something toward the bridge and come running back toward the car, yelling at us to get in and go. He told us that he saw a horrible monster-woman standing in the middle of the bridge, looking at him. He said that he was so scared that he had thrown his pocketknife at it.

As we headed back over the bridge, we suddenly

stopped laughing as we found our way blocked by a box that was sitting in the very center of the narrow bridge. There was no way it was there before, or we wouldn't have been able to get over the bridge in the first place. We were all scared witless, so half of us got out to move the box. We could see dark liquid dripping down the sides, and when we lifted the lid, we freaked! It was filled with blood, bloody organs, pieces of bone, hair, and other stuff. I recall clearly seeing an eyeball! We sped out of there as fast as we could and pulled over at the first place we found—an old bar—where we ran in, asking to use the phone.

We were all panicked and freaked. We called the cops, who came out and met us and asked us to lead the way. To our surprise the bloody box was still there (we half expected it to have disappeared). As soon as they opened the box, the cops un-holstered their guns and called for backup. More cops came and took statements from us, and then we had to leave. The only explanation they gave us when we left was maybe it was "bait" left by a fisherman.

That was one of the most bizarre things that has ever happened to me. My friend still insists that he saw La Llorona, and he's convinced that she left the box there for us. My other friends think we almost stumbled across a murderer who was dumping what was left of his victim. Another friend even has a theory that someone was leaving an offering for La Llorona. I don't know what I believe, but that was something I'll never forget!—*Shady*

The Devil's Looking Glass

Not far from Jonesborough in eastern Tennessee is a place known as the Devil's Looking Glass. This pile of rocks in the mountainside looks ordinary by day, perched along the Nolichucky River in Unicoi County, but as the moonlight hits it at night, the face of Satan himself appears.

Spirit in the Rocks

Terrifying tales are told of the Devil's Looking Glass, a sheer rock wall rising hundreds of feet over the rugged Nolichucky River in Unicoi County, Tennessee. One story tells of a young Indian woman who, having lost her beloved husband in battle, flung herself off the precipice in a fit of anguish. Her ghost is said to haunt the base of the cliff. Another Cherokee story is that a cave about halfway up the face of the cliff was home to a horrible demon. He lay in wait to pounce upon a passing canoe.

After the whites settled Unicoi (then Washington) County, stories about the Looking Glass became even more numerous and frightening. Strange cries of agony came from the rocks. Sometimes the glowing wisps of spirits could be seen among the cracks. Everyone gave the Looking Glass a wide berth—except for a local witch called Ol' Miz Wilson, who lived near the site in a tiny cabin, where evil spirits were said to visit her in the dead of night. She would entertain them with various incantations and spells. The unholy revelry would continue until the first rays of the morning sun sent the evil spirits scurrying back to their home among the rocks.

—*Tennessee Haints, Hauntings and Hoodoos*

The More Things Change...

As an example of how tales travel from place to place and change, here's a letter from a reader that relocates La Llorona to Arizona, changing the Rio Grande to the San Pedro River.

She Killed Her Kids, and She Just Might Kill You

Back in the 1800s in Arizona, when Tombstone was in its heyday, this lady thought her kids were possessed by Satan. She threw them off a bridge into the San Pedro River; then she threw herself off. Ever since then she's been walking around looking for her kids. It's said if you see her and pick her up, you'll be fine; she'll just leave flowers on the seat of your car, and the seat will be wet. But if you don't pick her up, watch out, because you're going to get into an accident.

My cousin, my friend, and I were going out to the desert one night, and we came upon this lady standing on the side of the road. She was standing there with old 1800s clothes on, her hair was this bright, freaky red, and her face was so white she looked like a mime. In her hands were what looked like some desert weeds. We were too scared to pick her up. Right after that my cousin's car wouldn't come out of first gear. The next night a black dog came out of nowhere and started chasing our car. The car went out of control for no reason, and we ran through a barbed wire fence. I guess we should have picked her up.
—*Dave Stratton*

The Devil's Tower

The town of Alpine in Bergen County, New Jersey, is home to a local legend known as the Devil's Tower. Dozens of legends surround the evil edifice, including a past filled with satanists, marital infidelity, suicide, and conjuring ghosts.

Some readers have told us that attempts to tear down the tower have led to deaths in the work crew. Some have experienced cold gusts of wind that sent them screaming for their cars. Others say that if you drive around the tower three times in reverse, the ghost of a woman will appear. One person said that if you walk backward around the tower six times at midnight, the devil will appear.

According to the Alpine Historical Society, the Devil's Tower was the centerpiece of an estate built in the first half of the 1900s by Spanish sugar plantation owner Manuel Rionda. The estate was called Rio Vista and was the largest on the Palisades, with a mansion on the cliffs where the present-day Alpine Lookout is located. There was even an elevator to take Rionda's guests up for the view.

After Rionda died in 1943, the estate was subdivided and was mostly just woodlands through the 1970s. The name Devil's Tower probably came about around that time, when kids used to break into it. Eventually the tower was sealed up. Just off to one side of the tower was a chapel and an ornately decorated mausoleum where Rionda's wife and sister were interred. Their bodies were removed after Rionda died.

The tower is on a public road called the Esplanade, accessible from Route 9W, about a mile north of the Tenafly-Alpine border.

He Cheated; She Jumped

The Devil's Tower was built by a rich man so his wife could see New York without really going to New York. One night the wife saw her husband on the tower with another woman, so she jumped right down the center of it. The husband was so upset that he stopped all the work on the tower. Now if you drive around the tower backward six times, the ghost of the wife is supposed to control your car and drive it straight into a tree.–*Nick G.*

For Whom the Tower Tolls

The tower was started as a birthday gift for Rionda's wife, but she passed away before its completion. It was fitted with a clock that never was used but was set to the time of her death. When strolling through the woods on Halloween night, a person could actually hear the tower clock ring at the appropriate hour!

–*Letter via e-mail*

Helpful Plan to Summon the Devil

I have been to Devil's Tower in Alpine many times. If you go around the tower three times with your headlights off and three times in reverse, then turn your car off, you can see the devil in the tower.–*Mike Pirone, River Edge*

Albino Gleep Guards the Devil's Tower

Visiting the Devil's Tower in Alpine, New Jersey, also known as Rionda's Tower, was a rite of passage for groups of young idiots to work off their testosterone surpluses. Rionda's gorgeous young wife, for whom he allegedly built the tower, died at quite a tender age. Old man Rionda, the Cuban sugar baron, was inconsolable. Legend had it that he had her embalmed, then put under glass, Snow White–style, in the top of the tower, and then he would visit her during the full moon.

We kids believed it and would go off on nighttime expeditions, braving storm fences, cliff overhangs, and the guards with Dobermans and salt guns, and then try to scale the tower itself to see the Lady Under Glass. The caretaker on the estate in those days was an albino whom people called the Gleep. He headed up the salt-gun and dog teams. These people were quite real—I'd seen them myself, marching the perimeter of the estate during the daytime.–*Bob de Marrais*

The Devil's Tree

The devil is said to frequent a certain tree in the Martinsville section of Bernards Township, Somerset County, New Jersey. This sinister-looking tree stands alone in the middle of a large field off Mountain Road, its trunk scarred by axes and chain saws. Supposedly, anyone who tries to cut down the tree comes to an untimely end, as it is now cursed. According to the locals, numerous suicides and murders occurred around the evil arbor. It is said that the souls of those killed at the spot give the tree an unnatural warmth, and even in the dead of winter no snow will fall around it.

When we here at *Weird U.S.* visited the Devil's Tree, we noticed evidence that many attempts had been made over the years to fell the unholy oak, but all have failed. Why no one has yet been successful in toppling the timber we cannot say for sure, but one reader said that the tree is a portal to hell guarded by a sentinel. He drives an old black Ford or pickup truck and will chase you down the road until a certain point. You will see headlights one second, and the next nothing—the car is just gone.

Devil's Tree More Than Just a Tree

We went up to the tree and noticed that all the snow around it was melted. After we'd touched the tree and gotten back on the road, a black truck with some very bright lights started tailgating me like crazy, doing 85 mph down the windy road. I was scared. All of a sudden, just as the truck's lights and the truck disappeared, my fan belt snapped. Then just last week we went up to the tree with a bunch of friends. We took a Polaroid picture of it, and to our astonishment, when the picture developed, on the right side of the tree there was a lady with a red dress hanging from what looked like a noose.

—Kirk Sporman

Don't Mess with the Devil Tree

A local youth decided to debunk the Devil Tree with a bunch of his pals. They gathered around the tree at midnight and proceeded to urinate on it. Next morning the boy ended up getting broadsided, and his truck rolled over. Later he went up and apologized to the tree.

—George W. Rappelyea

Devil's Tramping Ground

There is no doubt about it . . . America is a strange and haunted place. The early explorers and Native Americans knew this and left behind evidence of it in the names they gave certain locations. As the explorers started to roam the vast reaches of the rugged land, they discovered areas that Native Americans had known for centuries and treated as sacred spots or terrifying places better left untouched. These mystery sites became the first "haunted" places in America, where people witnessed unsettling sights and sounds, such as unexplained balls of light, apparitions, and screams in the night.

The first idea that crossed the minds of Bible-reading, God-fearing folks was that the devil was involved, and they promptly gave these places names that would alert other visitors to the dangers. The peculiar American phenomenon of naming unusual or cursed places with devil names is apparent in Chatham County, North Carolina, where the Devil's Tramping Ground lies.

In the woods not far from the town of Siler City is a circular gap, forty feet in diameter, where the devil is said to have walked the earth. No plant or tree will grow inside this circle. The surrounding brush grows up to its edges and no farther. Animals do not come here, for no food grows, and they shy away from the area as though it were tainted. The only living thing within the mysterious circle is sparse growth of a variety of wire grass that residents say has not successfully been transplanted elsewhere.

The first settlers who came to the area attributed the strange spot to the Indians who held their tribal ceremonies here. It is said that the tramping of the Native Americans' feet wore a circle into the ground. But, strangely, the circle has remained long after the Indians departed. Over the years, the Tramping Ground has become the stuff of legend. It is said that no birds will nest in the nearby trees, no wild game is ever found here, and for decades no traveler would pass this way after nightfall.

Indeed, modern experiments conducted to determine what caused the unusual circle have not yet succeeded. Perhaps the most logical solution came from Dr. J. L. Stuckey, a state geologist whose soil tests revealed a high level of salt. This could certainly cause the land to become barren—but why in such a perfectly circular pattern? Could the mysterious patch of earth known as the Devil's Tramping Ground have once been a UFO landing site or an ancient crop circle? Who knows? This site, like so many other such places throughout the country, will probably remain a mystery for the ages.

—Troy Taylor

Devil's Circle

There is a tale told by old-timers in Lake County, Florida, of a circle twenty feet in diameter called the Devil's Circle, located deep in the Black Water Swamp, near where the Wekiva River meets the St. John's River. Reportedly nothing grows inside this circle; it has always been totally barren of plant life and remains extremely dry, even after heavy rains. Folklore has it that objects placed inside the circle overnight will vanish. Such circular places exist in many states, and Florida has several, another being in the Green Swamp, west of Orlando.

Soil sample tests in two such circles found that, in both cases, there was a zero level of nitrogen and an extremely high level of sodium and iodine content when compared to the surrounding soil. This would affect the growth of plant life. Another observation is that insects such as ants and beetles normally found in the same areas are seldom found within these circles.–*Charlie Carlson*

Devil's Stomping Ground

Off Highway 521 in Lancaster County, South Carolina, is a patch of land so cursed that it is said the devil himself frequents it. No plant life grows within this forty-foot-wide crop circle, and no animals cross through it. People who stand within it reportedly experience feelings of dread and intense nausea. Other reports say that any objects left within the circle will disappear or be inexplicably moved around.

Stomping and Tramping on the Devil's Ground

The Devil's Stomping (or Tramping) Ground is a circle of barren earth in the woods. There's no plant or animal life living within the circle. It's rumored that if you put rocks or sticks in the circle, they'll disappear or will be moved outside of the circle during the night. Also, if you place a live plant within the circle at night, in the morning it will be dead. The same thing is supposed to happen to you if you sleep within the circle during the night. Okay, enough of this—my skin's starting to crawl!–*Nancyz*

The Water Babies of Massacre Rocks

Outside my hometown of Pocatello, Idaho, is a tragic, frightening spot known as Massacre Rocks. Long ago it was the scene of an incredibly awful incident, and now it is the home of the ghosts of that event. When Native Americans inhabited this area, there was a famine so intense that the villagers decided there wasn't enough food to feed any new mouths. As babies were born, their mothers were forced to take them down to the nearby river and drown them. Today these so-called Water Babies still make their presence known. If you go to the banks of this river and sit for a while in silence, you will begin to hear the unmistakable sound of babies crying for their mothers. *–TechnoTempo420*

Witch Dance at the Natchez Trace

For centuries the mysterious pathway known as Natchez Trace has crossed the middle southern states. Many strange tales and legends have grown up around the trail, which takes its name from the city of Natchez, Mississippi. Just south of Tupelo, the National Park Service placed a sign that reads WITCH DANCE. Old folks say that witches once gathered here to dance and that whenever their feet touched the ground, the grass withered and died, never to grow again. The sign appears to be right. You can actually find scorched spots on the earth, where the grass will not grow. And these spots have been there since the days of Andrew Jackson, who noted the spots in his journal after a trip along the Trace on the way home to Tennessee. *–Troy Taylor*

Purgatory Chasm

They say that the devil himself has visited Purgatory Chasm in Middletown, Rhode Island. His footprints are supposedly scattered about the area. A few people have died by falling into the chasm, and others have jumped on dares. Some may have been tossed off intentionally. They say the blood of some of these unlucky souls still stains the walls of the chasm.

A Second Salem

I live in Whitewater, Wisconsin, and, according to legend, the whole town is haunted. Whitewater has been referred to as the second Salem. Its university was originally built as a school for mediums and paranormal research. I have been told that all possible ways to leave town require going over running water and that, when looked at from above, the cemeteries form a five-pointed star. And a coven of evil witches is supposed to meet on the hill behind the student dorms.

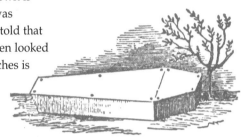

The problem is this: The town council has made sure that documentation of all these weird events no longer exists in town. I have even been told that someone wrote a book on the town and all of the freaky things that have happened. Can anyone direct me to where I can find out more? *–Jeff Woosley*

Jeff's letter about his highly haunted town intrigued us. So we tracked down some of the more famous legends surrounding the school and town from an article in the University of Wisconsin–Whitewater's newspaper, the *Royal Purple*. Here is what we learned from the *Royal Purple*'s account:

The first school dedicated to communicating with the spirit world, the Morris Pratt Institute, once stood in Whitewater. Large crowds would gather outside the Pratt Institute on Sunday nights for raucous public séances. The school moved out of Whitewater in 1946, but its legends remain part of the town's folklore.

Here are some true but strange Whitewater stories. The town cemeteries form a perfect isosceles triangle, not a five-pointed star. On Halloween in 1970 the community was shocked to find that one of the cemeteries was missing a young girl's coffin; it had been placed on the mall of the university's campus. The previous night two fishermen had seen strange lights floating around one of the cemeteries.

A series of underground tunnels form an intricate maze below Whitewater. Some believe that they were used as part of the Underground Railroad. Others say the tunnels have a much darker purpose—witches use them to avoid public knowledge of their black arts.

Speaking of witches, they reportedly use two spots on campus as meeting grounds. The field where the Wells Hall dormitory now stands was once a major meeting place for witch covens. Rumors claim that somewhere underneath Wells Hall there is an altar around which a number of bodies are buried upright. The other witch hotspot is the water tower in Starin Park, known colloquially as Witches Tower. Rumors persist that witches meet there—the police received calls one Halloween about candlelit ceremonies by the tower—though it is locked up and surrounded by barbed wire.

The most fascinating rumors about the dark side of Whitewater concern the secret literature in the university's library. Apparently, the contents of one book are so volatile that four people killed themselves after reading it. Three were university students, and one was a local resident who was found in a gas station with his wrists slashed. The luckier readers merely went completely mad. The library now keeps this powerful book under lock and key. Its contents remain unknown.

The Dead Boy Beneath the Waters

The village of Ola'a on the Big Island of Hawaii is a quiet community. An outside observer would never guess that this was the site of a tragedy that still haunts the village's children. In 1947, while neighborhood kids were playing on the shore of a local pond, one of them fell in and disappeared beneath the surface of the water. The boy, whose name was Tanaka, did not resurface. His companions rushed to find help, and when divers entered the water, they were disturbed by what they saw.

The dead boy was at the very bottom of the pond, sitting upon a rock with his arms by his sides. His eyes and mouth were open. His body was swaying back and forth with the currents. It was as if he had calmly sat down on the rock and waited to die. The divers retrieved the corpse, and everyone tried to put the strange and tragic death behind them. But the drowned boy refused to let them forget. People who traveled by the pond complained that something would tug at the bottom of their pants as they walked. One boy was actually dragged into the pond.

Rumors spread that the boy's spirit is trapped beneath the dark waters and tries to pull unsuspecting victims into his watery grave. Nowadays children are warned to avoid this pond. Who knows when the spirit will become restless once again and claim another young life? *–John Kawikonu*

The legend of this eerie pond was documented in the work of the late great storyteller Glen Grant. In his book, *Obake Files, Ghostly Encounters in Supernatural Hawaii* (Mutual Publishing Company, 1999) Grant writes:

"On some evenings the villagers could hear a cry emanate from the pond in the middle of the night. At first most everyone believed that the haunting cry was the wind blowing through the tall sugar cane fields. But a few of the older people said they knew better. The high-pitched whining was not wind but the spirit of the Tanaka boy—cold, wet, and desolate at the bottom of the pond. The soul was crying out for help and deliverance. Trapped in this world by accident, he sought someone's spirit as a substitute. They would take his place at the bottom of the pond so that he could be free to go on to the otherworld.

"Those who were present at the second accident swear that the other boy was pulled into the water against his will. It was the noon hour. He was walking about 50 yards behind his father along the edge of the pond, occasionally picking up a flat stone to skim across the water. When he fell, he screamed out to his father that something was pulling him into the pond. He clawed at the earth, trying to hold on, to fight back. But in what seemed like an instant, the force tugging at his legs pulled him into the watery depths of the pond. By the time the young boy's body had been located, it was found sitting naturally on a rock on the bottom of the pond. He seemed so natural sitting there—arms placidly at his sides, eyes and mouth open, swaying gently to and fro in a light current. Fortunately, the rescuers were able to bring him to the surface in time to be resuscitated.

"A Shinto priest was brought from Hilo to bless the waters, and the haunting cries finally ceased. Yet, on peculiarly dark nights when the evening skies seem bathed in black ink, those who live closest to the pond say that they sometimes hear the Tanaka boy's cry. But are the cries melancholy or sinister? And will the Tanaka boy ever find peace?"

The dead boy was at the very bottom of the pond, sitting upon a rock with his arms by his sides. His eyes and mouth were open. His body was swaying back and forth with the currents.

Ancient Mysteries

Some might think that mysterious rock formations and cryptic inscriptions from lost civilizations are confined to remote parts of the world, but they can be found right in your backyard.

Native American petroglyphs have been discovered in caves, crevices, and rock shelters throughout the country, but in addition to these postcards from indigenous cultures, there is evidence that visitors from Europe and Asia may have come and even settled here long before the travels of Christopher Columbus. Some inscriptions appear in ancient languages like Libyan, Celtic, and Phoenician. Others are of a mysterious origin yet to be determined. Some actually predate the arrival of Indian tribes on the North American continent.

How did the authors of these puzzling texts and the builders of these stone structures get to this land? Why did they come and where did they go? Nobody can say for sure, but these ancient New World sojourners have left behind their sacred sites and cryptic messages for us to decipher.

Examining these lost pages from the book of history opens up a new realm of possibilities that are just as fascinating as the heritage we thought we knew. Whether or not you choose to believe that an ancient civilization once inhabited the land we now call the United States, one thing is for certain: This country we call home has been a very weird place for a very very long time!

Standing Stones and Rocky Ruins

Throughout the country enormous stones stand in strange and seemingly premeditated arrangements. How they were put in place remains a mystery. Were they erected by the hand of man, or are they merely natural formations? Although the debate still rages about the origins of these stone structures, the fact remains they are awesome sites to behold. If prehistoric cultures did construct them, they are a testament to the ingenuity of primitive man. And even if some natural force put them where they now stand, they are no less awe-inspiring for having remained in place for thousands of years.

Dolmens, or perched rocks, are found all over the world. While some believe that these formations are nothing more than erratics dropped in place during the movement of glaciers, others argue that they are the last remaining remnants of prehistoric people. Many show evidence that some ancient culture did have a hand in their placement, because they are aligned with significant celestial events such as solstices and equinoxes.

The American Stonehenge of New Hampshire and Gungywamp in Connecticut, for example, are unquestionably the handiwork of some long lost colony of people. Other structures, though, like the Rock Lake Pyramids of Wisconsin, are not so easy to classify as man-made. Were they erected by prehistoric cultures as places of worship or perhaps even worshipped themselves by virtue of their awesome stature? It is a question as old as the hills on which they still stand.

America's Stonehenge

Standing on a hilltop in North Salem, New Hampshire, is one of America's most ancient and most mysterious sites. This series of stone chambers, walls, secret underground passages, and strange inscriptions is known as America's Stonehenge. Rather than having standing stones like its English namesake, this area consists of a number of enclosures constructed using stacked stones in conjunction with existing natural rock formations.

The site, which is also known as Mystery Hill, lies on twenty acres of hills and features twenty-two stone enclosures that go by such names as the Oracle Chamber and the Watch House. The origin of this strange lithic structure has been debated for years. Some say a group of Irish Culdee monks landed there in the tenth century after fleeing the Vikings and established the site as a Christian monastery. Most scholars have dismissed this as highly unlikely. Because the formations can be used to track various astrological, lunar, and solar movements, one theory is that it was an ancient place of worship. Another feature that has fueled this idea is the presence of the Sacrificial Stone, a flat rock with a deep groove thought to enable the blood of victims to run off.

It is difficult to estimate the age of America's Stonehenge, since many stones were removed, displaced, or damaged by early European settlers who plundered the area for building materials. However, some have hazarded the guess that the site is over 4000 years old, which would mean it existed even before Native Americans inhabited the area.

This odd spot has been adapted for many uses since the colonization of New Hampshire. In the 1830s local farmer Jonathan Pattee owned the land and, according to rumors, used some of the hidden chambers to hide the moonshine he distilled on the side. The spot was also said to be a stop on the famous Underground Railroad. Archaeologists have unearthed shackles there that they believe were left behind by slaves on their flight to freedom in the North.

The Mysterious Land of Gungywamp

Near Groton, Connecticut, are twenty unusual acres of land known as Gungywamp. The area features odd arrangements of standing stones, rock houses, earthen mounds, and underground stone chambers—and many mysteries. The unusual structures are man-made, though no one really knows what men made them. Are they the primitive work of Native Americans? Or are they the handiwork of Colonial, or even pre-Colonial European settlers, as shards of china found during archaeological digs at the site indicate?

Strange tales circulate, attributing certain powers to the area. It's said that there are magnetically charged fields there and a certain cliff that inexplicably induces depression in those who go there.

Because it stands on private land, access to Gungywamp is limited. For $5 one can take a tour through the area, led by the Gungywamp Society, a nonprofit educational research organization that conducts excavations and gives lectures on its findings. Visit www.gungywamp.com for more details.

Tripod Rock

People from Morris County in New Jersey call Tripod Rock the Morris Stonehenge, because they feel the place possesses the same mystical powers as those ancient pre-Celtic monoliths. Perched high atop Pyramid Mountain near the border of Kinnelon and Montville, Tripod Rock is a massive boulder balanced precariously upon three smaller stones. The formation looks as if it might topple over and tumble down the mountain at any moment.

From the south you can see two stones placed thirty-nine feet beyond the dolmen; they line up into a V shape with two hills three quarters of a mile away. On the summer solstice the sun appears right between the V. Looking west, you can see a standing stone forty-five feet from the dolmen that lines up with the peak of a hill half a mile in the distance.

Tripod Rock is part of Pyramid Mountain Natural Historical Area, a county-maintained park. Thanks to the conservation efforts of many local residents, geologists, and archaeologists, the area has been spared from development. Put on your hiking boots for this trip—it's about two miles into the woods on a slow incline. Maps of Tripod Rock can be found at the beginning of the trails.

Hogback Ruins

Just south of Morrison, Colorado, lies a mountain ridge that is home to an intriguing series of stones. The U-shaped structure called the Hogback Ruins has captivated hikers for decades with its unobstructed view to both the east and the west. According to author Sal Trento, it is clear that the stones were removed from a ledge close to the area and intentionally placed in their current formation, but there are no signs that tools were used to remove or arrange the stones. This suggests that they are of such an old age that they predate the use of metal tools.

Balanced Rock

In North Salem, New York, there is a dolmen, a huge boulder that is unbelievably balanced on smaller rocks. It was reputedly built by ancient Celts who crossed over to the New World long before ol' Chris was a sparkle in Mr. Columbus's eye, though some less enlightened scientists claim it is an erratic, left over from the glacial retreat thousands of years ago. To that I say poppycock! I have done years of research on this and have concluded that only humans could have created such a monument; only ancient drunken Irish or Scots would have wanted to.

Do the stones mark the solstice? Are they huge graves? Did someone have a big party there some thousand years ago and get carried away? Who knows? But you can draw your own conclusions after you too see the dolmen in North Salem.–*Dr. Seymour O'Life*

The Silent City of Rocks

The site has been an Idaho landmark since the days of the Oregon Trail when westward-bound pilgrims were both intrigued and frightened by this nine-square-mile region. This area west of Almo features outcroppings of rocks that look like small villages and are inscribed with intricate carvings. While the "city" seems to have been created by the hands of man, some believe that the granite shapes occurred naturally as the result of many millions of years of erosion.

Mysterious Line of Celestial Stone

The Blue Mounds State Park near Luverne, Minnesota, is home to a very old, very odd set of rocks. Nobody knows who is responsible for placing this quarter-mile-long line of rocks, but on the spring and fall equinoxes the sun rises directly on the east end of the line and sets on the west.

Some say that Europeans lined up the rocks before Norse explorers ventured into the area. Others speculate that the stones predate the known Indian tribes and were put in place by a more ancient culture.

Blue Mounds State Park is located in the southwestern part of the state near the South Dakota border, off Highway 75, four miles north of Luverne.

On the spring and fall equinoxes the sun rises directly on the east end of the line and sets on the west.

Hexenkopf: The Witch's Head

In eastern Pennsylvania there is a hill called Hexenkopf, the German word for witch's head. A slew of local legends revolve around this place, including tales of cults and witches. Some speak of a witch who lived on the forested hill and placed a curse on her rowdy neighbors for interfering in her affairs. When people started falling sick, the nearby farmers and villagers decided to take justice into their own hands and hanged the witch. She was later seen wandering the hill looking for a chance for vengeance.

This neat little tale is probably not true. What is true, I discovered, is even stranger and more worthy of notice. Apparently, Hexenkopf Hill was long of importance to the local Indian tribes, whose shamans would perform rituals to draw the evil spirits out of the sick or afflicted. These evil spirits would then be imprisoned in the mountain. It is said the hill used to glow at night from all the evil trapped inside it. Early settlers to the area were so impressed with the shamans' results that they began to learn the rituals. For the next century or so, long after the Indians were gone, local witch doctors performed "powwows," as they called them, to drive the evil spirits from sick people.

While working for the area's daily paper, *The Express-Times*, I wrote a story on the hill's history and met the daughter of one of the last powwowers of Hexenkopf. This elderly lady told me her father was a skilled powwower and had worked the rituals well into the early twentieth century. She remembered an incident that happened when she was a child. Her older sister had just given birth, and the baby was sick with a fever. Her father "took the fever out of her and put it in the rock." She told me that the spirits dance on the rock on All Hallows' Eve and that she was planning on going up and joining them. I never did find out if she did.

The hill itself has long lost its eerie night glow. Skeptics speculate that the glow had been caused by a coating of a mineral that has eroded away. But some say it's because the spirits aren't in the rock anymore—they're out in the woods roaming free and looking for a new "host."

All I know is that I have been up there at night, and it makes your flesh crawl. I've encountered strange lights and shadows (as well as a weirdo with a machete who was sitting alone on the rock in the dark. . . . He was friendly to us, but I was pretty freaked out the entire time we talked to him). Others who went there with me reported seeing figures walking alongside them in the night woods.

Hexenkopf is easy to find. Just take Route 78 to the Easton exit. Turn left at the exit stop and head up Morganhill Road into Williams Township. About five miles down this road is Hexenkopf Road, on the right. While driving down Hexenkopf Road, the hill will be on your left.–*Rick Cornejo*

Alien Enclosure

In 1999, I visited a friend in Puerto Rico. He lives way up in the Cordillera Central in the center of the island. Aside from the alleged chupacabras and elephants in the jungle, there is an interesting phenomenon to which I can attest firsthand. In the rain forest adjacent to my friend's property, there is a small stone enclosure upon a steep hill. It's a perpendicular T made with stones, leaning against the hill, obviously man-made. Inside this structure is a series of hieroglyphs on the wall, including a face that looks strikingly like the stereotypical alien head, accompanied by weird writing. (Bear in mind there were no indigenous pre-Columbian writing systems in Puerto Rico.) Apparently, a farmer related to my buddy discovered it after a big hurricane a few years back.–*Alex M.*

Lost Pyramids of Atlantis?

The southern end of Rock Lake near Aztalan State Park, in Jefferson County, Wisconsin, is the site of an unexplainable series of rock formations that for centuries has baffled everyone who has seen them.

When European settlers first took up residence in the area, Native Americans told them of "rock tepees" on the lake's floor that had been constructed by "ancient foreigners." In 1900 local duck hunters verified the existence of the rocks when they caught sight of massive conical structures from their boat. The stone pyramids were entirely submerged and stood thirty feet high and one hundred feet long.

Explanations for the formations vary. Some say that they are simply the result of natural glacial action, while others say that they are man-made and were constructed by an ancient civilization before the area was flooded with water. Proponents of this theory point to the archaeological evidence found nearby in Aztalan State Park, where an ancient and mysterious tribe known as the Mississippians built pyramidal mounds over one thousand years ago.

The passage at right comes from the Rock Lake Research Society, an organization dedicated to the investigation and documentation of these enigmatic pyramids.

1900: Two local residents, the Wilson brothers, spot mysterious structures underwater while duck hunting. Unusual clarity exists as it is late fall and rainfall was low for the year dropping water levels below normal. The two men advise the other residents of Lake Mills and dozens of people in boats converge on the lake to witness the underwater structure. Several boys dive a short distance and touch the pyramidal structure. It is described as a long tent shaped structure of undetermined height and approximately 100 feet long. The next day water conditions change and the structures are lost to the murkiness and silt of the lake. . . . Lake Mills then becomes a center of statewide attention as newspapers ran articles.

(Years later) Famous Diver Max Nohl, the true inventor of the 'SCUBA' tests his equipment in Rock Lake. He came upon a tall cone shape pyramid in the south end of the lake. The structure made of small stones looked like an upside down ice cream cone that was definitely manmade according to Nohl. Nohl plans to come back to further explore the pyramid legends of Rock Lake. Nohl dies in car crash with wife several years later before he could return.

Due to murky water conditions, the structures are rarely visible, even with high-tech equipment, but fishermen and divers do catch glimpses of the mysterious structures from time to time, and the Rock Lake Research Society has documented their existence using sonar and aerial photography.

Fountain of Youth Burial Ground

On April 13, 1934, workers planting an orange field in St. Augustine, Florida, uncovered human bones. They had stumbled upon an Indian burial ground from the period of the Spanish occupation under Don Juan Ponce de Léon, shortly after St. Augustine was established in 1565. These graves are considered to be North America's first Christian Indian burial ground.

Eventually more than a hundred skeletons were excavated and formed an attraction in the Fountain of Youth National Archaeological Park. The skeletons were arranged in the exact positions they were found and were housed in a building similar to an early Indian settlement. There they would remain until 1991, when the Timucua Indian Nation asked for the bones to be reburied.

Archaeologists have excavated Fountain of Youth Park and have found many Indian artifacts in the area. Some antedate Ponce de Léon's arrival by more than a thousand years. The park is the site where Spanish conquistadors first came ashore in what is now the continental United States. The Ponce de Léon expedition sighted land in the present locality of St. Augustine and named it La Florida.

The Hills Are Alive with the Sound of Moodus

In Connecticut, centered in the area of the Haddams where the Salmon and Moodus rivers converge, is a strange phenomenon that has baffled local residents for centuries — the Moodus Noises. Every so often a trainlike sound emanates from the caves in and around town. Some liken the sound to that of far-off thunder.

Moodus's name actually comes from the Wangunk Indian word "machemoodus," which translates to "place of noises." Native Americans used the sounds as a sign that a tribal meeting should be held. Early Puritan settlers attributed the phenomenon to the work of the devil. Modern scientists say that the sounds, which are most noticeable around Mount Tom, are caused by low-level seismic activity within the mountains.

Indian Burial Ground, Fountain of Youth Park, St. Augustine, Florida

The Oldest City in the United States

Huge pyramids, giant temples, primitive calendars, sprawling cities in ancient times, bustling with people. Where would this be? Ancient Egypt? The mighty Incan or Mayan civilizations? Wrong on all counts.

When early American settlers started their westward expansion, they came upon huge earthen mounds. Many farmers from western Pennsylvania all the way past the Mississippi leveled the mounds they encountered, not giving them any significance at all. But in the late 1800s Americans got caught up in a new spiritualism. Psychics and mediums, mostly charlatans, were everywhere. Talk of ancient Atlantis fired the imagination of many, and somebody reasoned that these mounds were the last remaining remnants of the lost Atlantean culture—for surely the common Indian could never have made such structures. Wrong!

Other explanations were equally ludicrous. Take, for example, the Serpent Mound in Ohio. Some "scholars" of the day insisted that this was proof that ancient Egyptians had made it to the New World thousands of years ago; there was no way that the natives could have created something so precise. Others believed the natives who built these mounds were a lost tribe of Israel.

The Mormons have a much more complicated backstory. They believe that Jaredites came to America about 2000 B.C. and built a thriving civilization that was destroyed in a great battle at Hill Cumorah. The Lamanites and Nephites followed, and they became the mound builders. The Lamanites, who were red-skinned as a mark of their sins, eventually won when warfare broke out.

Today we can acknowledge that not only did Native Americans create these incredible structures, they had vast and thriving societies. In fact, the remains of the most sophisticated prehistoric native civilization north of Mexico are preserved at Cahokia Mounds State Historic Site. Within the 2200-acre tract, located a few miles west of Collinsville, Illinois, lie the archaeological remnants of the central section of the ancient settlement that is today known as Cahokia.

Cahokia—the Mecca of the Mounds

Near Cahokia , Illinois, across the Mississippi River from St. Louis, Missouri, stands one of the most significant prehistoric sites in the United States—the Cahokia Mounds. This place is so remarkable that in 1982 UNESCO—the United Nations Educational, Scientific, and Cultural Organization—designated it a World Heritage Site. But although these earthworks are most important in our understanding of the prehistory of

North America, you could almost miss the place as you drive by, because it is bisected by a state road.

The site is named for a subtribe of the Illini, the Cahokia, who occupied the area when the French arrived. Archaeological investigations and scientific tests have revealed that the city was inhabited from about A.D. 700 to 1400. At its peak, between 1100 and 1200, it covered nearly six square miles, with houses arranged in rows around open plazas. The main agricultural fields were outside the city, which had a larger population than London at that time. Bigger than one of Europe's largest cities? You betcha!

The reasons for the disappearance of the Cahokians and their city are unknown. Depletion of resources probably contributed to the city's decline. A climate change after the year 1200 may have affected crop production and the plant and animal resources needed to sustain a large population. War, disease, social unrest, and declining political and economic power may have also taken their toll. After two centuries of gradual decrease in population, the site had been abandoned by the 1400s. The timing is significant, because at the same time, the pueblo-dwelling peoples of Mesa Verde abandoned the cities they had inhabited for hundreds of years. There must have been an ecological catastrophe.

Today there is a wonderful museum on the site, where visitors will learn much about our land. Cahokia Mounds is managed by the Illinois Historic Preservation Agency.

—Dr. Seymour O'Life

The Moundsville Mounds

Just south of Wheeling, West Virginia, is the town of Moundsville, home of the largest conical burial mound in the United States. Built some time before 150 B.C., the Grave Creek Mound is sixty-two feet high and some two hundred forty feet in diameter, and was once even larger. Over the border in Ohio, just east of Columbus, stands the Newark Earthworks State Memorial. This massive system of mounds contains the Octagon Earthworks and the Great Circle Earthworks (formerly known as the Moundbuilders State Memorial). You can still make out the different earthworks at this great site, but time and ignorance have taken their toll on many of these old mounds.*—Dr. Seymour O'Life*

A shaped stone *inscribed with Hebrew letters—popularly known as the Keystone—was found in June 1860 at the bottom of a pit adjacent to the Newark earthworks.*

Florida's Lost Volcano

For hundreds of years stories have persisted about a lost volcano in northwest Florida. The volcano is allegedly in Wakulla County, about twenty-five miles southeast of Tallahassee, at the intersection of the Wacissa and Aucilla rivers. It takes its name from the town of Wakulla, an Indian word meaning "mysterious." Wakulla Volcano is well named: This is some of the least explored wilderness in the Sunshine State, a virtually untouched subtropical jungle, dotted with sulfur springs and quicksand bogs.

Long before any white settlers appeared in the region, Seminole Indian legends told of smoke rising in the swamp. Over the years each generation came up with a new explanation. During the second Spanish period, settlers thought the smoke came from a pirate camp. In 1860 people theorized that it was from a camp of runaway slaves or Civil War deserters. Superstitious folks believed the column of smoke was "the devil stirring his tar kiln." Eventually people came to believe that it was a volcano.

The chimney of smoke could be seen from twenty miles or more out on the Gulf of Mexico. Ships' captains would navigate by it. The smoke varied in shape and color, sometimes swirling upward, sometimes hazy, ranging from bluish white to white and occasionally black. Explorers tried to reach the source of the smoke but never succeeded.

Unfortunately, this is a mystery that can no longer be seen. On August 31, 1886, an earthquake in Charleston, South Carolina, shook up north Florida, and the smoke has not been seen since.

Was there ever a volcano in Florida, and did the earthquake seal it? Several explorations have not uncovered any hard evidence. In 1949 workers building Highway 98 through the swamp came upon a large hole surrounded by what appeared to be molten rock. But the site was never examined by geologists—and thirty-four dump trucks covered the evidence with six hundred tons of crushed rock.

In response to a query, the University of Florida's department of geology stated, "We are unaware of the Wakulla Volcano as described in lore, certainly there is no evidence of volcanic activity in this region."

Perhaps that 1886 earthquake removed all signs of the volcano, or maybe it never existed at all. But if the smoke was not from the Wakulla Volcano, then it had to come from some source that lasted for over a century.–*Charlie Carlson*

Cryptic Inscriptions

When the past speaks to us, its messages are often written in stone. Sometimes these voices from long ago provide a record of a lost and forgotten civilization. In other instances the curious markings we see in rock are the work of some geological anomaly. Trying to figure out which is which is usually the best part of the game. But sometimes, deciphering the hidden meanings is like trying to piece together a jigsaw puzzle with missing pieces and without the benefit of a picture from which to work.

Of course, scrutinizing anything prehistoric is bound to raise unanswerable questions that lead to some heated debate. The fact is that we just don't know the meaning of many cryptic inscriptions handed down to us through the misty veils of time. Some will be forever shrouded in mystery and will continue to be the subjects of speculation and conjecture for generations to come.

The Mysterious Judaculla Rock

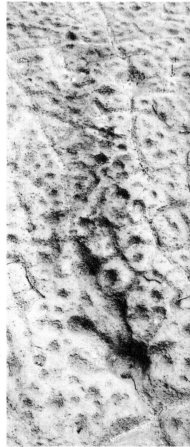

Just outside the town of Sylva, North Carolina, is a puzzling boulder known as the Judaculla Rock. This stone behemoth measures about forty feet around and is adorned with ancient and indecipherable symbols. The markings look like stick figures, swirling curlicues, and thousands of pockmarks, and modern archaeologists are mystified about their meaning. It's believed that Native Americans made them between one thousand and three thousand years ago, though Cherokee legends say the carvings are the handprints of the mythical Indian figure for whom the rock is named—the fierce giant Judaculla, who ruled the Balsam Mountains. The stone can be found nine miles south of Sylva on the unpaved lane called Caney Fork Road, which is about three and a half miles off NC 107.

The Puzzling Pemberton Wedge

Not all Native American artifacts are readily identified. Things that are not obviously arrowheads, spear points, and the like are labeled enigmatics. Then there are the rarer stones, inscribed with pictures or other symbols, which are known as pictographs. Sometimes these symbols are found to be ancient forms of writing left by an unknown or obscure people. In Tennessee an ancient form of Hebrew was found inscribed on a stone that is now in the Smithsonian Institution. In other states pictographs have been found and deciphered as Egyptian hieroglyphics, Roman Latin, and an unknown form of ogham, an ancient Celtic alphabet.

One such amazing inscribed stone was found in Pemberton, New Jersey, along the Rancocas Creek, an area that has been populated for more than ten thousand years. In 1859 Dr. J. W. C. Evans found an ancient wedge-shaped six- by four-inch sandstone axe head, which was inscribed with ten characters. An illustration of the engraved stone appeared in the *American Ethnological Society Proceedings* in 1861, and epigraphic study of the markings revealed that the Pemberton Axe pictograph was most likely Phoenician.

In 1861 archaeologist James Whittall read the published report of the artifact in a Boston library and subsequently published an interpretation of the markings in the Early Sites Research Society's bulletin. He claimed that the script was from the Tartessian Kingdom and said, "Stand firm, on guard, parry, close in and strike." The language is believed to be ancient Iberian, used by the Neolithic tribes that once inhabited the peninsula that today is Spain and Portugal. These Stone Age mariners from 3500 to 4000 years ago were a mixture of Celtic, Libyan, and Carthaginian cultures and sailed the waters of the Mediterranean and Atlantic. Several inscribed stones found in North America have been attributed to these prehistoric sailors, who perhaps ended up here by accident after being blown off course. It is also possible that these people had intentionally colonized this continent, only to leave again long before the arrival of their Spanish descendants in 1492.

Beguiling Smiling Stones

The discovery of a set of strangely carved stones in central Massachusetts is baffling researchers. So far three granite stones have been found, ranging in size from six to twenty-five pounds, all carved with an odd smiley face, which features two sunken eyes and a wide grinning mouth. They appear to be ancient and don't seem to have been carved, but chipped away by other stones, a process that would have taken months with rocks of this size. After examining them, a former state geologist estimated that the stones are hundreds of years old. Local Native American tribes have said that the carvings are not their handiwork.

Riddle of the Voynich Manuscript

Not all mysterious transcripts are written in stone. Some puzzling documents are much more modern, yet prove just as hard to decipher. In 1969 a private collector named H. P. Kraus donated a tiny six- by nine-inch manuscript to Yale University that has troubled and puzzled academics ever since.

This diminutive book, known as the Voynich Manuscript, contains 235 pages of writing and drawings that nobody has been able to decipher. The text is written in a twenty-eight-letter alphabet that has never been seen anywhere else. Some cryptologists say that the manuscript actually contains two separate indecipherable languages. Many of the drawings are of nonexistent plants and animals; others include miniscule images of women taking baths, as well as crude zodiac symbols adorned with pictures of people.

The manuscript was created sometime between the thirteenth and fifteenth centuries, and since then it has had some distinguished

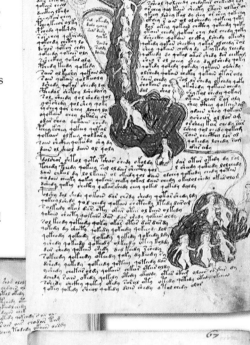

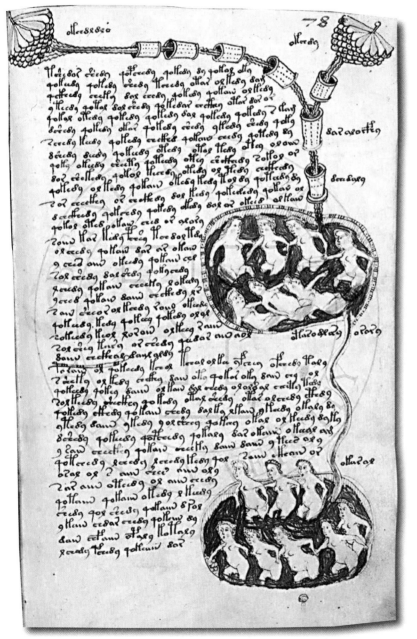

The Voynich Manuscript contains 235 pages of writing and drawings that nobody has been able to decipher.

owners. For some time it was the property of Petrus Beckx S.J., the twenty-second general of the Society of Jesus. Another owner was Emperor Rudolph II of Bohemia (who practiced alchemy, surrounded himself with dwarfs, and recruited giants for his army). Some say it was once owned by English astronomer Roger Bacon, who may have been its author. Bacon was the type of man who would invent his own secret language. In his *Letter on the Secret Works of Art and the Nullity of Magic*, he wrote, "The man is insane who writes a secret in any other way than one which will conceal it from the vulgar and make it intelligible only with difficulty even to scientific men and earnest students. . . . Certain persons have achieved concealment by means of letters not then used by their own race or others but arbitrarily invented by themselves."

The Voynich Manuscript has certainly confounded its readers over the centuries. Some think it is a guide to alchemy. Some think it is a text detailing the downfall of the Cathars, a religious group purged from Europe years earlier. Others think it is a clever hoax, meant to frustrate and confuse scholars; if so, it has been wildly successful.

The Devil's Footprint

Manchester, Maine, is the home of an infamous piece of stone known as the Devil's Footprint. Efforts have been made over the years to chisel down or sandblast away the marks on this stone, but no amount of work has been able to remove them.

The story of the first Devil's Footprint goes like this: Construction workers were laying down a new road in Manchester when they hit an unexpected snag. A large boulder blocked their path, and no amount of effort or equipment could budge it. Fed up, one man began cursing and proclaimed that he would give his soul to the devil to move the rock. The next morning the workers trudged back to the spot to find the rock had miraculously been moved yards away, onto the property of a local cemetery across from the Manchester Meeting House. Imprinted on it were some strange shapes. One was a man's footprint, and the other was a three-toed footprint, supposedly that of Satan himself. The man who challenged the devil was never seen again.

Another version of the story tells of a local farmer who had fallen upon some very hard times. He made a deal with the devil to sell his soul if he would be able to harvest enough crops to pay off all of his debts. His harvest was successful, but when the devil came to collect his soul, the farmer refused. A chase ensued, and the man wound up climbing atop a structure on his property. The devil followed. Both of them jumped off at the same time, landing on top of a large stone next to the building. Their footprints have been embedded in the stone ever since.

New Harmony: Where Angels Tread

Many residents of New Harmony, Indiana, don't even know about the miracle in their own backyard. The town was founded as a religious colony, under the leadership of one Father Rapp. Rapp was desperately trying to get new settlers to move into his then desolate settlement, when he saw a vision. The angel Gabriel was walking atop a stone slab in the forest and left footprints that are still visible today in a large piece of stone, which lies in the backyard of a private home. Unfortunately, a fence surrounds the property, which is not open to the public.

Darwin Be Damned!

The Creation Evidence Museum of Glen Rose, Texas, has some startling footprints on display. Fifty-seven giant human footprints are shown in the same strata as footprints of dinosaurs. This apparent evidence that humanoid creatures existed alongside the ancient extinct reptiles disproves the theory of evolution—at least according to the creationists who run the museum. The footprints can be seen along with other exhibits, including a fossilized foot in a boot.

Fabled People and Places

Once upon a time in a land called America . . .

The quest for mythical lands and fabled people has obsessed people across the world and down through the ages. Among medieval knights the quest was for the Holy Grail. Spanish conquistadors sought the Fountain of Youth and El Dorado, the city of gold. And Lewis and Clark longed to find the Northwest Passage.

Here at *Weird U.S.,* we yearn for more humble places, but they are often just as elusive. We seek out legendary colonies of little people or people without pigmentation. But we set out on our expeditions with all the fervent conviction of Don Quixote going forth to face the windmill giants. And we keep an open mind, just in case these storied people and places must be believed to be seen, and not the other way around. For we want to believe in them, even though we know these things we seek may only exist in our nation's collective imagination.

The Hideous Melon Heads

For as long as anyone can remember, northern Ohio has resounded with tales of a strange race of subhuman creatures in the woods near Kirtland. These mutated beings are known as Melon Heads because of their disproportionately bulbous craniums. Local children are warned not to venture into the forest, where these vicious little monsters are said to kill and even eat anyone who wanders into their turf.

One sick man is responsible for the physical and mental condition of the Melon Heads—a malevolent physician known as Dr. Crow. The story goes that the government commissioned Dr. Crow to treat children suffering from hydrocephalus, a rare condition in which large pockets of water gather within the brain. But Crow began a series of cruel experiments on the sick children placed in his charge. He injected their brains with even more water, abused them, and exposed them to radiation. Many of the children he tortured in his twisted experiments died—you can still see numerous graves of babies in the nearby King Memorial Cemetery.

The surviving Melon Heads suffered severe physical and mental retardation from the experiments. They continued to mutate until they became little more than wild animals, and like all wild animals, they had no ability to reason and acted purely on instinct. Their main instinct, to survive, led them to attack their tormentor. One day they snapped and overran Dr. Crow in his lab, pummeled him, tore his body apart, and ate him. In the process of the attack the creatures destroyed electrical devices and knocked over vats of chemicals, causing a fire that engulfed the laboratory.

The Melon Heads escaped by fleeing into the surrounding forest, where they now roam in packs. They rule these woods. Dozens of reports come in each year about creatures staring out from the woods on the edges of local roads in the dead of night. Many hikers and outdoorsmen routinely find slaughtered animals in the trees, which they blame on the swellheaded hordes. Many claim to have been attacked by Melon Heads, especially along the banks of the Chagrin River.

Bad Moon Rising

The story I have heard is that Dr. Crow (possibly spelled Crowe; I have seen it both ways) practiced medicine out of his house in the early-to-mid-1800s. He had either been given kids with mental problems or kidnapped them (again I have heard it both ways). He kept them locked away in cages in a green barn next to his house and injected their brains with water. A few of them escaped, and some say the barn burned down. Anyway, these Melon Heads still roam the area out near the Holden Arboretum (on Wisner Road, from what I have been told). Supposedly, they come out only at night. If it is a full moon, they will attack any humans they see—however, they have a hard time seeing. If you wear dark clothes, you will be safe. But if you have on any bright colors or white, you are a prime target.—*Justin V.*

Mental Melon Heads

I just read your story on the Melon Heads of Ohio, and I have to say that we here in Connecticut have a Melon Head story of our own. It goes something like this: In Southbury, Melon Heads are said to roam the woods and back roads. They are supposedly escaped mental patients and have gotten their seriously bulbous heads from years of inbreeding in the woods of Southbury. A few years ago I heard a variation based around a mental institution in Newtown. Though I've never heard that they ever hurt anyone, the warning was always to stay out of the woods and off the back roads late at night lest you run into a Melon Head.—*Millie*

These next couple of stories of firsthand encounters with the Melon Heads were contributed courtesy of Chuck from Creepy Cleveland.

Local Authorities Deny Existence of Melon Heads

At Wickliffe High School in the mid-'60s, we heard a different version of the Melon Heads story. Some kids were driving around one day and saw a Melon Head watching them from the side of a country road. They stopped, and he ran into the woods. They followed deep into the woods and came to an old farmhouse.

On the porch sat a middle-aged couple and several Melon Heads. The kids asked what was going on, and the man explained that he had been a nuclear scientist during World War II. After the war he married, but the exposure to radiation caused all of his children to be born as Melon Heads. The government gave him a lot of money to keep quiet and bought this secluded farmhouse where they could live away from prying eyes. He asked the kids to tell no one what they'd seen and never to return.

Someone told this story at a party in the summer of 1964, so we all crammed into cars and headed out to find them. We got stopped by the police in Waite Hill. When they found out where we were going, they gave us a stern lecture that there were no such things and that we should tell all our friends so. We were taken to the police station, where we had to call our parents to come and get us.

We all agreed that the police were so intense in trying to convince us that there were no Melon Heads that there had to be. If not, why were the police so upset that we were looking for them?—*Paul I.*

Ditched Melon Head Along Roadside

On October 5, 2001, my stepfather, mom, stepbrother, and I were driving down Chillicothe Road in Chardon. We came up on this stretch of road with fields on both sides and an irrigation ditch running parallel to it. I looked out my window and saw him—a Melon Head! He, or it, was running next to the ditch. We were going about 45–50 mph, and the Melon Head was actually keeping up with us. It didn't look anything like I've heard in the stories. It looked about the same height as me (five feet seven inches) and was wearing ripped up brown pants held together by what looked like corn husk. It wore a white shirt with brown and red stains all over it. (I'm hoping that the red stains weren't blood.) Its head was a very light brown tint with two holes in the sides that I think were ears. Its head was swelled up, and its eyes were very big. Just as we turned a curve, it jumped into the woods.—*Tony*

Solving the Melon Head Mystery

My father's house rests in a secluded, thickly wooded area off Mitchells Mill Road in Chardon, Ohio. When my family relocated there in the mid-'70s, my older sister's middle school classmates turned white as a ghost when she told them where our house was.

"You live in Melon Head Country!" they exclaimed. She was then frightened with tales of Dr. Crow, the evil man who had performed cruel experiments on hydrocephalic children to make them into cannibalistic fiends. As I grew older, I discovered that these legends had traveled to nearby parts of Geauga and Lake counties. By then I had heard conflicting locations for Dr. Crow's laboratory and institution.

The legend states that the events occurred on Wisner Road near a bridge, but this road is actually split in half due to a washout. One half is in Chardon, one is in Kirtland, and each features a different bridge as a landmark. I also became aware that high school students from Chardon often disguised themselves as Melon Heads to frighten necking teenagers. Despite the passage of several years and my relocation to Los Angeles, I was still haunted by the secrets of the woods in northeast Ohio. After stumbling upon the *Weird U.S.* website, I decided to get to the bottom of the Melon Head myth once and for all.

The first step I took was to contact an old family friend who was the oldest resident of Chardon that I knew. She recommended a woman who had several interesting stories to tell. According to her, the real Dr. Crow had studied hydrocephalus (a condition in which children are born with excess fluid in the brain) thirty years ago, at a place called Sumner Cottage near the natural spring on Wisner Road. The cottage burned down in mysterious circumstances. No mention was made of escaped patients with deformities.

Stories tell that Dr. Crow was either killed by his patients or perished in the cottage fire. Another tale has him swinging by the neck from a beam of the Arch Barn on Mitchells Mill in an apparent suicide.

I went to the library and found a newspaper article from the *West Geauga Sun* claiming that a Dr. Kroh had been influenced by Gregor Mendel and was experimenting on humans to

increase the size of their heads. His experiments failed, and in a fit of pique he piled his genetic mutations into his car and left them by the side of Chagrin River Road in Kirtland, where they presumably fled into the woods and have remained to this day.

I next visited the health department to look up death certificates on any Chardon residents named Crow, Crowe, or Kroh. There were records of people with these names, but none of them appeared to be doctors and all had died of natural causes. My investigation was further hindered by the fact that I could not pin down these events to a specific time period or location, assuming they had happened at all.

Just when I thought I would be returning empty-handed, I tracked down an expert on local folklore who was able to give me the official version of the Melon Head legend. The legend, according to her, was that Dr. Crow and his wife had lived together in a cottage where they cared for children afflicted with hydrocephalus. The children adored Mrs. Crow but weren't so keen on her husband. One night the couple got into an argument, and Mrs. Crow fell against a cabinet, suffering a fatal blow to the head. Thinking Dr. Crow had murdered his wife, the children attacked and killed him. They then proceeded to tear the place apart, setting fire to the cottage in the process. Some of them survived to dwell in the surrounding woods, living off animals and occasionally attacking humans when threatened (or really hungry).

The cold hard facts of the case, though, left me a bit disappointed, so skip this next part if you want to remain pleasantly disturbed by the myth. In the late '50s and early '60s a few children with hydrocephalus lived in northeast Ohio. One of them lived on Wisner Road and was enrolled in the Kirtland school district. The boy and his "normal" friends, who were all preteens, would creep up on parked cars and scare away the older kids. The frightened students would tell their peers at school that they had been "chased by the Melon Heads!" Children afflicted with hydrocephalus do not live very long, so the original Melon Head died of natural causes. He is buried in Kirtland South Cemetery. His friends are now businessmen in Kirtland.

While I may have discovered the origin of the Melon Head legend, I felt as though I'd just scraped the tip of the iceberg as far as the folklore of northeast Ohio is concerned. As my plane took off for Los Angeles, I could feel the magnetic pull of those mysterious woods drawing me in for further adventures. I knew that the next time I returned, it wouldn't be just the home-cooked meals calling me back to Melon Head Country.

—Ryan Orvis

As strange as the legend of the Melon Heads may seem, it is not a tale that is unique to Ohio alone. The following story hails from Michigan.

Melon Heads Menace Michigan

I have heard about Melon Heads before, but I thought they were only around west Michigan. I haven't experienced them personally, but I have heard stories about them in the county of Allegan, near Grand Rapids.

The story goes something like this. There once was this kid with a giant head, and everyone mocked him, so the parents ended up moving into the middle of the woods. There, the family started to inbreed and develop a grudge against normal society, so they are violent toward people. I hear they make a loud, high-pitched scream right before they attack. If you go into the Allegan woods, you can find weird carvings in trees, cats hung by nooses, and animal skulls in trees. I saw a pentagram made out of stones in the middle of the woods.

A young virgin girl was sacrificed at a campground in the Allegan woods, near Silver Creek. They never found out who did it, but some believe it was Melon Heads. I spoke to some locals up near the campground where the murder occurred, and they said that near an abandoned insane asylum and jail in the woods, there were caves in the sides of the hill that lead up to a trail into the woods. They said the caves were constructed in the '60s due to the cold war and that Melon Heads inhabited these caves for a period of time. It was also said that the local government put brush over the cave entrances and sealed them up to block any civilians from trying to get inside them.—*Ben Dawg*

All in the Name of the Devil

Connecticut has no shortage of locales named in honor of the Evil One. There is the Devil's Kitchen in Burlington, the Devil's Pulpit in Hamden, and the Devil's Mouth in Redding. You can taste the Devil's Dripping Pan in Branch Brook, jump the Devil's Gap in Brookfield, and spit into the Devil's Gorge in Weston. There's a Devil's Jump in Derby, a Devil's Plunge in Morris, and a Devil's Rock in Old Saybrook and another in Portland. There are five Devil's Dens, four Devil's Backbones, and two Devil's Footprints.

The Devil's Den

Within the town of Sterling, Connecticut, is a circular cave one hundred feet around, said to be one of the devil's hideouts. Known as the Devil's Den, the cavern has two fissures fifty feet deep, one of which serves as an entryway. Curiously, this entryway also features a depression that extends to the outside, forming a natural chimney. Within the den there is a natural staircase that extends from the top all the way to the bottom of the rock wall. The constantly cold cave has often been explored, and many stories have been told of sightings of evil beings within it.

Satan's Kingdom

Just outside New Hartford, Connecticut, is the most colorful and majestic of the Prince of Darkness's places—Satan's Kingdom. Local clergy gave the area its sinister name centuries ago due to its rugged and isolated terrain. Legends say that Satan once claimed the area as his own stomping grounds, until the angel Gabriel decided the area was too idyllic and cleared out the dark lord and his band of demons.

Descriptions of the area from the eighteenth century tell of the sort of people who were attracted to the forbidding wilds there. "Indians, Negroes, and renegade whites" claimed the area as their own home turf, from which they would venture out to rob, steal, and otherwise terrorize the more law-abiding local citizens.

These days this once infamous bastion of lawlessness is a tranquil and scenic state recreation area, famous for hiking and canoeing. Though it no longer seems to deserve its demonic nickname, it does offer canoers some wicked class III rapids to shoot along the west branch of the Farmington River.

The Devil's Hopyard

Just a few miles north of the point where Routes 82 and 156 intersect in East Haddam, Connecticut, is a notorious spot known as the Devil's Hopyard. Stories of its strange nature have been told since before European settlers moved into the area in the seventeenth century.

Native Americans claimed that this 860-acre area, which features the Chapman Falls of the Eight Mile River, was home to a god. Puritan settlers thought that the wild land was more likely a home for the devil and gave it its present moniker.

Under the Chapman Falls are rocks with perfectly round potholes in them. While geologists might tell you that these strange pockmarks are the result of swirling eddies of water boring away at the stone, local lore has it that these curious depressions were drilled into the stone by the tail of Satan himself. Some say that the evil one has been seen sitting on a boulder at the top of the Chapman Falls. Others have seen and heard strange moving shapes, and in 1999 five men claimed to have been accosted by demonic creatures.

Not the Devil, but Avoid Him Anyway

For more than a century the Winsted area of Winchester, Connecticut, has been the stomping ground of a strange bigfootlike creature called the Wild Man. The first written account of the Winsted Wild Man appeared in 1895, when a local politician saw a large, naked, hair-covered man emerge shrieking from some brush and sprint into nearby woods. The creature stood upright at over six feet tall. Much the same description came from eyewitnesses four generations later in the early 1970s. The Wild Man was spotted on several occasions, usually around the Crystal Lake and Rugg Brook reservoirs. Accounts of the creature all agree he stands erect like a man, is covered in dark black hair, and weighs over three hundred pounds.

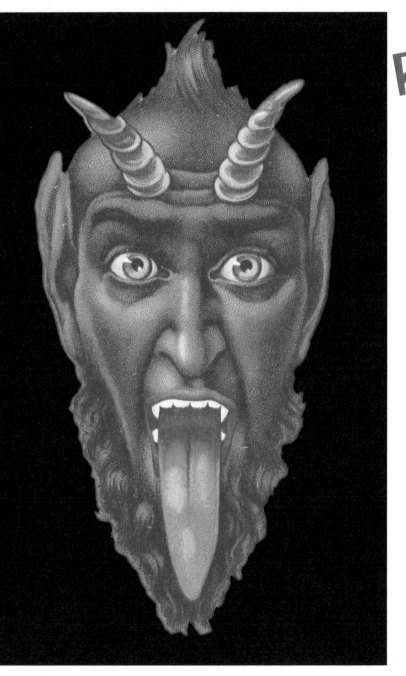

Buried Beneath the Devil's Tree

In Port Saint Lucie, Florida, there is a little park called Oak Hammock Park. There's a Devil Tree there with many legends associated with it, but this is the true story. In January 1973, before the park or any houses were built in the area, the serial killer Gerard John Schaefer abused two nineteen-year-olds, Collette Goodenough and Barbara Ann Wilcox, before hanging them and burying their bodies. Over the next five days Schaefer (known as the Killer Deputy because he was a deputy for the Martin County Sheriff's Department) returned to the scene to commit necrophilia. The bodies weren't discovered until 1977 when two fishermen came across a tree with two ropes tied around a low branch and bones protruding from the ground.

Ever since, people have reported hearing screaming coming from the woods and seeing hooded figures chase thrill-seekers from the area. When the city built the park, they decided to cut down the tree. But when the men came to cut it down with their chain saws, all malfunctioned. When they brought in the manual two-man saw, its teeth chipped off. When they tried an axe, the axe head came off the handle.

I get creeped out when I go there, and I refuse to set foot in the woods. I have heard of people feeling cold spots along the trails during the hottest days in July. If you're ever in the area, the park is located at 1982 S.W. Villanova Road, Port Saint Lucie.–A.C.Y.

The Mysterious Jackson Whites

Since the Revolutionary War, legends have circulated about a motley group of social outcasts living in the Ramapo Mountains of Mahwah and Ringwood, New Jersey, and the southern New York State towns of Hillburn and Suffern. The tales tell of a group inbred to the point of mutation, descended from renegade Indians, escaped slaves, Hessian mercenary deserters, and refugee prostitutes. They are known as the Jackson Whites. But the story of these peoples has been confused by less-than-scholarly historical texts that present local legends as authenticated fact.

Probably the earliest written reference to this group is in an article entitled "A Community of Outcasts" in *Appleton's Journal of Literature, Science and Art,* dated March 23, 1872. The relevant passage reads:

> In relation to this particular people, there are half a dozen legends current, all possessing more or less romance and attractiveness; but the most favored one is, for a rarity, the most reasonable.
>
> The people will tell you that this stain upon their fair country was first put there by fugitive slaves, more than a hundred years ago.
>
> There was gradually added to these fugitive slaves, fugitives of other descriptions, and the general antagonism to the world made each individual endure the others. They buried themselves deep in the fastnesses and gorges of the mountains, and reared children, wilder and more savage than themselves.

An early written reference to the Ramapo people as Jackson Whites dates back to 1900, in J. M. Van Valen's *History of Bergen County,* which states:

The Ramapo Indians sometimes visited the settlements in the township of Franklin. They were known formerly as the Hackensack Indians, but are more properly described as the 'Jackson Whites.' They bear little resemblance to the Indians, yet as tradition gives it they are descendants of Hessians, Indians, and Negroes, but know nothing of their ancestry, so ignorant have they become.

Arthur S. Tompkins's 1902 history of Rockland County, New York, told the saga of the Jackson Whites this way:

> The Jackson Whites originated when the Indians were yet living in the lowlands along the Ramapo Mountains. The first race came by a union between the Indians and half breeds on one side, and colored laborers brought from the lower part of the county to work in the Ramapo factories on the other side. The colored people were either freed slaves or their children grown up, and many of the names today may be traced as identified with some of the old Holland pioneers of Orangetown, for the slaves in old times bore the surnames of their masters. Intermarriage among these people has caused them to degenerate intellectually if not physically.

In 1906–07 the New Jersey historical society's annual report contains this passage explaining the Jackson Whites' curious lineage:

> The Secretary wrote that his understanding had been that they [the Jackson Whites] were a people of mixed Indian and Negro blood. . . . They are supposed to be the offspring of former Negro slaves, runaways, and free Negroes, who sought refuge in the mountains where they could eke out a living by cutting hoop-poles and wood for charcoal, in the days of charcoal iron furnaces. They have been regarded as outcasts, and hence have been allowed to sink into a degraded state. . . .

In 1911 the Jackson Whites' story took on a pseudo-scientific authority when a University of Pennsylvania anthropologist named Frank Speck published an article that claimed that the Jackson Whites were

> Algonquian Indians, probably Minisinks of the Delaware, with some of the Tuscarora who lingered for a rest in the Ramapo Valley on their way from Carolina in 1714 to join their colleagues, the Iroquois, in New York State. To this small nucleus became added from time to time runaway Negro slaves and perhaps freed men from the Dutch colonial plantations in the adjoining counties in New Jersey. Vagabond white men of all sorts also contributed a share to the community from the early days until now. The Jackson Whites may be regarded, therefore, as a type of triple race mixture.

Also written that same year was an even less well-researched study by the head of New Jersey's Vineland Training School, Henry Herbert Goddard, entitled *The Jackson Whites: A Study in Racial Degeneracy*. Taking his liberties with history, Goddard gave his own slant to the Ramapo people's lineage.

> The Indian blood found in the Jackson Whites, whether it came down through individuals held as slaves or through isolated free Indians who intermarried with the emancipated Negroes, is supposed to have belonged to a remnant of the Algonquin Tribe — to the Minsi, or Wolf Clan, who were natives of the Upper Delaware Valley in Pennsylvania,

New Jersey, and New York . . . there were also a few families of the Tuscarora Indians who remained in the Ramapo mountains after their tribe had made there a three years sojourn, from 1710 to 1713, on its way to join the five nations in New York State.

The document that solidified the Jackson Whites' legend was a 1936 book self-published by John C. Storms, a

small-town newspaper editor. *The Origins of the Jackson Whites of the Ramapo Mountains* contended that the first ingredient in the Jackson Whites' racial stew was a group of Tuscarora Indians who had fled North Carolina between 1711 and 1713. Storms drew upon the day's prevailing mythology more than on any personal investigation, and he had a well-known penchant for embellishment and romanticism. According to Storms:

> Originally the Ramapo Mountain region was a favorite resort of the Hagingashackie (Hackensack) Indians, part of the Leni Lenape family of the Iroquois [in fact, they were part of the Algonquin language group, not the Iroquois] . . . . These aborigines had practically all disappeared by the end of the seventeenth century. However, a few remained together with a scattered population that had sought the security of the mountains to evade their brother white man, his laws and customs. Thus it was a sort of No Man's Land.
>
> The first real influx of a permanent population in the Ramapo Mountains was in 1714. This was a remnant of the Tuscarora Indians . . . perhaps it was because there were to be found congenial spirits among the remaining Hagingashackies and the wild renegades who were hiding there. But the ultimate object was to unite theirs with the powerful Five Nations that ruled the country to the northward.

The second strain in the Jackson Whites' bloodline, according to Storms, came from Hessian mercenaries fighting for the British during America's Revolutionary War.

Reaching America under duress, placed in the forefront at every important battle in which they were engaged, beaten by their officers with the broadside of swords if they attempted to retreat, made to do the menial labor of their British companions, their fate was a particularly cruel one. With no interest in the outcome of the military struggle . . . they proved unfaithful, and deserted the army at every opportunity.

In the fighting that took place in the vicinity of New York City, from the camps scattered throughout this region, and at the marches across New Jersey, these men, known by the general name of Hessians, fled to the nearest place of safety—the Ramapo Mountains. There was no possibility of escape, no opportunity to return to their native land, so they made for themselves homes in their retreat, mated with those they found already there, and reared families.

The third genetic element in the Jackson Whites' lineage, according to Storms, derived from English and West Indian women brought to New York to serve as concubines for British soldiers.

The British War Office had a problem on its hands—keeping New York City loyal to the Crown as a Tory city, while keeping thousands of its soldiers in the military camp that General Clinton had established there. . . . But there was a way out of the difficulty, a way that had long been in vogue by warring European nations, in fact, by England herself. A little judicious questioning and a man was found who would accept the undertaking. The man's name was Jackson—history has not preserved for us anything more about him than this, not even his given name.

A contract was entered into that Jackson was to secure thirty-five-hundred young women whom England felt it could very well dispense with, and transport them to America to become the intimate property of the army quartered in New York City. . . .

Jackson set his agents at the task of recruiting from the inmates of brothels of London, Liverpool, Southhampton and other English cities along the sea coast. . . . If a young woman or matron chanced to be on her way home from her occupation, or on the street on an honest mission she fared the same fate as the inmates of the houses of ill fame, and many a respectable working girl or young housewife was shanghaied, and carried off to a life of shame across the sea.

In 1783, when New York was repatriated by American army forces, the stockade of women was evacuated, and the prisoners beat a hasty retreat along with British soldiers and Tories.

Across the Hackensack Meadows, up the Saddle River valley, these derelicts made their way on foot. . . . At last, with Oakland past, the crowd entered the Ramapo Pass and soon found itself in a country that, while wild and inhospitable in character, yet offered the boon of peace; there was no one to drive them away. Here the

colony scattered, finding shelters in the woods and among the rocks. Here the individual members found companionship of peaceful Indians, escaped outlaws, Hessians, runaway slaves—there was ample companionship and it was readily accepted.

Storms cites a New York Tory newspaper, known as *Rivington's Loyal Gazette,* as the first publication to coin the name Jackson Whites and adds that escaped slaves would contribute the final piece to their ancestral puzzle.

The Dutch settlers kept these bondsmen as servants principally, and the bondage was not particularly hard in most cases. Still, it frequently happened that these escaped slaves would seek their own freedom, and the most accessible place and most secure was the fastness of the Ramapos. . . . These people carried with them names of former masters, white acquaintances, or those that they had adopted. Thus we sometimes find family names among them that are borne by prominent and socially acceptable white persons.

It is unclear how much of Storms's account of the Ramapo Mountain people's origins is historically accurate and how much was merely transcribed from oral folktales. It is certain, however, that his account influenced people's perceptions and tainted many works that would follow. The famous writer of dog stories, Albert Payson Terhune of Pompton Lakes, vilified his mountain-dwelling neighbors in his 1925 book, *Treasure.* And in his epic 1947 poem, "Paterson," William Carlos Williams concocted his own version of the Jackson Whites' legacy, drawing obvious inspiration from the Storms history.

Violence broke out in Tennessee, a massacre by the Indians, hangings and exile. . . . The Tuscaroras, forced to leave their country, were invited by the Six Nations to join them in Upper New York. The bucks went on ahead but some of the women and the stragglers got no further than the valley-cleft near Suffern. They took to the mountains there where they were joined by Hessian deserters from the British Army, a number of albinos among them, escaped Negro slaves and a lot of women and their brats released in New York City after the British had been forced to leave. They had them in a pen there—picked up in Liverpool and elsewhere by a man named Jackson under contract with the British Government to provide women for the soldiers in America.

The mixture ran in the woods and took the general name, Jackson's Whites. (There had been some blacks, also, mixed in, some West Indian negresses, a ship-load, to replace the whites lost when their ship, one of six coming from England, had foundered in a storm at sea. . . .)

The Ramapo Mountain people themselves will tell you a variety of stories to explain their own ancestry, intertwining elements of the Dutch, Hessian, and Tuscarora Indian sagas into their own legacy. Most insist that they are really a tribe of Indians called the Ramapough, though they bear little physical resemblance to Native Americans (most appear to be light-skinned African Americans). They have been petitioning the federal government for twenty years to be recognized as a legitimate American Indian tribe. The state governments

of New Jersey and New York have recognized them as such, but the federal Bureau of Indian Affairs has denied their petitions. Such recognition is considered crucial because it brings certain federal benefits, such as housing and health care assistance and the right to operate a casino.

According to the bureau, though, the Ramapoughs are not a tribe at all, but rather descendants of settlers with African and Dutch blood who moved to the area, beginning in the late 1600s, from Manhattan in search of farmland. The bureau asserts that they have failed to show that they are descendants of a historic Indian tribe and cannot prove that they have led a continuous existence as a separate band of people since the time of their first contact with Europeans.

In the end, there is not much historical evidence to support any version of the Jackson Whites' legend. It is almost certain that many tales were originally told to create a derogatory stereotype of the mountain people among their white neighbors. While the Ramapough show a fierce pride in their unique identity, you would be hard-pressed to find a person in Mahwah, Ringwood, or Hewitt who would call him—or herself—a Jackson White. "Those people," it would seem, are always to be found just over the next mountain.

Defending the Jackson Whites

I went to school with these people. They work for the Wanaque Reservoir, drive our school buses, are lunch aides in our elementary schools, and are overall a big part of our community. Granted they are their own people. If you don't bother them, they aren't gonna bother you. Oh, and they have phones and cable, which is more than I have. I have a phone and electricity, but no cable!

–Liz from Caldwell College

Melungeons: Jackson Whites' Southern Cousins

I am currently going to college in North Carolina. Back home in Ramsey, New Jersey, we all knew about the infamous Jackson Whites, the reclusive mountain people of the Ramapos, and while growing up, we all feared them. I came to realize that they were not the miscreants we were led to believe. So imagine my surprise when I began college down here in NC and started to hear similar tales told about the Melungeons. They are supposed to be a strange-looking group of people who avoid contact with outsiders and sometimes even get violent when people venture into their domains. The similarities between the description of the Melungeons and the Jackson Whites piqued my interest, so I did a little research into their history. It is believed that there are about fifty-five thousand of them living in the mountainous regions where North Carolina, Kentucky, Virginia, and Tennessee converge.

I went looking for the Melungeons a few times with friends of mine. We have stumbled upon some very isolated, run-down, and intimidating groups of shacks. One time we were chased down a mountainous dirt road by a dilapidated pickup truck with five hillbilly-looking people in the bed. To be fair, I don't know if they were Melungeons or not, but if they were, they certainly lived up to the fearsome legends I have heard.—*J. P. Figeuroa*

> **They are supposed to be a strange-looking group of people who avoid contact with outsiders and sometimes even get violent when people venture into their domains.**

The Melungeons: Lost Colony or Lost Tribe of Appalachia?

In grade school history classes we are all told the same story of how Europeans came to settle this land. The story begins with two forays onto American soil—Jamestown and Plymouth Rock. But this history overlooks the existence of earlier European-influenced settlements and the people who inhabited them—the Melungeons.

Who were the Melungeons? For years that question has left many historians scratching their heads. As early settlers and explorers ventured westward, they encountered isolated bands of people living in desolate areas of the Appalachian Mountains in North Carolina and Virginia. These people spoke broken English—and, in some cases, Elizabethan English—mixed with Indian dialects. Many had the dark skin of Native Americans, but some had red hair or blue eyes. They grew beards like Europeans and lived not in Native American style dwellings, but in log cabins. They were regarded as a triracial isolate—incorporating Caucasian, African, and Native American bloodlines.

There are concentrations of Melungeons in Tennessee, Virginia, Kentucky, North Carolina, and South Carolina, and many of them added to the mystery of their origins by intentionally hiding or obscuring their family histories. In the south, where racial antagonism ran high, many hid their ancestry in an effort to retain the rights to own land and vote.

One popular theory has it that they were the descendants of the settlers of the Lost Colony of Roanoke, Virginia. When this thriving colony, settled at roughly the same time as Jamestown, was found completely empty, all efforts to track down the colonists were in vain. The word Croatoan had been carved into a tree nearby, so some assumed the pilgrims had fled to the Croatoan Indian tribe nearby. But they were never found. Speculation has it that they fled to the Appalachian Mountains and the Melungeons are their descendants.

Another theory says that the Melungeons are the survivors of a Portuguese shipwreck in the 1700s. Early records of Melungeon encounters state that they claimed to be "Portyghee," and the

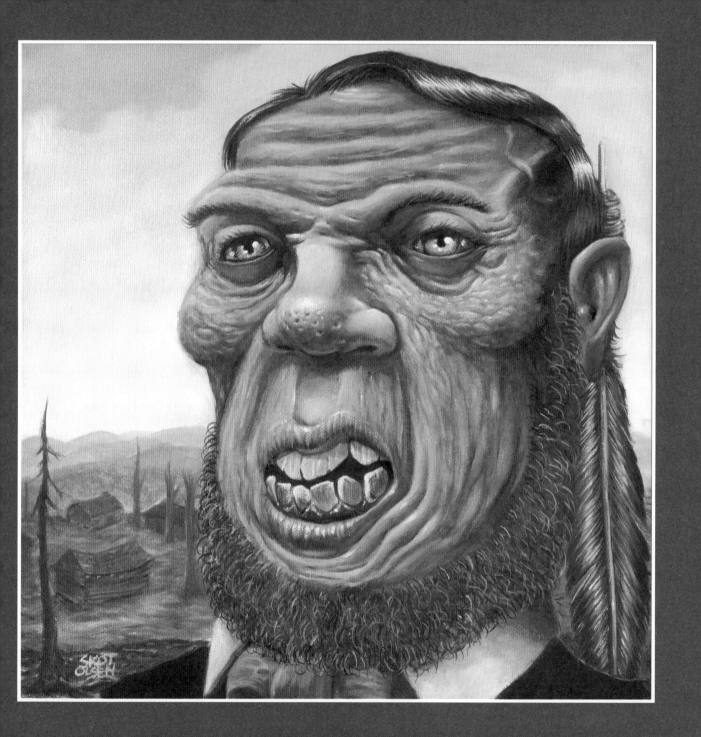

word Melungeon may be a corruption of the Afro-Portuguese word for shipmate, *melungo.* (Other possible origins of the name are the French *mélange,* meaning "mixture," or the Turkish *melun jinn,* meaning "cursed soul.") Many popular Melungeon surnames may be anglicized versions of Portuguese names—Brogan could have been Braganza, Mullins could have been Mollen, and so on.

In his book *The Melungeons: The Resurrection of a Proud People: An Untold Story of Ethnic Cleansing in America,* author Brent Kennedy suggests that they descended from Turkish slaves brought to America by Portuguese sailors in the 1500s. These slaves, whom Kennedy counts among his ancestors, joined local Cherokee Indians, who gave birth to the first Melungeons. Kennedy also asserts that Abraham Lincoln, Elvis Presley, and Ava Gardner may have had Melungeon blood. Unfortunately, Kennedy offers little hard evidence to support his claims, and critics assert that his research draws more on the prevailing mythology of the Melungeons than on any historical facts.

According to an article by Monica Whitaker published in *The Tennessean,* Melungeons have been maligned for centuries. It began, writes Whitaker, with the first children of Middle Eastern and Mediterranean laborers and Indian wives. European settlers and the native tribes alike mocked them, so they hid their Indian features and tried to fit in with the white communities—or retreated into Appalachia for several generations. The author goes on to describe the discrimination suffered by one modern-day Melungeon woman who was kept from knowing her ancestry by the "white" side of her family.

"Growing up she heard about the 'lungeons,' a dangerous people akin to the bogeyman, who could take you away and do terrible things if you were bad. Sometimes, people pitched rocks at her. She started researching her Melungeon ancestry four years ago. 'I was always told I was a half-breed, that I wouldn't amount to anything,' she said."

Wayne Winkler, president of the Melungeon Heritage Association, agrees that Melungeons have been maligned. "Being in the same geographical region and being non-white, they had to come up with something to call us," said Winkler. "That's what white folks did then, so they could segregate you and treat you differently."

These days many southern families can trace some Melungeon connection in their heritage. There are two unique genetic traits that are said to be dead giveaways of Melungeon ancestry: a condition known as "shovel teeth"—a curvature of the front teeth into a shovel-like formation—and a lump on the back of the head.

Though in the past there may have been a stigma attached to those of Melungeon descent, today communities with high Melungeon populations celebrate their heritage and culture. Newman's Ridge, Tennessee, an early Melungeon town, abounds with affectionate Melungeon lore, most famously the stories of Mahala Mullins, a woman infamous for bootlegging liquor and being incredibly obese. Some communities, they say, still speak a hybrid version of Elizabethan English, centuries after the tongue has died out elsewhere. And like the so-called Jackson Whites or Ramapo Mountain people of New Jersey and New York, they strive to be recognized as a unique and distinct culture of Indian descent, albeit of mixed ethnicity.

History books and grade school lessons may be telling us only half the story. It's possible that the history of the first true European settlers in what would one day become America can be traced back to the mysterious Melungeons.

There's Something About Albinos

For some reason, a lack of skin pigmentation really freaks some folks out. Evidence of this fear can be found in the hundreds of letters we have received at *Weird U.S.* relating frightening encounters people have had with albinos.

Albino Village

One of the most fabled of all locations in New Jersey lore is the so-called Albino Village in Clifton, where whole families of these pallid people are said to live.

"Albino Village is a truly weird place that I visited often in my teens," says Carl S. of Paramus. "At that time there were only a few albino families left. By the early 1960s, all that was left were the entry tunnel and a few shacks." Even so, Carl explains, it was a fearful place. "You would have to fight off the urge to scream and flee after riding through the tunnel entrance. It was very scary."

Once you emerged from the portal, you would drive as quietly as possible, gawking at the albinos' cottages. The road was a dead end, and the only way out was back through the tunnel. Most drivers would turn their car around before proceeding to the next phase of the Albino Village ritual.

At this point it was customary to turn on your headlights; honk your horn; hang out the car's windows, beating on the doors with your fists; and scream at the top of your lungs. Of course people came out of their houses to see what all the commotion was about (wouldn't you?). Nobody really knows if they were albinos or just annoyed homeowners, because folks didn't stick around long enough to get a good look. Most had already put the pedal to the metal and were through the tunnel and speeding away from Albino Village.

Albinos Will Net You

I remember taking dates through the tunnel in the mid-'70s, but with a twist. Early in the day we'd hang pieces of string or old netting from the bridge and tell our dates that the albinos would net us if we screamed! Of course with the windows fogged up, this trick made it even spookier!–*Cousin G.*

In His Pink Eyes We Were the Strange Ones

I want to share my experience with the Albino Village. Back in 1966 I went there with about five other guys in a friend's car. It was late at night, and as we pulled through the tunnel, we drove very slowly with the headlights off. Just as we got to the end of the block, a young teenage boy came out from the side of one of the yards. He was very tall, thin, and about fifteen to seventeen years old. He had short white hair, pale white skin, and pink eyes. I remember we all just sat there in the car looking at him in amazement. I will never forget the look on his face and his pink eyes. He stared at us as if we were the strange ones, and I remember a feeling of guilt. He looked at us for a while through the car window and then walked off into the darkness. No one in the car said a word. We just drove off in complete shock.

–*Frank Fiore, Nutley, NJ*

I have been known to hop into my car at all hours of the night and drive aimlessly. On one of my nocturnal travels, I wound up on a deserted road in the upper regions of Passaic County, New Jersey. To my horror a gang of baseball bat-wielding albinos emerged out of the woods and surrounded my car, threatening to kill me if I didn't get out of there. I hit the gas pedal and sped off into the darkness, never once looking back. I am not a troublemaking wise guy. I would never bother anyone who was different, but this frightening experience in the New Jersey hinterlands has restricted my nightly drives to local diners and Laundromats. —*Stephen*

Beware the Midget Albino Cannibals

A few years ago my friend's mother was driving down a back road in Boonton, New Jersey, with her two kids. A gang of midget albinos emerged from the woods and grabbed her son from the back seat of the car. She drove off, and a few months later the boy's body was found. As my friend tells it, it appeared they had eaten him. I'm not sure how true this is, but he has promised to find me some newspaper articles from when it all happened.—*Rebecca K.*

Albino Village Resident Speaks Out

I was out when Henry Pimley barged through the door of our office. He pointed to the front page of our newspaper and said, "I want to talk to the guy who wrote this story."

That was me. I'm a reporter for the local weekly. He was referring to a feature I had written on the "Albino Village" in Clifton, New Jersey. Some locals called the area Frogtown.

Turns out Mr. Pimley—there was nothing albino about him—had lived there more than forty years ago. He remembered the honking horns, the hollering drunks. "Albinos!" the rowdies would yell, and they wouldn't shut their mouths until they got a glimpse of Henry or his family or his neighbors. Then they'd speed off thinking they'd seen an albino in the flesh. Maybe it was the way the moon was shining.

With time, the locals got creative. To access their quiet dead end on the Passaic River, one had to go through a giant stone tunnel. At the outlet of the tunnel, residents would pile leaves and sticks. Carloads of rowdies would ride over those piles on their way in, with their headlights turned off. They'd do the Albino Village ritual—turning around at the end of the road, coming to a stop as they neared the tunnel for a quick getaway, then flicking the lights on, honking, and shrieking as if to rouse the dead. Once they got scared enough or ghostly figures emerged from the homes to give chase, motorists would speed toward the exit—and the piles of sticks. Little did they know that, while the cars were turning around, residents had hidden farewell presents inside those piles, often nice-sized rocks. The troublemakers wouldn't leave albino village unscathed.

Other times residents would wait atop the stone tunnel with an albino-looking stuffed doll on a rope. As cars crept in, down came the doll. Screaming in horror, the invaders would retreat. Once, Pimley said, he greeted several outgoing cars with a harpoon and held them up until police arrived to escort them to safety. You don't want kids taking Sunday drives with all those crazy albinos in the brush.

Yeah, Pimley remembered those times. And he wanted to share his memories with me, the reporter who put his former neighborhood on the front page of the local paper and back into the imaginations of infernal rowdies. I was gonna get it. But to our surprise he just wanted to help me dig up more secrets about his former home. He even offered some old photos. We owe our thanks to Henry Pimley for taking the photos and for being willing to share them. And for taking the years of sleepless nights so well.—*Dan Prochilo, Clifton, NJ*

The Essex Road Albinos

Essex Road is a strange and lonely back road in the Tinton Falls/Neptune area of Monmouth County, New Jersey.

Essex Road's lore includes tales of albinos hiding in the woods, waiting to attack unsuspecting motorists who wander onto their turf. To enhance the road's mystique, there are body outlines drawn on the blacktop to mark the places where the ambushed have fallen.

Strange Encounter

Ever since I was a kid, there were all kinds of stories about the wooded mile-long road. Apparently there were two albinos, brothers I believe, who lived in the woods there. People always talked about them being insane, so I stayed away from there until I was old enough to brave the road. My friend's house was nearby—walking distance easily—and his older brother told us about his encounter with the albinos.

Actually, he saw only one. He was walking along the road during the day, and a man in the woods yelled at him to leave. The man then shot his BB gun at him to scare him off. Of course he ran away.—*Dave T.*

"So, You Want to See the Albinos"

While working in Freehold, New Jersey, my cousin and her friend told me about Essex Road in Neptune. They said that in the late 1800s, families of albinos lived deep in the woods along the road. People used to come from all over just to get a look at them. I guess they got fed up and began murdering curious onlookers and putting the bodies in a slaughterhouse. At a local gas station we asked the attendant where Essex Road was, and he said, "So, you want to see the albinos."—*Jennifer B.*

Attacked on Essex Road

Albino families supposedly lived namelessly in the woods behind Essex Road. When development started in the woods, an accidental death of one albino caused a war between the workers and the albino family. Another tale tells of a romance between an albino girl and an "outsider," which was ended quickly and painfully by the girl's father. Essex Road has a very strange effect on many people. In reality, the road is only about a two-minute-long drive, but when you drive down at night, the trip seems infinite, as though you'll never get off the strange road.—*Joi C.*

The Albino Cannibals of Ghost Mountain

Every rural area in the country seems to be inhabited by a reclusive band of albinos. We here in Sellersville, Pennsylvania, have our own. These cannibalistic, child-stealing, rock-salt-shooting, circus-escaping, inbreeding clan of albinos are said to live high up in the woods on Haycock Mountain and were the stuff of legend in my childhood. They're said to waylay unwary travelers and eat them. They supposedly sometimes raid area farms for livestock and leave gruesome evidence behind. Local police know of their existence and are scared to go up the mountain.

They live in a huge concrete house with no windows and throw firecrackers at passing cars in the middle of the night. They hide in trees and drop down onto unsuspecting hikers, dragging them away to become dinner for the rest of the clan. They block back roads and perform unspeakable rites on moonlit nights. They cavort like fairies among the trees, frightening passersby with their unnatural complexion. Sightings of them flitting from tree to tree and being mistaken for errant specters supposedly gave one local road its name: Ghost Mountain Road.

My own investigations into this have turned up plenty of stories and supposed eyewitness accounts, with some proof in the form of rock-salt residue blasted into the cheap paint jobs of local high schoolers' Camaros; but of the albinos themselves, not a trace. Although I did find two abandoned houses, one with all the bathtubs and sinks filled with a mixture of mud, leaves, and what may once have been water. A search of local newspaper archives has revealed a depressing lack of corroborating evidence. But, hey, not all the news gets reported, y'know?—*Amy McCormick*

Albinos Under Glass

There's a place we call Ghost Mountain, near a town called Haycock, Pennsylvania. There is an old covered bridge there where local legend has it that someone hanged himself. It's also said that if you turn your car on and off three times, it will cease to start. You can really get bad vibes around that area. There is a glass house nearby where albinos live. If you go on their property, they will chase you away with a shotgun. A couple of my friends found this to be true.—*Melissa*

Midgetville

It is human nature to be captivated by miniature versions of everyday things. This is evident nowhere more than in the fascination with miniature people and their homes. Little people have always been showstoppers, from General Tom Thumb in P. T. Barnum's circus, through the Munchkins of Oz, to Mini Me in the Austin Powers movies. And in our experience there is perhaps no more fabled place than the mythical village of Midgetville. We have investigated dozens of locations in search of Midgetville, but most have come up short; they usually turn out to be cottage communities of vacation homes.

But other sites that we've investigated have had dwellings with suspiciously small doorways and windows and looked inconvenient if not impossible for an average-sized adult to live in comfortably. According to legend, such houses and communities were custom-built for groups of little people who had retired from a circus or the vaudeville stage. We have heard many tales of a scaled-down town with tiny inhabitants driving downsized vehicles past diminutive traffic signs.

One aspect of these stories that remains fairly constant is that the occupants are usually hostile toward outsiders. This is undoubtedly because the residents of these rumored Midgetvilles get annoyed at the late-night gawkers who plague them year after year. That's why we never give the exact locations of the supposed Midgetville communities.

Our quest for a real Midgetville is one of the main reasons why we are still out on the road after all these years. For us it is like the Holy Grail of *Weird U.S.*, our El Dorado. If there is any truth to the rumors, we must see it with our own eyes.

Midgets Play Small Role in War Effort

When I was a kid, we used to ride our bikes down from Cliffside Park to the Midgetville on River Road in Edgewater, New Jersey. There were midgets living there at one time. The stop signs were also nailed low. I have driven through there once or twice in recent years, and a lot of the small houses have been replaced with newer, larger houses. The area is prime real estate.

My father told me that in the late '30s, before the war, industry along the Hudson River began contributing to the war effort. The midgets were vaudeville and circus workers who found their niche in the war industry for specific tasks, such as rivet men crawling inside the wings of planes.–*Ernest P.*

Attacked by Midgets

When we were growing up, in North Bergen, New Jersey, one kid told us the story of Midget Town and how he had been there and was nearly killed. We all wanted to go and see this village for ourselves. The kid was hesitant to show us, but he finally agreed. I'm not sure exactly what town we were in, but it was real close to the entrance to the George Washington Bridge. The houses were unusually small. The doors were just about five feet high, and the roads were very tight. All of a sudden we saw little midgets running after our cars throwing rocks. We didn't stay, because the kid who owned the car didn't want it to get messed up.–*Polo Bear*

The Right to Bear Small Arms

Recently I visited this small place, and there were many, many little people there. I was driving by, and I heard bangs as I saw a few dwarfs. I thought they were throwing cans at my car, and when I got out to check the damage, it was much more than I had expected. I found nine bullet holes on the passenger's side of my brand-new car. I went to the police. They told me that I wasn't supposed to be down there and that any car that entered without a permit was shot at.–*Jessica M.*

Don't Be Fooled by the Size of Their Houses

If you go there late at night and you honk your horn, a few select midgets come out and will literally chase you down. Now, not to sound funny or anything, but for little people they sure can run. They chase you with baseball bats and knives, until they have chased you out of their part of town. Now, don't be fooled, but there are no little houses, they live in the same-sized houses as everyone else.–*Kristie*

So Small and So Cute!

There is a Midgetville in San Diego, California. We found it by accident, so I couldn't give you directions, but it is located on Mount Soledad. Even though the people that live on this very prestigious mountain deny Midgetville's existence, I have seen it! The mountain has a large white cross at its top. There is a little section where the houses and the doors and the mailboxes are so much smaller. You can stand by the houses and be almost as tall as they are. It is so cute! *—Teresa*

This photo shows the cast of freaky performers employed by the Ringling Bros. circus in the early 1920s.

RINGLING MANOR - 1916
PRE-REVOLUTIONARY PETERSBURG FORGE, LATER THE SITE OF ALFRED T. RINGLING ESTATE. CIRCUS ACTS AUDITIONED IN MANSION. ANIMALS AND CIRCUS EQUIPMENT OFTEN HOUSED IN OUTBUILDINGS.

NATIONAL REGISTER OF HISTORIC PLACES
NEW JERSEY REGISTER OF HISTORIC PLACES
MORRIS COUNTY HERITAGE COMMISSION

The Real Midgetville?

The most credible reports of Midgetville that we've investigated center around a remote enclave of houses in the woods of Jefferson Township in northern Morris County, New Jersey, near the St. Stanislaus Friary. That's because this monastery used to be the estate of circus mogul Alfred T. Ringling.

In 1913 Ringling purchased nearly one thousand acres of land in the area, then known as Petersburg, to build an estate and winter home for his performers (many of whom were little people). The estate proper consisted of one hundred acres, with a stately twenty-six-room stone mansion overlooking the grounds, barns, and cobblestone elephant houses. The circus would arrive at the nearby Oak Ridge train station each autumn and trek four miles down the dirt path of Berkshire Valley Road on foot or by horse-drawn wagon to the Ringling estate to spend the winter months. When Alfred died in 1919, the circus moved to Bridgeport, Connecticut, then to Sarasota, Florida, its winter quarters to this day.

When we went in search of the Jefferson Midgetville, we stopped in to ask the monastery's Capuchin fathers for information. Though they were gracious enough to give us a tour of the old mansion, they said they knew nothing of any nearby midget colonies.

But down a narrow dirt road leading through a pine forest, we found a group of small houses, a few of which were no larger than the prefabricated backyard sheds that you find at Home Depot. But these were actual houses—cozy little cottages at that—some decorated with flower boxes and Pennsylvania Dutch style ornamentation. An average-sized adult would be able to stand upright only at the very center of these houses, where the pitched roof was highest, and would definitely have to stoop down to look out a window or get through a doorway. We knocked on the little doors and peeked through the tiny windows, but unfortunately, there were no residents, midget or otherwise, to be found anywhere.

Is it merely a coincidence that a cluster of extremely small cottages is located so close to the estate where a circus that employed many little people once wintered? Or is it possible that Alfred T. Ringling had these homes custom-built to make his tinier attractions more comfortable?

Carrot Wielding Little People

There are NO TRESPASSING signs all over Midgetville in Jefferson. I've been there, and two midgets came out with carrots and chased me out. I have also seen the midgets outside shoveling snow. There are about ten midget homes with a two-foot-tall castle-looking statue in the middle.—*Letter via e-mail*

I See Midgets in California

There's a dwarf community in San Diego, somewhere in Coronado. The houses all look normal except the windows are low and the doors are small. Pretty dang nice houses too!—*Anonymous*

One Midgetville Gone, Another Thriving

I live in southern California, and there is an abandoned Midgetville here. It's old, and the trees are overgrown. Some of the houses have been demolished. What's strange is that the buildings are so oddly shaped and twisted. A friend of mine went to a Midgetville in Utah that was still thriving. Now that I've heard there is one in New Jersey, I have reason to believe they're all over the country!
—*Shireen Dada*

Midgets with No Manners

There is supposedly a Midgetville here in Virginia, located in the suburb of DC known as Tyson's. The Ringling Bros. circus is said to have built it, back when they had an office in the Tyson's Corner Mall. Supposedly midgets still live there and are rude as hell to outsiders. It's reportedly like a scaled-down town with small houses with short light posts.
—*Charlie*

Rich and Retired and Living in Midgetville

In high school we all knew about Midgetville, which was supposed to be somewhere in eastern Maryland. A bunch of rich midget actors from *The Wizard of Oz* retired there and built a completely miniaturized neighborhood of suburban excellence. But because they built the town in an isolated, hard-to-find place, the residents went insane, and their inbred children have insatiable desires for mischief and blood. They wait in the trees in front of their homes and jump down on lost motorists and bite their eyes.—*Dyna Moe*

Midgetville's Just a Short Hop from Downtown

We have a Midgetville here in Ridley, Pennsylvania, across from Taylor Hospital (it's about fifteen minutes from Philadelphia). Midgets, I mean little people, still reside in this private community, and trespassing is prohibited, but there are ways of getting inside. In this small town are streets of tiny little houses; even the mailboxes are tiny. It's a must-see.–*Carol*

The Yellow Brick Road Leads to Salt Lake City

In Salt Lake City, Utah, the term "hobbit" is not so much about Tolkien movies and books as about a strange and dangerous neighborhood in the northeast corner of town. For decades rumors have swirled about a diminutive community known as Hobbitville, a secluded, guarded portion of Salt Lake City supposedly inhabited exclusively by dwarfs, who built their houses in a private neighborhood away from judgmental eyes.

Local teens often become enraptured with this story and go on late-night rides to see Hobbitville for themselves. The stories they bring back are usually strange and often frightening. One rumor has it that the hobbits have created a system of communication to alert each other to the presence of outsiders and yell to each other in a strange dialect. They will also confront intruders, often throwing vegetables and fruit at them. In fact, it's said that they have cultivated large stockpiles of foods for the express purpose of pelting the curious with them. Some stories say that the hobbits are very vicious and have killed intruders. A large, unkempt man called the Ogre also patrols the area.

There are many NO TRESPASSING signs posted throughout the neighborhood, and Hobbitville is patrolled by both police and private security (not to mention the Ogre). Whether or not little people really are living there, big fines are levied against those caught exploring this mythical land after dark.

What the Squatters Ate

There is a Midgetville in Kentucky, and I've been there on several occasions, both at night and during the day. It's in the sticks on US 42, just south of Louisville, on the road between Shepardsville and West Point. It's really an interesting little place. The cottages are arranged on a big square, high on a hill right off the main road. Most of them are built on the edge of a steep cliff and are supported by wooden stilts. The cottages are tiny and come complete with miniature doors, windows, porches, and the smallest furniture I've ever seen this side of a Toys "R" Us summer sale. There are about thirty or so little cottages. In the center of the square is a rather large, funky-looking church.

Lots of squatters mill about during the daytime and give you funny looks when you drive by. Though all of them appear to be of normal height, that's where the normalcy of their appearance ends. One theory is that they are a wandering tribe of gypsy cannibals who ate the previous residents before settling their digs. One drive around the square is enough to convince the astute observer that this is entirely feasible.–*Eric Crump*

Small Wonders: The Miniature Menehune of Hawaii

The folklore of many nations around the world includes stories of magical little people. The most famous are the leprechauns of Ireland. In Hawaii it is the mischievous menehune who are said to haunt the deep forests or the mountains of Pu'ukapele. They come out mostly at night—to play tricks on people or to serve them if they feel inclined.

The mythology of the menehune is as old as Polynesian history. Some say that the great god Maui himself was one of the tiny creatures. When the first Polynesians arrived in Hawaii, they found dams, fishponds, and even temples, all presumably built by the menehune—who were already there, living in caves.

The creatures are said to be about two feet high, although some as small as six inches have been seen. They are naked, but the long, straight hair that falls to their knees keeps them warm and discreet. Apparently no two are the same, and they can be moody—malicious and dangerous one day, harmless the next. But they are always tricky and therefore should be avoided unless a special favor is needed of them. They are expert builders and craftsmen and many a major project, such as the preparation of a wedding feast, has been completed in a single night by the superstrong little gods.

On the island of Kauai the menehune pull many tricks. But then the owl god summons all the owls of Kauai to chase the menehune back into the forest. Menehune are afraid of owls.

—*Hugh D. Mailly*, Encyclopedia Mythica

Pygmy People

For centuries Native Americans have told tales of a fearsome race of people who exist in secret throughout the American West. Myth says that these warlike, reclusive, and aggressive people are best left alone. Legend also says that these people are at most a few feet tall. Some claim to have encountered small, strange, manlike creatures in the mountains near Casper, Wyoming, and the mummified corpse of an inexplicably small man was discovered there early in the twentieth century.

In October 1932 two men prospecting for gold unearthed an extremely peculiar corpse in the San Pedro Mountains, sixty miles southwest of Casper. It was found sitting cross-legged on a ledge in a small cave with its hands folded in its lap. While only fourteen inches tall, the creature was otherwise a fully preserved and fully grown human male. The mummy was small and shriveled and its skin was loose and wrinkled. It had a broad nose and thin lips, and its head was covered in a dark gelatin.

Dubbed "Pedro," the mummy was put on display, sold, and before long had changed hands many times from one owner to another. Most people disregarded the find as a hoax early on, thinking that it was created in order to sell tickets to sideshow attractions.

The Pedro Mountain Mummy was eventually purchased by a Casper businessman and taken to New York City where the remains were X-rayed at the American Museum of Natural History and certified as genuine. The examination showed that this was indeed a small man.

According to the doctor's report, Pedro possessed an "irrefutably manlike skeleton, despite its tiny stature." It had fully formed arms and legs and a perfectly formed spine and rib cage. In addition to the damage to the skull, it was also determined that Pedro had a fractured collarbone.

"It seems as if this little person met its death through some violent attack, accounting not only for those injuries but also for its flattened head and the dark gelatinous substance covering its head," the doctor said.

Upon hearing that the mummy was not a hoax, skeptics rationalized the corpse as being that of a child or fetus. These theories were also debunked when it was revealed that the mummy had a fully grown-in set of teeth. Scientists speculated that it was not a child but close to sixty-five years of age! Since these tests were conducted, the mummy of Pedro has been lost, making further tests impossible.

Did a mysterious race of tiny warlike tribesmen once roam the mountains of the American West? Shoshone Indian legends tell of an ancient race of little warriors called the Nimerigar, who once inhabited the land and attacked with tiny bows and poisoned arrows. According to some stories, they were so fierce they would even kill their own kind by crushing their skulls if they became ill. Could this have been the fate of poor little Pedro? And since many have reported encountering the so-called Little People in Wyoming, Colorado, and New Mexico, could a prehistoric race still roam the remote reaches of the Rockies?

The Frog People

They live alone in a desolate compound that no outsiders dare enter. Years of inbreeding have given them hideous features that make them look more like amphibious creatures than human beings. They come out only at night. They are the Frog People.

"I remember some family around Danbury," Connecticut native Brian Hines told *Weird U.S.* "I don't know much about them, but I remember parents, a very young girl, and a boy maybe around fifteen at the time. They looked like frogs, mostly because of the bugged-out eyes. A science teacher in junior high told me they were inbred."

The *Fairfield County Weekly* ran a short mention of the Frog People in 1998, placing them in nearby Bethel. "For years, rumors of an inbred family of large-eyed freaks have been circulating throughout the town, even seeping into the gossip of neighboring burgs," the article read. "It is said that this mysterious family lives together on a decrepit compound not far from Bethel's center, and that members of the clan have been observed milling about the place, spilling from open doors and windows and performing various bizarre, unspecified acts. They even venture into town from time to time, we hear, for the occasional shopping trip."

One of the most pervasive legends regarding the Frog People is that they do not take kindly to outsiders, so few dare to venture near their secluded enclave. *Weird U.S.* has managed to locate a man who bucked this trend by personally visiting the homes of the Frog People. Redding native Curtis Gwinn told us what he has seen with his own eyes.

"When I was growing up, everyone knew about them. They were described as having their eyeballs on the sides of their heads, thin crusty lips and wide mouths, and sunken noses with nostrils that were just thin slits. They had patchy hair that sat upon heads that were too big for their bodies. Their bodies were frail and weak. They wore clothes from the Salvation Army and came out only at night because they were afraid of being tormented. It was rumored that they looked this way because of continuous inbreeding.

"The summer before my junior year of high school a friend's mother was running a version of meals-on-wheels at a local church. I volunteered to help. Two friends and I would go around Danbury door to door to give out lunches to unfortunates. In one of my houses were the Frog People. They share a family name I can't remember. They wouldn't come to the door; we were told to knock on the door and then leave the food there. Being mischievous kids, we would hide and wait. I never got awesome views, but the door would crack open and a hand would come out. They would snatch the food.

"A year later, I'm at my local grocery store around eleven p.m., with the same two friends. We were walking down the canned goods aisle, and there's a Frog Person. He has penny loafers and a short-sleeved dress shirt tucked into khaki pants. He was going through soups. We gasped. He turned and saw us, and I'll tell you what—it was not as horrific as described.

"His head was lemon-shaped. He had a bad lazy eye. His face was sort of stretched, and his eyes and nose looked far apart. He had sores on his very thin lips. He really did have a very froggy appearance. However, he had a normal head of hair. I'd go so far as to say it was even sort of nice, parted on the side. He had a bobble head sort of appearance and was very gangly.

"Then a girl came around the corner—blond hair, pretty well groomed. That added to the creepiness of it. If you saw them from behind, they would look totally normal, but if you turn one around, it's a monster! I know it sounds mean, but they did look like two frogs. They darted away and quickly made their way out of the aisle."

Unexplained Phenomena

"There are more things in heaven and earth, Horatio, than are dreamt of in your philosophy." —William Shakespeare, *Hamlet*

Charles Fort (1874–1932) is sometimes referred to as "the father of strange phenomena." This complex and odd fellow would scour newspapers and magazines looking for stories of extraordinary events, often spending hours at the Public Library in New York City collecting notes about weird observations. He and his wife, Anna, traveled to seek out strange stories, and he published several articles and books on his findings.

In New York in 1929 he met up with Tiffany Thayer, a young novelist with whom he'd been corresponding. Fort's massive collection of shoeboxes filled with scribbled notes and newspaper clippings inspired Thayer to form the Fortean Society, dedicated to chronicling Fort's work and research.

Today, more than seventy years after Fort's death, numerous societies and publications are dedicated to Forteana, the contemporary term for anything that is classified as unexplained. These groups attract scientists and scholars, deranged crackpots, and the occasional visitor from Mars. But, as we say at *Weird U.S.*, keep an open mind and anything is possible.

Like Charles Fort, we have found unexplained phenomena in every locale. Through our research we've gathered some amazing accounts of America's truly odd hot spots. But unlike pseudo-scientific organizations that try to solve or, worse, debunk reports of unexplained happenings, we prefer to simply record the events and report our findings. We leave it to you, the reader, to contemplate the possibilities and draw your own conclusions.

Mysterious Handprint of the Carbon County Jail

In the town of Jim Thorpe, Carbon County, Pennsylvania, there's an infamous legend dating back to 1877. It is the story of a miner sentenced to death for conspiring with the Molly Maguires against the avaricious coal barons. During the trial and while on death row in the old Carbon County Jail, he vehemently proclaimed his innocence. On hanging day, before he was taken from his cell, he rubbed his hand on the dirty floor of the cell, placed it on the wall, and proclaimed, "This is the hand of an innocent man!"

Innocent or not, he was hanged that morning. To accommodate the next guest, the cell was cleaned and the handprint was scrubbed off the wall. Strangely, however, it reappeared. Over the next hundred-plus years the handprint has remained on the cell wall despite repeated washings, repainting, and even being plastered over. No matter what, the handprint reappears in a day or two.

The Carbon County jailhouse is now the Old Jail Museum and offers public tours. You can actually see the ghostly handprint in cell 17, testifying to an innocence proclaimed over a century ago.

—George Wylesol

As the home of Benjamin Franklin, the brilliant scientist and statesman, Philadelphia has a long and proud history as a technologically advanced city. However, Philly is also the birthplace of some scientific experimentation that would have shocked even old Ben, the father of electricity.

The Philadelphia Experiment

The Philadelphia Naval Yard harbors a hidden history beyond its role as a docking point for military vessels. It might just have been the site of one of the strangest scientific experiments of all time.

The infamous Philadelphia Experiment defied the laws of physics as we understand them and, according to some, cost several servicemen their lives. Did this top secret experiment ever really happen, or is it only a high-tech myth of our modern age?

Those who believe it tell the story this way: In 1943 the Germans had the advantage on the high seas. Their fleets of U-boats wreaked havoc upon Allied military and merchant vessels in the Atlantic. The United States decided to pull out all the stops with a device that could electronically cloak vessels from being picked up on radar. In Philadelphia a small destroyer known as the U.S.S. *Eldridge* would test this theory.

In June the *Eldridge* was fitted with tons of strange equipment. Generators and coils were mounted throughout the ship in order to produce encompassing electromagnetic fields. When the devices ran in unison, this setup would theoretically bend the light and sound waves around the ship, making it virtually invisible. At nine a.m. on July 22, 1943, this theory was tested for the first time. When the generators were turned on, a green fog surrounded the ship. In a blink of the eye the fog and the ship itself entirely vanished! Fifteen minutes later the generators were turned off and the *Eldridge* reappeared.

The crew was in a state of shock and was violently ill.

They reran the test in late October. This time, when the generators were turned on, the ship disappeared again but left a clear impression upon the water. There was a blinding flash of light; then even that disappeared. Meanwhile, miles down the coast, in Norfolk, Virginia, witnesses saw the ship materialize off their shore. For several minutes the U.S.S. *Eldridge,* moments ago docked in Philadelphia, sailed the Virginia coastline. Just as suddenly as it had appeared, it vanished and was seen once again in Philadelphia.

When the ship was boarded, the entire crew was ill. Some of the crew had disappeared, and five were fused into the walls of the ship. Some had been emotionally and mentally stripped to the point of insanity.

No one knows how the physical teleportation of the U.S.S. *Eldridge* could have happened. The government quickly covered up the results of the experiment, although over the years many witnesses have verified the strange tale as authenticated fact. Some say that the Philadelphia Experiment is nothing more than a sci-fi fantasy. Others swear that it is terrifyingly true.

Bottomless Pits: The Hole Story

For centuries, stories and legends have surrounded the mystery of what lies beneath the surface of the earth. From lost civilizations to strange artifacts that can't be explained, tales range from weird to downright spooky.

For example, there are regional stories of what are usually called sinkholes — depressions or pits in the ground that never seem to be filled. In some instances people have been throwing extra dirt from gardens and yards into these holes for generations. The situation seems harmless until you begin to question the implications. Where is the dirt actually going? Why does the pit only sink so far, even though it is filled over and over again? Why doesn't the sinkhole continue sinking until there is a deep shaft into the earth?

These pits often become the source of local legend or supposed curse. In many of these cases the story goes that a man was hanged, and, when the weight of his body stretched the limb of the hanging tree too close to the ground, his executioners were forced to dig a hole. The story normally concludes that this hole — the sinkhole — has not filled since, no matter how much dirt has been tossed into it.

Where Have All the Tires Gone?

In Tacoma, Washington, a man named Johnson discovered a hole in his yard that was about four feet in diameter, with the sides of the top three feet all bricked. He didn't notice the hole until he moved into the house and his dog found the opening. The man decided to drop about fifty feet of rope into the hole, but failed to reach the bottom. Assuming that it was an abandoned well, he loaded it with old tires, and it actually seemed to be getting close to being filled.

Johnson asked his neighbors about the hole and was told that the previous owners of the house had dumped a load of marble into it, and a short time later an explosion blew everything out. The former residents moved away soon after.

Eventually Johnson saw that the tire level in the hole began dropping, as if it were digesting the tires. Soon the top of the pile disappeared from sight. Neither Johnson nor anyone else was inclined to get into the hole to see where the tires had gone.

Not a Good Slide

For years, tales have circulated about a hole near Hannibal, Missouri, that was rumored to be bottomless. According to the stories, cattle and other animals had been lost in the hole, which was located in the woods outside of town, and had never been found. It became a scary place that residents avoided. Legend has it that the fellow who owned the land decided to check it out for himself one day. He tied a rope around a nearby fence post and slid down into the blackness. Some friends discovered him shortly after he surfaced from his adventure in the pit. His hair had turned completely white, and he was wildly insane. Whatever he had encountered down in the hole had caused him to lose his mind! *–Troy Taylor*

Those Magnificent Men Are Flying Machines

Those Magnificent Men **Are** Flying Machines

C'mon, Baby, Light My Fire

Puerto Rico is full of funky stories. I thought you guys might enjoy this one. My neighbor's daughter lived with her little girl in a wooden house. One afternoon she put her daughter to sleep and fell asleep herself. She woke up smelling smoke coming from her little girl's room. When she opened the door, there was fire all around except for immediately around the crib. The mother was able to grab her child and run out, but the house burned. The funny thing is, though the house burned completely, charred black, it didn't fall. The baby burned down three houses in the same manner. The mother would leave her in the crib and come back to find the room in flames. I had the opportunity to see one of the houses. It was burned to a crisp but was still standing. I don't know what happened to the little girl; she must be about fourteen now. I hope she's not burning any more houses. –*D. Musseb*

High above the state of Washington soars a peculiar oddity that residents have reported three times in the past sixty years. Early in 1948 a Chehalis resident heard a strange noise while out in her backyard. She looked up to see a man hovering two hundred feet above her. Attached to his shoulders were long wings, which he was controlling with a device that covered his chest. After only a few moments he abruptly ascended and flew away.

Many people dismissed this report as a hoax or hallucination, but a few months later two citizens of Longview saw not one, but three flying men. According to their reports, these men were flying roughly two hundred and fifty feet above them, wearing goggles, and carrying what appeared to be guns. They were traveling fast and seemed to be observing what was going on below them with great curiosity. The two witnesses called for their co-workers to come join them, but by the time anyone had come outside, all three flying men had vanished.

All was quiet on the flying-man front until the mid-1990s, when a teenager driving near Lake Kapowsin encountered a manlike flying beast standing nine feet tall. The creature was coated with blue fur and descended from the sky on large wings, landing on the road in front of the youth's car. The beast had birdlike feet but a human's legs and torso. After a few tense minutes the creature flapped its large wings, shaking the boy's car, and flew off into the night sky.

So what exactly are flying high in Washington? Men, beasts, or whatever, they're certainly a weird addition to the state.

Ghost Lights

One of the most common and widespread unexplained phenomena in the United States is the appearance of ghost or spook lights. These mysterious illuminations are most often seen along railroad tracks, and consequently, many have given rise to tales of apparitions of dead lantern-waving railway workers. Other spook lights are seen dancing around farm fields or hovering on a distant horizon. Many think these beguiling orbs are more extra-terrestrial than spectral in nature. Unlike most ghost sightings, ghost light stories actually offer a site where you can go to witness the phenomenon for yourself! For years these mysterious lights have drawn generations of curiosity-seekers like beacons. They flocked to reported spook light hot spots around the country, hoping to catch a glimpse.

There will probably never be a satisfactory answer to the question of whether such lights are of a scientific or metaphysical nature. But we here at *Weird U.S.* don't really care what causes these bizarre lights to appear. As long as they continue to shine and fascinate late-night seekers of the light, that's enough for us. Why not just sit back and enjoy the show?

Hookerman Lights

It is a moonless night in Flanders, New Jersey; leafless branches sway in the chilly November breeze. Through the mist ahead you see something: a dim white ball of light. It appears for a second, then dissipates into the dark. Suddenly it appears again in a different spot, almost beckoning you to join whoever is up around the bend. In the distance you hear the faint sound of a whistle. Is it just your imagination, or could a phantom train be riding on the tracks?

Just then the light appears to be coming down the tracks. Is it someone with a lantern or a flashlight? It starts to look like a bouncing ball. It gets brighter as it approaches, then passes over your head and fades into the dark. You've just witnessed what people around Flanders call the Hookerman.

The legend of the Hookerman is a familiar tale among aficionados of the supernatural. This odd phenomenon occurs in more than sixty different locations throughout the United States alone, and explanations for it fill Fortean notebooks and magazines throughout the world. Many sightings are associated with railroad tracks, although some occur on open farmland and hillsides, and sometimes over water.

In New Jersey the Hookerman legend is that of a railroad worker who lost his arm in a train mishap over a century ago. Some say he was a night watchman on the Bartley–Flanders spur, who was either signaling an oncoming train to stop or was traveling on the train itself. He fell and lost consciousness. When he awoke, the train had run him over and cut off his arm. Now, fitted with a hook to replace his lost hand, the Hookerman's spirit appears on the tracks, carrying a lantern, still searching for his lost arm.

For more than a century the Hookerman has been sighted in Flanders on North Four Bridges Road but more recently on the Naugherton Road railroad tracks in Washington Township, Warren County, and off Roycefield Road in Hillsborough, Somerset County. Other reports have come in from Boonton and from Budd Lake. Anthony Muller, a science teacher in Mount Arlington, has witnessed these lights on several occasions.

"The effect is a bright, rose- to amber-colored light, ball-like or disklike in shape, with a diameter of about four feet," said Mr. Muller. "It seems to be ten to twelve feet above the tracks and moves in one direction, I would estimate at 25 to 40 mph.

"I was quite interested in this phenomenon and began some research. Geologists and electrical engineers told me that quartz-bearing rocks, under pressure and stress, produce electrical discharges in what is known as the piezoelectric effect. The railroad tracks may focus this electrical energy into ball lightning or at least something close to it."

In 1976 the New Jersey–based organization Vestigia conducted a study of the Long Valley mystery lights. The group included experts in meteorology, physics, optics, photography, and chemistry. They set up a Geiger counter and methane detectors, and laid four thousand feet of copper wire between the rails, attached to amplifiers and oscilloscopes. At ten p.m. on November 20 their instruments registered drastic changes as a small but distinct light appeared a foot above the ground and hovered there for about two minutes before disappearing. The team's cameras photographed a pinpoint of light, with infrared photographs that showed more density and light range of the object. The team then turned to geophysical science for an explanation. The geodesic maps of New Jersey revealed a major fault, the Ramapo Border Fault, which runs through Peapack and ends at Indian Point, New York. Since 1962 there have been no less than thirty-three minor earthquakes along this fault. Because quartz-bearing rock produces an electrical charge under seismic stresses and the railroad bed in Long Valley is granite, which is a very good conductor of electricity, a scientific explanation had been reached.

Sadly, Conrail, which owns the Flanders railroad bed property, decided to rip up the tracks in 1977 because of all the people looking for the Hookerman lights. Conrail did not want to take responsibility for anyone getting hurt or losing arms along the railroad bed. Fortunately for New Jersey night riders, this doesn't dampen the mystique of the legend. As long as there is some place to drive to see ghost lights, New Jerseyans will set out to find the Hookerman, as they have done for over a century.

I Saw the Light

Three of my friends and I went down to Four Bridges Road in Chester to look for the Hookerman. We parked where the railroad tracks would have crossed and headed down the abandoned bed. A few minutes later we thought a car was coming down the tracks, until the four bright lights merged into one, then came down the bed toward us. It got real faint as it got closer. It was the Hookerman! As it came close to us, we ran for that foggy light. We got within about twenty feet or so; then it disappeared. As we looked down the bed past the car, the light reappeared. We ran past the car and down the bed on that side of the road. The light had disappeared again. This part really scared us. We looked back at the car, and the light was doing loops around it. It started as foggy light, changed to a green, then bright red, then shot up about ten feet and disappeared for good. Three of us swear on our grannies' graves about what we saw. The fourth is in denial. He says the bright lights were from a helicopter and the light looping around his car was a radar detector! Go figure.—*Don in Andover*

A Shout out to the Hookerman

When I was in high school in about 1983, some friends and I would drive down to the tracks, face east, and yell for the Hookerman. We would then see a light flash in the distance. The light would appear in colors of blue, red, green, and white. If you yelled enough and had the courage to stay long enough, the light would appear to come closer each time it flashed. We would see it almost every time we attempted to draw out the Hookerman.—*Letter via e-mail*

Hookerman vs. Fishermen

I have a cousin who lives about a mile from the Hookerman trail. I always thought it was just an old folktale, until I actually got out there. It is a very freaky place. The train tracks have been unusable for ten years now, yet you can hear the train whistle blow and the tracks feel like there is a train in the area. It is true that the trail is haunted.

We were out there one night fishing off the bridge, and we came in contact with the Hookerman. It was the scariest moment of my life. At first I thought it was just the cars passing by, but then there was a light that looked like someone or something was carrying a lantern. Then the light went into a circular movement and turned colors. We all left our poles and booked to the car and left and have not been back since.—*Mike*

Hunting for the Hookerman

Back in the 1960s and 1970s the Hookerman site was a big teen attraction. A friend of mine would often go down to see the lights, and on hot summer nights there would always be a crowd of fifteen to thirty teens! The Hookerman, he said, generally appeared right before a train was to pass by. Usually it appeared as a yellowish, hazy ball that bobbed about the tracks. One particular night my friend became a true believer. As a train approached, the Hookerman light appeared about thirty feet down the tracks from where the crowd were standing. The train got closer, and the light moved slowly down the tracks as well. Just before the train reached the group, the engineer dimmed his headlight, then turned it up to full brightness. For about a second, in the rays of the bright light, the group saw a translucent figure of an overalled railroad worker with one arm, and that arm was waving a lantern side to side.

As the train passed, a train crewman stuck his head out of the window and shouted to the group, "Did you see that?" As soon as the train's caboose rolled past, the group started running toward their cars.

One last intriguing fact: In the 1920s and 1930s the Central Railroad of New Jersey, which owned the tracks, had a notation in their employee timetable not to stop for any lantern signals in this area. That's how common the Hookerman lights were!

—Paul Tupaczewski

Hookerman Roams the Southern Rails

I found striking similarities to a story my friend Beau told me about a ghost in Gurdon, Arkansas. This town was founded in the 1880s, and it's very small—not more than three thousand people, I think. Anyway, a guy named William McLain was the head of a railroad crew. One night he and a crew member were out fixing a problem when this guy—the one he's working with—chopped William's head off with an axe. It's said that he still walks the tracks at night looking for his head. If you go out there, you can see him waving his lantern, searching for it. If you bang on the railroad ties, he appears and comes toward you. My friend Beau told this story to a producer from some TV channel, and they actually did the story on television.*—Roxane*

Ghost Light of Bragg Road

While Hookerman Lights seem to bounce around railroad tracks all over the country, there are plenty of other spook lights hovering far from any tracks. For decades residents of southeast Texas have flocked north of Saratoga to Bragg Road, or Ghost Road as they call it. Ghost Road stretches eight miles through the area known as the Big Thicket, near the Texas–Louisiana border, and is surrounded on both sides by the dense, foreboding woods for which the area is named. Travelers come in search of the famous Ghost Light, a glowing ball spotted in this area since the early 1900s.

Most people who encounter the Ghost Light see it from hundreds of yards away, although some stories tell of those who came face-to-face with the glowing, hovering ball. Descriptions of the light vary: Its color reportedly ranges from orange to blue to white. It sometimes moves slowly, almost remaining stationary, and at other times is said to move at speeds up to 50 mph. Many believe that the Ghost Light is downright malevolent. The light, they say, is known to chase and terrorize moving vehicles, sometimes leaving burn marks on their exteriors.

Some theorize that the Ghost Light is the lantern of a railroad man who was beheaded in an accident and now wanders this desolate area for all time, hoping to recover his now nonexistent noggin. Others say that a hunter once wandered off by himself into the wilds of the Big Thicket, never to be seen again. The light is his hunting torch, and he is using it to try to make his way out of the woods.

Green Fireballs

Between 1948 and 1951 strange green fireballs in the skies above New Mexico had government officials baffled. Military pilots first spotted the lights, which they said looked like pale green flares but larger and with more movement. The lights were not the result of any military activity. Top officials confirmed that no tests—not even top secret ones—were under way at the time.

Military officers and scientists converged on Los Alamos and decided that these lights were not meteorites and were therefore of an unknown origin. The boldest among them theorized that the lights were test firings of some sort of extraterrestrial weaponry. Washington weighed in and proclaimed the lights as natural, despite the protests of qualified scientists. Sightings continued, and investigations proceeded despite government efforts to quell the curiosity. A program entitled Project Twinkle was established to investigate the lights. It found no conclusive results and was shut down in 1951.

Marvelous Marfa Light

Many Texans have seen the light. It's not a hard thing to do if you travel to Marfa. The Marfa Lights are some of the best-known mystery lights in the United States. To see them for yourself, travel east from Marfa on US 90 until you get to the Marfa's Mystery Lights Viewing Area. From here most people can see strange white lights on the horizon, appearing one at a time, then fading away quickly. Though they are miles off in the distance, they're easy to see.

Some people say the lights are simply reflections from stars or cars. The town of Marfa makes no effort to explain the lights—it just tries to cash in on them. Capitalizing on the number of tourists who come from all over to see the lights for themselves, the town has taken to holding a Marfa Lights celebration each Labor Day.

Devil's Promenade and the Hornet Spook Light

Twelve miles southwest of Joplin, Missouri, a roughly paved road known as the Devil's Promenade runs through a narrow canyon. This track runs about four miles along the Oklahoma border near the village of Hornet. A light has been seen along this road since 1866, and the Army Corps of Engineers officially concluded it was a "mysterious light of unknown origin." It is known as the Hornet Spook Light. This ball of fire spins down the center of the gravel road at great speed, rises up high, then bobs and weaves to the right and left. The light retreats when it is pursued. Does it have some sort of intelligence? That remains one of the many mysteries surrounding it.

One legend claims that the light was connected to the spirit of two young Quapaw Indians who died there many years ago. Another claims the light is the spirit of an Osage Indian chief who was beheaded on the Devil's Promenade. The light was said to be his torch as he searched for his missing head. Another legend tells of a miner whose children were kidnapped by Indians; he set off looking for them with only a lantern to light his way.

In 1958 a writer for the *Ford Times* noted that the light seemed to change from the size of an apple to that of a bushel basket. He also saw the light split off into three different lights and then settle on a tree and change to a single blue light.

What is it? The most popular suggestion is that it is will-o'-the-wisp, the name given to a light caused by the decay of wood and other organic materials. But a will-o'-the-wisp does not give off intense light. Another suggestion has been marsh gas. Unfortunately, marsh gas does not ignite spontaneously. Even if it did, wind and rain would soon extinguish any flame that appeared.

One suggestion theorizes that electrical fields in areas where earthquakes and ground shifts take place may cause the light. This is a possibility, since there are fault lines in the region and four devastating earthquakes took place here in the early 1800s. Author Raymond Bayless embarked on an extensive study of the Devil's Promenade in October 1963. Around dusk on the evening of the seventeenth, he reported a bright light at the end of the roadway. It fluctuated in intensity and at times became two separate lights. The light disappeared, then returned about an hour later and was so bright that it caused a reflection on the dirt surface of the road.

A few minutes after the light appeared, Bayless and his investigation group pursued it. The light vanished and did not reappear until they reached a point near an old museum. The Spooksville Museum, then operated by Leslie W. Robertson, offered not only photographs and a collection of accounts about the light but also a viewing platform for people to observe it. A member of Bayless's group set up a small refracting telescope on the platform. The telescope revealed that what appeared to be a single light was actually composed of a number of smaller lights. The lights were goldish amber in color and sometimes had a reddish tint. The edges of the light were observed to be like a flame in that they were not uniform and constantly changed.

Several authorities on the Hornet Light have stated that they believe it is fading away, or at least appearing less regularly. I hope that this is not the case. The Hornet Spook Light is one of America's greatest mysteries, and we need the light to be around for future generations to ponder for themselves.—*Troy Taylor*

Chased by the Greenbriar Light

For many years, people have reported being chased by a strange ball of light on a rural dirt road called Greenbriar Road, in St. John's County, near Mandarin, Florida. In 1987 a scientific investigation was conducted but found no explanation for the luminescence phenomenon. *—Charlie Carlson*

Spook Light Spotting Is a Family Affair

My mother was raised in northeast Oklahoma during the Depression. Most summers in the early '60s she and I and my older brother would venture up there from Texas. Even when I was little, I remember all of us driving out of Fairland, Oklahoma, to this deserted country road where we would sit for hours waiting for the Spook Light to appear. There were the usual explanations—swamp gas, car lights refracted somewhere, and so on. My mother told us her father used to see it when he was a kid, before cars were invented. His generation believed the Spook Light had something to do with lost and wandering Cherokee spirits. Others claimed it was the ghost of a Civil War soldier with a lantern, out looking for his decapitated head.

My favorite story involved a couple of policemen who witnessed the light come close enough to pounce on the hood of their patrol car, then the trunk, before disappearing.

Most of the time I remember falling asleep in the car, waiting and waiting, then waking up on the way home, my mother telling me if they had seen the light or not. Finally, one night when I was about six, I got to see it for myself; it was exactly as everyone had described it to me over the years. It started out way down the road, and it took a while to get your eyes focused on it. What was cool was hearing other car doors opening and realizing about five or six other families had come out there late on a summer evening for the same thing.

I was frightened at first, but that faded as the phantom light came closer and more focused in intensity. I could see why some people described it as the front light of an approaching train. Except as a train's light grows in intensity and illumination, it also increases its circumference, which helps you to keep it in perspective as to its proximity. The Spook Light, however, grew only in illuminated intensity; it never grew in size. It consistently appeared to be the size of a bowling ball.

This first time I saw it was cool because I really thought this thing would dance or bounce around like I had always heard. I wasn't disappointed, because the closer it got, the more you could see that it wasn't taking an entirely straight course; it veered and dipped ever so slightly.

As my family and I watched it approach, I heard the excitement of the other families around us, particularly the random "boo" and the high shrill squeak from some poor little kid, followed by laughter. But I didn't take my eyes off the Spook Light. What happened next was the part that made that night even more memorable.

The light just veered off to its left in a wide arc, cutting across a field, but fast, like a big round rocket hitting a booster stage, and BOOM. Everyone sort of "ewwww"-ed and "awww"-ed together when that happened. It was the only time I observed the light seeming to change in its size and intensity as it faded off. I did see it other times later, but it was never so cool as that first time. *—Nick Beef*

The Maco Railroad Light

A famous and strange light is found at a railroad crossing near Maco Station in Maco, North Carolina. While this has many of the characteristics seen in other railroad ghost lights, it has puzzled witnesses and scientists for many years.

The legend of the Maco railroad light dates back to 1867, when the Atlantic Coast Line Railroad was rebuilt and the small station once called Farmer's Turnout became Maco Station. One night the train was steaming along with Joe Baldwin, the conductor, riding in the last car of the train as usual. Joe realized that his coach was slowing down and saw that it had come uncoupled. There was another train following behind that he was sure would crash into his slowly moving car. Joe ran out onto the rear platform and started wildly waving his signal lantern to get the attention of the engineer of the train behind him. But the engineer paid no heed and crashed into the coach, killing Joe and severing his head from his body.

A witness to the accident reported that Joe stayed where he was, waving the lantern, through the entire wreck. Just seconds before the engine collided with the car, Joe's lantern was hurled away as if by some unseen, but mighty, force. It hit the ground and rolled over and over again, finally coming to rest in a perfectly upright position.

Shortly after this horrible accident the Maco light began to appear along the train tracks. It has been appearing there ever since and has become a popular curiosity to seek out on a warm summer night. Rarely is anyone disappointed, because Joe Baldwin, or whatever is the ghostly source for the Maco light, still continues swinging the lantern and signaling the train that journeys from this world to the next.

Maco is northwest of Wilmington on U.S. Highway 74/76. The railroad crossing is located outside of town.

–*Troy Taylor*

The Maco Mystery Light

There is a story of a mysterious light along the railroad tracks at Maco, North Carolina. The Maco light has been seen by almost all the people I know who grew up in that section of North Carolina. Maco is about twenty miles west of Wilmington. Apparently some railroad yardman was supposed to have been killed in a bizarre accident years ago—some say in the 1920s; others say in the 1880s. He was decapitated by a fast-moving freight train, and ever since he makes regular walks along that stretch of track where the accident happened, looking for his lost head.

I have never seen the Maco light, but I do know that driving around that part of the world with a huge "Green Swamp" just south of the place can be a very spooky experience late at night. David Lynch sort of people live there— *Blue Velvet* and *Wild at Heart* were filmed nearby.—*Letter via e-mail*

Brown Mountain Lights

In the western hills of Burke County, North Carolina, stands a mountain that plays host to perhaps the strangest mystery in the state. Brown Mountain is in the foothills of the Blue Ridge Mountains and, for many years, it has attracted the attention of people all over the nation. Even the government's interest was piqued, and it conducted a U.S. Geological Survey of the strange anomalies of the mountain. The unusual events are called the Brown Mountain Lights, and they appear along the ridges of the mountain on almost any clear night.

The best place to view the lights is at Wiseman's View on Highway 105 near Morganton. Curiosity-seekers are rarely disappointed. By looking to the southeast, watchers will suddenly see a light that appears to be about the size of a basketball. The reddish light will hover in the air for a moment and then disappear. In a few minutes it will appear again, but in another location, and then all through the night the lights will come and go, appearing and vanishing against the night sky.

Almost every person sees the lights in a different way; some see them as white and bobbing, others as pale and stationary, while yet others see them coming and going quite rapidly.

Many have tried to explain the lights. Some have suggested will-o'-the-wisp, that elusive gas that resides in swamps. Yet no swamps are in the area. Others have suggested fox fire or some sort of phosphorus, radium rays, strange gases, or geological anomalies with the rocks. Some have even suggested that the lights could be from the firing of moonshine stills by liquor makers on the mountain. However, it has been quite some time since moonshine was made there. Always popular is the explanation that the lights are simply headlight reflections, but this ignores the fact that they were reported well before automobiles were even invented.

A spooky legend explains the source. This story dates back to a night in 1850 when a woman disappeared in the area. Suspicion fell on the woman's husband, and everyone in the community helped search for her body. During the search, strange lights appeared over Brown Mountain, and many believed they were the spirit of the dead woman, coming back to haunt her killer. The search ended without success—and the lights ended with it. Shortly after, the husband disappeared. A number of years later, a woman's skeleton was found on Brown Mountain and the lights started to appear again.

Brown Mountain is located between Morganton and Lenoir, in the western part of the state.—*Troy Taylor*

Paulding Light over Lake Superior

Every night just after dusk a strange phenomenon spreads inland from Lake Superior. It's called the Paulding Light, and it can last anywhere from a minute or two to more than half an hour. Some nights it is white, and some nights it is red. Believers in the supernatural attribute the light to the death of a railroad worker. After he failed to throw a switch, causing a train accident that killed dozens of people, he wandered off into some nearby woods. Shortly after that the lights began appearing.

The legends of the Paulding Light are so widespread that signs have been erected around Watersmeet, Michigan, to guide visitors to good vantage points.

Dog Meadow Ghost Lights

One or more strange lights have been appearing near Eagle River, Wisconsin, since as early as 1966. A variety of theories claim to explain the lights, from swamp gas to the usual railroad worker with a ghostly lantern, but no one actually knows what causes them to appear. They usually show up on the northwest horizon northeast of the area known as Dog Meadow — a marshy lowland about thirty miles from Eagle River. The light appears as a glowing white orb that sometimes turns red. It is also said, on occasion, to break off into two smaller lights. According to reports from the region, the lights can be seen on almost any clear night.

To get to the area where the lights are seen, travel north of Eagle River to Watersmeet, Michigan. Go four to five miles north of town on Route 45 and turn on Robbins Pond Road. Drive up just over the second hill and park. A roadblock prevents anyone from driving all the way through.

—Troy Taylor

Can You Hear Me Now?

Want to hear a voice echoing inside your head? Visit the amphitheater outside the Navajo Museum's Library and Visitors Center in Window Rock, Arizona. This theater features an acoustic anomaly that the locals call a vortex. If you stand on the raised platform in the theater's concrete circle, just at the point where the two guidelines intersect, you will experience the vortex. Speaking in a normal tone makes your voice echo in your head. It sounds loud and unnatural to your ears, but you sound normal to listeners a few feet away.

Yellowstone Whispers

A strange natural phenomenon takes place in the high country above Yellowstone Lake in Wyoming's Yellowstone National Park. Travelers in the area hear a disturbing whining noise that is said to last up to thirty seconds. The Yellowstone Whispers are heard most often between the hours of dawn and ten a.m., usually when few people are around. There's nothing new about this phenomenon — early trappers in the region knew of it, and Native Americans regarded the Whispers as a sacred occurrence.

Covering Up the Montauk Project

I recently became aware of an old military base at the easternmost tip of Long Island, in Montauk, New York. The base stood in what is now a state park at the very end of Route 27. During World War II it was known as Camp Hero, and its large guns and bunkers were used for coastal defense. After the war the air force took over the base, which was renamed Montauk Air Force Station.

Reportedly, it was used as a radar station during the cold war, but it actually lost its funding in the late 1960s because its radar technology was obsolete. Yet it was still open until the mid-'80s. The buildings are still intact, and radar equipment remains standing.

But what is really strange is this: While the land belongs to the state, the military still owns whatever lies under the ground, where there are apparently many levels that were used for research—a subterranean city still in use today by secret branches of the military. People say that the radar equipment was built as a cover for military experiments in time travel and mind control, and that is what all the electronic equipment was for. It seems that this base cooperated with Mitchell Field air base and other research laboratories on Long Island. Some even say the base and the Montauk Project had something to do with the Philadelphia Experiment and the Rainbow Project. *–Derden*

Meat Bath in Bath County

Bath County, Kentucky, residents experienced one of the strangest storms in history in March of 1876. It lasted only a few minutes and fell on only a few people. What makes this storm so noteworthy is that it was not rain that pelted the locals in the area of Carrington Rock, just south of Olympia Springs. It was meat! Where the thin-sliced red meat came from is a mystery. This was before the days of air travel, so it could not have fallen from a plane.

See What Happens When Worlds Collide

Want to see a police car that was mauled by a UFO? You can do just that in Warren, Minnesota. Marshall County deputy Val Johnson has not repaired his vehicle since a close encounter in the summer of 1979.

Johnson was approaching Highway 220 on County Road 5 when he noticed an object in the sky that looked like it was in distress. As he followed it south on MN 220, it lowered in the sky, hovered for a moment, and then headed straight for his car. He was knocked unconscious for forty minutes, and when he came to, his car was standing sideways in the middle of the road, three hundred yards from where the collision occurred. The car had suffered considerable damage, including a smashed windshield, headlight, and siren light, and a dented hood. Johnson found that his watch and the car's clock were running fourteen minutes behind the actual time. His eyes were burned by exposure to a bright light. He radioed for assistance, telling the dispatcher that his car had collided with something that was not another car.

Because of the national attention to this incident, the car was never repaired and was put on display. You can see it at the Marshall County Museum in Warren.

Bizarre Beasts

"They are terrible looking things . . . with GREAT big ears, great big mouths . . . and long claws. Come back, there's nothing to be afraid of."
—Ollie Dee in *March of the Wooden Soldiers*

Lizardlike bipeds, hairy malodorous primates, serpentine water monsters and shadowy red-eyed demons—do mysterious creatures like these roam the American countryside? It hardly seems possible that they could lurk in our forests, swamps, and mountainous regions without ever being captured or photographed. Could enormous sea serpents swim the dark waters of our lakes, rivers, and sounds without ever being netted and hauled ashore?

Despite widespread development and the destruction of natural habitats, there remain remote areas of the nation where sightings of unusual beasts are reported every year. Stranger still are the reports of mysterious animals that appear in the heart of our densely populated urban areas. Cryptozoologists, who search to uncover unknown species of animals, are constantly on the lookout for evidence of never-before-documented wildlife. But are these fanciful creatures real or merely the product of our own imaginations and fears? Often the only evidence we have to support their existence is eyewitness accounts. Researchers suspect that only one sighting in every ten is ever reported, however, because most witnesses fear ridicule. In other words, most sightings never become public knowledge.

If eyewitnesses to these mysterious beasts are courageous enough to report their encounters, we believe they are telling the truth—or what they believe is the truth. That gray area between fact and fantasy is where you, the reader, have to make your own decision of whether or not to believe. After reading some of these tales, even the most diehard skeptics out there might find themselves thinking twice before entering the woods alone on a dark moonless night.

Mothman: The Enigma of Point Pleasant

The story began on November 12, 1966, near Clendenin, West Virginia. Five men were in the local cemetery, preparing a grave for a burial, when something that looked like a "brown human being" flew over their heads. The men were baffled. It looked like a man with wings. A few days later more sightings took place, electrifying the entire region. Mothman, as the bizarre beast has come to be called, is one of the strangest creatures to ever grace the annals of weirdness in America.

Late in the evening of November 15 two young married couples were driving past an abandoned TNT plant near Point Pleasant, West Virginia, when they spotted two large eyes attached to something that was "shaped like a man, but bigger, maybe six or seven feet tall. And it had big wings folded against its back." The couples panicked and sped away and moments later saw the same creature on a hillside. It spread its wings and rose into the air; they followed in their car, which by now was traveling at over 100 mph. "That bird kept right up with us," said one member of the group. They would not be the only ones to report the creature that night. Another group of four witnesses claimed to see the "bird" three different times!

Another sighting had more bizarre results. That same evening Newell Partridge, who lived ninety miles away, was watching television when the screen went dark. A weird pattern filled the screen, and then he heard high, loud whining sounds from outside. Partridge's dog, Bandit, began to howl out on the front porch, and Newell went to see what was going on.

When he walked outside, he saw Bandit facing the hay barn. Puzzled, Partridge turned a flashlight in that direction and spotted two red circles that looked like eyes or "bicycle reflectors." The sight of them frightened him. Bandit, an experienced hunting dog, shot off across the yard in pursuit of the glowing eyes. Partridge went into

the house for his gun, but was too scared to go back outside. The next morning Bandit was gone and had still not shown up two days later, when Partridge read in the newspaper about the sightings in Point Pleasant.

One statement in the newspaper chilled him to the bone. Roger Scarberry, a member of the group that spotted the strange "bird" at the TNT plant, said that as they entered the city limits of Point Pleasant, they saw the body of a large dog lying on the side of the road. A few minutes later, on their way back out of town, the dog was gone. Newell Partridge immediately thought of Bandit, who was never seen again.

On November 16 a press conference was held in the county courthouse, and soon news of the strange sightings spread around the world. The press dubbed the creature Mothman, after a character from the Batman television series of the day.

The abandoned TNT plant became the lair of the Mothman in the months ahead, and it could not have picked a better place to hide. The area was made up of several hundred acres of woods and large concrete domes where explosives were stored during World War II.

Tunnels honeycombed the site and made it possible for the creature to move about without being seen. The area also included the McClintic Wildlife Station, an animal preserve filled with woods, artificial ponds, and steep ridges and hills.

The Ralph Thomas family lived in the area. One day they spotted a "funny red light" hovering above the TNT plant. "It wasn't an airplane," Mrs. Marcella Bennett (a friend of the Thomas family) said, "but we couldn't figure out what it was." Mrs. Bennett drove to the Thomas house a few minutes later and got out of the car with her baby. Suddenly a figure stirred near the automobile. "It seemed as though it had been lying down," she later recalled. "It rose up slowly from the ground—big gray thing. Bigger than a man, with terrible glowing eyes."

Mrs. Bennett ran to the house. The family locked everyone inside, but hysteria gripped them as the creature shuffled onto the porch and peered into the windows. The police were summoned, but the Mothman had vanished by the time they arrived.

For nearly a year strange happenings continued in the region. Researchers, investigators, and "monster hunters" came, none so famous as author John Keel, who has written extensively about Mothman and other unexplained anomalies. Keel chronicled the case and wrote that at least one hundred people witnessed the creature between November 1966 and November 1967. According to their reports, the creature stood between five and seven feet tall, was wider than a man, and shuffled on humanlike legs. Its eyes were set near the top of the shoulders, and it had batlike wings that glided, rather than flapped, when it flew. Strangely, it was able to ascend straight up "like a helicopter." It had murky gray or brown skin and emitted a humming sound when it flew. The Mothman was apparently incapable of speech, but gave off a screeching sound.

Before long most of the sightings came to an end as Mothman began to fade away into the strange twilight zone from which he had come.

So who was Mothman, and what was behind the strange events in Point Pleasant?

It was clearly not a hoax since there were too many credible witnesses who saw something. John Keel, who believed the creature was genuine, suspected that a few of the cases involved people who were spooked by recent reports and saw owls flying along deserted roads at night. Even so, Mothman remains hard to dismiss. The case is filled with an impressive number of multiple-witness sightings by individuals that were deemed reliable, even by law-enforcement officials' standards. —*Troy Taylor*

According to their reports, the creature stood between five and seven feet tall, was wider than a man, and shuffled on humanlike legs.

The Goat Man of Prince Georges County

There exists a creature in Maryland known as the Goat Man. Whether it is Maryland legend or Maryland reality, there are enough witnesses and circumstantial evidence to keep the Goat Man's name alive. As recently as August 2000 a group of construction workers sighted a Sasquatch-like creature traversing an area of Washington's suburbs. In their estimate it stood twelve feet in stature.

So what the heck is the Goat Man? Some have claimed that he has a human body with a goat's head, like the popular portrayal of Satan. Some insist that he has a goat's lower body with the torso of a human, like the satyr of Greek mythology. Other observers (or speculators) say simply that he is an exceptionally hairy humanoid creature roughly six feet in height.

The most persistent accusation against the Goat Man is that it assaults pets. The area has suffered several rashes of mutilated or missing animals. Some people claim to have witnessed the Goat Man throwing dogs off Interstate 495 overpasses near secluded areas.

Since the late 1950s the Goat Man's territory has included several localities in Prince Georges County — with a focus on the Bowie area, which is largely forest, with a number of main highways running through it to other, more populous, parts of the state. At the heart of the matter is the bridge known as Crybaby Bridge on Governor's Bridge Road, where motorists can hear the shrill cry of an infant ghost — or the Goat Man. The Goat Man also frequents Lottsford Road and Fletchertown Road and the locale around Lottsford–Vista Road and Admore–Ardwick Road.

Some have claimed that the Goat Man broke into their homes while they were out, and they startled the belligerent creature on their return. The Goat Man also shoulders the blame for attacking cars left near the woods, often with an axe.

More often than not the Goat Man's origins are linked to the United States Agricultural Research Center of Beltsville, Maryland, on the outskirts of the Washington, D.C., suburbs. Two common variations involve a scientist working with goats at the facility. In one story the scientist goes mad, for reasons often improvised by the storyteller, and runs off screaming into the woods, where he stalks to this day with an axe. The second and more fantastic version claims that the scientist's experiments went horribly wrong and mutated him into a goatlike

appearance, whereupon he fled to the relative peace of the woods with an axe and a chip on his shoulder. There is a third assertion involving a botched attempt at creating a cure for cancer.

And finally there is the assertion that the Goat Man is the embodiment of none other than the archfiend himself, summoned to this earth from time to time by the rituals of satanists.

The story of the Goat Man doesn't thrive just in Maryland. In the Texas town of Marshall, hunters reported seeing a Goat Man in 1972. In Alabama another Goat Man was reported, roughly seven feet tall, with hoofs, claws, and a lumpy bald head. Stories have also poured in from Oregon, Oklahoma, Kentucky, and California. Cryptozoologists, those who study so-called extinct or nonexistent animals, have been drawn to the story in droves. Until the myths can be sufficiently proved or disproved, the Goat Man will continue to be the object of both ridicule and fear.—*John Lawson*

Far from Human Goat Man

As a kid growing up in Kentucky, I heard of the Goat Man, a half human with a goat head. My grandfather told of a screaming devil jumping a fence, grabbing two pigs, and running off with them. On Highway 69 outside of Dundee, I was heading home and I saw something leap across the road. I hit the ditch to keep from hitting it. It was far from human, with a monkeylike face, small horns, strange arms like a kangaroo, thick legs, and a long tail. I think this was the Goat Man.—*Doug Oller, Paducah*

Why It May Be Known as Helltown

About twelve years ago three friends and I were driving around in an area I know as Helltown, in farm country in Westmoreland County, Pennsylvania, near Irwin. It was about twelve thirty at night and we were on a bumpy and rutted road with woods on the left and a fenced-in pasture on the right. A few hundred feet ahead of the car, we saw something crossing the road. My friend put the car in reverse to see what it was. The headlights hit it just as it was approaching the woods. It was walking on four legs and was about the size of a cow, but much thinner. It was black with white near its feet. As it neared the tree line, it stood on two feet and proceeded to walk into the woods just as a person would. I would estimate it to be seven feet tall on two legs.

The next afternoon some of us returned to the same spot. All of the trees were shredded from about six feet down to the ground, and there were heavy footprints imbedded in the damp ground.—*Susan Wallace*

Bardin Booger Beast

Something big and hairy is walking around the backwoods of Bardin, Florida, just northwest of Palatka. Locals claim this bear-size beast has a pig's nose, a long red tongue dangling out of its mouth, and a stride longer than humanly possible. And they call it Booger.

The two-thousand-strong population of Bardin has come to embrace their neighborhood creature. They sport T-shirts, hats, and cups emblazoned with its likeness. The local restaurants offer Booger Burgers, and songs have been written in the monster's honor. And whether it is a beast or just bull, Booger has put Bardin on the map. Locals celebrate—or commercialize—their resident whatsit by dressing up as Booger for store grand openings and often scare visitors and farmers by donning Booger costumes and masks.

So is it a product of an imaginative advertising campaign, or does the Booger beast really exist? Old-timers of the area swear that this legend has been around for many years. But when the wind is right, you can smell an offensive odor that the townsfolk claim to be the Booger Beast foraging for food. Maybe he's just hungry for a good Booger Burger Deluxe.

Here a Lizard Man, There a Lizard Man

These strange creatures have been spotted in many locales, often in southern Atlantic states with their low-lying roads that cross through swamps. But you don't need a swamp to find a Lizard Man.

A Stalking Lizard Man

If one didn't know better, they'd see Bishopville, South Carolina, as just another small southern town surrounded by swamps. But what happened there one summer fifteen years ago made the sleepy place rife with frenzy and fear.

In 1988 the eyes of the world focused on Bishopville in hopes of catching a glimpse of the mysterious and dangerous Lizard Man. The sensation began in June when seventeen-year-old Christopher Davis was on his way home from working the late shift at McDonald's. As he drove along the outskirts of town, along the border of Scape Ore Swamp, a tire blew out. It was already approaching two in the morning, and the exhausted teenager simply wanted to go home and get to bed. The events that occurred as Chris labored to change his tire would make it difficult for the young man to ever sleep soundly again.

Suddenly Chris heard a loud thump in a bean field across the street from his disabled car. A few days later Davis described his experience this way to the AP wire services:

"I looked back and saw something running across the field towards me. It was about 25 yards away and I saw red eyes glowing. I ran into the car and as I locked it, the thing grabbed the door handle. I could see him from the neck down—the three big fingers, long black nails and green rough skin. It was strong and angry. I looked in my mirror and saw a blur of green running. I could see his toes and then he jumped on the roof of my car. I thought I heard a grunt and then I could see his fingers through the front windshield, where they curled around on the roof. I sped up and swerved to shake the creature off."

When Chris arrived home, he woke up his parents, who found him to be absolutely panicked. Chris insisted he had been assaulted by some sort of strange beast. His father checked the car in an effort to figure out what exactly was going on. The mirror on the car door was twisted and hanging off; the roof had deep scratches and grooves etched into it. Police were contacted, and Davis told them that the creature was seven feet tall, had red eyes, and lizardlike skin and scales.

In the ensuing months hundreds of people claimed to have encountered the Lizard Man in one fashion or another. Numerous three-toed footprints were found in the area, some as long as fourteen inches. Posses formed and hunted the swamps for any sign of the reptilian creature. The Lizard Man was also spotted outside Bishopville, as residents in all parts of the greater Lee County area claimed to have witnessed him.

By August of '88 the hype had largely died down, though there are sightings every once in a while. Was this an elaborate hoax? Or perhaps an angry black bear misperceived in the dark of the night, as some have alleged? Or is it possible that a strange reptilian humanoid creature still stalks the swamps of South Carolina?

Next time, call AAA

We were driving down Joe Miller Road, on our way home to Columbia, South Carolina, from my grandmother's house. The car started pulling to the left, and my dad realized that we had a flat. He went out to replace the tire, and something large darted across the road. It was dark, so none of us saw exactly what it was.

My dad just shook it off and put the spare from the trunk on the car. He placed the flat in the trunk and was just about to open the front driver's-side door when all of a sudden the creature darted back into the middle of the road and turned to look at the car. Then it froze, startled by the headlights, which were on so my dad could see what he was doing.

My mom and I got a clear look at it. It was about seven and one-half feet tall, with webbed feet and hands, red eyes, brownish green skin, and scales covering every part of its body. It stood up like a man on two feet. Then it just turned and ran back into the swamp. My dad jumped into the car and drove off as fast as the spare would let him.—*Tennisdog*

Green and Tall and Lipless

A motorist driving through Wayne, New Jersey, in the 1970s reported seeing a green, scaly Lizard Man, with bulging eyes and a lipless mouth. Another motorist, traveling west on Route 80 near Great Meadows in 1974, reported seeing a huge humanoid creature standing beside the road. The beast was described as having a towering green body that was covered with scales. As the driver sped past the animal, he could see its reptilian face, bulging froglike eyes, and broad lipless mouth illuminated in his headlights.

Man-Eating Piasa Bird

I'm a longtime New Jersey resident but I was born in Alton, Illinois, and I spent many of my formative years there. Just about everybody in or around the city of Alton knows the story of the Piasa Bird, Illinois's answer to the Jersey Devil.

In 1673 French explorers Father Jacques Marquette, a Jesuit priest, and Louis Jolliet made a famous expedition down the Mississippi River in an attempt to discover whether the river connected to the Pacific. As they passed the great stony bluffs near what is now Alton, close to the settlements of the Illini Indians, they discovered a vast painting on the cliff side. The painting depicted a monstrous winged creature—green, black, and red—with an evil red-eyed face, huge antlers, a scaly horselike body, a long beard, sharp claws and teeth, and a tail so long it wrapped around its body several times. The explorers even documented the sighting in their journals.

Many legends surround the origin of the portrait. The oldest and most famous of these tales tells of a great chief named Ouatoga, the respected elder of the Illinwek tribe. However, even Ouatoga was at a loss when, on a peaceful morning, a great terror swept down from the sky. As big as a horse and with vast reptilian wings and a menacing scream, a devil-bird swooped out of the clouds and snatched up a human from the tribal village. The Illini warriors fired arrows upon it, but the beast seemed invulnerable.

Nearly every day thereafter the creature terrorized the Illinis and surrounding villages, snatching up victims before returning to its lair in the bluffs to devour its prize. The tribe called the creature "Piasa" (pronounced Pie-a-saw), or "bird that devours men."

Finally, Ouatoga set out into the deep woods for contemplation and prayer. For an entire moon he fasted and implored the Great Spirit to save his people. At last, the Spirit whispered to him that the terrible bird had a weakness. Ouatoga tearfully thanked the Great Spirit, returned to the village, and told the tribe of his plan.

That very night, Ouatoga and a group of his bravest warriors climbed to the top of the highest bluff. A piercing scream was soon heard, and the Piasa

appeared in the sky, and swooped down upon Ouatoga, who fell to the ground and gripped a tree root with all his might.

The warriors released a volley of poisoned arrows into the delicate scales just beneath the bird's outstretched wings—the weak spot revealed by the Great Spirit. The Piasa screamed and attempted to take to the air when another hail of arrows found their mark. At last the Piasa uttered a final shriek and plummeted over the cliff, into the river below. The triumphant Illini braves and their wounded chief cheered as the body sank into the churning waters.

To honor this historic occasion, the tribe painted a depiction of the Piasa on the bluff. From then on, every Indian who passed the painting fired an arrow at it for good luck. Years later, passing Indians would fire a rifle at it, and historians wrote of a painting etched into the cliffs that had been worn away by "ten thousand bullet holes."

Over time the painting of the Piasa faded, and land developers in the nineteenth century quarried away the portion of the bluff upon which the remains of the painting could be seen. However, decades later a metal likeness of the bird was created and affixed to the bluff, becoming a local landmark. Eventually traffic on the Great River Road became so heavy that the sign became a nuisance, and it was removed. However, historians and local advocates protested, and today the great painting on the bluff has been restored in all its former glory.—*Brendan Middleton*

Giant Penguins, Anyone?

Numerous people reported seeing a giant penguin on Clearwater Beach, Florida, in 1948. The huge bird was described as fifteen feet tall and supposedly left big tracks along the beach. During this same period, people in a boat off the Gulf Coast reported seeing an extremely large penguinlike bird floating on the water. In the same year another big penguinlike bird was seen by a private airplane pilot on the banks of the Suwannee River in north Florida. The famed investigator of the unknown, the late Ivan Sanderson, conducted a scientific inquiry into both cases. No conclusion or explanation was ever reached.—*Charlie Carlson*

Big-toothed and Hissing

On August 1, 2002, a group of offshore swimmers in Portsmouth, Rhode Island, met with more than they bargained for when a hissing, serpentine creature attacked them. "I was deep out in the water and kept hearing this hissing sound. Then I saw its head come up showing me its big teeth," one of the victims told the local paper, the *Herald News.* "It kept rolling while it was swimming and knocking into my feet. I just froze."

The creature was described as being fifteen feet long, with four-inch-long teeth, green skin, and a white stomach. "My heart is still pounding. I don't want to seem scared, but people should know to keep their children close, because that thing was definitely big enough to kill us," another victim told the paper. "I thought I was dead."

Seven-Foot Creature

Three buddies and I spotted a creature near a man-made pond called Five Points in St. Pauls, North Carolina. As we approached the pond, I saw a reflection in the water. It was a seven-foot-tall bipedal creature. He spotted us, then darted toward the edge of the woods near our truck. At this point we were already in reverse and tearing out of there. Many others have also spotted this creature.

—*Nicholas J. Woodall*

Dover Demon

In the late 1970s a strange, inhuman creature set upon Dover, Massachusetts. On April 21, 1977, three teens driving through town saw a peach-colored creature with round, orange eyes, an oversized head, and a thin, gangly body. The four-foot-tall creature, soon to be known as the Dover Demon, was spotted later that same night by another teen, who was walking home. The creature approached him, then ran into a nearby patch of woods. The boy noted that as the creature walked over rocks or touched trees, its hands and feet seemed to mold around the objects it touched. Although investigators attempted to dismiss the sightings as a series of hoaxes, their interviews indicated that all the witnesses believed they were telling the truth.

Ilies

Iliamna Lake in Alaska is known to host a whole family of strange creatures, known as Ilies. The creatures are more fishlike than serpentine, and their enormous size has stunned many witnesses. A pilot who spotted an entire school of the monstrous beasts while flying over the lake in the 1950s stated that the fish were anywhere from fifteen to twenty feet in length.

I'm Not Wild About Herry

Lake Herrington, in Harrodsburg, Kentucky, is home to its very own unusual monster, an enormous catfishlike creature known as Herry. First seen in 1972, Herry has since been spotted dozens of times. Reports state that he is fifteen feet long, with a curly tail and the face of a pig. Unusual indeed!

Face to Face with South Bay Bessie

I have a boat on Lake Erie near Vermilion, Ohio, and I can tell you that there is a monster in that lake. Many people have seen it over the years, and I am one of those people.

Pretty much every weekend or free day, I'm out on Lake Erie. One night two summers ago I anchored the boat a few hundred yards offshore and fell asleep. I was awakened by something rubbing against the bottom of the boat. I immediately heard the rushing of water followed by the slap of something against the surface of the lake. I grabbed my lantern and held the light over the water. I will never forget what I saw.

There was a long, thick creature a few feet beneath the keel of my boat. This thing was at least twenty feet long. It darted with incredible speed away from my skiff as I struggled to make out its form beneath the surface of the water. When it was about thirty feet away, the beast reared its body up out of the lake. It was a clear night with a full moon, so I could make out the long, serpentine body and large round head before it submerged again and disappeared.

The thing slammed into my boat. My first instinct was that I had invaded its territory and it was letting me know. Perhaps like a common eel, it had been attracted to the glow of my lantern. That was the last night I ever spent alone on Lake Erie.

The town of Huron has tried to make money off this monster. They call it Bessie and try to get tourists to come look for it. I think this is irresponsible and downright dangerous. The thing I saw was vicious and dangerous. Giving it a cute name and trying to get people to come and search for it is only going to lead to a tragedy.–*Franklin P. Wainwright*

Bear Lake's Monster

Bear Lake straddles the border between Utah and Idaho. One of the oldest bodies of water in the American West, it may also be home to a prehistoric creature that has terrorized humans for centuries. Reports of a serpentine monster lurking in the waters began circulating in 1868. The beast was said to be huge, with pronounced ears. Over the years many reliable and respected people—including a Boy Scout—claim they have spotted the beast. One group of people tell of seeing ten of the animals speeding around the lake; other reports claim the creature is over two hundred feet long. Some even say the beast is amphibious, but while it swims at incredible speeds, it's thought to stalk the land around Bear Lake quite slowly.

On the Trail of the Thunderbirds

There are many more accounts of winged creatures attacking and carrying off people. One took place in Tippah County, Missouri, in 1868. According to the report, an eight-year-old child named Jemmie Kenney was carried off by what was described by his teacher as an eagle. The teacher's account states that he was summoned by the other children, but by the time he had run outside, he could only hear Jemmie screaming as he vanished into the sky. The teacher and the children on the playground began to raise the alarm in town; apparently, the noise frightened the bird, and it dropped the boy, dead.

Could this really have been an eagle? Even the most powerful eagle cannot lift more than a rabbit. So how do we explain this mysterious encounter—and those that took place eighty years later around Alton, Illinois?

On April 4, 1948, a former army colonel named Walter F. Siegmund saw a gigantic bird in the sky above Alton. "It was definitely a bird and not a glider or a jet plane. From the movements, I figured it could only be a bird of tremendous size." A few days later a farmer named Robert Price, from Caledonia, saw a similar bird, and on April 10 in Overland, so did Clyde Smith, his wife, and a friend. They said they thought the creature was an airplane, until it started to flap its wings furiously.

A few days later a St. Louis chiropractor named Kristine Dolezal saw the bird from her apartment window as it swerved to avoid crashing into a plane, then vanished into the clouds. The next day the bird was reported by instructors at a flight school at the Lambert–St. Louis International Airport. On April 28 a salesman named Harry Bradford spotted it while turning onto Kings Highway. When Clifford Warden and Mary and Charles Dunn saw it on April 30, the creature was giving off a dull glow.

The bird was reported for the last time on May 5, when Arthur Davidson in Alton and Mrs. William Stallings of St. Louis called authorities to report it. "It was bright, about as big as a house," said Mrs. Stallings.

Ironically, just when the public excitement over the bird reached its peak, the sightings came to an end. Until the Lawndale incident of 1977, that is.

Giant Swooping Birds

One of the best-documented encounters with giant birds occurred in 1977 in Lawndale, a small town in Logan County, Illinois. On the evening of July 25 reports came in of two huge birds swooping in the sky. Finally they headed straight down and reportedly attacked three boys who were playing in the backyard of Ruth and Jake Lowe. One of the birds grasped the shirt of ten-year-old Marlon Lowe. The boy tried to fight the bird off, then cried loudly for help.

Marlon's mother ran outside to see the bird actually lift the boy three feet from the ground and carry him about thirty-five feet. She screamed, and the bird released the child. Luckily, although scratched and badly frightened, Marlon was not seriously injured.

Four other adults appeared on the scene within seconds of the attack. They described the birds as black with bands of white around their necks. They had long, curved beaks and wingspans of at least ten feet. The two birds were last seen flying toward some trees near Kickapoo Creek.

Ruth Lowe spent long hours looking through books, certain that the creature had not been a turkey vulture, as an area game warden tried to convince her that it was. "I was standing at the door," she told the investigators, "and I saw Marlon's feet dangling in the air. There aren't any birds around here that can lift him up like that."

controlled airplanes he and his friends were flying. He claimed the bird dwarfed the small planes that buzzed close to it.

The next sighting took place near Bloomington when a mail truck driver named James Majors spotted the two birds. He believed they were very large condors. He saw one of them fly into a nearby field and pick up a small animal, which he believed to be a pig.

Officials from the department of conservation insisted the birds were merely turkey vultures, but wildlife experts and cryptozoologists refute this statement. The only North American bird with a wingspread of up to nine feet is the California condor—but the condor is an endangered species found only in a few areas in California. There is little chance that a few stray birds traveled to Illinois to attack small children!

Another witness reported looking out the window of her home near Chester and saw a huge bird resting in the top of a tall tree in her back yard. The bird was much larger than anything she had ever seen before. A few minutes later it flew off, gliding toward the Mississippi River. Its wingspan, she guessed, was at least ten or fifteen feet. After that the rash of 1977 bird sightings in Illinois came to an end.

We have to be puzzled as we read such tales. Are these mysterious flying creatures actually real? If not, then what have so many people seen over the years? One thing is sure: The sightings have continued, and occasionally an unusual report still trickles in from somewhere across America. So next time you are standing in an open field and a large dark shadow suddenly fills the sky overhead, ask yourself this question: Was that just a cloud passing in front of the sun—or something else? —*Troy Taylor*

Experts tell us that there aren't any birds on the North American continent capable of it either. Yet something appeared in Lawndale that day and managed to do the impossible. And the Lawndale incident would not be the last sighting in central Illinois!

Three days later a McLean County farmer named Stanley Thompson spotted a bird of the same size and description flying over his farm, close to the radio-

Big Hairy Men

Everybody has heard of Bigfoot (also known as Sasquatch). But did you know that this eight-foot-tall, long-haired, foul-smelling man-ape tramping the ancient forest of the Pacific Northwest has kin all across the country? That's right, from the Deep South to the Midwest to the Great Plains, reports of these big hairy creatures seem to come from all corners.

The Wild Man of the Big Thicket

Since the first Europeans settled the dense forests and swamps of the Big Thicket in southeastern Texas, stories have circulated of a large, naked, hairy, humanlike beast that stalks the area. This strange creature is most often called the Wild Man, but is also known as the Ape Man, Mossyback, the Route Monster, and the Raggedy Man.

Some say the Wild Man is a prison convict or mental patient who fled into the woods to escape imprisonment. The Big Thicket has long been known as a haven for unsavory fugitives from the law; perhaps the Wild Man is one of these ruffians. Others say he's a hermit who shunned society by retreating into the forests, his hatred of humanity causing him to terrorize and attack whatever hunters, campers, and hikers he has encountered over the years.

Most who come upon the Wild Man get only a fleeting glimpse of him, often at dusk, before he flees into the depths of the Thicket. But all who see him agree on his general appearance: He is larger than average, hairier than average, and sports a scraggly beard. Some say he looks more like an ape than a man, and makes a haunting, high-pitched howl. He stays around bodies of water within or close to the borders of the Big Thicket Nature Preserve. He also seems to be a bit of a voyeur, peering in parked car windows along secluded roads and startling teenagers as they make out.

Watery Creatures in the Sunshine State

Between 1955 and 1961 there were numerous reports in Florida newspapers of a monster in the Saint Johns River. All reported seeing a giant creature whose descriptions fit either a brontosaurus or big manatee-like thing, depending on who was doing the reporting. Most sightings occurred between Astor Park and Lake Monroe, with their center being located around the Blue Springs area.

One Lake County man claimed to have seen the monster on land, grazing on plants. He reported that it left a wide, mashed-down path through the bushes. The animal's skin was described as gray and elephantlike and very leathery-looking.

In 1975 a group of boaters on the Saint Johns River near Jacksonville claimed to have seen a dragonlike creature that reared its head from the river, then disappeared into the deep water. It was described as having a head like a giant snail, with two horns. In an 1891 newspaper report a sea serpent chased bathers from the ocean at the Jacksonville beach. That monster was said to have had a doglike head and a long, skinny neck.

In 1962 a scuba diver reported a bizarre story of Florida sea serpents, off the Gulf Coast near Pensacola. In that incident the monster attacked a group of divers and overturned their small boat, allegedly killing all but one of the men. The surviving victim claimed that the creature had a long, rigid, ten-foot neck, like a telephone pole. It had small eyes, a wide mouth, and whipped about like a large snake. Evidence of a Florida marine monster was hauled up from the New River Inlet in 1885. A ship's anchor brought up the carcass of a creature with a long neck that

resembled an extinct plesiosaur, very much like the descriptions given for the infamous Loch Ness monster. Who knows what lurks beneath Florida's waters? Something to think about on your next swimming trip.—*Charlie Carlson*

Highway 13's Reptile Man

Several years ago a Department of Natural Resources warden traveling down Highway 13 just south of Medford, Wisconsin, saw a figure standing in the road. He couldn't believe what he was seeing. Staring at him was a shiny, green-scaled, manlike figure. As he got within several yards of it, wings popped out from behind the creature's back. It zoomed straight up and over the vehicle and landed on the road behind the warden. A group of highway workers also had an encounter with the creature while driving along the same stretch of road. As they approached, wings shot out from behind its back, and it flew into the trees. Maybe some day, while driving down a lonely stretch of Highway 13, you'll look up and discover a clue to this creature's existence.

—*Rick Hendrick, Weird-WI.com*

Beast of Bray Road

Shaggy. Manlike. Wolf-headed. Staring. Sneering. Wicked claws. Fangs. These are the words eyewitnesses use to describe a creature that lurks mostly by night in the cornfields and thickets of southeastern Wisconsin. The Beast of Bray Road has shocked Walworth and Jefferson county residents ever since its sudden appearance in 1936.

That was the year Mark Schackelman, a security watchman at a Catholic facility for the developmentally disabled, made an unsettling discovery on his midnight rounds. Schackelman spotted something digging on an old Native American burial mound behind the main building. Thinking it was a dog, he aimed his flashlight toward it and saw a man-size shaggy creature with a doglike head, pointed ears, and three long claws on each hand. After a short standoff, the beast walked off into the woods, but Schackelman encountered it again the next night and heard it utter what sounded like a word: "gadara." He considered it a "demon from hell" and never told anyone about it until his later years when he divulged it to his son Joe, a Kenosha newspaper editor.

Through the '60s, '70s, and '80s, other sightings led to puzzled and frightened witnesses calling local police or the state's department of natural resources to try to find out what they had seen. Surrounding communities whispered about a humanlike creature known by such local names as Bluff Monster and the Eddy.

It was in December 1991 that a local school bus driver told me about a shaggy, manlike, wolf-headed creature haunting the cornfields and woods of Bray Road around Elkhorn in Walworth County. At the time, I was working as a staff reporter for a county newspaper, *The Week.* My editor and I agreed it would be an entertaining story, though I was skeptical, to say the least.

My skepticism began to thaw a bit, however, when I discovered that our local animal control officer, Jon Fredrickson, had been keeping track of the eyewitness queries in a file labeled WEREWOLF. Witnesses like Lori Endrizzi, who saw the manimal kneeling by the side of the road holding what looked like roadkill, had asked Fredrickson if he was aware of some really strange "thing" wandering the farm fields east of Elkhorn. It was news to Fredrickson, although he speculated that perhaps the witnesses were seeing something like a deformed coyote. But Endrizzi insisted that if werewolves exist, they would look exactly like the creature she had spied.

Though Fredrickson's use of the term werewolf may have been tongue-in-cheek, his role as Walworth County's official animal control officer was enough to slide the story into the province of public news. And public it soon became. Within days of my initial story in *The Week,* the tale hit the Associated Press and made lurid headlines all over the country. All the Milwaukee TV stations showed up to interview the witnesses, and the television show *Inside Edition* came to do a half-hour segment on what came to be known as the Beast of Bray Road. I was interviewed on radio stations coast to coast and by many magazines. I even had an offer to write a screenplay based on the story.

The publicity drew out other witnesses. As the tales began to pile up, it soon became apparent that the hairy phenomenon went back decades and crossed county lines. Either there existed a family of such creatures or the thing was very long-lived.

The witnesses, with one or two exceptions, all seemed like trustworthy citizens. Most were reluctant to talk, none of them had anything apparent to gain, and most of them faced ridicule once their stories were out. There was no single "type" of witness either. They ranged in age from children to the elderly, in profession from white- to blue-collar, and were both male and female, local folk and those just passing through. After finishing their stories, almost all of them would say something like, "I know what I saw, and nothing is going to change that."

The descriptions stayed fairly consistent too. The beast's height was estimated at between five and seven feet. Its hair was described as shaggy and often extremely wild, with coloration usually said to be dark brown, sometimes with gray or silver streaks or tips. Those who had a good look at its head usually reported that it looked like that of a wolf or German shepherd, with pointy ears. The most compelling characteristic, though, was the creature's aggressive stare. They said that the beast made eye contact and almost seemed to be sneering at them. This was what seemed to frighten the witnesses most.

One witness, a Williams Bay businessman, was able to corroborate the other sightings with a story of his own from 1981. On an August afternoon he was driving along Highway 11 near Bray Road when he became aware of a creature staring at him from behind a fallen tree not far from the road. He pulled over and looked at it from the window of his van. It looked right back at him. Unnerved by its stare, he sped off, but he made a drawing as soon as he got home. He showed me the yellowed paper he has saved ever since. The drawing is exactly like that of all the other witnesses, although this was ten years before the newspaper story broke.

Does the beast still live? There haven't been any reported sightings on Bray Road since the early '90s, but there was one in tiny Hebron, north of Whitewater, Wisconsin, in February 2002. Two gentlemen saw what they described as an enormous creature placidly crossing the community's main intersection at about two o'clock in the morning.

Cryptozoologist Loren Coleman has speculated that the beast may be a smaller species of bigfoot. Others theorize that the beast is a hybrid wolf-dog, a bear, a large wolf, a denizen of another dimension, a true werewolf, a hoax by someone in a hairy costume with a very determined and decades-long obsession, or even a holdover large carnivore from the Ice Age.

Probably only time and perhaps a lucky capture or video will be able to solve the mystery once and for all.

– Linda S. Godfrey

Slimy Slim

Lake Payette in Idaho is home to a fearsome creature known as Slimy Slim. Over the last century he has been sighted only sporadically, but in the summer of 1941 more than two dozen people claimed to have seen the beast. At that time, one area resident told a local paper that "his head, which resembles that of a snub-nosed crocodile, was eight inches above the water. I'd say he was 'bout thirty-five feet long."

The Gow-Row of Devil's Hole Cave

In the northern part of Arkansas in Boone County is a small village called Self. This remote and not very accessible place is home to a story that is both elusive and fascinating. It centers around the strange and largely unexplored Devil's Hole Cave. One day, a number of years ago, the owner of the land decided to explore the cavern. He climbed down a rope about two hundred feet to a ledge. There, the shaft narrows so that it's only possible to get through it by crawling. He suddenly heard a vicious hissing from the darkness, and he made a hasty retreat.

Sometime later he and some men from town tied a flatiron to a rope and dropped it down to the same place in the cave. They heard a hissing sound and the rope was pulled hard. When they hauled it up, they found that the flatiron had been badly bent and scored with scratches and teeth marks. Next they tried a stone, and the rope was yanked taut again. They pulled it back up to find that the stone was gone and the rope was neatly severed. Not surprisingly, no one dared to climb down to see what was in the cave, but the locals still gave it a name—the Gow-Row.

The story dates back to around 1900, and many believe the monster may be some sort of giant lizard, but nobody knows for sure what it is or even if it is still alive. Arkansas spelunkers have informed me that they have visited this cave, and while much of it remains untouched, they have yet to encounter the Gow-Row!

Caution is advised when entering the Devil's Hole Cave. It can be very dangerous—whether the Gow-Row exists or not!–*Troy Taylor*

Momo

The town of Louisiana, Missouri, had only 4600 residents in 1971. That is, of course, if you're counting humans. The town tallies in at 4601 if you count its resident monster, Momo. This hairy, foul-smelling beast first appeared in the summer of '71, when he emerged from a thicket and scared off some picnickers. As they watched from a locked car, Momo ate the remains of their food.

Momo wasn't seen again until the following summer, when he made a series of appearances. First, a group of children saw the beast amble by carrying a dead dog under its arm. A few nights later a local farmer witnessed a flash of light that was accompanied by a foul stench and loud growls. For the next two weeks people reported seeing Momo and experiencing other unexplainable phenomena, such as hearing disembodied voices warning them to stay out of the woods.

For a while Momo gained national attention as papers far and wide covered the sightings—mostly in a humorous fashion. But for the past three decades Momo has been keeping a low profile.

Beware the Fouke Monster

The town of Fouke, Arkansas, would normally be easy to miss on a map or speed past on a highway. But hordes of tourists travel fifteen miles southeast of Texarkana to this sleepy southern town with a population of just over six hundred. People flock here in hopes of catching a glimpse of the deadly, strange, infamous beast known as the Fouke Monster.

Since the 1940s local newspapers have reported a creature resembling a hybrid between a human and a gorilla in the swamps surrounding Fouke. According to eyewitness accounts, it stands between six and seven feet tall, weighs over three hundred pounds, has fiery red eyes, and gives off a terrible odor. It has killed livestock and terrorized humans in their own homes. In 1965 fourteen-year-old James Lynn Crabtree claimed he was unable to slow the beast down even after shooting it three times in the face. Some say there is only one monster, while others claim that whole families of them inhabit Fouke's backwater swamplands.

While the creature has been hanging around Fouke for six decades now, it first drew national attention in the 1970s. In May of 1971 a family living near Jonesville was startled when a huge hairy claw came crashing through their screen door. They chased the creature into the woods, but it returned again later that night. Local law-enforcement officials took plaster casts of its distinct, flatfooted, seventeen-inch-long footprints. Later that week the youngest son of the same family was tackled outside his house but luckily managed to escape. The same distinctive tracks were found in the area of this tussle. At the end of the month several motorists were stunned to see a seven-foot-tall creature sprint across Route 71. The attacks drew national headlines, and bigfoot hunters from across the country descended upon Fouke. None were able to hunt down the creature.

A production company traveled to Fouke in 1975 and filmed a motion picture, *The Legend of Boggy Creek*, featuring the Fouke Monster as its main subject.

In March 1978, Appleton residents found huge footprints near caves in their township. Ten miles away, in Center Ridge, livestock disappearances were reported around the same time. On June 26, a ten-year-old resident of Crossett, Arkansas, named Mike Lofton went face-to-face with the Fouke Monster. While the boy was feeding his dog, he noticed his pet was trembling. Just then he saw the monster emerge from the woods. He ran to his father's room, grabbed his father's rifle, and fired on the creature. It fled into the woods.

Many residents of Fouke swear that they've seen the monster. Many others brush off the stories as tall tales and an annoyance. Still others have managed to cash in on the creature's popularity. The local deli is known as the Monster Mart and sells monster-related kitsch items. Just outside stands a metal replica of the Fouke Monster in which tourists can place their own face and have themselves photographed as the vicious, malodorous beast.

Fouke Monster–mania had died down in recent years, but in 1998 there was a rash of over forty sightings, with twenty-two of them in a single day! Had monster-mania reached a fever pitch again and affected the collective imagination of this small rural community? Or is it possible that there really is a strange subhuman beast lurking in the backwoods of Arkansas?

Skunk Ape

Tales of Florida's own bigfoot creature, the Skunk Ape, go back centuries to early pioneer lore and even to Indian legends. We could dismiss these early accounts as folklore if it were not for more recent sightings. In 1955 three Boy Scouts emerged from the Ocala National Forest scared out of their wits, saying they had been routed from their campsite by a big hairy monster with a human face. It wasn't the first sighting in that region; more than twenty other witnesses had reported encountering what they called a man-ape in various parts of the same forest.

On a November evening in 1966 a woman motorist had a flat tire on a remote road near Brooksville, Florida, and got the scare of her life. While she was changing her tire, a big, shaggy-haired, manlike creature came out of the nearby swamp and sat down in the road to watch her. Fortunately, another car came along and the beast lumbered off.

In a 1999 interview with this author, J. B. Johnson, eighty-seven, of Lake County, Florida, recited his tale of a 1947 encounter with a strange apelike creature. According to J. B., he and four other companions were hunting bears in the Wekiva Swamp. They had split into two groups when "I heard something in the palmetto bushes and saw what I thought was a large bear." He picked up his gun and "brought the critter down."

But J. B. soon found out that it was no bear. "It looked more like a gorilla, it was long, about seven feet . . . and had hair all over it, except its face, it looked like the face of a man." J. B. and his partner hurried off to get the other

The elusive beast is generally seven to eight feet tall, with shaggy hair and an obnoxious odor like rotten cabbage, rotten eggs, or skunk musk. Hence the nickname Skunk Ape.

men, but when they returned, the thing was gone. "There was dragged marks on the ground," explained J. B. "We followed the trail until we came to a creek too deep to cross. We could see on the other side where it had been dragged out. I figured that one of its own kind came to get it." The hunting dogs refused to follow the trail and "cowered down and just whined like pups." All four men kept their story secret for fear of ridicule. J. B. is the last living member of the group, and he still believes that what he shot was something half man and half ape.

The descriptions given by witnesses indicate that the elusive beast is generally seven to eight feet tall, with shaggy hair and an obnoxious odor like rotten cabbage, rotten eggs, or skunk musk. Hence the nickname Skunk Ape.

Shawn Scott of Bithlo, Florida, saw what he called a "monkey man" on Highway 520 west of Cocoa, Florida. He said that for a short distance it kept up with his pickup truck, going about 45 mph. Shawn recalled that "whatever it was caused a smell like a polecat inside my truck." Scott was not the only one to see this thing; several callers to an Orlando radio show reported similar sightings on the same road.

In 1971 five members of an archaeological expedition in the Everglades claimed that a manlike beast came crashing into their camp in the middle of the night, then ran off. They described it as seven to eight feet tall, with a man's face, and covered with shaggy white fur. As in the other accounts, they complained about the obnoxious stench that seemed "to linger in the air long after the thing was gone."

There are thousands of alleged sightings of the Florida Skunk Ape, some by very credible people. While some have been proven hoaxes and others simple misidentifications of Florida black bears, a significant number of sightings remain as mysterious as the Sasquatch encounters of the Northwest. There are still remote areas of Florida that are difficult to explore, but these are falling fast to the developer's bulldozer. Perhaps there's some unknown primate species that inhabits Florida's swamps, emerging on occasion to come face-to-face with the encroachment of civilization. We can only speculate; however, with the thousands of reports it is obvious that some people have encountered something that cannot be easily explained.–*Charlie Carlson*

Encounter with the Blue Thing

On an August night in 1999, Michelle of Madison, Wisconsin, was hiking with her companion along the Ice Age Trail, just outside of Lodi, off Riddle Road. They had hiked nearly to the Lodi Cannery when they turned around to return to their car. Michelle stopped to wait for her friend to catch up when she saw a flash of motion some fifty feet ahead along the trail. Her first impression was that it was someone dressed in a blue jacket, perhaps a rider on a bike rolling along the trail. But the trail was posted as off-limits to bikes. Miffed, she was readying herself to step aside, when the blue thing abruptly glided to her right and disappeared into the trees. As it turned, she noticed a long blue plume of something waving from behind its head. Whether it was feather or hair or scarf, she didn't know. It was waving blue, then gone.

Startled, she turned to her companion, who had come up behind her. She told him what she had seen, and the two went along the path to where the Blue Thing had disappeared into the bushes. Nothing to the right. Nothing to the left. And there was no path through the woods—just unbroken scrub brush and trees.

— *Rick Hendrick, Weird-WI.com*

Caddy of Puget Sound

A terrifying sea serpent has long terrorized the shores of Washington in the vicinity of Puget Sound. This titanic creature is known as Caddy. His two most notable features are an elongated neck and an undersized, horselike head. Terrified spectators estimate that he is nearly forty feet long. Caddy sightings have taken place for decades now, although their frequency increased in the 1990s, especially in the area of the Saanich Inlet in British Columbia.

Chupacabra – Bloodsucker of the Southwest

One of the most famous beasts in all of cryptozoology has made many an appearance in the Rio Grande Valley area of Texas. He is the Chupacabra, legendary throughout Puerto Rico, Mexico, and Texas as a hairless, black-eyed beast that survives by sucking the blood of goats. Hundreds of farmers have reported finding their goats slaughtered and eerily drained of every drop of blood. Appropriately, the Spanish word *chupacabra* means bloodsucker. Most describe the beast as a reptilian creature about three feet tall, with razor-sharp fangs and claws. Some say that the Chupacabra is a life-form left behind after an alien visit to this planet.

Local Heroes and Villains

Colorful characters and local loonies—every town has at least one. Their exploits may garner fame outside their communities, even earn them a place in the history books, but most of them achieve celebrity only in their own hometowns.

We feel that the people featured in this chapter have done something to set themselves apart from the crowd, and that makes them worthy of attention. In many instances these folks are probably better known to the residents of their communities than are their own mayors!

We hold these unique individuals in the highest regard and mean no disrespect in any form. We appreciate their presence and the fact that they help make each of our towns and cities a more interesting place to call home.

Carnival Comes to Town

Florida has long been home to freaks of all kinds—especially the professional kind! There is even a town for them to go to when their sword-swallowing days are over. It's called Gibsonton, known more commonly as Gibtown.

In 1924 sideshow performers started spending their nontouring winters in Gibtown, where they could have all the solitude and fishing they wanted. It started with Al "the Giant" Tomaini, who was eight feet four and one-half inches tall. Al opened the Giant's Camp Restaurant, which established the small town as a haven for performers. He was joined by his wife, Jeanie the Half Girl, a legless woman two feet six inches tall. Each year more and more performers and carnival workers would travel to Gibtown, park their trailers, and put down roots for a few months.

At one time, Al the Giant served as police chief, and a dwarf known as Colonel Casper was the head of the fire department. Gibtown is the only town in the United States whose post office features lowered counters to accommodate little people.

It became commonplace to see performers out on the streets, and no one batted an eye at the sight of even the strangest of sideshow freaks. Among those who have called Gibtown home are Percilla the Monkey Girl, the Anatomical Wonder, Melvin "the Human Blockhead" Burkhardt, and Johnny "the World's Most Famous Half Man" Eck.

The most infamous resident in Gibtown's storied history is Grady Stiles Jr., known better as the Lobster Boy. Stiles's family possessed a rare genetic mutation called ectrodactyly, which caused the fingers of their hands to be fused into claws and deformed their legs into flippers. Stiles's father toured the sideshow circuit and brought Grady into the freak show lifestyle. But although he became one of the industry's most famous performers and shrewdest businessmen, Stiles was a severe alcoholic who beat his wife and children. Grady even murdered his daughter's fiancé, but served no jail time, partly because prisons couldn't accommodate his needs and partly because his neighbors, a 712-pound man and a bearded woman, testified to his upstanding character. In 1992 scandal struck Gibtown when a news report stated that a local thug hired by Grady's wife and son-in-law had killed Grady in his trailer.

As the older freaky folk of Gibtown have died off, it has become less

The Tinfoil Man

Residents of Portland, Maine, have embraced a once homeless resident with a quirky grasp of art. His real name is Robert Wilson, but he is much better known as the Tinfoil Man.

The Tinfoil Man creates sculptures out of—you guessed it—tinfoil. He began doing so as a child in the South and continued his hobby through adulthood. By the time he was an adult, he had mastered the art of making extremely lifelike representations of animals and people—his most well-known pieces are large scorpions.

These days the Tinfoil Man's work can be seen in many shop windows and displays throughout the city.

He charges up to $25 for a single sculpture. Always keep your eyes peeled—periodically the Tinfoil Man spreads out his works on a sidewalk just to amaze the crowds who pass by.

common to see three-legged men or human torsos out and about town. But their memories live on. The Giant's Camp Restaurant still stands on Route 41 and is open twenty-four hours a day. Al and Jeanie, the Giant and the Half Girl, the World's Strangest Couple, stare down from a photo on the wall. And performers and carnival workers still populate the town. Clowns, fire-eaters, ride operators, and their ilk still congregate at Showtown USA, a local bar, to discuss life on the road, and tell stories of times and people gone by. Just nine miles south of Tampa, Gibtown is truly one of a kind. Just like many of its residents.

Underdog

Most local heroes gain celebrity only within the borders of their hometown. However, one New Jersey legend attained national celebrity after appearing on the Howard Stern Show in 1992. She is choreographer and dancer Suzanne Muldowney, better known as Underdog.

Ms. Muldowney has been a south Jersey celebrity since the 1970s, thanks to her elaborate homemade outfits and her frequent appearances in south Jersey parades. Muldowney portrays pop culture icons, such as the 1960s cartoon superhero Underdog, which she regards as performance pieces.

After twelve years of public appearances as Underdog, Muldowney was contacted by the producers of the Howard Stern television show in 1992. She had never heard of Stern but agreed to appear in a segment called "Howie-wood Squares" that satirized the game show Hollywood Squares. She regretted the decision when she discovered that the other participants included scantily clad women and members of the K.K.K., and that the show focused on sex, vulgarity, and the bizarre. She couldn't leave her square, because she was seated in the top row of the three-story set and the ladder had been removed. Muldowney was visibly angry with Stern and launched into aggressive arguments with him on the show.

Needless to say, this performance satisfied Howard's rabid fans, and

has haunted Muldowney for the past decade. "I became a laughingstock and an outcast," she said. At parades and other public appearances she has been bombarded with taunts, often including Stern's name for her—Underdog Lady.

Muldowney worries that this infamy affects the integrity of the Underdog character. Most present-day youths know Underdog only as the eccentric, angry person on Stern's program. "They think Underdog is Howard's invention," says Muldowney, "and that the character and I are lustful cads."

So Muldowney has set about correcting these injustices, promoting Underdog's super-heroic nature and casting Stern as an adversary. "Howard Stern and his minions have committed very real deeds of super-villainry," she proclaims. "How many countries over the world could have gotten brainwashed via Stern? Underdog has to be detoxified worldwide!"

She May Be Underdog, But She Ain't No Lady

Suzanne Muldowney performs as the cartoon superhero Underdog and responds kindly only to being called Underdog and not Underdog Lady, as some folks have attempted to call out to her.—*Anonymous*

Rooting for the Underdog

Miss Suzanne, as I called her growing up in Delran, is a very unusual woman. Highly educated and from an affluent Boston family, Miss Suzanne still lives in the same sparsely furnished apartment that she originally rented in the early '70s. She does not drive and can be seen most mornings walking along Route 130, looking to catch the bus to her job in Philly. Her eccentric trait of playing dress-up first materialized in the mid-'70s when she appeared in the *Burlington County Times* as an avant-garde Dracula, complete with an aluminum-foil sword and fruit punch on her mouth to simulate blood. She takes these characters very seriously. If you see her on the boardwalk in her costume or walking along the highways in her cape, show some respect for a true south Jersey icon.—*Monica St. Clair*

Don't Mention Howard Stern

I saw her on a corner in Ocean City, and I approached her, telling her how I had just seen her on the *Howard Stern Show*. She yelled at me. She loudly began telling me to get lost or shut up. She is truly a bizarre person. —*Anonymous*

The Devil Made Them Do It

Murder is unquestionably the worst crime one person can perpetrate. Different people kill for different reasons. For the most callous, cold-blooded murderers, it's a business and merely a way to make a buck. There are other killers, though, whose motives don't seem as logical to the outside observer. Their reasons for killing, while almost certainly crystal clear to themselves, baffle the rest of us.

The Bender Family: Bleeding Kansas One Body at a Time

In its early days Kansas was notorious for its violence and bloodshed. The intense rivalry between abolitionist and proslavery forces earned the territory the nickname of Bleeding Kansas. Even after conflicts over slavery were a thing of the past, southeast Kansas in particular was known as a rough area. But one case in Kansas history rises above all others in the gruesome and bloody stakes. It is a tale of deception. It is a tale of greed. It is the tale of the mysterious, murdering Bender family of Cherryvale.

The Bender family—parents, son, and daughter—hailed from Germany and settled just northeast of the miniscule town of Cherryvale, Kansas, in 1870. They built a small inn to provide shelter and food for travelers and their horses. With so many settlers making their way through the relatively young and unsettled state in those days, inn-keeping was a lucrative business. But apparently it was not lucrative enough for the Benders. They decided to supplement their income through incredibly treacherous means.

When a traveler would enter the Benders' home, they would seat him at a dinner table with his back to a canvas curtain. While engaged in conversation by the young and attractive Kate Bender, the unsuspecting traveler would be attacked with a hammer by one of the Bender men, who rained blows down upon the skull of his victim. Then all four of the Benders would loot any money and possessions on the victim's person, slit his throat, and dump him through a trapdoor into a well-like enclosure beneath their house. Later, under the cover of darkness, the body would be removed and buried in the Benders' orchard out back.

Soon the Benders began preying upon the townsfolk of Cherryvale. Kate Bender hung posters in town proclaiming herself Prof. Miss Katie Bender, with the capacity to cure blindness, deafness, and other infirmities.

She also claimed to possess psychic powers, including the ability to communicate with the dead. The Bender men would set upon her clients in their usual manner.

In all, the Benders murdered eleven people, including George Lochner and his daughter, who in a truly disturbing incident was buried alive with the mutilated corpse of her father. The *Kansas City Times* described the discovery of her body:

"The little girl was probably eight years of age, and had long, sunny hair, and some traces of beauty on a countenance that was not yet entirely disfigured by decay. One arm was broken. The breastbone had been driven in. The right knee had been wrenched from its socket and the leg doubled up under the body. Nothing like this sickening series of crimes had ever been recorded in the whole history of the country."

Others narrowly escaped being killed by the Benders. When one William Pickering refused to sit with his back to the canvas because of its disgusting stains, Kate Bender threatened him with a knife, at which point he fled the premises. Out of the corner of his eye a Catholic priest stopping at the inn saw one of the Bender men hiding a large hammer, and the priest escaped, using the excuse that he needed to tend to his horse.

After the disappearance of a prominent local doctor in 1873, suspicions fell on the Benders, so they disappeared overnight. Soon after, eleven shallow graves were discovered in their orchard and the nature of the murders was uncovered. Here is how the *Kansas City Times* described the initial investigation of the pit beneath the Benders' home:

"[The men] groped about over these splotches and held up a handful to the light. The ooze smeared itself over their palms and dribbled through their fingers. It was blood-thick, fetid, clammy, sticking blood—that they had found groping there in the void. Blood perhaps, of some poor, belated traveler who had laid himself down to dream of home and kindred, and who had died while dreaming of his loved ones."

The Bender murders quickly became national news, and rewards totaling in the thousands of dollars were offered for their capture. Surprisingly, the fate of the Benders is unknown. Rumors quickly sprang up that a posse captured and hanged all four members of the family, though no such posse ever came forward. Some said that other criminals dispatched the Benders. In the early 1880s two females thought to be the Bender women were brought from Illinois to Kansas but were released after a short period, as it was impossible to prove that they were part of the murderous cadre from years before. In fact, it's possible that the family was not a family at all, just four criminals working together.

Today little remains to remind us of these macabre incidents of Kansas's past. The inn was destroyed soon after the discovery of the bodies, as souvenir hunters combed and dismantled the building. A marker describing the incidents stands on US 169, near the former site of the inn; it very accurately proclaims the fate of the Benders as "one of the great unsolved mysteries of the Old West." —*Chris Gethard*

Law-Breakin' Lawman

We all know what role the sheriff played in a Wild West frontier town. When the bad guys rolled in, he was the last line of defense. When the saloon erupted into mayhem, he got everyone back in line. When the stagecoach was hijacked, he thwarted the crooks and escorted the women to safety. That's what we've all learned from movies and comic books; in the real world the sheriff was sometimes the town's biggest crook!

The small mining town of Bannack, Montana, was a rough-and-tumble place. By the early 1860s the residents were looking for someone to keep order and peace. When Henry Plummer came to town in 1862—well dressed, well groomed, and well spoken—the townspeople embraced him almost immediately. He was a perfect gentleman, and by July 1863 he had been elected sheriff. The people trusted him. And that is exactly how he wanted it.

Immediately after being elected, Plummer quietly brought his gang of thieves and murderers into Bannack. He was the kingpin of a pack of criminals known as the Innocents, for their password, "I am innocent." In the six months that Plummer served as sheriff, they proved themselves to be anything but, killing at least one hundred people and perhaps a hundred more that were never reported. Plummer would use the townspeople's own jail against them, shackling people and locking them up if he needed information from them.

By December the people of Bannack had no choice but to fight back. When Plummer murdered a well-liked young Dutchman on the outskirts of town, the townspeople formed their own gang, the Montana Vigilantes. They hunted down and hanged the murderers. Over the next two weeks the Vigilantes hanged twenty-four members of Plummer's gang. Most of the rest fled west.

On January 10 they finally caught Plummer himself and swiftly exacted their revenge. Legend has it that Plummer cried like a baby before being hanged and muttered his last words, "Give me a good drop."

Today Bannack is a completely abandoned ghost town and a state park of Montana. One can visit the buildings, even the jail Plummer used against those trusting townspeople. People say that Plummer's ghost still wanders the empty buildings to this day, proclaiming his innocence. But the people of Montana won't be fooled again.

Satanists, Vampires, and Evil Clowns

Vampires and Satan worshippers exist in fact as well as legend. But they don't always look like the screen image of Bela Lugosi pulling the cape over his face and hypnotizing his helpless victims before biting into their neck. There are weird people out there who live the role of a vampire, acting not quite human, and claiming the ability to channel and manipulate life forces. These lurkers of the darkness tend to drain the lives of the people they associate with, rather than their blood. And speaking of lurkers of darkness, let's face it, deep down inside we all always suspected that clowns were up to no good. Whether it's the frightening wigs, the garish outfits, or the nightmarish face paint, there's just something disturbing about these happy hobos and harlequins. Satanists, vampires, and evil clowns—none of them are up to any good.

Anton LaVey and the Church of Satan

Like any good satanist, Anton LaVey needed a place to worship and to discuss the daily rigors of evil curses, rites, and rituals in praise of the Unholy One. So in 1966 he opened the Church of Satan, known as the Black House, at 6114 California Street in San Francisco. With his clean-shaven head and diabolic black goatee, Anton LaVey was called the Black Pope by his followers. But was the author of *The Satanic Bible* really a practitioner of the black arts or merely the P. T. Barnum of the satanic set?

Most of LaVey's stories seem to be fabricated—from tales of an early career as a lion tamer to his friendship with Sammy Davis Jr. and his affairs with Marilyn Monroe and Jayne Mansfield. But the devil is not known for his truthful tongue, is he?

Even LaVey's real name seems to have been of his own invention. Though he says he was christened Anton Szandor LaVey, his 1930 birth certificate from Cook County, Illinois, states his given name as Howard Stanton Levey. And while LaVey claimed it was his Transylvanian Gypsy grandmother who introduced him to the Dark Side, his grandmother was actually Ukrainian and had no Gypsy blood.

To see two very different pictures of the man, just compare excerpts from his official bio offered by the Church of Satan to the personal remembrances of his daughter, Zeena.

According to the Church of Satan's literature, written by Magus Peter H. Gilmore:

LaVey worked for a while as a photographer for the Police Department.

Zeena LaVey begs to differ: *San Francisco Police Department past employment records include no "Howard Levey" nor "Anton LaVey."*

Church of Satan: *LaVey was . . . attracted to the keyboards. . . . This talent would prove to be one of his main sources of income for many years . . . in bars, lounges, and nightclubs.*

Zeena LaVey: *According to LaVey's first wife Carole, his only income of $29.91 a week was generated by his regular engagement at the "Lost Weekend" nightclub, where he was the house Wurlitzer organist.*

So how did this cocktail lounge organist come to be the high priest of satanists? The answer to this question too seems to be debatable.

Church of Satan: *Through his frequent public gigs as an organist . . . LaVey became a local celebrity and his holiday parties attracted many San*

Francisco notables. . . . From this crowd LaVey distilled what he called a "Magic Circle" of associates who shared his interest in the bizarre. When a member of his Magic Circle suggested that he had the basis for a new religion, LaVey agreed and decided to found the Church of Satan. And so, in 1966 on the night of May Eve — the traditional Witches' Sabbath — LaVey declared the founding of the Church of Satan.

According to Zeena LaVey, his reasons were more monetary than philosophical: *In 1966 ASL supplemented his income by presenting lectures on exotic and occult topics . . . and he charged $2 a head. Publicist Edward Webber suggested . . . that he "would never make any money by lecturing . . . it would be better to form some sort of church and get a charter from the State of California. . . . In the summer of 1966 . . . a newspaper article about ASL's lectures offhandedly referred to him as "priest of the Devil's church."*

LaVey's media blitz began when Avon Books approached him to write *The Satanic Bible,* hoping to cash in on the satanism fad. LaVey borrowed passages from various authors to meet Avon's deadline. In 1968 he released a record album, *The Satanic Mass.* LaVey emblazoned the symbols of pentagrams and goat heads on his book and record jackets. He followed *The Satanic Bible* with several more books.

Despite LaVey's claims that church membership was in the hundreds of thousands, it apparently never exceeded three hundred. But his seminars attracted '60s subculture types including Manson family member Susan Atkins.

The Church of Satan was run out of LaVey's modest house in San Francisco's Richmond District. The church's black-and-purple façade stood out on the residential street. The interior was painted glossy red, black, and purple, and had secret passages and rooms. LaVey's grotesque paintings were hung in the entrance hall, and murals depicting the devil were displayed throughout the house. The fireplace had a trapdoor that led to the "Den of Iniquity" where the more bizarre activities of the church allegedly occurred. With its secret openings, chambers, and ritual rooms, LaVey had created the ultimate "nightmare of the psyche" dwelling.

So in what does a practicing satanist believe? Is the "religion" all about animal sacrifices and carnal orgies, as the low-budget cult films would have us believe? In 1967 Anton LaVey laid down eleven commandments for being a good satanist:

The Eleven Satanic Rules of the Earth

1. Do not give opinions or advice unless you are asked.
2. Do not tell your troubles to others unless you are sure they want to hear them.
3. When in another's lair, show him respect or else do not go there.
4. If a guest in your lair annoys you, treat him cruelly and without mercy.
5. Do not make sexual advances unless you are given the mating signal.
6. Do not take that which does not belong to you unless it is a burden to the other person and he cries out to be relieved.
7. Acknowledge the power of magic if you have employed it successfully to obtain your desires. If you deny the power of magic after having called upon it with success, you will lose all you have obtained.
8. Do not complain about anything to which you need not subject yourself.
9. Do not harm little children.
10. Do not kill nonhuman animals unless you are attacked or for your food.
11. When walking in open territory, bother no one. If someone bothers you, ask him to stop. If he does not stop, destroy him.

There is evidence that LaVey himself might have had some difficulty practicing what he preached. His daughter Zeena stated that he routinely beat and abused the female disciples with whom he had sex, and his fits of rage and cruelty extended to animals.

In 1991 LaVey filed for bankruptcy. He lived the rest of his life subsidized by California state aid and handouts from friends and relatives. The Black Pope died on October 29, 1997, though the date was changed on his death certificate to Halloween. After his death the church fell into disrepair, and the building was demolished in October 2001.

So was Anton Szandor LaVey the spokesman for the devil here on earth or simply a master showman? Perhaps he was a bit of both. The Church of Satan has the last word.

LaVey was a skilled showman. . . . However, the number of incidents detailed in his biographies via photographic and documentary evidence far outweigh the few items in dispute. . . . The Church has survived his death, and continues, through the medium of his writings, to continually attract new members who see themselves reflected in the philosophy he called Satanism.

Mercy Brown, the Rhode Island Vampire

"There are such beings as vampires, some of us have evidence that they exist. Even had we not the proof of our own unhappy experience, the teachings and the records of the past give proof enough for sane peoples," read Dr. Seward's diary in Bram Stoker's *Dracula.* It was Bram Stoker who took the vampire of folklore and made him beautiful, powerful, and sexy. There were cases of vampires all over the world before, during, and even after *Dracula*—and one of these cases was Mercy Brown, the Rhode Island vampire.

Mercy Brown has the distinction of being the last of the North American vampires—at least in the traditional sense. Mercy Lena Brown was a farmer's daughter and an upstanding resident of rural Exeter, Rhode Island. She was only nineteen years old when she died of consumption on January 17, 1892. On March 17, 1892, Mercy's body would be exhumed from the cemetery because members of the community suspected the vampire Mercy Brown was attacking her dying brother, Edwin.

Dr. Michael Bell, a folklorist, wrote *Food for the Dead,* a book that explores the folklore and history behind Mercy Brown as well as several other cases of New England vampires. "A vampire is your classic scapegoat . . . a corpse that comes to the attention of a community during a time of crisis, and is taken for the cause of that crisis."

Attacking vampires was a way

for a community to fight an evil that was plaguing them. In the case of Mercy Brown, that evil was consumption. During the 1800s one out of every four deaths was attributed to consumption, or pulmonary tuberculosis. The victim becomes pale, stops eating, and wastes away. At night the condition worsens because when the patient lies down, fluid and blood may collect in the lungs. During later stages breathing becomes labored as the body is starved of oxygen, and victims may wake up to find blood on their face, neck, and nightclothes.

"You look the way vampires have always been portrayed in folklore," says Dr. Bell. "Like walking corpses . . . skin and bones, fingernails are long and curved."

In December of 1883 Mercy's mother, Mary, died of consumption. Seven months later the Browns' eldest daughter, Mary Olive, joined her. The Browns' only son, Edwin, came down with the disease a few years later. Although he was sent to live in the arid climate of Colorado to arrest the disease, it got worse, and he returned to Exeter in 1891. Mercy's battle was considerably shorter—she had the "galloping" variety of consumption that took her life in a few months, and she was laid to rest in Chestnut Hill Cemetery behind the Baptist church on Victory Highway.

After Mercy's funeral her brother Edwin's condition worsened. Their father, George Brown, grew more frantic. He had lost his wife and two of his daughters, and now he was about to lose his only son. Science and medicine had no answers for George Brown, but folklore did. So much death had plagued the Brown family that poor George probably felt he was cursed. Maybe the family was under vampire attacks from beyond the grave. Was Mercy Brown the vampire, or was it Mercy's mother or sister? Because he felt he had no other choice, George Brown was willing to try the old European practice of slaying the "walking dead." He would exhume the body of his recently deceased daughter, remove her heart, burn it, and feed the ashes to his son.

In his book Dr. Bell recounts an extensive interview he conducted with Everett Peck, a descendant of Mercy Brown and lifelong resident of Exeter, Rhode Island. "Everett said that after they had dug her up, [they saw that] she had turned over in the grave—but there's no mention of that in the newspaper or the eyewitness accounts."

Mercy Brown died before embalming became a common practice. During decomposition, it is possible for bodies to sit up or jerk. We don't know exactly what position her body was in on that day in March when George Brown, and some of his friends and family, came to examine Mercy's body. We do know that she looked "too well preserved."

The group cut open her chest cavity. "They cut her heart out," Dr. Bell said, "and burned it on a nearby rock. Then according to the newspaper, they fed them [the ashes of the heart] to Edwin."

The community's vampire-slaying failed to save Edwin—he died two months later. But maybe it helped others by absorbing the fears and guilt that people felt.

As Dr. Bell said, "Folklore always has an answer—it may not be the scientifically valid answer, but sometimes it's better to have any answer than none at all." –*Jeff Belanger*

Vampires, Pirates, and Glowing Graves

Apparently Rhode Island (from the 1800s up to the discovery of disease-causing germs) was the capital of digging up loved ones to dismember their bodies in hopes that this practice would curtail any further deaths in the family.

Mercy Brown is the easiest case to verify, since her gravestone still stands. There are others: Nellie Vaughn, whose gravestone reads I'M WATCHING & WAITING FOR YOU, is a Rhode Island favorite located on Devil's Road. People say that you can see eyes watching you from the cemetery as you drive by. The eyes are two pieces of mica in one of the gravestones that reflect cars' lights. Another story relates to the Black Tillinghast, the meanest pirate of his time. Tillinghast's grave still stands on its original site because people are still freaked by this guy. The grave is right in someone's yard on Benefit St. in Providence's East Side. The story goes that all the Rhode Island vampires had Tillinghast bloodlines. Sara Tillinghast was the first popular vampire case.
—*Brad Maloney*

Phantom Clowns Accost Our Kids

In the spring of 1981 Boston, Massachusetts, appears to have been the port of entry for a strange new version of the Pied Piper story. During the first week of May some individuals in multicolored clothes began trying to entice schoolchildren into coming along with them. School committees, area police, and scores of parents were openly discussing reports in the local newspapers of clowns in vans bothering children. On May 6, 1981, the police, responding to persistent complaints, warned that men in clown suits were harassing elementary school children. One of the men was seen wearing a clown suit just from the waist up; from the waist down, he was naked. According to reports, the clown had driven a black van near Franklin Park in the Roxbury area of Boston between four and six p.m. He also appeared in the Jamaica Plain neighborhood of Boston near the Mary E. Curley School.

A day earlier, in the adjoining city of Brookline, two clown men reportedly had tried to lure children into their van with offers of candy. The Brookline police had a good description of the van: older model, black, with ladders on the side, a broken front headlight, and no hubcaps. After the clown men and van had been seen near the Lawrence Elementary School in Brookline, the police told school administrators to be "extra cautious."

The previous week Investigative Counselor Daniel O'Connell of the Boston Public School District had sent a memo to the district's elementary and middle school principals. He wrote, "It has been brought to the attention of the police department and the district office that adults dressed as clowns have been bothering children to and from school. Please advise all students that they must stay away from strangers, especially ones dressed as clowns."

By May 8 reports of clown men in vans harassing children had come in from East Boston, Charlestown, Cambridge, Canton, Randolph, and other cities near Boston. Police were stopping pickup trucks and vans with clowns delivering birthday greetings and "clown-a-grams," but no child molesters were arrested. Frustrated policemen pointed out that virtually all the reported sightings originated with children age five to seven. The headline in the May 9 issue of the *Boston Globe* told the story: POLICE DISCOUNT REPORTS OF CLOWNS BOTHERING KIDS. The public had been calmed, and that was the end of the story. Or so the papers would have had us believe.

However, fifty miles south, in Providence, Rhode Island, similar reports were coming to the attention of psychiatric social workers counseling the city's youth. Perhaps these were spillovers from Boston, but subsequent reports are more difficult to dismiss. The focus of activity shifted a thousand miles west to Kansas City, Kansas, and Kansas City, Missouri. On May 22 a yellow van on the Missouri side stopped by two girls, who ran screaming from the knife-wielding clown inside. Dozens of similar reports came in, involving six different elementary schools, and by that afternoon police cruisers were trailing the yellow van across town. The calls did not taper off until five o'clock that afternoon.

The previous week in Kansas, schoolchildren said a clown had chased them home from school and threatened them if they didn't get into his van. Some reports claimed that the clown brandished a sword instead of a knife.

Before long the "Killer Clown" affair spread to the Hill District of Pittsburgh and became tied up with reports of someone wearing a pink-and-white rabbit costume in a blue van and other weird stories involving a costumed "Spiderman" joining forces with a "gorilla" and a "clown" in Arlington Heights, Pennsylvania, and trying to entice a boy into a vehicle.

I began to sense that we were in the midst of a major flap of a new phenomenon. Through the Fortean underground, I was able to ascertain the depth and breadth of the phantom clown drama. Phantom clowns in at least six major cities, spanning over a thousand miles of America in the space of one month is quite a mystery. Were the "clowns in vans" being sighted elsewhere in the United States? Are they still being seen? Only time will tell, but new reports keep popping up, and one of the most recent ones comes via Fortean researcher Richard Hendricks. The *Wisconsin State Journal* of Madison reported on June 20, 2000, "A man dressed in a complete clown costume and holding three helium balloons tried to lure children into woods near the King James Court Apartments at about 12:30 p.m. Monday, Fitchburg police said."

Then two days later the *Wisconsin State Journal* ran this article:

SUSPICIOUS CLOWN HAD UNIQUE FACE PAINT
Fitchburg police, investigating a man in clown costume who tried to lure children into the woods on Monday, have concluded he's not a "legitimate" clown. Detective Todd Stetzer, who said he's learned a lot about clowning since the man appeared near the King James Court Apartments, said the man's black face paint set him apart from any of three mainstream styles of clown costumery. "That's extremely,

extremely unique," he said. "It isn't in the legitimate style of clowning, which kind of leads us to believe the person was using it as a costume only for this purpose (enticement)."

The denizens of the netherworld have apparently dreamed up a new nightmare to shock us. Leagues of phantom clowns in vans have now joined the scores of Fortean, ufological, and flying saucer people. The cosmic joker is alive and well, and living in a clown suit.–*Loren Coleman*

Some people seem to move through this world slightly out of step with the rest of society. Perhaps it's the pace at which they move or the mannerisms they employ while in motion that sets them apart from others around them. But whatever it is, there is something out of sync about these folks that makes the rest of us notice them. And once they have been noticed, inquisitive minds start trying to explain their curious behavior. Stories are invented, told, and retold. Some of these tales stay close to home, but others have proved to be not only far-reaching but also endowed with a surprising longevity.

Here are some tales that have transformed certain more or less ordinary people into the stuff of legend.

Leatherman: One Weird Wandering Hobo

Since 1862 many have heard the tale of a vagrant who traveled in an endless 365-mile circle between the Connecticut and Hudson rivers. This strange man spoke only in grunts or gestures, and dressed in a crudely stitched suit of raw leather. The suit must have weighed more than sixty pounds in total from his hat to his shoes—a coat of armor to protect him from the sometimes harsh New England elements. Leatherman, as he came to be known, would sleep outside year-round and mostly in caves around Connecticut and New York. Some claim old Leatherman is still making his endless journey today, through the woods, mountains, and river valleys of the two states.

A wandering eccentric is nothing surprising in American folklore. There are enough to fill a thousand railroad boxcars. But what makes the Leatherman unique is his incredible precision in daily routine. He would arrive in the same location every thirty-four days.

Though the Leatherman was first seen in Connecticut in 1862, his tale begins in Lyons, France, in the 1820s, when the young Bourglay family had a son, Jules. The Bourglays were a family of woodcutters, which afforded them a place in the lower middle class at a time when one's social station was all-important. A family's wealth would determine its children's entire future—whether they got to go to school, what kind of job they would have, whom they would marry. Young Jules Bourglay met and fell in love with Miss Margaret Laron, the daughter of a somewhat wealthy leather merchant. Jules and Margaret had to keep their courtship a secret because of the difference in their class. Eventually Jules worked up the courage to approach Margaret's father and ask for his daughter's hand in marriage. Monsieur Laron objected to the match.

But Jules Bourglay didn't give up easily. After much negotiating, he was given the opportunity to work in the Laron family leather business. If he could learn the trade and be successful, he would be granted permission to marry Margaret. If he failed, he would have to leave France.

Jules Bourglay worked hard. Monsieur Laron began to trust young Jules so much so that he was given more responsibilities, including the purchase of leather on the open market. Jules speculated on the leather market in much the same way that traders speculate on the stock or commodities markets today, with similar results. But he neglected to keep an eye on technology and missed the introduction of a new chemical tanning process in 1855. Before then leather tanning had been done with tree bark and was extremely labor-intensive.

Though he would occasionally be invited to sleep indoors or in barns by good Samaritans, he always chose to sleep outside or in one of his many caves.

Jules made a large leather purchase, and almost overnight the price dropped by forty percent. As the price of leather continued to fall, Jules continued to buy, in hopes that a rebound in the market price would net him a good profit. Laron's leather firm was ruined.

Too ashamed to go back to his own family, the disgraced Jules became a homeless wanderer in Lyons. Then he disappeared and was never seen in the city or anywhere in France again. For the next few years the story of Jules Bourglay is a mystery. One could speculate that he simply wandered Europe as a beggar for a while. Then, in 1862, someone fitting his description and background showed up in the town of Harwinton, Connecticut.

The Leatherman Arrives in Connecticut

The man fitting the Leatherman's description began a clockwise trek between the Connecticut and Hudson rivers. His 12-mile-per-day, 365-mile-per-month circuit began at Harwinton. The route took him through Bristol, Forestville, Southington, Kensington, Berlin, Middletown, and south along the westerly side of the Connecticut River to the shore towns. He then traveled west to Westchester County in New York, coming within a few miles of the Hudson River and then back east into Connecticut. From Danbury, he went north to New Milford, through Roxbury, Woodbury, Watertown, Plymouth, and back to his starting point in Harwinton.

Modern-day public transportation can't hold a candle to the schedule the Leatherman kept. He arrived at the same place in precisely thirty-four-day intervals and at the same time of day. Many people were startled the first time they saw the mountain of a man covered in leather, but as he became familiar, some would have a meal prepared for his arrival. Many different families took it upon themselves to feed the Leatherman when he passed by. He never spoke, but would grunt or make appreciative gestures, then quickly move along to keep his schedule.

A true outdoorsman, the Leatherman didn't survive on handouts alone. He would hunt for food, gather berries, and take his water from streams and rivers. Though he would occasionally be invited to sleep indoors or in barns by good Samaritans, he always chose to sleep outside or in one of his many caves.

Bourglay tended to every detail before leaving each day's sleeping location. He would gather wood and safely store it in the cave so when he returned he could quickly get a fire started with dry wood. His bed was made of the rocks by his fire, and his thick leather suit added some padding.

For almost three decades Jules Bourglay made his journey through heat, rain, drought, and bitter New England winters. The Leatherman's routine would suffer only one setback. The blizzard of 1888 slowed his cycle by four days and made him ill. Bourglay, who was now in his mid-sixties, made it through the rest of the winter but finally died in a cave on the George Dell farm in Briarcliff Manor, New York.

The Leatherman's Caves Today

The Leatherman's caves still exist. One of the most famous is located on the Mattatuck Trail in a section of state forest in Watertown, Connecticut. A good starting point to reach the cave is the Black Rock State Park on Watertown Road in Thomaston. Leatherman Cave is approximately a two-mile hike into the woods from the state park. It is a blue-blazed trail and well marked, but it is rocky and at times very steep.

Making the hike in the summer wearing good hiking boots, shorts, a T-shirt, and a backpack with water and snacks in it makes one truly appreciate what the climb

must have been like in winter while wearing sixty pounds of leather.

Could the Leatherman's lost love for Miss Margaret Laron have kept him going for almost thirty years of perpetual, methodical motion to forget his past? Could his troubled spirit still be making that same journey today, as some have claimed? While hiking through the Leatherman's trails and caves, one can only imagine the broken-hearted anguish he must have suffered to drive him to this endless journey an ocean away from his homeland.

—*Jeff Belanger*

A Man and His Pet Ham

P. D. Gwaltney Jr. was a pretty average guy—except, of course for his pet ham. Gwaltney worked curing meats in Smithfield, Virginia, and took a particular liking to one of his hams after it survived two decades in the rafters of a packing house. He began carrying it with him wherever he went. He even put a collar on it so he could chain it up to avoid its theft. The ham can still be seen at the Isle of Wight Museum in Smithfield.

Dream Writer

Everyone, it's said, has a story in them somewhere. The average person never takes time to let that story out. Writers, however, put it into words and give it a life of its own. And then, if they are any kind of writer, they repeat the process and do it again. That's how John Thieme of Phillips, Wisconsin, has accumulated volumes of stories—simply by writing one after another throughout his eighty-four years. But while some writers strain for story ideas, Thieme never has to. He literally dreams things up.

"Most of 'em came to me in dreams," he says. "I'll dream something, and then I'll wake up and go scribble it on a little piece of paper, and a few weeks later I'll find the paper and make it into a story. You have to write 'em down as soon as you wake up, though, or you lose 'em."

Thieme has a rich dream life—from alien visitors to Native American spirit creatures, to small-town life gone very strange. And, oh yes, talking apple trees. They're all in a volume he calls *Fantastic Stories,* printed out on his home computer and bound neatly with duct tape. He's down to the last few copies of his first edition of one hundred and is hard at work on the second edition.

Thieme's stories are grounded just enough in the lore of the northwoods town of Phillips to seduce a reader into believing them, but the tales don't lead where you'd expect them to. Reading his stories, you're down the Yellow Brick Road and well into Wonderland before you even realize you've left the Elk River Valley.

I met Thieme in Phillips on Czech/Slovak Fest weekend, when people of the town take advantage of the tourist influx to sell their castaways. In the center of his garage stood a table filled with home-printed books bound in tape. "If you buy the big book for three dollars," John told me, "the book of poems is free."

I bought the big book and accepted the free *You Must Read My Poems* and scanned them as we drove around looking for other rummage sales. After a quick survey of the contents I insisted we go back. I had to get *Yarns of Yore* too.

His wife, Eva, peeped through the screen door as John climbed off his riding lawn mower and ambled over. They'd been married fifty-eight years, he said. "I picked up that little gal in Louisiana," he added, smiling. He was stationed there in the air force, and he and Eva were married in 1942. He then served in England as a mess hall sergeant during World War II. When he came home, he and Eva moved back to Wisconsin and started a family.

They raised five children while John worked first as manager, then owner, of Gamble's Hardware Store before "retiring" at the age of fifty-eight. He set up a bicycle repair shop in his garage and kept on writing stories.

The first story in *Fantastic Stories,* "Buried Treasure," was written in 1930 for his eighth-grade English class. "A bloody pirate rests not until he dies," wrote the young Thieme, "and seldom do we die of old age." Thieme went on to live a life of adventure and fantasy, at least in his imagination.

He began to spin tales of Native Americans who lived in the valley around the Elk River in Price County, which he says became known as Scokum Valley because of a prototypical animal spirit called the Scok. "There were rumors that all the animals we know today are descendants of the Scok," says Thieme. "The Scok could take any form or shape that it chose. So numerous were the tales, and so unbelievable that soon all the white settlers just ignored all the tales, and the Scok was forgotten."

But not by John Thieme. Of course, Thieme was the one who thought up the Scok in the first place, so he would be much less likely to forget it.

I read on to learn how Thieme's apple tree communicates with him in his dreams. "The apple tree is bending down," he wrote, "as if it wants to talk to me. In the branches there is a face, with a large mouth, and little chic-a-dees are picking food from between the face's teeth. Words come forth, but I cannot hear them. I try hard to understand just what the tree is saying to me, I get closer. . . ."

Then he writes that the tree talks to him through a blue jay clinging to his window.

Thieme tapes the blue jay's chatter, then plays it back. "Later when I put the tape in the player to check if I had really heard words, it came out very clear, 'I'LL BE CHECKING ON YOU.' Now I knew that the old apple tree really had been talking to me."

There are also tales of abductions by aliens, giant asteroids hitting the earth, outrageous fishing stories, and a hilarious farce about ordering Viagra off the Internet. All of John's stories are first written out by hand. "Then I rewrite 'em, add paragraphs maybe. . . . Lots of times you can take out or add a paragraph, and it changes things quite a bit. That's one of the secrets of writing, I think."

Copies of John Thieme's books are available to read at the Phillips Library. He invites other writers to contact him at 416 S. Argyle St., Phillips, Wisconsin 54555, but he does not sell books by mail. –*Linda Godfrey*

Hail to the Chief: Emperor Norton I

Most Americans assume that the Declaration of Independence did away with the rule of kings on these shores. Perhaps so, but less than a century after the declaration was signed and the War of Independence won, an English emigrant named Joshua Abraham Norton declared himself the Emperor of the United States—and reigned in San Francisco, California, for twenty-one years.

Born in England in the early 1800s, Norton moved to San Francisco in 1849, where he used a $30,000 fortune he made in South Africa to provide the city's growing population of gold miners with the supplies they needed. Within six years he had become a highly respected businessman and landowner. It was then, in 1855, that he hatched a bold scheme to supply San Francisco's other large population—the Chinese. He quickly cornered the market on all the rice in the Bay Area, and it looked as though he was going to make another fortune. But then two supply ships laden with rice steamed into the bay, and Norton was ruined. For the next three years his fortune and holdings vanished in a series of court actions, and by 1858 he was broke.

Norton disappeared for nine months. Then, in the summer of 1859, he strode into the offices of the *San Francisco Bulletin* and handed them a prepared statement. The newspaper dutifully ran the declaration on their next edition's front page:

"At the peremptory request of a large majority of the citizens of these United States, I, Joshua Norton, formerly of Algoa Bay, Cape of Good Hope, and now for the past nine years and ten months of San Francisco, California, declare and proclaim myself Emperor of these U.S., and in virtue of the authority thereby in me vested do hereby order and direct the representatives of the different States of the Union to assemble in Musical Hall of this city, on the 1st day of

February next, then and there to make such alterations in the existing laws of the Union as may ameliorate the evils under which the country is laboring, and thereby cause confidence to exist, both at home and abroad, in our stability and integrity."

Norton I
Emperor of the United States
September 17, 1859

Thus began the reign of the first and only Emperor of the United States, Norton I. In the years that followed, he abolished Congress, dissolved the Republic, and declared himself the Protector of Mexico. He also called for a convention to purge the Bible of its "false lights" and promote a universal religion. And he banned the Bay Area's most heinous "F" word—Frisco—the use of which was named a High Misdemeanor, punishable by a $25 fine to be paid to the Imperial Treasury.

Although clearly off his rocker and initially given newspaper space simply for a lark, he was treated with great respect by many in the city. A Sansome Street print shop issued treasury certificates in the emperor's name, which many local merchants accepted. He dined well, and gratis, at the finest restaurants, which took to putting up plaques reading BY IMPERIAL APPOINTMENT.

But like all empires, Norton's was not always peaceful. For a time the Grand Hotel gave him lodging, though they eventually evicted him in a move he called rebellion. He decreed "We, Norton I, do hereby command the Water Companies to close down on them, and the Gas Company to give them no light, so as to bring them to terms."

The Grand Hotel was not the only faction to rebel. When Congress reconvened in 1860, the year after it had been abolished, his Imperial Highness was forced to call in the army by the following declaration.

WHEREAS, *a body of men calling themselves the National Congress are now in session in Washington City, in violation of our Imperial edict of the 12th of October last, declaring the said Congress abolished;*

WHEREAS, *it is necessary for the repose of our Empire that the said decree should be strictly complied with;*

NOW, THEREFORE, *we do hereby Order and Direct Major-General Scott, the Command-in-Chief of our Armies, immediately upon receipt of this, our Decree, to proceed with a suitable force and clear the Halls of Congress.*

And there was real-life turmoil too. In the 1860s, during an ugly race riot against the Chinese population, Norton intervened directly and quieted a mob. He stood between the rioters and their intended victims and recited the Lord's Prayer until they dispersed.

But by and large the emperor's duties were fairly straightforward. Usually dressed in a blue naval uniform with gold-plated epaulets, wearing a beaver hat decorated with a rosette and a peacock feather, often carrying a cane or umbrella, he performed daily inspections of San Francisco neighborhoods. He would examine the condition of public property, sidewalks, and cable cars, inspect police officers, and philosophize at length to whomever would listen.

One incident in the eighth year of his reign showed just how much of a local hero Norton had become. In 1867 a young police officer named Armand Barbier arrested Norton and intended to commit him to involuntary treatment for a mental disorder. The citizens were outraged, and a series of scathing newspaper articles forced Police Chief Patrick Crowley to order the emperor's release with a formal apology. From that point on, all police officers would salute the emperor as he passed.

In 1880 Norton collapsed and died in the street. The following day the newspapers ran front-page obituaries with headlines like LE ROI EST MORT (THE KING IS DEAD). A local businessmen's club bought him a handsome rosewood casket, and the city paid for him to be interred at the Masonic Cemetery. The funeral procession was two miles long, and as many as thirty thousand people paid their respects.

Joshua Norton's remains have now been moved to the Greenlawn Cemetery in Colma, off the Junipero Serra Boulevard. But his impressive gravestone is not the only testament to this towering presence in the world of the weird. In the fourteenth year of his reign he commanded the cities of San Francisco and Oakland to appropriate funds for a suspension bridge from Oakland Point via Goat Island to San Francisco. Although it opened sixty-four years after Norton's decree, the five-mile bridge stands today as a memorial to this true visionary. But how many of the 259,000 drivers that jaunt across the San Francisco Bay Bridge realize that they owe their commute to America's first and only emperor? —*Matt Lake*

Fred Birchmore's Great Wall

Some people fear growing old, knowing that their best days lie behind them. Others embrace the opportunity to retire, relax, and enjoy some peaceful times. At ninety-five years of age, Fred Birchmore of Athens, Georgia, has chosen neither of these options. He continues to approach the world with endless energy, a positive attitude, and the idea that anything is possible if he puts his mind to it.

The most permanent testament to Fred's attitude is his home, Happy Hollow. In 1983 a neighbor suggested that he build a fence between their two yards. Fred did him one better. The septuagenarian spent five years single-handedly constructing a massive stone wall that reaches twenty feet high in places. The five-foot-six, one

In 1936 he became the first man to ride his bike around the world.

hundred and thirty pound Birchmore hunted down suitable stones, loaded them into his car, and placed them in the wall. Fred brushes off the titanic task of handling the stones, some of which were twice his body weight. "It's all attitude, mind over matter," he says.

This approach has helped Birchmore perform incredible feats throughout his life. In 1936 he became the first man to ride his bike around the world—an exploit he wrote about in his book *Around the World on a Bicycle*. The bike in question, which he christened Bucephalus, after Alexander the Great's horse, now resides in the Smithsonian. Birchmore has climbed the Andes and the Swiss Alps. He once walked from Georgia to Toronto to attend a Kiwanis convention (he has been a member for seventy-one years). Perhaps most amazingly, he walked down the stairs of the Washington Monument—standing on his hands!

Athens resident Eric Harris describes a recent visit he paid Mr. Birchmore.

"Fred Birchmore's house lies at the end of a nice suburban street in the Five Points area of Athens. We went through the Happy Hollow gate, down a marvelous path lined with low stone walls, and knocked on Fred Birchmore's door. His wife answered and politely told us

that he was out walking the trails with his great-grandchildren. So off we went down the trail, gawking at the gigantic stone wall that Fred built. The trail takes you first along the outside of the wall and then cuts through some beautiful woods, and after two and a quarter miles it looped us around back to Fred's wall where we began. It was very enjoyable, but we hadn't run into Fred.

"I decided to try the bell again. Mr. Birchmore answered the door this time, and he immediately invited me in and offered me a chair on his back porch. Lying around the porch and on the walls were many photos, newspaper clippings, and mementos concerning his exploits over the years. On the back of one chair hung a red vest, every inch of which was covered with medals and patches. Apparently he's received every award and honor from the Kiwanis Club.

"Fred is remarkably effervescent and friendly, a bit nutty, and, to say the least, excited to talk about his achievements. He quickly shifted into tour-guide mode, motioning us back through the gate to the great stone wall. Just inside he has mortared into the wall rocks that people have sent him and that he himself has collected from around the world—pyrite from China, a rock from the South Pole, a river stone from the northernmost point

of Europe, one from beneath the sea two miles off the California coast, and even a stone from the summit of Mount Everest.

"The wall itself is immense and remarkably well constructed. The stones fit together tightly (if they didn't, he sledge-hammered them into shape), and you can hardly see any of the concrete mortar between the boulders. He hauled and lifted every stone into place with only a wheelbarrow and some ladders—no pulleys or winches whatsoever. Every so often triangular stone buttresses containing steel beams provide reinforcement on the inside of the wall as the massive stone construction flows free-form around trees and curves in the landscape. The top of the wall is a smooth concrete path two or three feet wide that you can walk on confidently. Notable travelers from all over the world (even the president of Romania with an entourage of heavily armed bodyguards) have come to Fred's property to 'walk the wall.'

"He spoke at length of his construction methods and how he was able to lift three-hundred-pound rocks just with the power of positive thinking. 'You just gird your loins and say, I think I can, I think I can!' he exclaimed.

"One particularly large stone that Fred calls the Blue Whale was impossibly immense and four feet high in the wall. Apparently a policeman pulled him over because the gigantic boulder wouldn't fit inside his car and he was driving it home with his doors wide open.

"As my visit with Fred came to an end, I told him I'd sometimes seen him exercising at the local YMCA. He told me that his only problem with the Y was 'when I get on those Cybex machines, I just can't stop! It just creates so much energy!' It must be nice."

If you'd like to see the wall for yourself, it's fine by Fred: In 1969 he donated part of his property to the city, which created the 2.5-mile Fred A. Birchmore Nature Trail around the wall.

Personalized Properties

O Give Me a Home on the Strange!

"Let me live in the house by the side of the road and be a friend to man." – Henry Warren, 1972
Plaque at Shangri-La, Hightowers, NC

They say a man's home is his castle, but in this great land of ours that home could just as easily be made of beer cans or be someone's version of the Garden of Eden. For some, landscaping a property with manicured shrubs and flowering plants is simply no way to personalize a living space. These are the people who make their property a statement of individuality. These unique homeowners are artists who do not limit their work to a studio space—it spills out into their eccentric abodes. Most often, these folks have no connection to the mainstream art world—or any other outside world for that matter. They are usually self-taught, self-styled, and draw on their own personal vision for inspiration.

Of course, some of these homes just creep out the average person. We can only wonder what the owner might have been thinking. (Perhaps it's best not to know.) Found on the fringes of everyday culture and society, these properties are extensions of the creator's personality, and in them we see a reflection of the homeowner's soul. Each one reflects a singular vision and creates a one-of-a-kind, slightly off-center environment in which these unique individuals are happy to spend their lives.

The Coral Castle

In the town of Homestead in Florida is an amazing complex of over 1100 tons of coral stone called the Coral Castle. It's the work of one man, Edward Leedskalnin, a Latvian immigrant with a fourth-grade education, who quarried and carved each stone single-handedly, using tools fashioned from wrecking-yard junk. Nobody knows how he manipulated the coral blocks, many of which are several feet thick, some weighing over twenty-five tons.

Inside the Coral Castle, which Leedskalnin originally called Rock Gate Park, you can see some truly bizarre structures. There is a nine-ton swing gate that is so perfectly balanced that it can be opened with the push of a finger. The stony home features a variety of coral furnishings. There is a table shaped like the state of Florida, complete with a water basin where Lake Okeechobee would be, and also a rocking chair weighing thousands of pounds that can be rocked with a single finger. Then there is a piece described by Robert Ripley (of "Believe It or Not!" fame) as the "world's largest valentine," a five-thousand-pound heart-shaped table with a blooming red flower growing from its center.

The Coral Castle also features pieces that reveal Leedskalnin's interest in celestial bodies. An arrangement called the "moon pond" consists of three enormous blocks of coral that represent the various phases of the Moon. Other stones depict Mars, Saturn, and Jupiter. The most remarkable is the Polaris Telescope, a twenty-five-foot-tall tower weighing thirty tons that follows the North Star across the hemisphere. It is said that Leedskalnin used this device to set his sundial, which is calibrated to noon on the winter and summer solstices and to this day is still accurate to within two minutes.

Edward Leedskalnin's architectural prowess is often compared to that of the mysterious builders of Stonehenge, the Easter Island statues, and the pyramids of Egypt.

Leedskalnin was a Latvian immigrant with a fourth-grade education, who quarried and carved each stone single-handedly, using tools fashioned from wrecking-yard junk.

"See" ROCK GATE and Have a New Experience
ROCK GATE is located 27 miles southwest
from Miami on Key West Highway

Is the Man Who Made the Place

Ed himself said of his accomplishments, "I have discovered the secrets of the pyramids and have found out how the Egyptians and the ancient builders in Peru, Yucatan, and Asia, with only primitive tools, raised and set in place blocks of stone weighing many tons!"

But as with those architects of old, there are no reliable eyewitness records of Edward carving any of the stones.

Weirder still, Leedskalnin began his creation in Florida City, a few miles away. When developments started creeping up around him, he decided to move, and spent three years transporting the castle on an old truck chassis, reinforced with two steel rails and pulled by a tractor. Although many people recall seeing the stones being moved along Florida's Dixie Highway, no one actually witnessed Edward unloading them at the new property. He would work at night by lantern light, reconstructing the castle under cover of darkness.

To understand the Coral Castle, one must first delve into the life of its creator. In 1913 the twenty-six-year-old Edward Leedskalnin was engaged to the love of his life, sixteen-year-old Agnes Scuffs, whom he called his Sweet Sixteen. But on the eve of the nuptials the bride-to-be called it off. Leedskalnin sank into a spiral of depression and over the following years suffered a bout of tuberculosis that prompted him to move to Florida. There, he set out to create a monument to the yearnings of lost love.

Between 1923 and his death in 1951 he labored on his unrequited-love shack, living alone and never marrying. The most touching pieces of all of Ed's carved coral furniture are the three beds carved for a family that was never to be. They are lined up side by side—one for him, one for his wife, and a small cradlelike bed for a child. His Sweet Sixteen knew about the castle for years but never once visited it.

Ed was a bit of a philosopher. He wrote pamphlets with titles like "Magnetic Current," "A Book in Every Home," and "Sweet Sixteen, Domestic and Political Views." Most of his money came from the sale of these pamphlets and from the twenty-five-cent admission fee he charged visitors to walk through his property and view his creations.

One theory is that Leedskalnin not only tapped into an energy grid to perform his amazing feats, but that he did it with the help of UFOs.

Ed was a small man, not more than five feet tall and one hundred pounds, and not well educated. Whenever he was asked how he was able to move great weights of stone, he replied that he knew the laws of gravity and weight well. He explained that "all matter consists of magnets that can produce measurable phenomena, and electricity," and he claimed to have "rediscovered the laws of weight, measurement, and leverage."

His secrecy would lead to some pretty far-out speculation. Some neighbors claimed to have witnessed him trying to lighten the stones by singing to them while his hands were placed on them. Others claimed to have seen him levitating the massive stones through thin air. One author with a theory is B. J. Cathie, who believes that Leedskalnin not only tapped into an energy grid to perform his amazing feats, but that he did it with the help of UFOs.

Coral Castle researcher Kathy Doore takes an even more metaphysical approach to try to explain the baffling mystery. She writes: *Ed Leedskalnin showed every indication of being a natural geomancer, one who senses the unique telluric forces of the earth. He was highly intuitive and knew how to observe nature for signs of anomaly, ultimately leading him to the discovery of vortex energy and the ability to harness the natural elements of magnetism. . . ."*

At the age of sixty-four Ed Leedskalnin fell ill and put a sign up on the door that said GOING TO THE HOSPITAL. He took a bus to a hospital in Miami, where he was diagnosed with stomach cancer. He died in his sleep three days later and was buried in Miami Memorial Park Cemetery. After his death the castle was given to his relatives, who sold it to a family from Illinois. During the cleanup of the property, the new owners found a box containing instructions that led to a cache of thirty-five hundred-dollar bills, Ed's life savings.

Had Ed Leedskalnin rediscovered the knowledge of the ancient Egyptian pyramid builders? Did he possess the power of antigravity levitation, and was he in cahoots with UFOs? Or was it memory of his long lost love, Sweet Sixteen, that gave this little man the superhuman strength to move mountains of rock? We will never know the answers to these questions. Edward took his secrets to the grave with him, leaving behind his mysterious Coral Castle—a riddle for the ages.

Yvonne's Garden of Love

Yvonne Leow lives life a little bit off the beaten path. She hears voices, and she pays attention to them. She obeyed their requests to record a gospel album in her native Guyana and later listened when they told her to buy an acre and a half of land in Maxton, North Carolina. This property is now a garden dedicated to her love of Christ. Yvonne lives there in a trailer decked in flowers, surrounded by ceramic figures, arches, and a multicolored altar. She sometimes invites religious singing groups to perform free concerts in her garden. *Weird U.S.* field scouts Chris Musto and Kim Childrey visited Yvonne's garden and filed this report:

"Yvonne Maria Leow is the most energetic seventy-two-year-old we've ever seen. She has never fallen ill and never been to the doctor (unless you count her one checkup when she immigrated to America). Her secret, she says, is that her diet consists mostly of raw vegetables. She does not eat pork, because Jesus once banished evil spirits into the pig, and that, she says, is why people who eat it get sick. Her belief in God also keeps her energetic. She has her own 'Stairway to Heaven' in her front yard, with a word on each step illustrating the path to heaven. Every single word that she's written, whether it's for a gospel album or her writings, she's heard in her head and written down verbatim. She's a staunch Republican, with a red-white-and-blue elephant pin on her lapel and an autographed picture of Mr. and Mrs. George W. Bush. But she hasn't forgotten her native land: The whole place and even her outfit are the colors of Guyana's flag.

"When visiting the Garden of Love, be sure to purchase a memento or two from the trailer. Oils, teas, and perfumes are among the items for sale."

The Paper House

Early in the Roaring Twenties, Massachusetts resident Elis F. Stenman was in the process of building his own home. The wooden frame was complete, and it was time to outfit it with insulation. An amateur inventor, Stenman settled on an unconventional material for the purpose—newspaper. He mixed old papers with glue and varnish and formed the concoction into one-inch-thick material that he stuffed into the home's frame to construct the walls. Then he left it that way. No wood, no clapboards, no siding—just paper. And thus the Paper House of Rockport, Massachusetts, was born.

Completed in 1924, the Paper House was Stenman's home until 1930, and it still stands today, some seven decades later. Except for its construction material, the house is rather normal. It has regular electricity and even had running water when it was inhabited. But it's still all paper: The furniture is made of pressed paper. Even the mantel over the brick fireplace is paper. And though the piano isn't made of paper, it's coated in the stuff.

Nowadays the house is open as a museum and is run by Stenman's family. Upon entering Rockport, follow Route 127 to Pigeon Cove. Take a left onto Curtis Street, then another onto Pigeon Hill Street. It costs $1.50 to get in. They accept paper, not plastic.

Winchester Mystery House

Death sends many people over the edge of sanity, but it seldom makes them move to San Jose, California, and begin a major construction project. In Sarah Winchester's case it did. She built an estate riddled with a labyrinth of stairways to nowhere, underground tunnels, and secret rooms specifically designed to contact the dead.

At the height of the Civil War, Sarah Lockwood Pardee married William Wirt Winchester, son of the founder of the Winchester Repeating Arms Co. The family was extremely wealthy, but wealth could not protect them from tragedy. The couple's only child died at the age of one month. Fifteen years later Sarah's husband died of tuberculosis.

Grief-stricken, Sarah visited a psychic. The medium informed her that she was being punished because the rifles that had furnished her vast fortune had taken the lives of many people, and the spirits of the dead held the producer of the weapons responsible.

But the psychic offered Sarah a solution to her torment. She told her to move west and build an elaborate house. The house would have to be huge—big enough to provide the good, friendly spirits with a home of

their own and immense enough to confuse the evil, vengeful spirits so that they couldn't find her.

Sarah agreed to build the house, and in 1884 she purchased an eight-room farmhouse from Dr. Robert Caldwell of San Jose. Over the next thirty-eight years — twenty-four hours a day, three hundred and sixty-five days a year — additions were built to the house. At any given time from ten to twenty-two carpenters were at work.

Sarah never used blueprints. Instead, she took her ideas

from direct communications with spirits in the séance room. She spent every night from midnight to two in the morning there, finding out what to build the next day. Sarah often felt that her projects did not satisfy the spirits, and an estimated six hundred rooms were knocked down immediately after construction.

What survived the constant construction and demolition process is a bizarre, confusing mansion. There are stairways that lead to doors with ten-foot drops on the other side. Many of the doors are only four feet high. Because of a folktale that said ghosts exited and entered houses through chimneys, Sarah became obsessed with adding them to her house. There are forty-seven fireplaces and seventeen known chimneys within Winchester House.

The house has two basements, two ballrooms, over ten thousand windows, six kitchens, skylights built into both the ceilings and floors, and forty bedrooms. Sarah's practice of sleeping in a different bedroom each night ended in 1906, when an earthquake trapped her in her room. Rescue workers spent more than an hour searching for her. After this she slept in the same room each night and closed off over thirty bedrooms as a precaution.

When Sarah Winchester died in 1922, workers' hammers fell silent for the first time in thirty-eight years. There are many spots where nails are only half driven into a wall, as workers quit immediately upon hearing of Sarah's passing.

Today, tours are given through portions of the house. Tour guides and tourists alike often report hearing strange sounds coming from hidden parts of the building. One time a visitor thanked her guide for the realistic actors portraying Winchester and her staff. Of course, no actors were employed at the house. Perhaps the spirits that demanded all that construction are not the only ones associated with the Winchester Mystery House.

Sarah Winchester Doesn't Pose for Pictures

During my last California trip, my best friend, Liz, and I explored the Winchester Mystery House. The weirdness started almost immediately. . . .

As we waited for our tour to begin, I decided to shoot a few pictures of the place. I used my LCD screen to line up the shot, but the second I aimed the camera at the house, my LCD went wacky. As soon as I panned away from the house, the screen would clear up. Yet every time I aimed it at the house again, it started giving a staticlike, almost negative effect. I called Liz over to verify what was happening, and she couldn't believe it either.

Once we entered the house, the camera weirdness continued. We had three fully charged batteries between the two of us, yet we both started losing battery power as soon as we entered the house. Also, my camera's power kept switching off. I continued to snap pictures inside, but I kept getting blacked-out shots or this strange, colored, negative-like effect. Liz was also having problems—many of her pictures were blown-out from too much light, despite the shadowy interior. We both felt goose-bumpy when our guide explained to us that when Sarah Winchester dwelled here, she did not allow any photographs to be taken of her. Perhaps she was hanging around during our tour, letting us know that she was still the lady of this house!

It took over an hour to make our way through all the rooms, and without our guide, I feel sure that we would have gotten hopelessly lost. There are so many twists and turns, false passageways, and hidden doorways—it's unbelievable! We saw the bizarre stairway that led literally into the ceiling, the bathrooms with windows in their doors, and the Daisy Room where Sarah was trapped during the earthquake that leveled the top three floors of the house, leaving only four floors standing.

Time seems to stand still in the Winchester House; an air of secrecy permeates every wall and every floorboard. The confusing, mind-bending twists and turns and perplexing mysteries inside its walls left Liz and me puzzled and intrigued when we stepped back out into the warm California sunshine with three completely dead camera batteries, a handful of bizarre photos, and a whole bunch of questions.—*Shady*

Shangri-La

It seems that once the ball was rolling, Henry Warren of Hightowers, North Carolina, saw no reason to stop. At the age of seventy-seven in 1960, Warren built a waterwheel to accompany his yard's goldfish pond. Once that was done, he began construction on a motorized miniature mill to connect to it. From there he built an elaborate village he called his Shangri-La, with stores, churches, and water towers—all made from white quartz that Warren quarried on his own land. When it was opened to the public, hundreds of people converged on the site to take in its miniscule magnificence. Henry's wife was quoted in the book *Roadside America* as saying, "As long as he had a cigarette and a Coca-Cola, he'd keep building." Henry Warren died in 1977, but his family has kept Shangri-La open to visitors. It's located on NC 86.

The Lawn of 2093 Milk Jugs

Along Route 40, near the town of Mizpah, New Jersey, you'll find 2093 multicolored milk jugs meticulously arranged into a Technicolor work-in-progress known as the Art Lawn of Buena Vista. Thirty-three years ago lawn artist Josephine Stapleton started placing one-gallon plastic jugs containing food and fabric dyes in her yard to keep her kids off the lawn. The resulting display now attracts art lovers and lactose enthusiasts from all over the country. Out-of-state visitors have even taken to donating their used jugs to Ms. Stapleton. She hopes one day to use the containers to represent the home states of these art patrons in a map of the U.S.

Josephine's display reflects different holidays with seasonal Easter, Halloween, and Christmas themes.

There's even a Disney-themed Mickey and Minnie design. (Better watch out for those copyright lawyers, Josephine!) She has even fashioned a self-portrait of sorts out of (you guessed it!) milk jugs, which she calls Jug-a-Bell. The longest-running motif in this front-yard gallery is the enormous red, white, and blue American flag, which Josephine maintains on a daily basis. If you're thinking of paying her a visit, she recommends coming on Flag Day, when Old Glory is unfurled in its full splendor.

Making a Molehill Out of a Mountain of Rocks

Navy veteran and railroad worker Louis Wippich lived a normal life in Sauk Rapids, Minnesota, until 1932. It was then that this son of immigrant farmers became enraptured with the teachings of Madame H. P. Blavatsky, founder of the Theosophical Society. Despite having only a fifth-grade education, he began constructing an architectural fantasy cathedral on his property at the corner of Third Avenue North and Sixth Street. With simple levers, pulleys, and a few hired hands, Wippich built a temple that he christened Molehill—complete with two towers, one of which is forty-five feet high. The structure also boasts seven Doric columns, a Grecian temple, a Romanesque stairway, and a reflecting pool. There is even a labyrinth of passageways leading through the four-block-wide monument. Most of the stones used in the construction came from local quarries and demolition sites, and some of the larger ones weighed in at well over a ton.

After Wippich's death at the age of seventy-eight in 1973, Molehill fell into a state of neglect, became hopelessly overgrown, and was even used as a dump. Fortunately, some of his descendants have now taken it upon themselves to clean up and maintain the property. Though the interior of Molehill is not open to the public, it is an awe-inspiring site when viewed from the street. And it stands as a fitting monument to its creator, the man who referred to himself as the "Clown of Molehill."

The Seashell House and the Metal Mansion

Stumbling across oddly shaped homes is no rare occurrence, but usually they're spread out, isolated, and proudly individualistic. But on East Canyon View Drive near Lubbock, Texas, you'll find not one but two personalized properties of the highest caliber. The first is made of rock and has a cone-shaped roof. It's adorned with blue, red, and yellow tiles—many say it resembles a seashell. And just down the street is a steel house created by sculptor Robert Bruno. This curvy metal structure has been a work-in-progress for more than thirty years. As soon as it's finished, Bruno plans to move in.

The Pine Menagerie

Clyde Jones of Bynum, North Carolina, loves animals and tree stumps—and he's combined the two passions. Clyde, who is known locally as Jungle Boy, uses a chain saw to carve stumps and roots into animal shapes, including pigs, elephants, cows, snakes, and even gorillas. He then displays his creations all over the front, back, and side lawns of his property on Thompson Recreation Street.

Prairie Moon Garden

Herman Rusch of Fountain City, Wisconsin, created more than forty bizarre sculptures on a tiny site he called the Prairie Moon Garden, and then enclosed them all behind a 267-foot-long fence. Rusch passed away in 1985, but in 1994 the Kohler Foundation restored all of his statuary and opened the site to the public. The garden is open daily, although the accompanying museum is only open on Sunday afternoons during the summer and early fall. The Prairie Moon Garden is located off Highway 35, between Cochrane and Fountain City, Wisconsin.

The Petersen Rock Gardens

Rasmus Petersen (1883–1952) created his Rock Garden in Redmond, Oregon, as a tribute to America. Among his many creations are facsimiles of Independence Hall and the Statue of Liberty. There are castles and bridges made of malachite and thunder eggs. There are ponds and peacocks. The constructions are very sophisticated, the landscaping is incredible, and the site is well maintained by the family. One of the most underrated folk art environments in the United States, it's still a little hard to find. Just look for the patch of bright blue Oregon sky above 7930 SW 77th Street, off US 97, southwest of Redmond. And don't miss the fluorescent rock display in the museum!

The Orange Show

Jefferson Davis McKissack's Orange Show in eastern Houston, Texas, is commonly described as a fun, colorful, mini-amusement park dedicated to the orange. But the attraction is one of the most architecturally sophisticated folk art sites in the U.S. Its multilayered, multispatial, mazelike environment is composed of the program elements of a classic Greek city: theater, museum, agora, and temple.

McKissack, a postman who ventured into many side businesses, started building the Orange Show in the 1960s, after giving up on plans for a plant nursery or a beauty parlor. He envisioned his new construction as a monument to health and good living, specifically that wonderful package of vitamin C, the orange. Using cast-off materials from scrap yards and demolition sites, McKissack began to piece together a rich collage of tiles, bricks, stairs, corridors, wagon wheels, and flags.

When he opened the Orange Show to the public in 1979, McKissack predicted that it would rival the Astrodome as a city tourist attraction. Unfortunately, the crowds didn't come, and he passed away just a few months later. Luckily, a group of art patrons saw the site's importance and purchased it from his nephew. The show reopened with support from a foundation that sought not only to preserve the monument but also to promote activities that would realize McKissack's dream of a citywide gathering place. Through its twenty years of existence, the Orange Show Foundation has become a center for visionary art awareness, art workshops, mural projects, lectures, films, an Eyeopener Tours program, and a nationally renowned Art Car Weekend held annually in May. As a long-time volunteer, all I can say is come to Houston and enjoy The Show!–*Larry Harris*

Salvation Mountain

Salvation Mountain, outside San Diego, California, is a decades-old project built by Leonard Knight. This man-made mountain stands three stories tall, is one hundred feet wide, and is covered in trippy bright colors and Biblical messages. Knight lives nearby in a home that's towed behind the Salvation Truck, which is decorated like the mountain.

Salvation Mountain was once threatened when officials decided it was highly toxic. They sought to have it removed. Luckily, their plans fell through. Toxic or not, the mountain still stands tall, reminding sinners that it is time to repent. Visitors are welcome. Knight does not ask for monetary donations, but is more than willing to accept gifts of paint.

The Temple of Tolerance

Over the past fifteen years I've seen many amazing visionary sites, but none quite like the one Jim Bowsher has created on Wood Street in Wapakoneta, Ohio. The Temple of Tolerance is two separate but interconnected structures. The first is Bowsher's home, an incredible museum of artifacts from the America that wasn't written about in your school history books. It's the secret Smithsonian, a Grand Central Terminal for the Underground Railroad, an invisible library of unwritten books on Freemasons, Harry Houdini, and Neil Armstrong. The actual temple complex is in his backyard, and the structure feels as though it has been unearthed rather than constructed. Massive glacial boulders mound up to form the central monument, dedicated to tolerance. There's a Vietnam War memorial and a Tree of Life constructed by local kids. Surrounding the main temple is a stage for summer music performances. Throughout the grounds you'll also find the archaeology of good and evil: boundary markers from a Shawnee Indian reservation, slab steps from a Klan meetinghouse, stone dragons from Ireland, fragments from the first baseball park in Cincinnati, even a marble countertop from a bank that John Dillinger robbed. As Cathy Schreima wrote in the *Wapakoneta Evening Ledger* on April 7th, 2001, "Perhaps more than anything, the Temple stands to remind us, as well as future generations, to have compassion for others as we continue to explore our dreams, follow our spirit, and search for answers in the hope of scaling new heights."

I can't wait to go back. –*Larry Harris*

Totem Pole Park

Totem Pole Park is a tribute to Native Americans that was built ten miles north of Claremore, Oklahoma, by the late Ed Galloway. The crown jewel of the nine-acre park is the world's largest totem pole, a ninety-foot-tall, 134-ton structure that took eleven years to build. The park also features an eleven-sided house known as the Fiddle House, so named because it was once the home of Galloway's hand-carved fiddles. He lived in the park until his death in the early 1960s. It is now owned by the Rogers County Historical Society.

Vollis Simpson's Whirligigs

In 1985 Vollis Simpson's career as a house mover in North Carolina was winding down, and he needed something to occupy his time. So he decided to use the very machinery he was using to transport homes—and virtually any other kind of discarded materials he could find—to make art. He made spinning machines known as whirligigs, devices he first experimented with during World War II while stationed in Saipan, when he built one to power a washing machine. Now Simpson's property on Wiggins Mill Road in Lucama is littered with them, along with the scaffolding, model airplanes, and reflectors he uses to build them.

Simpson's whirligigs have made quite an impact in the folk art community. They can be found in a number of museums, and four of them were installed in downtown Atlanta during the 1996 Olympic games.

Aluminum Siding: The Beer Can House

Many people struggle with the problem of drink. Drinking too much can tear a home apart, but in the case of John Milkovisch, late of Houston, Texas, drinking too much actually built his home. Milkovisch began coating the exterior of his house at 222 Malone Avenue with flattened beer cans in 1968, and he didn't stop for twenty years. This artist didn't particularly favor any one type of beer: Bud Light, Pabst Blue Ribbon, Texas Pride, and Buckhorn are just a few of the many different brands that decorate this odd dwelling. Although Milkovisch is now deceased, an arts organization has purchased the house and plans to keep it in its current condition while operating it as a museum.

Wildlife and Much More

There's much more to the Hanson Wildlife Museum of Lenora, Minnesota, than its humble name suggests. Its founder, Bruce Hanson, displays pretty much anything that he has gotten his hands on over the years. Except for its driveway, which is lined with bowling balls, the museum's not much to look at from the outside. It consists of eighteen farm outbuildings—weathered woodsheds and chicken coop—with some deer skulls tacked up on them.

But on the inside it's a different story. There's a shed full of knives, one full of axes, and one that has close to 1500 wrenches. There are pelts, horns, antlers, and skulls from a variety of exotic and common critters, not to mention the fossil of a giant squid that Bruce uncovered on his own property. Another shed displays a dazzling variety of seashells from around the world, as well as collections of horseshoes and license plates. And don't miss the five hundred different brands of beer represented in Bruce's collection of cans!

The Hanson Wildlife Museum is on County Road 24, just west of Lenora.

Richart's Ruins

Dick Tracy isn't just a square-jawed detective in comic strips. Another (much weirder) Richard Tracy is the mastermind behind a larger-than-life yard in Centralia, Washington, that's filled with some of the world's strangest art. Even his name is his own creation—he prefers to be called Richart (as in "rich art"). As Styrofoam sculptures began appearing in Tracy's front yard in the mid-1980s, his neighbors quickly came to realize that Richart was a bit eccentric. These days his home is the centerpiece of the neighborhood. Sculptures stand in front of, above, and around his house. Tracy offers tours of the property by appointment, but his willingness to do this is tied to his infamous obsession with the number five. He gives tours only to groups of five people and only for five minutes. He offers art lessons and classes, but they last for only five minutes. And his work is for sale. The asking price? Five dollars. Richart's home—and his art—is located on M Street, within a stone's throw of Interstate 5.

The Forevertron

Words can't adequately describe the Forevertron. Sure, people have thrown around stuff like "a masterpiece of visionary folk art," or "that thing's way cool." But one thing's certain: It's the only 320-ton, 50-foot-high antigravitation machine in south-central Wisconsin.

Back in 1983 Dr. Evermor (or Tom Every, as he was known back then) began to draw on his years of experience as an industrial wrecker to build the environment, using a ready supply of materials at Delaney's Surplus yard. It now includes a giant spider, a customized barbecue-pit vehicle, and a forty-six-member Bird Band. But who knew that old survey markers, quantum physics, and art could be "way cool"?

Dr. Evermor described how he was inspired to create the Forevertron in a 1998 interview. "The Forevertron was conceived with the idea of a professor or scientist who in the time frame of about 1890 thought that he could perpetuate himself inside a glass ball, inside a copper egg, back into the heavens on a magnetic lightning force beam. That's the crux of the concept."

The Forevertron is about nine miles south of Baraboo, WI, on U.S. 12.–*Larry Harris*

The Garden of Eden

Samuel Dinsmoor, born in 1843, didn't begin sculpting his masterpiece in Lucas, Kansas, until he was in his mid-sixties, but his age didn't hold him back. He created one of the most bizarre, gossip-inducing pieces of public art the state has ever seen: the Garden of Eden.

Despite its religious-sounding theme, the Garden was conceived to promote the political philosophies of the Populists, a political party that had already by and large died out. For twenty-one years the self-taught sculptor built concrete commentaries on the economy, religion, and other aspects of society. Some of the concrete creations include forty-foot-tall trees, Adam and Eve, and a devil with electrified light-up eyes.

All of them were put on public display, not too far from the center of town, visible from the railroad tracks.

Originally Adam appeared without anything covering his sizable genitalia—Dinsmoor told the curious townsfolk that he himself had been the model for the statue. And now Dinsmoor himself is unarguably part of the display. Upon his death, he stipulated that he be placed in a concrete coffin near the entrance to the Garden of Eden. His coffin is encased in glass and adorned with an angel and a water jug. The site is located at 305 East Second Street.

The Hartman Rock Garden

The garden is a living history lesson built in Springfield, Ohio, during the Great Depression. It's filled with castles, cathedrals, scenes of American history, and images from 1930s popular culture. Ben Hartman started the garden in 1932 with only his own hands and in seven years created a 35-foot by 140-foot spectacle with more than 250,000 individual stones. Although somewhat deteriorated, the garden still stands, its impressive displays adorned with flowery paintings to welcome all visitors. The Rock Garden is at the corner of McCain and Russell streets.

House on the Rock

Alex Jordan chose a rocky perch one hundred and fifty feet above Spring Green, Wisconsin, as the spot for his dream house. It was there, in the 1940s, that he completed a spectacular Japanese-style home that became known as the House on the Rock. But the personalization of the property had only just begun.

Jordan began expanding his home and filling it with thousands of curiosities. The House on the Rock is now a dizzying collection of just about anything one can imagine, from musical instruments and clocks to weapons and dolls, arranged in random chaos décor. This reflects its owner's credo concerning collecting: "It doesn't have to be good, it doesn't have to be bad, it just has to be." There are hundreds of dollhouses, thousands of Santa Clauses, and winged mannequin angels fluttering overhead. A full-sized carousel features countless carved animals, flickering lights, and swirling chandeliers. The famous Organ Room is filled with the instruments, constantly blaring their tunes. There is the Unique Weaponry exhibit, the Heritage of the Sea wing (complete with a two-hundred-foot-long sea monster), and a life-size animatronic marching band.

All in all, the complex now includes sixteen buildings, and it takes over four hours to tour the whole site. The last stage of the tour is a walk through a huge glass enclosure called Jordan's Infinity Room that reveals the valley floor fifteen stories below the visitor's feet.

The House on the Rock is open to the public for an admission fee and is located on Highway 23 between Spring Green and Dodgeville.

Kenny Hill's Sculpture Garden

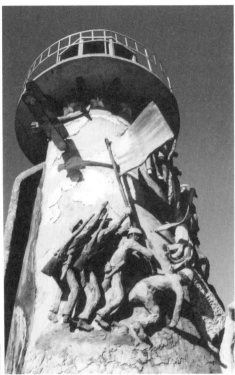

Kenny Hill, an artist from Chauvin, Louisiana, seems to enjoy his privacy. Very little is known about the former bricklayer—he prefers to let his magnificent sculpture garden do the talking for him.

When Hill moved to Chauvin in 1988, he lived in a tent while he built his home—but he didn't stop building in 1990 when it was completed. Instead, he turned his attention toward building large-scale sculptures with religious themes. By 2000 Hill had more than one hundred sculptures packed onto his cramped piece of property. The most imposing sculpture is a forty-foot-tall lighthouse decorated with figures of cowboys, military men, religious icons, and Kenny Hill himself.

Hill scattered sculptures of himself throughout the garden. Reportedly a deeply troubled man, he had a falling-out with the local parish in 2000. Soon after, he beheaded a statue of Jesus and walked off the property, never to return.

The site is now owned and operated by Nicholls State University and is open to the public.

Pasaquan

Just outside the tiny town of Buena Vista, Georgia, is Pasaquan, a monument to one of the most eccentric men America has ever known. Edward Owens Martin, who came to be known as St. EOM, grew up just three miles from Pasaquan, but at the age of fourteen he left dirt farming behind to seek a new way of life in New York. He certainly found it. At various times he was a pimp, a gambler, a homeless person, and a drug dealer. He also worked on merchant ships bound for India, where he learned about yoga and the occult.

In 1957 Martin had a vision of a long-haired man telling him to return to his childhood home. When he did, this turban-wearing and tattooed artist took the town by storm. Counterculture youths flocked to hear his rambling preaching with its talk of astronaut levitation suits and other far-out theories. Dogs would follow him around his compound, and when he drove to town, he often brought a cadre of cats that would all come running and jump back into his car when he beckoned them.

St. EOM became known locally as a fortune-teller, and a booming business soon developed around this talent. He used his earnings to purchase concrete and paint with which he built twelve-foot-tall totem poles to guard the entrance to his home. Inside he began creating statues, many of naked men and women. He adorned the walls with planets, snakes, rocket ships, and other outlandish adornments. He also included elements of Mayan temples and Japanese pagodas, as well as sections that were distinctly Egyptian. One writer refers to his work as "Dr. Seuss on Peyote."

St. EOM lived until 1986, when he took his own life due to depression.

Margaret's Grocery

ALL IS WELCOME JEWS AND GENTILES reads the sign above Margaret's Grocery, a few miles north of Vicksburg, Mississippi, on old Highway 61. The grocery has been closed for several years, but the colorful architectural menagerie built by the Reverend H. D. Dennis still attracts visitors from around the world.

Dennis's hand-built temple to God has evolved through the years, the color scheme changing from Lego-block bands of red and white to its current pink-and-yellow palette. Now nearly ninety years old, the rail-thin Dennis is still eager to show visitors his holy land, pointing out his handmade Ark of the Covenant as well as the many Bible verses painted on signs that cover the complex. His eyes may now be clouded over with cataracts, and his hearing aid may need new batteries, but that hasn't slowed down the Reverend Mr. Dennis from delivering his powerful message. (Note: His sermons may run over an hour or more, so don't plan on a quick snapshot stop.) —*Larry Harris*

The Watts Towers

"With leftovers from his daily bread, he created a sculptural garden. Hail to the innocent Gaudí of California, who destroyed the myths of Disneyland and movieland in a swift, isolated competition."—Sculptor Gio Pomodoro

It has been called the finest example of a folk art environment in the world as well as the largest single artwork ever created by one person. In 1921, in the Watts district of Los Angeles, a poor Italian immigrant named Sabato (Simon) Rodia purchased a small house on a triangular piece of property and started building.

For the next thirty-three years and without assistance, Rodia constructed sculptural towers, embellishing walls with bent steel rebar, wire mesh, cement, and thousands of pieces of broken tile and pottery. He made many major modifications through the construction, even rebuilding entire towers. In 1955, with the two tallest towers nearly one hundred feet tall, Rodia left the home, property, and his towers to a neighbor and moved to northern California.

Four years after he left, the Los Angeles Building Department made plans to demolish the "pile of junk." A group of concerned citizens, the Committee for Simon Rodia's Towers in Watts, organized to prevent the destruction. In a court hearing the committee volunteered to conduct a loading test on the towers. In October 1959, with over a thousand people looking on, a force equal to a sustained 80 mph wind was applied to the tallest tower. The steel beam of the testing apparatus began to bend, but the tower did not. The test was stopped, the crowd cheered, and the towers survived.

The Watts Towers are today owned by the city that tried to tear them down. In October 2000, following a decade-long restoration project, the towers reopened to the public. They're located in Watts at 1765 East 107th St.—*Larry Harris*

Watts Towers Found in Houston

In 1996 (apparently with too much time on my hands) I started to piece together a scale model of the towers. Constructed of a combination of basswood, museum board, plaster, and gesso, the model took about nine months to complete. The accuracy of the layout and massing would not be possible without the help of preservation activist (and great friend) Seymour Rosen and his archive photographs, as well as site measurements and technical data from conservation engineer Bud Goldstone. The model is now on display on my dining-room table in Houston, Texas. Contact me at narrowlarry@aol.com to arrange for a visit.

Roadside Odyssey

When traveling around this great land of ours, the credo to adopt is "It's not the destination, it's the journey that counts." As Americans, we are fortunate to live amid quirky and imaginative roadside oddities, often right along the routes we travel every day. America has a roadside culture all its own—architecturally odd, eccentrically innovative, and sometimes downright beguiling.

Books have been written and TV programs produced about our nation's roadside attractions and highway hangouts. Most of them focus on the tacky and touristy or lighthearted and nostalgic aspects of the genre. We decided to take a different route. We want to take you on a trip that is just a bit different—one you may never forget—a sort of asphalt vision quest. Of course, on any twenty-first-century mystical journey of profound discovery, the places we seek must be conveniently located near a major travel artery. Hey, this is America we're talking about, after all. While previous generations of explorers may have had to scale steep Tibetan mountain ranges or bravely traverse angry seas in their quest for enlightenment, all we modern-day adventurers need do to satisfy our wanderlust is jump into our car and drive.

We asked our long-time back road buddies Jeff Bahr and Dr. Seymour O'Life to hit the trail on their motorcycles and head off to parts unknown in search of truly unique places. Then we took off in the opposite direction to see what we could find.

We'd like to take you now on a tour of what we discovered. There may be fun or just plain goofy sites that bring a smile to your lips, but they are there only to distract the unwary traveler, like the sirens that sang to brave Ulysses. Don't be fooled, friends, even these apparently frivolous novelties have weird tales to tell.

Sometimes the unknown is not to be found "out there"—it is just down the road. All you have to do is pack up your sense of wonder and go looking for it.

Curious Constructions

Everyone who has seen the film *Field of Dreams* remembers Kevin Costner standing alone in a vast cornfield and hearing the ghostly whispered words "If you build it, they will come." Well, apparently Costner's character is not the only one who has been hearing voices urging them to build things. Across the country we find strange and puzzling constructions built by visionaries and dreamers. But the reason they were built is often a riddle. Whether divine or delusional, the inspiration for these grandiose projects may always remain a mystery to all but those who created them.

The Haunted Pillar, or the Pillar of Prophecy

Motorists and pedestrians who pass the corner of Fifth and Broad streets in downtown Augusta, Georgia, invariably notice the lone column standing on the southwestern corner. Made of concrete-coated brick and measuring two feet in diameter and ten feet high, it is known as the Haunted Pillar, and many believe death awaits any who touch it.

The pillar is all that remains of the Market, two large sheds about two hundred feet long and one hundred feet wide that occupied the center of Broad Street from 1830 until 1878. They were known as the Upper and Lower Markets, and the citizens of Augusta flocked there daily to purchase food from farmers, grocers, and butchers.

In the late 1800s (a less authoritative source lists the year as 1829) an itinerant evangelist visited the city. The eccentric preacher was described as an elderly, white-haired, man whose clear voice was "incisive even to the piercing of the human heart," one witness declared. It is variously argued that no church would host his services or that he disdained them. Again the story varies — that he preached in the Lower Market for some time or that the managers refused him permission to speak or that he was run out of town by disbelievers. Whatever the circumstances, the preacher proclaimed that a storm would soon destroy the Market, and that only the southwestern column would survive. He then declared that anyone who attempted to move it would be killed.

The prediction came to fruition at one ten a.m. on February 8, 1878, when a tornado touched down in Augusta. It tore a two-hundred-foot-wide swath through the town. Two people were killed, and several houses were knocked down. The Lower Market was destroyed.

Perhaps prophecy was fulfilled, but the curse did not kick in until later, for the city council elected to rebuild the Market on its original site. The surviving pillar was moved to the corner of Fifth and Broad, which is where the legend of its being haunted/cursed began.

Reportedly, two workmen who attempted to move the pillar were struck by lightning or otherwise caused to die. Another version has a bulldozer operator dying of a heart attack while advancing against the pillar. However, a man who managed a liquor store across the street for fifty years denied the story, saying the pillar had "been moved [without injury to workers] several times because it was too close to the street."

It does seem to be haunted. Late at night visitors near the column have reported hearing whispered conversations between phantoms and the footsteps of invisible beings pacing alongside them. Police revealed that eleven traffic accidents had occurred at the intersection between January and October one year, so perhaps the pillar has an effect on cars or their operators—or perhaps careless drivers eyeing the column caused their own accidents. The pillar seems to attract its own bad luck—it twice has been struck by lightning and been hit by an errant car.

The pillar remains a great tourist draw, attracting individuals, buses, and walking tours. At times it seems to receive more publicity than the Masters Golf Tournament. On December 12, 1996, the Haunted Pillar received its own historical marker. —*Jim Miles*

Ozymandias Legs

Why are there two giant concrete legs standing in a field off Interstate 27 south of Amarillo, Texas? The simple answer is that local resident Stanley Marsh III read Percy Shelley's poem "Ozymandias." The poem states, *Two vast and trunkless legs of stone stand in the desert.* Marsh took this reference and made it a reality. He commissioned the building of two legs just like the poem's—one thirty-four feet tall, the other twenty-four. Marsh's quirky sense of humor extended to a fake historical marker at the site, claiming among other things that Shelley wrote his famous poem there and that the face of the statue now resides in the Amarillo Museum of Natural History. There is a natural history museum in Amarillo.

Troll Bridge

Seattle is known for its rainy weather, its grunge music . . . and the troll that lives underneath the Aurora Bridge.

The troll is seventeen feet tall and is made primarily out of two tons of concrete. He grips a Volkswagen Beetle as if he had just plucked it right off the road above him. The Fremont Arts Council commissioned him in 1989 to add some zest to a rather plain part of town. Now the troll is well known throughout the area and lends his name to the annual Halloween celebration Trolloween.

The Integratron: A Real-Life Time Machine?

Imagine, if you will, that beings from another world or galaxy choose you to enlighten and enrich mankind. What would you do? If you were George Van Tassel, you'd build a thirty-eight-foot-high, fifty-foot-diameter nonmetallic structure and call it the Integratron.

Van Tassel was a former test pilot for Howard Hughes and Douglas Aircraft, an engineer who lived at Giant Rock, California, and operated the Giant Rock airport. Between the 1950s and 1970s he led weekly meditations in a cave and hosted annual spacecraft conventions attended by thousands of UFO sighters and pioneers in the fields of antigravity, primary energy research, and electromagnetics. And he spent eighteen years creating the Integratron—a rejuvenating time machine inspired by UFO channelings and ideas from scientists such as Nikola Tesla.

Van Tassel tried to change the course of history and mankind with the Integratron. He published a paper on the subject, which you can read in the proceedings of the College of Universal Wisdom, 1950–1978. It states:

"The purpose of the Integratron is to recharge energy into living cell structure, to bring about longer life with youthful energy. This has been the goal of many people, since Ponce De Leon started looking for the fountain of youth. Our effort here, in this giant machine, is not the first idea of its kind. It is the first time that other research efforts have been brought together and applied simultaneously."

He picked a magnetic vortex as the spot to build the Integratron, using a complex set of theories involving the earth's magnetic field and the relative positions of the Great Pyramid in Egypt and Giant Rock, the world's largest freestanding boulder. He claimed that by using magnetometers you could measure a gigantic magnetic vortex of several miles' radius around the site. He believed that the great weight of the rock produced a piezoelectric effect on its granite crystals, creating the necessary magnetic field.

Many visitors say that because of its geographic location and off-world design, the Integratron is truly a wonder of the world. Others say it's just a neat roadside attraction. We'll leave it up to you to decide. The Integratron can be found on Belfield Road outside Landers, CA.–*Dr. Seymour O'Life*

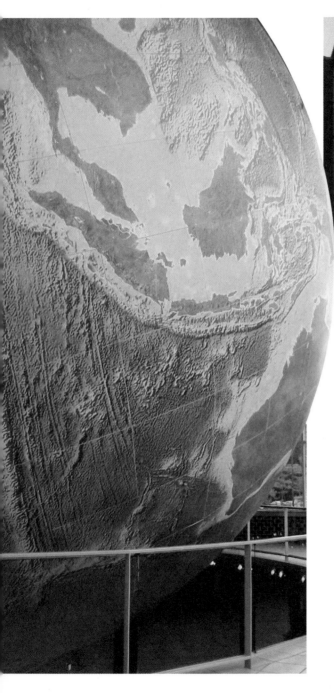

Eartha—The World's Largest Globe

If you are anything like me, you are fascinated with maps and globes. I can spend hours in a good map store and days poring over maps and charts, especially when preparing for a motorcycle trip. But I was unprepared for what I would find at DeLorme's headquarters just off Route 1 in Yarmouth, Maine. When you pull into the large parking lot, you cannot help but see a mongo-globe named Eartha through a wall of glass over three stories high. She has dominated the entire front of the building since July 23, 1998 — the largest printed image of the earth ever created. Designed on computers using more than 214 CD-ROMs' worth of information, the globe is over forty-one feet in diameter and weighs nearly six thousand pounds. At a scale of one inch to one mile, the surface area is a whopping 5310 square feet. If laid out, the Omni-Span Truss aluminum skeleton would stretch for nearly three miles. And more impressive still, she rotates exactly as the earth does at a degree of 23.5.

So if you are a fan of maps and globes, you owe it to yourself to head to the giant globe DeLorme calls Eartha. Looking at her and her beauty you'll realize, like I did, that the earth is not only mysterious but mesmerizing as well. Eartha is located at Two DeLorme Drive. *–Dr. Seymour O'Life*

The Georgia Guidestones
A Heavy Message or Towers of Babble?

Late on a Friday afternoon in May 1979 a man walked into the office of Joe Fendley Sr., president of Elberton Finishing Company, and introduced himself as R. C. Christian. He informed Fendley that he wanted to order a monument. Fendley explained that his company was a wholesaler and not involved in individual orders.

"Then he told me what he wanted," Fendley told Boyd Lewis, a writer for *Brown's Guide to Georgia.* "The size, as he described it, was so large that it was unreal. There had never been a monument this large done in Elberton, and Elberton is the granite capital of the world."

What Christian was asking for was a miniature Stonehenge that would be called the Guidestones. His motivation was that it would be for the "conservation of the world, and to herald the coming of an age of reason." As he left, he said, "My name isn't Christian. It's just that I follow the teachings of Jesus Christ. And I represent a group of Americans who believe as I do, in God and country." He emphasized that they were patriots who lived outside Georgia and stipulated that their organization would never be revealed.

"Then he said I'd never see him again, and I haven't." Fendley thought the mysterious stranger was in his fifties, spoke with a Midwestern accent and was well educated.

Mr. Christian then visited Wyatt C. Martin, president of Granite City Bank and made a large deposit to finance the monument. Martin required Christian to reveal his real name and his organization, but promised "I would never reveal their identity or where the money came from."

Mr. Christian sent two missives to Fendley and Martin during construction of the monument. The letters contained long-winded phrases such as "Make mankind more willing to accept the system of limited international law which will stress the responsibilities of individual nations in managing their internal affairs while assisting them collectively in regulating the international relationships," and "Every one of us is a small but significant bit of the infinite . . . we must live in harmony with the infinite."

The message to be inscribed on the Guidestones was divided into ten "guides," which some now consider a new age Ten Commandants. Introduced by "Let these be Guidestones to an age of reason," they read:

"Maintain humanity under five hundred million in perpetual balance with nature."

"Guide reproduction wisely, improving fitness and diversity."

"Unite humanity with a living new language."

"Rule passion–faith–tradition and all things with tempered reason."

"Protect people and nations with fair laws and just courts."

"Let all nations rule internally resolving external disputes in a world court."

"Avoid petty laws and useless officials."

"Balance personal rights with social duties."

"Prize truth–beauty–love–seeking harmony with the infinite."

"Be not a cancer on the earth—Leave room for nature—Leave room for nature."

The nondenominational wording was intended to appeal to all religious, cultural, and political groups and would appear in eight languages—English, Spanish, Chinese, Arabic, Hebrew, Russian, Swahili, and Hindi.

Christian returned once to see Martin, bearing a model of the Guidestones. It incorporated the astronomical alignments of England's Stonehenge. The stones were cut,

appropriately, at Pyramid Quarry. Foreman Joe Davis said the unique shape of the stones, and the fact that they were only nineteen inches wide, required a week of work to produce each.

The ten guides were engraved on the eight sides of the slabs, while the capstone contained the following inscription: "Let These Be Guides to An Age of Reason" in four archaic languages—Egyptian hieroglyphs, Babylonian cuneiform, Sanskrit, and classical Greek.

Frank Coggins, a local quarry owner, donated five acres of land to the county for the site of the Guidestones. The spot has commanding views to the east and west, the directions in which the stones are oriented, for the sunrises and sunsets on the summer and winter solstices. Workers excavating a foundation for the monument and those who erected it heard inexplicable sounds atop the windswept hill and complained of feeling dizzy or lightheaded during construction.

The finished stones were transported to their permanent location and laboriously hauled into position. After nine months of painstaking work, the monument was finished. It measures nineteen feet three inches in height—taller than Stonehenge—and weighs 119 tons. The complex rests on a base of five support stones weighing a combined 22,000 pounds.

Only one hundred people appeared for the March 1980 unveiling. When the ceremony concluded, one local minister proclaimed that he and his congregation "don't think Mr. Christian is a Christian." He believes the monument was "for sun worshipers, for cult worship, and for devil worship."

A wide variety of people visit the Guidestones, including witches and UFO buffs. Many are drawn by the belief that the unique astronomical alignments to the sun and moon and the location combine to emit a powerful energy field. A former mayor admitted that there "have been some occult-type things going on out there, also tribal ritualistic dancing and nude dancing." But, he emphasized, "there have also been Christian activities there and even a wedding." The curious by the thousands visit every year from across the United States, Canada, and Europe.—*Jim Miles*

Ave Maria Grotto

In the nearly fifty years between 1912 and 1958, the Benedictine monk Brother Joseph Zoettl built a miniature stone city known as the Ave Maria Grotto on the grounds of the St. Bernard Abbey in Cullman, Alabama. This Bavarian-born hunchback faithfully re-created one hundred twenty-five significant buildings on the four-acre hillside, including the Vatican's St. Peter's Basilica, the Leaning Tower of Pisa, the Tower of Babel, and even the Alamo!

Brother Joe's real job at the abbey was to work in the power plant, but his grotto-building hobby soon became an all-consuming passion. His diminutive city, sometimes called Jerusalem in Miniature, is constructed of concrete and decorated with all manner of junk, from marbles and costume jewelry to seashells and ceramic tiles, much of which has been donated by visitors from around the world.

The grotto is probably best described on the site's official web page, which states:

The gift shop provides entry to a forested trail, winding down past several miniature building clusters and junk-bejeweled shrines. Round a bend, and you see it — an entire hillside packed in urban splendor with cathedrals and famous building [sic]. One half of the hillside features building [sic] and scenes from the Holy Land. There's also a central artificial cave — the Ave Maria Grotto.

Among the numerous replicas which elicit admiration and wonderment from the visitor are the famous buildings of Jerusalem and the Holy Land, familiar to all from the Bible; Roman Landmarks, as St. Peter's and the Colosseum;

the famous Spanish Missions of the American Southwest, and replicas of the famous Shrines of Our Lady, Fatima and Lourdes.

Brother Joseph continued his work for over 40 years, using materials sent from all over the world. He built his last model, the Basilica in Lourdes, at the age of 80, in 1958.

Brother Joseph died in 1961 and is buried in the abbey cemetery a short distance from the grotto gift shop. The Ave Maria Grotto is still lovingly maintained and open to the public on all days except Christmas. It is located at 1600 St. Bernard Drive, S.E. (off U.S. 278), just east of Cullman, Alabama.

Tales of Shirtwood Forest

We found one of the best examples of a roadside head-scratcher right in our own backyard, just off Route 70 in the town of Brick, New Jersey. We had received several letters about a strange swampy area just a few yards into the woods, where dozens of men's starched white shirts hung suspended from dying trees above the stagnant marsh. Now, there's nothing weird about white shirts, but when you're alone in the quiet of the forest, facing neatly pressed and tailored laundry, it is very unnerving indeed. At just such moments, you ask yourself questions like, "Who would go to the trouble of doing such a thing?" "Why, are they mad?" and the inevitable question: "Could they be here somewhere right now — watching me?"

The Shirts Are One Weird Calendar

I live in Brick, and on the other side of town is a patch of woods right by a swamp. I have ventured there many times, and I always found the same weird thing. On October seventeenth there were seventeen white dress shirts hanging twenty feet high in the trees. On the twenty-ninth of October there were twenty-nine shirts hanging on the tree. At the bottom of the tree lay a strange bird with its neck snapped. Today is the thirty-first. I wonder what's gonna happen next?–*Evan Levinson*

Noises from the Shirts

When I went back there, white shirts were hanging all over the place. The shirts were hung as if a person would be inside them. I threw rocks at them, and they made a funny noise as if they were sprayed with some sort of starch. It just seemed a little strange to us.–*Joe*

Shirtwood South

As I was browsing the Shirtwood Forest story from Brick, New Jersey, on your website, I was filled with a sense of fear. I have seen that very same thing before in Gatlinburg, Tennessee. My bride-to-be and I were staying in a chalet off a gravel road just outside the city. As we pulled in, I noticed what looked like shirts attached to sticks. There were maybe four or five of them on both sides of the road, in two small clearings surrounded by woods. I made a joke about some "Blair Witch" tomfoolery, but I became quite uneasy. The next day some of the shirts were missing. Something simply did not sit right with me when I looked at them. The fact that someone was out there in the middle of the night fooling with these spooky-looking things bothered me. Needless to say, every sound at night had me bolt upright!–*Jacob O. Amos*

The Shoe Tree of NC

In the middle of a field here in North Carolina there is a gigantic tree from which all types of shoes are hanging. Most of them are nailed to the tree's trunk, and some are hanging by their laces. This is definitely the weirdest thing that I have ever come across. Why were so many shoes nailed to the trunk of the tree? Was some crazy murderer keeping track of how many people he killed? Was someone so obsessed with shoes that he wanted to display them? When we stopped at this tree and explored the area around it, there were dates and names written on some of the shoes. There was no one who knew what this was about, but my friend and I came to the conclusion it was some kind of memorial. *–Corinne O*

Flying Footwear in Fashion

On Old State Road 64 in Milltown, Indiana, stands the Shoe Tree. For four decades people have come from all over, even from different states, to toss their old shoes up into the limbs of this tall tree. No one has counted them all, but I think that there are several hundred pairs up there.

Flatfoots Eye Unlawful Soles

On Highway 131, north of Kalkaska, Michigan, is the famous Shoe Tree. Hundreds of pairs of shoes have been tossed into the tree. They first appeared early in 2001 and have multiplied in growth greatly since then. State police are keeping their eyes peeled for the perpetrator, although it's not too high on their list of priorities.

The Shoe Tree (with Pocketbook Accessories)

This Shoe Tree is behind the American Way Diner in Belvidere, New Jersey, on Route 46. There are thirteen pairs of shoes in one tree, and in another there are pocketbooks. *–Kate Barr*

Ever wonder where those enormous fiberglass statues you see standing alongside the road, advertising auto repair and sandwich shops, come from? Here's a hint: Cheddar is not the only cheesy export from the Badger State.

Land of the Giants

If you're ever in Sparta, Wisconsin, be sure to check out the grounds of FASTcorp. It's a landscape from another planet. The experience begins as you head into town past the statue of E.T. standing by a fourteen-foot Viking. Giant replicas of everything imaginable surround the FASTcorp building—some ready to be trucked off, some waiting for a coat of paint and a gob of lacquer, and others languishing against the side of the structure. Behind the metal building, acres of fields ringed with evergreens store massive molds. This fiberglass boneyard houses a six-foot-tall honey bear with its stomach wide open down the middle. Nearby a shark's head pushes up through the sod, angry teeth bristling over its empty maw. An oversized ice-cream cone nestles against the forest backdrop.

There's a sign that welcomes visitors to walk around and take pictures, but warns against touching, climbing, or other contact with the massive artworks. If it isn't Sunday, you can go inside and buy a catalog for $5. As I stocked up on film at the local Wal-Mart, the young clerk recalled that her high school class had gotten a free foam tornado from FASTcorp last year for its homecoming float. It appeared to tear through mannequins dressed as the enemy team. "The theme was 'Let's Rip 'Em,' " she explained.

I reluctantly concluded that even if I could afford one for myself, I could not fit any of them in my car trunk. So I left the big creatures to comfort one another in their mutual strangeness.—*Linda Godfrey*

WELCOME TO SPARTA, WISCONSIN

The Cardiff Giant: America's Greatest Hoax

The story of the Cardiff Giant is one of the greatest hoaxes in America. Back in 1866 an atheist by the name of George Hull decided to play a little prank on the gullible local folks. He and a partner, H. B. Martin, commissioned Chicago sculptors to make a twelve-foot-tall statue of a man using a block of gypsum from Iowa. They treated the stone with acid to make it look petrified and even created the image of skin pores using small needles. The finished work was secretly shipped to the farm of one Stub Newell, near Cardiff, New York, and buried some five feet below ground.

The giant lay there for a few years until the area was overgrown with shrubs and weeds. Then in October 1869 workmen were sent out to dig a well. They were told precisely where to dig, and before long, they found something. A man—a giant of a man—turned to stone. Word spread like wildfire, and a tent was erected over the giant. People came from hundreds of miles to see the "Giant from the Ancient Bible." Hull's prank had worked. The townsfolk had taken the bait hook, line, and sinker, and paid fifty cents to peek at the giant.

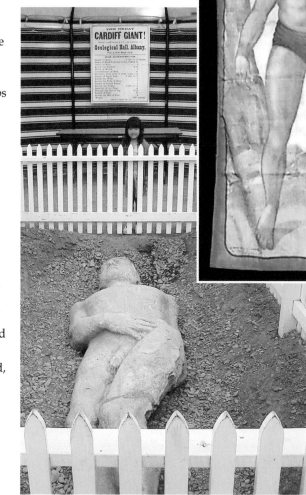

As media attention grew, the Cardiff Giant was put on display in Syracuse and eventually went on tour. P. T. Barnum offered thousands for it, but Hull refused, so Barnum created his own giant. Even after it was generally considered a fake, the Cardiff Giant still drew onlookers— as it does to this day at its home in the Farmers' Museum on Lake Road in Cooperstown. I know I happily shelled out a few bucks for it!—*Dr. Seymour O'Life*

Area 51

Back during WWII, two dirt landing strips were carved into the Nevada desert, right outside Groom Lake. Originally used for training flights, they were abandoned and all but forgotten after the war. From these humble beginnings grew the legendary Area 51.

As the cold war heated up during the 1950s, the CIA brought in Lockheed Skunk Works to build a top secret development and testing facility. A Lockheed test pilot called Tony LeVier rediscovered the old airstrips, and in the facility developed there, the U-2 spy plane was born. An executive order from President Eisenhower restricted airspace over the region. It was called Area 51, for the simple reason that it was the fifty-first area at the mammoth Nellis Air Force Base, which takes up more than a million desert acres.

Over the years the facility grew and grew. During the 1960s and '70s, SR-71 Blackbirds flew from here and testing was finished on the F-117 Stealth Nighthawk. Today the landing strip at Area 51 is 27,000 feet long. That's five miles!

Of course, it's not unusual to see things in the sky over the mountains along Route 375. After all, the SR-71, F-117, and other military craft were tested there in secret; you have to wonder what the government is working on these days. Whatever it is, they don't want you getting too close. Over the last few years the Feds have taken over more and more of the surrounding land. Area 51 remains clouded in mystery. And I for one am willing to let it stay that way.–*Dr. Seymour O'Life*

Haines Shoe House

There was an old woman who lived in a shoe. . . .

Do you remember that little snippet from your childhood? Well then, jump on your bike and follow me to the state of Pennsylvania, to the little town of Hallam, where a sliver of childhood endures in a most enchanting form!

The year 1947 found American huckster and self-proclaimed colonel Mahlon Haines presiding over an empire of forty shoe stores scattered throughout Pennsylvania and Maryland. This savvy promoter had a penchant for advertising and a keen eye for a gimmick, so he commissioned an architect to build the ultimate shrine to shoedom. Holding an old shoe in his hands, he said "Build me a house like this."

The result must have made old Mahlon smile, for where else in the world can you find a five-story shoe forty-eight feet long and seventeen feet wide, standing a full twenty-five feet tall, with three bedrooms, two baths, a kitchen, and a living room? The house is decorated with stained glass windows. In one of them, Mahlon is depicted holding up a pair of his beloved shoes. All the other windows showcase—you guessed it—still more shoes.

Over the years the shoe house has been a pure gimmick, a private home, an ice-cream stand, and a bed and breakfast. Current owner Ruth Miller will be happy to lead you on a heel-to-toe tour and sell you some homemade ice cream along the way. So go ahead, take a trip over to Shoe House Road, take a run through the shoe house, and become a child once again. But try not to leave any footprints—they may clash with the décor!–*Jeff Bahr*

Promise of a Brighter Tomorrow

The New York State Pavilion is located on the site of the 1964 World's Fair in Queens, NY. The original guidebook description of the site was: Above a huge "Tent of Tomorrow," housing state exhibits and shows, rise three towers, one of them an observation tower 226 feet high. Various displays are sheltered under the world's largest suspension roof, made of translucent plastic and hung from sixteen 100-foot columns.

Today the overgrown and under-maintained fairgrounds languish, still promising a bright future that has long since been and gone.

Carhenge

Carhenge was built near the town of Mojave, California, in the early 1990s as a set for a TV commercial. It was all taken apart right after this picture was taken. Talk about being in the right place at the right time!

—*Troy Paiva*

The Neon Graveyard

This is the world famous YESCO (Young Electric Sign Company) boneyard in Las Vegas, Nevada. This storage yard is where many of the old Las Vegas casino signs bake in the desert sun awaiting restoration for inclusion into the terribly underfunded Neon Museum. Many are junk; the fifteen-foot-tall silver slipper is one of the coolest things in the scrap heap of yesteryear's neon signs.–*Troy Paiva*

Weird Museums

Many people think of museums as stuffy places filled with musty old artifacts and all-but-forgotten relics of the past. There are probably some folks out there who have not even ventured inside a museum since their last grade school field trip to one. Well, we'd like to give those people a glimpse at what they've been missing. America has some truly bizarre and macabre exhibits in its museums, some of which offer the visitor an education they never could have gotten in any class!

Lizzie Borden House Museum

*Lizzie Borden took an axe
And gave her mother forty whacks.
And when she saw what she had done
She gave her father forty-one.*

This macabre and infamous playground rhyme describes a violent tragedy that befell an unassuming town in Massachusetts over a hundred years ago. It's a stanza repeated so often that even though most people are familiar with it, they can't recall the circumstances that prompted it or the players involved. And that's a darn shame, because as murder mysteries go, this one was a real humdinger—particularly for its time.

As I rode my motorcycle down Second Street through Fall River's business district, I almost skipped by the Borden house, the scene of the famous murders. It's a mistake that many make, for who would expect to find a nineteenth-century slice of Victoriana among modern-day office towers with a busy bus terminal directly across the street? But even if the setting was not the idyllic small town in my mind's eye, it still had something that drew me in. I forked over the entrance fee and joined up with the tour group, chop-chop, as they say.

As the tour began, our guide led us into the sitting room to set the stage for the historical recounting about to unfold.

August 4, 1892, began quite uncomfortably for the Borden family. Its members had been stricken with food poisoning, and the family physician, Dr. Bower, visited them early that morning. The familial patriarch, Andrew Borden, seventy, one of Fall River's wealthiest men, and his second wife, Abby, sixty-four, were resting on the first and second floors of the house respectively. The doctor treated them and left. He would be the last person to see them alive— except for their murderer, of course. Our guide explained

with a difference. We were treated to tales that departed from the usual written accounts—tales of incest between Lizzie and her father, hatred for her stepmother, and a lust for money. Added to the mix were theories of coconspirators and cover-ups. Soon we were led into the parlor where Andrew Borden's skull met the business end of an axe. The weapon was discovered in the basement, and its edge aligned precisely with his wounds.

that Andrew's oldest daughter, Lizzie, discovered her father's dead body. She summoned the Borden's live-in maid, Bridget, to seek help, exclaiming, "Come down quick, Father's dead! Somebody came in and killed him." Lizzie then directed Bridget and a neighbor, Mrs. Churchill, upstairs to her stepmother. There they discovered the lifeless body of Abby Borden, bludgeoned to death like her husband.

These horrific events soon set Fall River society abuzz with whispers and conjecture. Who could have done such a thing? Did Andrew Borden have enemies? Did Abby? They wouldn't have to wait long to find out. Within a few days the police notified Lizzie that her name was being placed at the top of their short list of suspects. Her alibi was weak; she said that she had been in many different rooms at the time of the murders, and her story in general was often contradictory. Soon she would be taken into custody.

All that information is pretty standard fare for anyone who is familiar with the case. But this was a tour

Upstairs, in the room where Abby Borden drew her last breath, our guide told us that since 1996, the house has been a bed and breakfast. The truly disturbing part? Not only do they rent the bedroom where Abby Borden was killed, but also a good many guests forego sleeping in the bed entirely, preferring instead to curl up on the floor, their bodies covering the precise spot where Mrs. Borden was hacked to death all those years ago. History shows that despite a preponderance of evidence against her, Lizzie Borden walked free—acquitted of all charges by a jury of her peers. I asked our guide if she believed Lizzie to be guilty or innocent. Her words left her lips with a measured cadence, with much thought and knowledge clearly applied to her answer. She said that in her opinion, Lizzie was undoubtedly . . .

Hey, wait a minute. If I divulge that, it might spoil the whole experience for you. Better that you don your tweed coat, stuff your pipe and magnifying glass into your tank bag, and motor up to 92 Second Street, Fall River, to decide for yourself.—*Jeff Bahr*

Mercer Museum

Some museums are unique for what they display. Some stand out because of where they are located. Still others gain fame for how they were designed and constructed. The Mercer Museum in Doylestown, Pennsylvania, embodies all that and so much more! Its construction and design are truly unique. Its displays are among the most fascinating you'll find anywhere in the United States, and the overall presentation—well, you'll have to see it for yourself.

Created between 1913 and 1916 by Henry Mercer, a young lawyer turned archaeologist and collector, the Mercer Museum is constructed solely out of poured reinforced concrete. Mercer built it by hand with help from eight laborers and a horse named Lucy. The impressive structure rises seven stories high, and with its towers and gables it totally dominates the landscape, a literal castle in Bucks County.

But as impressive as the Mercer Museum is on the outside, it was what I found on the inside that really got me excited. Henry Mercer realized that there were few, if any, historical records and artifacts of preindustrial America. Before the Industrial Revolution, many Americans excelled in a trade, such as woodcraft, fishing, metalworking, textiles, or farming. Mercer feared that, as folks became more involved with the newer technologies, America's past would simply vanish. His museum is filled to the rafters with everything and anything from classic America. Art, furnishings, and work implements of early America are all represented.

A Vampire Killing Kit *from the collection containing a pistol, silver bullets, an ivory crucifix, powdered flowers of garlic, a wooden stake, and a serum. Essential items "considered necessary for the protection of persons who travel into certain little known countries of Eastern Europe where the populace is plagued with a particular manifestation of evil known as Vampires."*

The museum is immense—and a bit on the chilly side, as heating up a concrete structure like this must cost a bundle. The immense center hall is seven stories high, ringed with rooms depicting lost American crafts. Giant sawmills, boats, fire engines, stagecoaches, and well sweeps stand or hang there. It feels like being in some weird and wild M. C. Escher drawing with winding stairways and multiple levels. Upstairs a real gallows stands with its trapdoor hanging open—execution was a craft all its own. There is even a vampire-killing kit on display! The museum also features an impressive number of local Native American displays, which proved to be some of the most interesting in the entire museum.

The Mercer Museum is an extraordinary place. It represents the heart of American history and the local heritage of eastern Pennsylvania. And, when you combine all that in a building that is altogether marvelous in its own right, then you truly have something of a wonder and a worthy destination. The Mercer Museum is found at 84 South Pine Street, Doylestown.

–Dr. Seymour O'Life

Morose Medicine at Philly's Mütter Museum

While some snooty academic types just can't accept that weirdness is a part of our lives, one scholarly institution in Philadelphia, Pennsylvania, embraces the weird. The Mütter Museum, part of the College of Physicians of Philadelphia, proves that academia can be totally weird too.

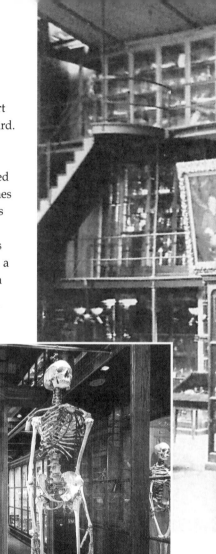

In 1856 Dr. Thomas Dent Mütter retired from teaching at the college and petitioned the school to make a museum out of his personal collection of teaching aids. His wishes were fulfilled three years after his death, when in 1863 the Mütter Museum opened its doors. Located at 19 South Twenty-second Street in Philadelphia, the museum has become a mecca of bizarre exhibits and medical oddities. One of the tamest exhibits is the museum's collection of outdated medical instruments, including an iron lung and a brain slicer, which was used to take samples of brains for slides. But they don't hold a candle to some of the other displays.

One stunningly graphic exhibit is the Eye Wall of Shame, home to wax reproductions of actual eye injuries, including a burned eye and one from an unlucky soul who managed to jam a toothpick through his retina. Another exhibit along these lines is the meticulously organized cabinet containing hundreds of swallowed items removed from people's stomachs. Some of the grosser items are rocks, pins, and fishhooks. One lovely wax model shows what a tongue infected with syphilis looks like!

The Mütter also displays some medical cases featuring celebrities from the era in which the museum was founded. There is a tumor secretly removed from President Grover Cleveland as well as a piece of the thorax of John Wilkes Booth, the man who shot Abraham Lincoln.

The museum is also strongly dedicated to putting freaky individual cases in front of the public. One of the more infamous items is the Soap Lady, an extremely obese woman who passed away after a bout of yellow fever. The alkaline soil she was buried in turned her body fat into soap. Another display features Chang and Eng, the world's most famous Siamese twins, whose autopsy was performed at the College of Physicians of Philadelphia. You not only can see the twins' conjoined liver but also can view a plaster mold of the link of cartilage that joined them at the chest.

If you're looking for freaks, this museum is your Shangri-la. You can see shrunken skulls, the skeleton of a seven-foot six-inch man, a

human skull with horns growing out of it, and the preserved skeleton of a man whose bones began to grow outside his body. Some of the museum's most morbid displays, such as its collection of deformed and injured male genitalia, are generally hidden from the public. However, rumor has it that the curators are sometimes willing to show off these secret displays if politely asked.

Perhaps the most over-the-top display at the museum is a colon removed from a deceased man who had suffered a severe blockage in his digestive system; this mind-boggling organ is over eight feet long and thirty inches in circumference. When removed from its former owner's body, it contained forty pounds of fecal matter.

Most museums are stuffy, quiet, and full of artwork and sculptures, and there's no way they'll ever make you lose your lunch. For a truly hard-core field trip, head over to the Mütter Museum.

More Museums of Medical Marvels

The Science Museum of Minnesota is home to the collection of Bob McCoy, a downright authority on medical quackery. His collection reflects his love of odd medical devices. Bob's got phrenology machines, weight-reducing glasses, fat-removing soaps, prostate warmers, and other devices you won't find being used anywhere today. The devices are on display in the Collections Room of the museum, which is at 120 West Kellogg Boulevard in St. Paul.

The Indiana Medical History Museum in Indianapolis is not for the faint of heart. Besides quack devices and outdated X-ray machines, this former asylum building houses diseased brains, damaged kidneys, and rotten livers. The museum is located at 3045 West Vermont Street.

The Wilhelm Reich Museum, Orgonon, in Rangeley, Maine, displays the works of an inventor who went to prison for his ideas. He invented a series of pseudomedical devices, which were banned by the FDA. After refusing to respect their ban, he was placed in the Lewisburg Federal Penitentiary, where he died in 1957. What were these volatile machines, you ask? They were devices powered by human orgasms. Orgonon is on Dodge Pond Road in Rangeley.

The Northern State Hospital for the Insane, in Oshkosh, Wisconsin, which has been in operation for one hundred and thirty years, is the home of an informative and sometimes sensational museum. The most striking display shows off different items that patients have swallowed over the years. Scissors, a bedspring, a toothbrush, and a thermometer are disturbing enough, but one patient took the cake by swallowing twenty-six spoons! The museum also attempts to show how their practices have changed over time. Besides the antiquated instruments and uniforms, you see how procedures like lobotomies were used and abused in the past, which is an admirable illustration of the progress made in the past century.

For those who want to know what happens to bodies when they die, the **Simpson Mortuary Museum in Newburgh, Indiana,** is the place to go. Embalming devices, body baskets, and other macabre tools of the trade are all on display.

Going to the **National Museum of Funeral History in Houston, Texas**, allows you to look at both the past and all of our inevitable futures. Founded in 1992, the museum displays strangely shaped coffins and funeral vehicles, among other things. Perhaps you've never considered being buried forever in a box shaped like a fish—well someone has, as the display of just such a coffin proves. Don't miss the San Francisco funeral bus, which was used only once to transport both a coffin and whole funeral party. The bus, unable to handle the combined weight of its living and dead passengers, tipped over, spilling the contents of the casket out onto the mourners. This must-see museum is located at 415 Barren Springs Drive.

The Mummies of Philippi

I had heard a story once about a pair of mummified women somewhere in the Allegheny Mountains, but I thought it was an old wives' tale. I was wrong. Back in the late 1800s, after years of experimenting with fruits, vegetables, and small animals, a Philippi, West Virginia farmer named Graham Hamrick successfully embalmed two recently deceased women from the West Virginia Hospital for the Insane. Hamrick's mummies traveled abroad in the 1890s as part of P. T. Barnum's tour to Europe. After their return to Philippi they were displayed at various fairs and local functions. Hamrick tried to donate the mummies to the Smithsonian but was turned down because he refused to reveal his techniques. All he would say was that the compounds were readily available from any country store and that a nickel's worth would mummify half a dozen bodies.

Today the Mummies of Philippi can be viewed at the Barbour County Museum at North Main Street, Philippi, WV. Cost of admission—$1. Well worth it to view one of America's greatest oddities, sealed in a back room in two wooden coffins with Plexiglas covers.–*Dr. Seymour O'Life*

Skullduggery in the Desert

The Giant Skull of Date Creek Road in Hillside, Arizona, was originally painted in 1900. Railroad workers with some leftover paint slapped a skull onto a large rock along a local passenger line, where it disturbed train riders for years. Now that the line has closed down, the skull is even creepier as it stares out in the middle of nowhere.

Mommy Mummy

For miles along Interstate 10 in Arizona, bright yellow billboards bombard travelers with messages beckoning them to come see the Thing. They never say what the Thing is, but every year, thousands of tourists find it too hard to resist. The curious stop at exit 322, about five miles west of Willcox pay their dollar, and go on a tour. At the end they finally see the Thing—a strange mummified creature of questionable authenticity. On display in a glass case stands something that looks like a mummified adult female corpse, holding a baby.

The Mysterious Boy

Janesville, Minnesota, is a small, quiet place known for one very strange boy in an otherwise normal house. In the attic window of a two-story house near Highway 14 is a life-size doll of a toddler. The detailed facsimile has disturbed and intrigued many who pass the house, wondering why the boy is there and what exactly he is staring out at.

The same family has owned the house for a century, but even they aren't sure when the boy was placed in the window—and they're not very interested in talking about him. But townspeople are. Many say that the doll is a memorial to a real boy who died in some gruesome fashion. Some say that the mannequin's clothes are changed daily. Others say that the figure is no boy at all, but an evil creature disguised as one.

Roads Less Traveled

"Two roads diverged in a wood, and I—
I took the one less traveled by,
And that has made all the difference." — Robert Frost

No matter what state you may call home, you will find roads that put you in touch with your most deep-rooted fears. Such byways may defy gravity, be subject to hauntings from the spirits of the dead, or play host to living cult members. With their archetypal nightmare imagery of ghosts, ferocious animals, and hooded figures around bonfires, they seem like windows into our own subconscious.

Maybe there is nothing at all scary to be found on such roads. Maybe these legendary routes serve as a conduit to our own innermost demons, turning a trip down one of them into a journey of profound self-discovery. Whatever the true story, people revel in the thrill of scaring the wits out of themselves and their friends. Who among us hasn't at some time, perhaps in their teenage years, piled into an overcrowded car and set off to some allegedly haunted nightspot?

Such jaunts usually build to a fever pitch long before you ever reach your destination, making your eyes play tricks on you.

So are these roads mystical epicenters or merely ideal destinations for rowdy joyriders? Or are they perhaps a little of both? That's a matter for debate, but since these roads are found all over the country, the forces behind them are not only geographically diverse, but awesomely powerful.

The Devil's Road and the Cult House

The most prevalent local legend among young people in Delaware involves a site that is not even located within the state. Just north of the border in southeastern Pennsylvania are the Devil's Road and a mysterious mansion called the Cult House. This narrow, two-mile stretch of rural road is lined with trees that mysteriously bend backward away from the street, as if recoiling from its impending evil. Skeptics tell you that the trees grow that way because they have been pruned to avoid contact with power lines. However, many of the strangely shaped trees are nowhere near the lines.

The most striking landmark of the Devil's Road is a tree that grows on an embankment along a treacherous curve. Erosion has exposed the roots, which look like an enormous human skull or the skeletal fingers of a hand clawing at the earth. The evil-looking arbor goes by several names, including the Skull Tree, the Devil's Tree, and, most chillingly, the Baby's Cradle, because of a dead infant once found in the hollowed-out crib of roots. The death of the child has been attributed to the cult's sacrificial rites. Decapitated baby dolls are sometimes found cradled within the tree's bony fingers.

Further down the road is the Cult House, a massive stone mansion apparently once owned by a member of the Du Pont family. It stands on a wooded hillside shrouded by dense evergreen trees. The branches, and even the trunks of the trees, lean away from the house, sometimes at a dramatic angle. The oddest architectural characteristic of the house is its windows, which most witnesses describe as inverted crosses.

At the beginning of the road a large barricade and sign are sometimes posted warning nonresidents to keep out and that trespassers risk incurring a heavy fine. According to locals, it was not uncommon for two hundred cars a night to visit Devil's Road before the ROAD CLOSED barrier was erected several years ago. Over the years frequent disturbances along the road, including a cross burning, caused local residents to complain to the police. They even hired a private security guard to patrol the lane, which might account for the numerous tales of visitors being followed and even chased down the road. Local police also patrol the road regularly, issuing tickets to those who violate the law.

Still, late-night caravans of thrill-seeking teenagers have long made pilgrimages to witness this local legend firsthand. The warning sign has apparently not been particularly popular with these night riders, who have carried it off on countless occasions, often depositing it in a nearby creek.

The Baby's Cradle

There is a legend in Delaware about a road nicknamed Devil's Road, located off Route 202 by Concord Pike. As rumor has it, there is a house or church used to perform satanic rituals. At the beginning of the road are two arrow-shaped pickets known to many as the Gates of Hell. On this road the trees are bent away from the church and there are many trees spray-painted with the numbers 666 and many other disturbing words and images. There is a gate to the side of the road, and off that road behind the gate is the church.

One of the most noticeable attractions on Devil's Road is a very large tree with a small hole hollowed out in the middle. Legend has it that this is called the Baby's Cradle, because a small fetus was once found inside the hole.

I have been on this road many times, and the only strange thing I saw was on Mischief Night (the night before Halloween), when I and my friends saw shadowy orange lights lighting up the house. I am pretty sure that it was candlelight, but we did not want to make any assumptions.—*CiCi*

Devil Worship and Dead Animals

Driving down Devil's Road toward the mansion, we noticed a pile of dead animals, mostly raccoons, slit from throat to genitals and completely gutted. When we finally approached the mansion, I was even more disgusted. Hanging from the black iron gate were more carcasses like the ones we'd just seen. It's also said that if you go at night, you can hear the satanic worshipping that goes on inside, word for word. Fortunately, we were there during the day.

—*Brooke Meadows*

Chased by Satan on His Very Own Road

Satan Road, as it is colloquially known, is a condemned road off Route 100 in Delaware. Its entrance is easy to miss, despite the bright orange warning signs, because of the way 100 bends and because of the overgrowth of the area. The state has attempted to blockade the road with signs that threaten a $1000 penalty to trespassers, but this has not stopped nosy teens.

The entryway and most of the first half of the road are so overgrown with trees and vines that they resemble a tunnel. Once you start down the road, there is no turning back. It is very windy and, despite being two lanes, is uncomfortably narrow for even a single car. About halfway down the road you come around one of the bends and you see it plain as day—the Cult House. All the trees near it grow up a few feet; then they all turn at an angle so sharp that they are almost parallel to the ground, always away from the house. It's not just two or three trees; it's every tree for several hundred feet. To the right of the road is a wall of rock covered in pentagrams. The house itself sits back from the road.

The Satan worshippers wait for your arrival at the entrance to the road in a black SUV. As soon as you start to slow down and turn, they turn on their headlights, pop out from hiding, and chase you out to a bridge on Route 100. I have been chased once by the SUV and have seen some sort of eerie bright blue flash when we were about to enter the road that scared us enough to not even bother with the road that night.—*Greg H.*

The Black Church of Satan Road

Supposedly, a Black Church constructed of solid jet-black stone with a black obelisk attached has sat on the Cult House property for almost two hundred years. It is visible only from deep inside the property. A historical article mentioned the eccentric son of a rich family that owned the land over two hundred years ago. This odd fellow was rumored to have dabbled in witchcraft and the black arts.—*Chris Trojak*

Chased Off Devil's Road

I have lived in Delaware my whole life and have been on Devil's Road at least a hundred times. I have been up to the Devil's House. The roof is lined with metal crows all facing in the same direction, and there is a white cement bench in the front yard with a demon's face carved on it. People really do chase you out of there. I remember one time around two p.m., I was driving with one of my friends on Devil's Road and a black SUV sped up behind us, then turned into the woods. There was no dirt road or anything; it just turned right into the woods. The next thing I knew, he was coming full speed right toward us. One time when there was a full moon, I could see a fire and the outlines of about twelve to fifteen people standing in a circle around it. Then I got chased off by two Bronco SUVs.—*Stephanie*

Gravity Roads

Tales of gravity roads or gravity hills are among the most popular road stories across the country. The stories are similar, yet all possess their own unique plot twists. Most involve at least one violent death and a spirit of some kind that pulls or pushes your vehicle uphill.

The preferred scientific method of testing these anomalous roads is to pull your car up to the spot in question, throw it into neutral, and remove your foot from the brake. Then, ever so slowly, your car will begin to travel uphill, as if forced by unseen hands. We've investigated several places where the forces of gravity are flouted. It really works, and the sensation can be very disorienting and unsettling.

Those seeking more concrete evidence of the spectral nature of the phenomenon will often sprinkle flour or baby powder on their car's hood or bumpers. Then, after the antigravity experiment, they check the car for signs of ghostly handprints in the powder.

Some claim that these sites of antigravitational pull are merely the result of optical illusions that make the viewer believe they are looking uphill, while in fact they are really facing down. To these people we say: We can tell our ups from downs and the high roads from the low. Sometimes all it takes is a little imagination to make a real joyride out of just another beaten path.

Rolling Up Burnt Mountain

We have a gravity hill in the foothills of the Blue Ridge Mountains of north Georgia. It's called Burnt Mountain, and it really works, although you'll get a ticket if you get caught testing it. I've done it several times. When you stop your car on the hill and put it into neutral, you'll start rolling up the hill. Eventually you'll reach a speed of between 8-10 mph.—*Tim L.*

Gravity Hill

When I was fifteen, I was taken down New Prospect Road in Jackson, New Jersey, to the very end, where it intersects with Farmingdale Road. At the stop sign my friend placed the car in neutral and let go of the brake. To my amazement we started to roll backward up the hill! About five houses down, a little girl and her father were brutally murdered by a stranger, and legend has it that when you are at this hill, the father is pulling you from the house to protect his daughter from harm.—*9Volt*

Gravity Hill of the Unknown Soldier

In Elkhorn City, Kentucky, the grave of an unknown soldier sits on a small hill overlooking the highway. Legend has it that if you stop near the grave on the road and put your car in neutral, the soldier will drag your car up the hill.

Serious Backward Action

I heard that a man on a motorcycle came over an overpass in Jackson, New Jersey, then ran through the stop sign and into the woods across the street, dying. So now he is protecting all the other motorists from going into the woods.—*Jesse*

The Magnetic Hill Mystery Spot

For more than a century Sussex Turnpike in Morris Township, New Jersey, has experienced a phenomenon known as Magnetic Hill. It sits at the entrance to the Bradford and Butterworth housing developments in Morristown, on the location of a Victorian mansion built in 1865. One legend said that inventor Thomas Edison developed a special formula that he poured on the road, and the remains of this special potion created the magnetic force. When *Weird U.S.* visited, a local man told us that the roadway had been regraded and repaved. This, he admitted with a sigh, has somewhat subdued its powers to distort the laws of physics.

Magnetic Hill

On Sussex Turnpike between Starlight Drive and Raynor Road in Morris Township is a stretch of road called Magnetic Hill. Traveling west by car, you are driving uphill. Take your foot off the gas, and you keep going up! My dad has a state-issued map from 1972 that marks the spot. Since then he has not been able to find another New Jersey map that mentions it.—*Anonymous*

The Gravity of Spook Rock Road

Spook Rock Road in Rockland County, New York, is a long, twisting road that starts in Suffern and eventually ends at Route 202. Near the end the road appears to go downhill, and if you park your car there, turn it off, and leave it in neutral, you will roll uphill. A while back a few people studied it and concluded that the last stretch of the road was an optical illusion. It only looks like a hill that is going down—it is really going upward. You could have fooled me.
—*Bonnie*

We Now Return Control of Your Car

A mile west of Manchester, Georgia, at the foot of Pine Mountain, a curiosity known as Magic Hill once stood. A car in neutral would appear to coast uphill for one hundred yards along a stretch of red clay road that extended across a spur of mountain. After passing over the apparent summit of the elevation, the vehicle then rolled to a halt on what looked like a downgrade. Water also seemed to defy gravity by running uphill and then flowing off the road and into a ditch instead of flowing on the downgrade.

When the wagons of early settlers rolled up the slope, they called the spot Ghost Hill, but during the Depression, journalists named it Magic Hill and brought it to national prominence. Robert L. Ripley made Magic Hill a "Believe It or Not!" entry. It was featured in a short film, and picture postcards helped spread its fame. Local officials placed signs to direct visitors, who arrived from a hundred miles around.

Surveyors solved the mystery over fifty years ago when they discovered that the ridge runs in a different direction from the road and the drainage ditch. That created an optical illusion that distorted a person's perception of the terrain.
—*Jim Miles*

Shaman's Grave Is a No Stopping Zone

To residents of Mooresville, Indiana, Kellars Hill Road is better known as Gravity Road or Magnetic Hill. Cars in neutral will ride backward from the bottom of the hill for close to one hundred feet. The phenomenon has worked since before the road was even paved. Supposedly, a Native American shaman buried at the foot of the hill pushes any vehicles that stop over his grave back up the embankment.

The Power of Christ Propels You!

Putney Road in Putney Corners, Michigan, is a well-traveled street—backward and forward. A portion of the road has strange powers that pull your car uphill backward. Legend says that the Blaine Christian Church at the top of the hill draws sinners toward its doors. To experience the phenomenon, make sure you are on the south side of Putney Road and that you can see the STOP AHEAD sign in your rearview mirror.

Gravity Bridge

In Jacob's Crossing, Texas, just north of Austin, there's a bridge out in the woods over a ravine. It used to be pretty well traveled before the interstates were built. Supposedly a bus driver drove his bus full of kids off that bridge, and no one survived. The bridge is flat for the first little way but then starts to slope upward at an angle. If you go out there, put your car in neutral at the base of the incline and sprinkle baby powder all over the back of your car. Then get back in and wait. The car will roll to the top of the incline, where the force will stop and the car will roll back across the bridge. If you look at the back of your car, there will be several tiny handprints that belong to the children and two large prints that are supposed to belong to the bus driver.—*DeargCeol*

Maryland's Ghost Hill

Near Boonsboro, Maryland, there is a gravity road known locally as Ghost Hill. You're supposed to go there at night, turn off your engine, and put the car in neutral. Then a ghost will push your car uphill.

Boonsboro is in the western end of the state, in Washington County, near Hagerstown. It's a one-stoplight, county fair, good-ol'-boy kind of town. Ghost Hill is actually on a lonely back road outside the town. This area is rich in Civil War history, and the story goes that the ghost was a Union soldier killed when he lost control of the cannon he was pushing. It rolled back down the hill and crushed him. Supposedly, the ghost is trying to push his cannon back up the hill.

I went to Ghost Hill once when I was a teenager, and guess what—it worked! It's not really a hill, more of a sloped section of road, but the car definitely seemed to be defying gravity and picked up considerable speed. Some have speculated that it's just an optical illusion or that there are large concentrations of magnetic rock in the ground nearby. Yeah, right.—*Travis*

Legends of Spook Hill

Central Florida is home to one of the nation's many gravity hills. Affectionately known as Spook Hill, it lies in a residential section of Lake Wales, in Polk County, and originates in a legend from the region's Seminole Indians.

The story goes that a large alligator in the nearby lake would raid the village and drag its victims into the murky deep. Under a shaman's guidance, the chief set forth to kill the alligator and battled with it for a month. As the Indians watched the lake turn bloodred, the chief emerged victorious. After this battle the nearby hill was haunted by the spirit of either the alligator or the chief, depending on who's telling the tale.

The antigravity phenomenon came to the attention of migrant farm workers, who noticed that their carts seemed to move backward uphill whenever they traveled the road. After the thoroughfare was paved, motorists experienced a similar phenomenon. This gave birth to a new attraction in Lake Wales. The town has set up signs and marks the spot in the road where the mystical journey begins, and the famous antigravity attraction gets many visitors.

Spook Hill is located off North Avenue. To find it, ask anyone where the Spook Hill Elementary School is. The road runs adjacent to it.

High Times on Lowe Street

Lowe Street in Leominster, Massachusetts, pulls cars uphill. When they are left in neutral on the street at the bottom of a slope called Magic Hill, cars roll close to fifty feet against the pull of gravity. The exact starting location has been lost over time, but many claim to have experienced it for themselves.

Rolling Toward the Border

Richford, Vermont, sits just near the Canadian border and is the home of a gravity-defying patch of land called the Mystery Spot. On the gravel road connecting East Richford to Route 105, cars are said to roll uphill at speeds close to 15 mph.

Racing with the Devil on Gravity Hill

Bucks County's gravity hill is one of Pennsylvania's legendary places. On maps this gravity hill is Buckingham Mountain, located in Buckingham Township, near the Mount Gilead African Methodist Episcopal Church. There, with a blatant disregard for the laws of nature and physics, things are said to roll uphill—cars, water, you name it. And dark legends say black magic and other evils are behind these amazing powers.

The church and graveyard at the hill are said to be the stamping ground of local satanists, and there's a cursed tombstone in the graveyard. As the story goes, once you touch it, you're supposed to run as fast as you can back toward the cemetery fence and hop over it. This dash is a race with the devil himself, and if you lose, you will be cursed with bad fortune immediately. Some say it means certain death.

Bedford's Gravity Hill

There is another Pennsylvania gravity hill, in New Paris, Bedford County. This one is actually touted by the town as a sort of tourist attraction. The town's official website encourages visitors to try out the phenomenon for themselves and offers advice on what to do once you reach the mysterious location:

Stay calm . . . keep cool. As you strain your ears to hear the laws of physics being shattered, put your car in neutral (after checking behind you for oncoming traffic, of course) and take your foot off the brake. Your car will roll, uphill. Some people like to take water or various other non-flammable, bio-degradable liquids and pour them onto the road. The liquids will flow uphill.

They even offer helpful directions to any would-be antigravity travelers: *Before you come to the town of New Paris (on Rt. 96), you'll come upon a small metal bridge. Turn left just before this bridge onto Bethel Hollow Road or S.R. 4016. Drive for 6/10th of a mile and bear left at the "Y" in the road. After another 1 1/2 mile, you'll come to an intersection that has a stop sign. Bear right onto this road and drive 2 tenths of a mile and look for the letters "GH" spray-painted on the road. Go past the first "GH" about .1 mile and stop before you get to the second spray-painted "GH."*

All the signs for the gravity hill are spray-painted on the pavement because the street signs that the town put up kept getting stolen. Apparently, gravity was not the only law being scoffed at late at night in Bedford County.

Gravity Hill near Melon Heads' Home Turf

I have some info about the gravity hill near where the Melon Heads live. If you leave Chardon, Ohio, on Mentor Road heading northwest, past Wisner Road (where the Melon Heads live), the road becomes King Memorial Road. At the bottom of the hill you'll stop at the Little Mountain Road intersection, in Kirtland Hills. Go about a hundred yards past the intersection on King Memorial. Stop your car and look in front of you. It will appear that the road ahead of you is at an incline. Now put your car in neutral and release the brake. Your car will start rolling forward, and it seems like you're rolling uphill. I've never tried it going the other direction, but I've heard it works both ways. The road obviously goes downhill, and it's just an optical illusion. I don't know what causes the illusion, but supposedly, this little trick was once explained in a Ripley's "Believe It or Not!" article —*Chrish*

The Long and Winding Story of Shades of Death Road

Can there be a more foreboding name for a road than Shades of Death? As with many places steeped in local lore, reality and legend about the Great Meadows, New Jersey, road have become intertwined over the years. This dark, mysterious thoroughfare has cut across one of the more isolated parts of the state for centuries, but how this street earned its curious name remains a mystery.

One of the earliest folktales that attempts to explain the name Shades of Death claims that the area was once home to a pack of vicious wildcats that often killed those who traveled along the road. According to one account, the ferocious nature of these beasts was so well known that early settlers referred to what is now Petersburg as Cat Hollow and Cat Swamp. There is still a road located nearby called Cat Swamp Road.

According to other legends, murder is at the root of the name. One tale says that the original inhabitants of the area surrounding Shades of Death were an unruly band of squatters. Men from this vile gang would often get into fights over women that would result in the death of one of the participants. When the civilized world encroached and the bandits disbanded, the name Shades of Death remained as the last evidence of their control over the meadows.

Yet another murder theory says that the road was originally known as the Shades, because low-hanging trees formed a canopy over it. Over time many murders occurred there, and many stayed unsolved, causing local residents to add a sinister twist to the formerly pleasant name. Anyone who has been around the area of Shades of Death can imagine that murderers would love the darkness and seclusion of the road.

Still other explanations involve death by natural

causes. Shades of Death traverses an area long known as the Great Meadows, which was a vast area of marshy swampland when it was first settled. Around 1850 malaria-carrying insects were discovered near a cliff face along Shades. As citizens around Shades came to expect deadly outbreaks of this terrible disease every year, the road's name came to reflect the morose attitude.

Today Shades of Death is still a mysterious place. Whether it owes its name to wildcats, wild men, or wild microorganisms, it issues a warning from beyond the grave to those who travel its dark path. Though we may never know for sure how the road actually got its name, it might be a good idea to heed those warnings and say a little prayer when traveling Shades of Death.

Dumped Bodies Still Plague Shades of Death

There are very haunted woods there, and the road is haunted. A plague killed most of these people in the town, forcing them to lay the dead bodies in the street so some sort of doctor could come pick them up. Some bodies were dumped in Ghost Lake, spreading the plague even more. –*Jennifer Bates*

Ghosts on Shades of Death Road

There's a legend of a girl who was murdered one night on that road while walking home. Her ghost asks motorists for rides, and if you do not give her one, you'll die in a car accident that night. A friend of mine was driving down the road when the passengers spotted a girl on the road. The conversation went as follows:

Girl: "Please, could you give me a ride?"
Driver: "I'm sorry! I really can't; the car is full."
Girl: "You don't understand. You want to give me a ride."
Driver: "I'm sorry. . . ."

The girl then walked off into the woods. Needless to say, all the occupants were freaked out. They stopped the car there at about two in the morning and waited until dawn before driving home. –*Matt, Long Valley, NJ*

All Turned Around on Shades of Death

I am from Sussex County and have had many experiences on Shades of Death Road. Although I have personally never seen anything, I have felt like there was someone watching me on that road. It is very hard to explain the feeling, but it is one of uneasiness. One of the last times I visited the road in the evening, I got very lost in the back roads of Sussex and Warren counties. I grew up there and know the roads like the back of my hand, but for some reason, that evening, I was all turned around and seeing the road signs was a very difficult task. It took nearly three hours for my friends (also Sussex County residents) and me to find our way back to Andover. The feeling I had was so intense that that trip was my last. –*Margie*

Chased by Phantom Pickup from Shades of Death

My friends and I went to check out Shades of Death Road. As we were driving, we made a turn onto a gravel road between two cornfields. The tiny road looked very creepy and scary. All of a sudden we saw headlights go on in front of us and begin coming toward us. We immediately put our car in reverse and began to drive back. (The road was so small that you couldn't turn around.) As we got back onto Shades of Death Road, we sped off, but the truck kept on following us. Everybody inside our car had an adrenaline rush, and every time we turned around, the truck was still there. Then all of a sudden it disappeared into nowhere. Shades of Death Road is nothing to mess around with. If you go there, make sure you know how to drive in reverse, just in case you make a wrong turn. –*Big C from the Crew*

Dark Hollow Road

In the deep forests of rural Carter County, Tennessee, by Roan Mountain, lies the infamous Dark Hollow Road. As you drive along it past Dark Hollow Cemetery, it is said you will feel a mysterious bump as if somebody had jumped into your back seat. It is the restless spirit of a woman named Delinda, buried in the Dark Hollow Cemetery over one hundred years ago.

Legend states that Delinda was very popular with the men of the town and had many husbands—though she was never married to any of them herself. Naturally, this upset the wives of the town, who branded Delinda a witch, and led to a tragic affair with a man called Jankins.

After trying to confront Delinda at her house and finding it empty, the wronged Mrs. Jankins returned home and shot her husband square in the chest, killing him. Delinda was never seen again, and the townsfolk thought she had beaten a hasty retreat to avoid an angry mob. But after Jankins's funeral the pallbearers remarked on the unusually heavy weight of the casket, leading some to speculate that Delinda had hidden herself in the coffin to follow her one great love to the grave.

Denied a proper Christian burial, Delinda can never be at peace in the consecrated ground of the cemetery, so her spirit is doomed to jump into cars as they pass. Some have even claimed that they have seen, through their rearview mirror, Delinda sitting in the back seat! And so here's a warning to late-night passersby on the shadowy Dark Hollow Road: Keep an eye out for beguiling spirits bumming rides.

Lurching Down Dark Hollow Road

In the wee small hours of a Sunday morning in the mid-'70s, my husband and I and two friends ventured along a country road called Dark Hollow, in Fall Branch, Tennessee. Our friend had walked the area at midnight, alone, and heard footsteps behind him, drawing ever closer and stopping when he stopped. He never knew what made the footsteps. My husband thought the legend was just a big story, so we drove slowly down the road for the two-mile stretch. Suddenly the car began bucking and jumping, as when you apply the gas and brakes simultaneously. This continued until we had reached the end of the area, when the car began to drive smoothly and normally. I was shaken and asked my husband not to return home through Dark Hollow. He said he was not driving an extra ten miles and turned the car around. The car began jumping and lurching again as soon as we reached the designated haunted area.—*Letter via e-mail*

Restless Spirits Haunt the Nation's Highways

Perhaps it's apropos that in our fast moving, highly mobile society many of our most notable ghosts are seen hanging out at the side of the road where it is said they met their untimely end. These roadside apparitions have been witnessed by countless motorists over the course of several generations. Unlike the popular urban legend of the Vanishing Hitchhiker who gets picked up only to disappear from the car's back seat, these street corner spooks don't seem to have any interest in bumming a ride. They seem content to wander their own stretch of highway year in and year out, eternally reliving their final living moments here on this earth.

Heavy Vibes and Little People on Old Pali Road

A group of us girlfriends left school at lunch one day and decided to drive around the island rather than go back for the second half of the day. I was sitting in the back seat with two other girls as we cruised down the Old Pali Road. This is located off the Pali Freeway, in Kailua, Hawaii, in a quick right turn surrounded by many plants and vegetation. Since we'd grown up here, we knew where to look, but otherwise it would not be easily found.

The place was well known for having heavy vibes. Like many teenagers, we did it in fun, but were always respectful of the Hawaiian legends. The strange thing about this road is that no matter how much fun you are having, after about a minute everyone inevitably becomes silent. The jokes either die down or are said weakly, without confidence. Even though the road is quite beautiful, there is something different in the air. It's hard to put into words—but it feels oppressive, as if the surrounding trees have created a tunnel. There is a strong feeling that every time you turn a corner, something will be standing in the middle of the road. Your body is tight with anxiety.

It was the same this day. I just wanted to get out. Okay, the next curve and then the road . . . but it kept going and going. Finally, we curved to the right, and there was the freeway! We started pulling out onto the main road, and just before we turned to merge onto the freeway, I looked out the window behind me and saw a dwarf walking out from the Old Pali Road! Where was he coming from? To this day I cannot think of a reasonable explanation. There were no other cars and no homes back there. This dwarf came out of nowhere into the middle of the road.

I'll never forget it but I eventually gave up trying to find explanations of where he could have come from.—*Paige*

The Half-faced Ghost of Old Pali Road

The desolate Old Pali Road in Kailua is haunted— and not by just any old ghost. The phantom in question is a young girl, with long black hair and only half a face, solemnly skipping rope as she floats down the street. According to eyewitnesses, her cheeks, nose, and mouth are completely nonexistent. Her eyes remain not only intact but wildly bulging out of their sockets.

She is said to be the wandering soul of a murdered teenage girl, strangled by her own jump rope and left to decompose in roadside bushes. They say that her eyes protrude because this is how she appeared in her last few terrifying moments on earth, and they attribute the missing portion of her lower face to scavenging animals that had eaten it away before the body was discovered. Now she is doomed to wander forever on the Old Pali Road.

The Red Eyes of Hansell Road

I am not generally afraid of anything or anyone—maybe sharks and God, but that's it! Anyway, that all changed one dark September night. I was working in Newtown, Bucks County, Pennsylvania, and some of the younger employees were talking about a road in nearby Buckingham called Hansell Road. The road is long and dark—with only a few houses that sit far off the road. It is not well traveled or lit. After you park and wait for a while, you see green mists appear and cross the road, followed by a black, shadowy entity. These are said to be the spirits of some youths who were murdered by an evil landowner for trespassing on his property.

So one moonless night in September four friends and I took a ride to Hansell Road. The road ascended on a slight incline, with large cornfields on both sides and dark woods looming ahead. The trees grew over the gravel road like a dark canopy. We parked the car on the grass shoulder about fifty feet from the tree line and sat on the hood for about twenty minutes. I got antsy and strolled up the road. I will never forget what happened next for as long as I live.

I was about fifty feet from the rest of the gang when a red, glowing orb began coming out of the woods from the left side of the road. It bobbed slightly up and down about fifty feet ahead of me, small but bright enough that they could see it from the car. The girls started yelling, "What the hell is that?" I shushed them and watched as it neared the road, as if it were going to cross. When it left the woods, it became two red, glowing orbs floating about six feet from the ground. They bobbed until they stopped directly in front of me, then just stayed there stationary. The hairs on the back of my neck stood up. I took two steps forward, and the "eyes" started to move off the road into the woods, then disappeared. I heard no foot or hoof on the gravel road or in the woods.

Now, bear this in mind: There were no lights at all, anywhere, so the theory that it was deer-eye reflections doesn't hold up. Besides, I never saw an animal with bright red eyes. I swear this account is true and that it happened exactly as described.—*Jim Bechtel*

The Ghost of Stone Church Road

There is a road about ten to fifteen miles from Bartonville, Illinois, called Stone Church Road that I had always heard was haunted. Rumor has it that a man died on that road and his spirit was stuck there with his car. Every time I go by that road, I see car lights just sitting there—not white lights, but yellow. One night my friends and I got the guts to check it out. We drove down the road, and in about twenty seconds we saw a car parked on the side and a man in the street. We couldn't turn around, so we had to keep going, but the guy wouldn't move. My friend Donnie got out and asked the guy what his problem was. The guy just looked at him without saying a word. Donnie was getting mad that the guy wouldn't answer him, so he kept yelling. I knew something was wrong. I told Donnie to get back in the truck and let's get out of there. He listened and got in the truck.

We kept staring at the guy, and he didn't move. I turned around for a second to turn on the music, and when I turned back to look again, the guy was gone—along with the car. I knew it was the ghost. To this day I get chills whenever I drive past that road. I still see the lights every once in awhile.—*Chris B.*

Blood Road

In 1990 my friend and I began hearing frightening stories about a road just outside Metamora, Michigan, called Blood Road. Kids driving down the road at night would witness trees following them or be chased by a truck with bright lights. The first time we went down the road, just after midnight, we noticed that it was wet, although it had not rained in days. The water was increasing as we watched, and it was strange and thick. We each opened our door and saw that the water was red in color. My buddy turned on his brights, and we saw that the whole road was covered in this bloodlike substance. He turned the truck around, and we began to leave; then we saw a fire off in the distance, with people in white robes standing around it chanting. As we kept driving, we saw a few of them run across the road. We got the hell out of there.—*Rypple*

Freaky Fermilab Compound Roads

I spend a good amount of time in Illinois each summer. I stay with my uncle in Geneva, Illinois, near a science center known as Fermilab. The government-run place speeds atoms up to nearly the speed of light. The weird part starts when you drive around on its roads. We came across a neighborhood of small houses with children's toys and cars in front, but no one was around. They were one story and were all painted cobalt blue and bright orange. Some had screen porches, and hanging from the walls were what looked to be either bio or radiation suits. It was a little strange to see these suits hanging on the walls of houses. Farther down the road was what appeared to be a preschool, with a yard full of toys, but no one to be seen.

Perhaps the weirdest part of that building was that right next to the door was a radiation-fallout shelter complete with an enormous metal door. We went through the scientific portion of the area, and right in the middle of the concrete buildings was a field full of grazing buffalo. We decided to leave to get some food and took a road that goes through a large field of nothing. By the side of the road were what looked to be manholes connected to concrete tunnels. I commented that the geese we had been seeing were fakes with cameras. We all had a good laugh, but when we turned the corner, there was a mutilated goose in the middle of the road—but no tire tracks on the body. We left after that and never found a reason to go back. But it was definitely one of the most interesting days I have had in a long time.—*Slojo*

Damn the Living Who Mock This Road!

Locals in Jacksonville, North Carolina, say that Highway 24 is haunted. The road is said to have been a Civil War trail used by the Union army, where they slaughtered a whole company of Confederate soldiers. I have witnessed much weirdness traveling this road at night. One time, right at the front gate of Camp Lejeune, my car's headlights dimmed real low; then the radio faded to nothing. At first I thought my car was breaking down, but then the gas pedal hit the floor by itself and the car took off straight at a tree. Right before I hit the tree, the car came to a dead stop and over the radio I heard a faint voice say, "Damn the living who mock this road."—*CoutuJA*

Route 666: The Highway to Hell

You would think that our nation's highway planners would know to avoid naming any road after the number of the Antichrist. But you would think wrong. There is a Route 666—it was originally the sixth branch of famed Route 66 that runs through four states in the west. The road, almost two hundred miles long, runs through Arizona, Colorado, and New Mexico, and ends in Utah. And although these states are making efforts to change the name of the road, nefarious happenings still occur along what locals have dubbed the Devil's Highway.

One enduring legend of Route 666 speaks of a young girl in a white dress who wanders the desolate dark road by night. When motorists stop to offer the girl help, she disappears into the thin night air. More malevolent spirits will climb into your car with you. It's said that the shape-shifters known to Native Americans as skin walkers terrorize motorists along Route 666. They first appear in front of moving vehicles as various animals, trying to make drivers swerve and crash. If this does not work, they appear in the back seat of the car, attempting to steal passengers' souls.

Linda Dunning, author of *Specters in Doorways: The History and Hauntings of Utah*, tells of an experience her husband had on this treacherous road. He was driving alone on Route 666 one night when suddenly "he saw a truck that looked like it was on fire heading straight for him, right down the middle of the highway. The truck was going so fast that sparks were flying up off the wheels and flames were coming from the smokestack." He estimated that the truck was traveling 130 miles an hour. He pulled off the road and fled into the desert until the imposing flaming vehicle passed him by.

According to Linda, the mad trucker is not the only apparition to be wary of along the way. She says, "Packs of demon dogs with yellow eyes have been seen on this highway as well, shredding the tires of those silly enough to stop. There are many other tales of people who either disappear along this route or suddenly appear out of nowhere. There are even tales of the same person disappearing at one point along the highway and then reappearing at another location miles away, without having any recollection of where they have been or what they have been doing."

After much public pressure, most of the highway has been rechristened with different number designations. The states included the following justifications for changing the road's name in their petition to federal officials:

"WHEREAS, people living near the road already live under the cloud of opprobrium created by having a road that many believe is cursed running near their homes and through their homeland; and

"WHEREAS, the number '666' carries the stigma of being the mark of the beast, the mark of the devil, which was described in the Book of Revelations in the Bible; and

"WHEREAS, there are people who refuse to travel the road, not because of the issue of safety, but because of the fear that the devil controls events along United States Route 666; and

"WHEREAS, the economy in the area is greatly depressed when compared with many parts of the United States, and the infamy brought by the inopportune naming of the road will only make development in the area more difficult."

In Arizona the road is now Highway 191. In Utah it will be known as New 491/Old 666. This new moniker has not stopped the strange incidents from happening on the road, nor has it stopped people from telling stories about it.

"Drive Route 666 at night, and you drive at your own risk," warns Linda Dunning. "Take a lot of people with you and don't leave any space for unwanted passengers who just might decide to appear in your back seat. Pull off the road if a huge diesel truck comes bearing down on you. Don't look for lights floating in the sky. Hope you don't see any young girls in white dresses. Never stop if you spot something peculiar, and don't pick up hitchhikers. Lastly, if demon dogs approach you in the night, just keep driving."

The Phantom Rider of Meshack Road
Just outside the small town of Tompkinsville, Kentucky, the old Meshack Road runs along a creek. For many years horse and motorcycle riders have reported an invisible presence clinging tightly to their waist along this road. This specter holds on for about a mile before it disappears. No one has ever been able to suggest an explanation for this phenomenon. Tompkinsville is located in the south-central part of Kentucky, about twenty miles southeast of Glasgow, a few miles north of the Tennessee border.—*Troy Taylor*

Gateways to Hell

T

here is no better way to prove one's courage than by walking straight into the gaping maw of hell itself. Luckily, the country is full of legendary passageways that lead there. What continues to amaze us here at *Weird U.S.* is not the number of supposed entrances to Hades, but how eagerly people seek them out. More curious travelers ask us for the exact whereabouts of these gateways than for any other location. It seems that everybody wants to go to hell these days. Generations of local teenagers have told tales of these darkened portals and dared each other to cross their thresholds. Are their stories an accurate reflection of what lies beyond? Or are they a window into the darkest fears inside us all? Only those who are brave enough, or foolhardy enough, to enter these dark recesses can say for sure.

Stull Cemetery

There are graveyards across America that go beyond merely being haunted and enter into the realm of the diabolical. They are places so terrifying that they say the devil himself holds court with his worshippers there. The cemetery on Emmanuel Hill in Stull, Kansas, is one of these places.

— And Now, in person, The Devil!

There is not much left of the small village of Stull, save for a few houses, a church, and about twenty residents. But some claim that the old graveyard is one of the "seven gateways to hell," which the devil himself visits every year. Such stories have been linked to Stull for more than a century, though none of them made it into print until the 1970s.

In November 1974 the University of Kansas student newspaper ran an article describing Stull as "haunted by legends of diabolical, supernatural happenings." It recounted legends that the cemetery was one of the two places on earth where the devil appears in person twice each year—at Halloween and on the spring equinox. The piece claimed that most students learned of Stull's evil reputation from their grandparents and elders but that many of them experienced firsthand things they could not explain. One student claimed to have been grabbed by the arm by something unseen, while others spoke of unexplained memory loss when visiting the site. Tales of devil worship and witchcraft also figured strongly in the article.

The residents of Stull and the pastor of the church in Stull dismissed the tales as the invention of students at the university. But such stories have a strong hold on people. On the spring equinox on March 20, 1978, more than a hundred and fifty people waited in the Stull Cemetery for the arrival of the devil. The word also spread that the spirits of those who died violent deaths would rise from their graves—but the only spirits that showed up that night came in bottles.

This did not stop the stories from spreading, however. One story told of two young men who were visiting Stull Cemetery one night and became frightened when a strong wind began blowing out of nowhere. They ran back to their car, only to find that the vehicle had been moved to the other side of the highway and was now facing in the opposite direction. Another man claimed he was knocked to the ground by this same anomalous wind, but inside the church rather than in the graveyard. Near the church lies a tombstone bearing the name Wittich, which gave rise to many witch stories. One tells of a grave that holds the bones of a "child of Satan"—born of the devil and a witch—who was so deformed that he lived only for a few days.

One of the strangest stories about Stull supposedly appeared in *Time* magazine in either 1993 or 1995. This story claims that

Pope John Paul II, while on his way to a public appearance in Colorado, allegedly ordered his private plane to fly around eastern Kansas. The reason for this, the story claims, was that the Pope did not want to fly over "unholy ground."

As the legends grew, so did the crowds. An estimated five hundred people thronged the graveyard on Halloween night in 1988, damaging the church and gravestones. This prompted the Douglas County sheriff's department to station deputies there the following year, handing out tickets for criminal trespass to anyone caught on the property. A chain-link fence was installed around the grounds, along with signs that warn against trespassing. The cemetery's late-night visitations have died down somewhat, except for in October.

But what about the stories? Strangely, the property owners have done little to debunk them. Although so many of the paranormal events supposedly involve the ruins of the old church, the owners let it stand vacant since 1922, instead of quickly demolishing it—and the legends that surrounded it. The roof blew off in 1996, and the church stood exposed to the elements until March 2002. Even when the church was torn down, the event was shrouded in mystery. It happened without witnesses and without the knowledge of at least one of the owners. Someone just slipped into the cemetery with heavy machinery and demolished the building. To this day the mystery is unsolved.

Other questions also remain: Why chase away those who come to the cemetery before the hour of midnight on Halloween? Why not allow the curiosity-seekers to see that no spirits run rampant, thus ending the legends once and for all? On Halloween night of 1999, when newspaper reporters and a television news crew joined the onlookers, a representative for the cemetery owners appeared at precisely eleven thirty p.m. and ordered everyone to leave the property. But if, as the owners stated, they did not want media attention brought to the graveyard, because it attracts vandals, why not allow the camera crew to show that the devil did not appear at midnight? Makes you wonder, doesn't it?–*Troy Taylor*

Legends of Stull and the Stairway to Hell

Stull had two major tragedies in the 1900s. The first is about a small boy whose father was burning a field of tall grass. After the field was burned, the charred remains of the boy were found. The other tragedy was of a man who was reported missing and was later found hanging from the limb of a tree. Stull also had a road in 1905 called Devil's Road.

I have heard many rumors involving the church, but here are a few that have been consistently repeated: If you take two bottles and make the sign of the cross with them, when you throw them against the church wall, they will shatter. However, if you make an upside-down cross, the bottles will not break no matter how hard you throw them!

Perhaps the most frightening rumor involves a set of stairs, believed to be located somewhere around the church, that are the true gateway to hell. According to different stories, the mystery stairs are underneath the rubble inside the church or back behind the church or in the cemetery in front. One rumor says that if you go down them, it will take two weeks to get back up, although it will seem like just a few moments. I have heard that some unknown force seems to pull you as if to drag you all the way down.–*Adam Schafer*

Campout on the Threshold to Hell

The stairs are behind the church on the right side if you are facing the church. They aren't easy to find, however, because they are well covered by grass that has grown on top of the lid that covers them.

If you really want to see or hear awful and weird stuff, try to camp out behind the church for a night. Do this behind the church to avoid the patrols that drive by there at night every hour or two. Take a flashlight and plenty of batteries, because you will have a ton of trouble keeping the flashlight working and it will go out a lot, trust me, I know.–*Ryan*

You Can't Move Away from Hell

It's a good thing there's a convenient gate to hell, because according to one Kansas resident, that is where we are all going. The following letter came to us from a reader who used to live in New Jersey, but now resides in Kansas. He just wanted us to know that his new home was just as weird as his old one.

This Place Is Goin' to Hell

To start off, the place I live in here in Kansas has a zip code that starts with 666—that should tell you something right away. How about a minister who some think is the devil himself? He has a private church open only to his family and their friends. He lives behind a barricade type of fence around his property, with security systems installed. The American flag flies 24/7—UPSIDE DOWN! His church group pickets on street corners and at funerals and weddings with the most disgusting signs. He has signs saying that 9/11 was sent by God to punish us and we deserved it because we're all homosexuals. He can get away with this because the whole family are lawyers and he himself is a disbarred lawyer and no one wishes to spend a fortune and the time in court. This may not be your typical weirdness, but it's weird enough.—*xjrzite*

Hades Beckons

Believe it or not, there are actually three locations in Pennsylvania that offer easy access to the dark netherworld. The surprising thing about these many storied passageways is how heavily traveled they are. Before compiling this book we never would have imagined what a popular destination Hades was!

All Link Arms in the Gates of Hell

The Twin Tunnels are located on Valley Creek Road in Downingtown, Pennsylvania. Back in the late 1800s or early 1900s a young woman was run out of town after giving birth out of wedlock. She ran to the tunnels and hanged herself from a tree that rose over them. She was holding the baby when she jumped, and when the rope ran out of slack the baby fell the rest of the way and died on impact. When you walk into the tunnel at night, you can sometimes hear the baby crying or see its ghostly apparition.

When we were in high school, we used to make trips to the tunnels every weekend. They were definitely creepy—pitch-black and deathly quiet except for the sound of dripping water. We would all link arms and walk to the middle of the tunnel where the girl hung herself.—*Nick Lombardo*

H Tree Marks the Spot

There is a story in Lansdale, Pennsylvania, of a tree in the shape of an H. It is actually two trees side by side connected in the middle. It's astonishing, really. The story goes that there are three H trees in the world and they all mark the gateway to hell. The tree stands on top of a twelve-foot-tall cliff, and the story is that if you walk under the middle of the trees and around the trunk of one of them six times and jump off the cliff, the ground will open up and take you to hell. The tree was knocked down during construction, and homes were put up. I certainly wouldn't want to be the family who lives in the house that was built over the tree!—*Jeff, Lansdale, PA*

Seven—Count 'Em—Seven Gates of Hell

In most respects York is exactly what you'd expect of a rural Pennsylvania town—a quiet place in the heartland of the state. Don't be fooled—there is a mysterious history and a dark underside of York. One site within the city limits of the town speaks to a sinister episode that betrays the city's tranquillity.

It is a story of death. It is a story of despair. It is a story about attempting to breach the very boundaries of hell itself. It is the story of Toad Road.

You will not find Toad Road on the map of York, because its name has been officially changed to Trout Run Road. This was done to dissuade curiosity-seekers from putting themselves in harm's way and to hide the grisly incidents that once occurred along the thoroughfare.

In the 1800s a colossal mental asylum stood in the woods of York off Toad Road. This was a hellish place and the home of only the most deranged, most unfortunate souls. The asylum was many stories high and contained hundreds of rooms. Buried in the desolate Pennsylvania woods, it was viewed as the perfect place to ship the insane from all across the state.

There was one major problem with this location, however; it was miles away from civilization. While viewed as a blessing by those who didn't want to face their fears, this also meant that the asylum was not easily accessible. This led to a great tragedy when it caught on fire one day.

Because of its remote locale, firefighters were unable to get there in time. Many patients burned to death in the upper floors of the building, and hundreds of others fled into the surrounding woods. The scene was true chaos—some of the most deranged and dangerous people in all of Pennsylvania had disappeared into the woods as an inferno spread throughout the area.

When officials finally put out the fire, they set out to capture all of the escaped inmates. Scared by the reputations of the asylum's inmates and unsure of how to handle the situation, the search party was extraordinarily aggressive, beating into submission some of those they found and killing others.

It's clear why no one in York acknowledges this publicly. The town changed the name of the road, stopped talking of the hospital, and tried to put the tragedy behind it. Unfortunately, this would be impossible.

The psychic impact of these horrible events forever cursed Toad Road. People today say that the area is so cursed that it is the location of seven gateways to hell. York officials had constructed seven barriers along the paths to the former site of the asylum. Most adventure-seekers never even locate the first one. For those who manage to find the path, it is said that, by the fifth barrier, the sense of evil and overpowering feelings of death will turn even the bravest explorer back. Apparitions are often seen along these paths. Strange noises and menacing screams are heard frequently.

Legends say that if one did manage to get past all seven gates, they would be standing upon the burned remains of the mental hospital, a bona fide passageway to hell itself.
—*Marcus Malvern Jr.*

The One and Only

You might think that Gates of Hell would be a common nickname for any dark and foreboding entrance to the underground. But in all of our years of research we have found only one subterranean passage in New Jersey with this moniker. It is a very old tunnel in Clifton with an arched stone ceiling about eight feet high. The light quickly vanishes behind you as you enter, and you are soon enveloped in total darkness. Even without the presence of Satan, it can be an extremely dangerous place. The tunnel system was built as drainage for a stream called Weasel Brook, and during heavy rain the usual trickle of water through the tunnel can almost instantly turn into a raging torrent.

Enter the Gates of Hell

My first recollections of this place were stories from the kids at the local BMX bike jumps. They would tell of people entering these tunnels and never returning. Satanic sacrifices, decaying carcasses, upside-down crosses, satanic graffiti—anything dealing with the darkness in human nature—was down there. There were seven layers of tunnels under the ground, and the lower you got, the closer you came to meeting the devil. Most chilling to me was a secret room many layers underground. This room was a dungeon that housed a human skull, or so it was said, and it could be entered only if you possessed the power to lift thousands of pounds of axes that blocked the door.

When I was sixteen, I was introduced to the gates for the first time. It was dark from all of the tree cover, and my stomach began to drop as we climbed down to the level on which the tunnel entrances were located. Unlike the other tunnels, which were round and had streams of water flowing from them, this entrance was square and had no water flow. At this point I was ready to leave and go home, but I realized that the only way to conquer the gates was to enter the tunnels.

Deep inside the dark tunnel we started to hear a strange knocking sound. My friend swears it was someone deeper in the tunnels whispering some chant. That's when we got the hell out of there. Years later I made several trips back to the Gates of Hell, but after telling my story, I could never convince anyone to venture into the tunnels as far as my friend and I did that one summer day.—*Ralph Sinisi*

The Portal to Hell Is Down in the Groove

There's supposed to be an area within the gates with some disturbing décor. There are dead trees planted exactly three feet apart with dead cats and birds tied around their trunks. Another story I've heard is that at the very end of the gates is the actual entrance to hell. There is a groove about twenty feet deep and about forty feet across. At the very center of the groove is a smoothed-out granite manhole, which is supposed to be one of the portals leading to hell.—*Richard M.*

Red-eyed Mike Guards the Gates to Hell

I have explored every inch of Clifton, and nowhere is as eerie as the Gates of Hell! It's said that a spirit known as Red-eyed Mike guards the tunnel. If you knock on the railroad ties above the entrance in groups of three, you will hear a loud horn sound from within the tunnel. I have heard this horn on occasion and have seen rocks hurling themselves out of the tunnel with no person visible inside. I also once witnessed a small human-shaped figure run out of the tunnel toward Weasel Brook Park with superhuman speed. I have been told that this is Red-eyed Mike.—*Jeff H.*

Those Gates are Everywhere

The great variety of passageways to hell is what makes our country so weirdly great. Whether you are cruising the interstate, retracing Charles Manson's steps, or even in a town called Paradise, you're not very far from hell.

Leave the Highway at Your Own Risk

The gateway to hell is by the I-75 ramp and the 826 expressway in southern Florida. There are many stories of kids going into the tunnel on a dare and not coming out. Strange writing on the wall warns them not to proceed. As you progress down the corridor, it gets darker and narrower. You have to climb over connected pieces of concrete, and you have to be very careful. There was also a very bad stench, and the sounds of babies crying in the night.—*Edward Clark*

Witchcraft and Murder in Hex Hollow

Hex Hollow, also known as Spring Valley Park and Rehmeyer's Hollow, is in southern York County, Pennsylvania. It is a maze of trails and dirt roads, old fieldstone walls that meander through the woods, paths that start and end with no particular logic. I would spend an entire day hiking, climbing, trying to learn the trails just as I'd first learned the stories of this haunted place.

Hex Hollow lies five miles from where my wife, Alison, and I live. People do not like to speak of Hex Hollow's legend. Most, when asked about it, give short answers if any at all.

Hex Hollow is not easy to find, but you know it when you're there: The world becomes a little darker. How much darker it must have been in 1928, when the hollow's one resident was Nelson D. Rehmeyer—a loner well over six feet tall, with deep-set eyes and a powerful presence. His wife lived outside the hollow because he was, in her words, "too damn peculiar." Rehmeyer was what is called in this area a pow-wow doctor. They are sometimes called Brauchers. In a more negative light they are called Hexenmeisters, Hex doctors, or simply Hexers. A strong tradition of faith healing and folk magic continues to this day among the Pennsylvania Germans.

With some searching, Alison and I found the Rehmeyer house. There is no grave here, no witch's burial ground, no pentagrams, and few hex signs (which are a common sight in these parts). The only outwardly "witchy" feature of the house is the red 13 painted on one of the barns.

Yet Hex Hollow has a feeling that Alison likens to a graveyard: peaceful and quiet, but with an undercurrent of foreboding. The romantic notion of Rehmeyer conducting black ceremonies in the basement of his sparse home greatly appealed to me. However, I found the truth by listening to an interview with Phillip Smith.

Phillip Smith, deceased, formerly of Jacobus, Pennsylvania, was the last in a long line of pow-wow doctors. When Smith was asked about the "hex" murder (and the trial that followed), he replied, "They said they found his [Rehmeyer's] hex book. That was no hex book. That was *The Long Lost Friend.*"

The Long Lost Friend, more accurately translated as *The Long Forgotten Friend*, was a collection of prayers, folk magic, superstitions, and rituals compiled by John G. Hohman in 1819. Still in print locally to this day, it is subtitled *A Collection of Mysterious and Invaluable Arts and Remedies Good for Man and Beast.* Its sources are diverse, including Gypsy magic and lore, ritual magic, German folk magic, and Albertus Magnus's book, *Egyptian Secrets.*

In Rehmeyer's time pow-wow was openly practiced. There were storefront pow-wow doctors in York City and hundreds of informal pow-wow practitioners throughout the area. One was named John Blymire, a sickly and sad man from a family of Brauchers who traced their spiritual lineage back to Pennsylvania's most famous witch, Mountain Mary. But John Blymire could keep none of his pow-wow

patients. He was reduced to working in a cigar factory. He had no explanation for his hardship, save perhaps the answer obvious to someone of his background: He must have been hexed.

Blymire visited every pow-wow doctor, witch, and faith healer in the area, trying to get his hex broken. He had no luck until he found Nellie Noll, a.k.a. the High Priestess of Marietta, a.k.a. the River Witch. After Blymire made many visits—and payments—to Noll, she revealed the source of his curse: Nelson D. Rehmeyer of Rehmeyer's Hollow. Blymire claimed that he handed Noll a dollar bill, and when she handed it back, he saw Rehmeyer's face in place of George Washington's.

Noll told Blymire that the only way he could break the hex was to get a lock of Rehmeyer's hair or his hex book or both, and bury them six feet down. Blymire quickly enlisted two teenagers to help. One was fourteen-year-old John Curry. Curry himself had a life full of hard times: a broken family, an abusive stepfather, poverty. It didn't take much for Blymire to convince Curry that he too was cursed and that Rehmeyer was the source. The other teen was Wilbert Hess. His family's farm was failing. It had flourished for years; the family could find no explanation for why the crops should fail and the cows not give milk—unless it was a hex. Blymire informed them that Nelson D. Rehmeyer was the cause.

This shocked the Hess family, who knew Rehmeyer. They had taken young Wilbert to Rehmeyer to be healed (successfully). Still, Blymire was sure of the hex and knew how to break it.

Blymire, Curry, and Hess went to confront Rehmeyer on a rainy November night in 1928. The old man invited them in, and the four men stayed up late talking of many things, from the weather to farming to pow-wow. Rehmeyer asked them to stay the night, then went upstairs to sleep while his three guests slept downstairs. In the early morning Blymire tried to convince Curry and Hess to go to the basement to find Rehmeyer's hex book. Curry and Hess wanted none of that. So after Rehmeyer fed them breakfast, the trio left.

They returned the following night. Again Rehmeyer invited them in. Blymire became agitated and more forceful. It took all three of them—Blymire, Curry, and Hess—to wrestle the powerful Rehmeyer to the ground. "Where is it?" they demanded. Rehmeyer said he would get "it" for them if they let him up. When they did, he handed them his wallet, which

angered Blymire even more. The three tied a rope around Rehmeyer's neck and beat him to death with a chair and a block of wood. Upon hearing his death rattle, Blymire exclaimed, "Thank God, the witch is dead!"

Even with Nelson Rehmeyer dead, the trio could not muster the courage to descend into his basement to look for his hex book. Instead, they decided to burn the body and the house. They poured lamp oil over Rehmeyer's corpse and the floor, set them ablaze, and left. Rehmeyer's nearest neighbor found his body two days later, on Thanksgiving.

The bizarre story of one witch brutally murdering another to break a hex was too good for the media to ignore. The whole culture was put on trial. Before the "hex trials," pow-wow was a strong cultural tradition. Afterward, worldwide attention often ridiculed the practice.

Nelson D. Rehmeyer is buried in the cemetery at the old Sadler's Church, just outside the hollow. His gravestone bears no epitaph, no pentagrams. He was a man of God. When I visit his grave, it's to pay respect, not to search for pentagrams or to light candles in midnight rituals. He might have pow-wowed for my ancestors, healed children, and given hope to the hopeless. I've decided that's a better legacy.

—*Timothy Renner*

From Hell to Paradise and Back

The next time someone tells you to go to hell, pack your handbasket and head toward Michigan. The 166-person town of Hell, Michigan, has existed since 1841. Hell isn't such a bad place to visit, really. They've got an ice cream shop, a liquor store, and a post office. Michigan is also home to a town called Paradise. Eerily enough, the round-trip distance between Hell and Paradise is 666 miles.

Tunnel of the Damned

In Boonesboro, Kentucky, three tunnels go straight into a mountain at three different angles. The main entrance is blocked off, and NO TRESPASSING signs are posted everywhere, but inside there are huge stone pillars that lead to the mine entrances. It's said that the site is used by local cultists who believe they are vampires.
—*Letter via e-mail*

Manson's Death Valley Gate to Hell

In Death Valley National Monument, Nevada, is a sinister place called the Devil's Hole. It's a fenced-in separation in a hill that many people think is a passageway to hell. Charles Manson searched for a bottomless pit in Death Valley to hide in during Helter Skelter, after which he would emerge as leader of the world.

You can get close to it and look into a small pool at the bottom. The pool connects to an underground lake containing a species of prehistoric pupfish. Biologists believe that the pool may be connected underground to other pools of pupfish located hundreds of miles away. Supposedly, reptilian creatures also live in the Devil's Hole and have emerged now and again.—*Anonymous*

Caught in the Web of the Spider Gates Cemetery

A gated dirt road in Leicester, Massachusetts, is all that blocks the outside world from the eighth gate to hell. Strange ceremonies take place there in the dead of the night. Tragic deaths have occurred. And the devil himself has appeared.

This Quaker resting place is officially known as Friends Cemetery, and its imposing wrought-iron front gates with their spiderweb pattern have ensnared many adventure hunters. The most widely told story is that the Spider Gate is the eighth gate to hell, and that seven others are hidden somewhere nearby. Find them and walk through them in the right order, and you will immediately find yourself in the netherworld. Stories about satanic practices also exist, always linked to a raised square patch of earth marked by granite posts and called the Altar. The devil may be summoned with an incantation by placing a piece of alabaster in a forked tree on the cemetery grounds.

Earthly tragedy also abounds at Spider Gates. One can see a piece of string hanging from a tree near the entrance. This is the Hanging Tree, so called because a local boy is rumored to have hanged himself from it in the early 1980s, and the string is a remnant of this macabre incident. And stories surround a small cavelike outcropping of rocks on the outer edges of the cemetery, where, they say, a teenage girl was murdered, mutilated, and abandoned.

The group that maintains the cemetery, the trustees committee of the Worcester-Pleasant Street Friends Meeting, adamantly denies all these stories. The raised ground in the graveyard is no satanic altar, they say, but the site of the old Leicester Meeting House. No tragic deaths took place there either.

But many other horrors and unexplained occurrences take place at Spider Gates. There is a strip of land where grass refuses to grow. At times a mysterious white ooze seeps up from the ground. Strange roaring sounds are often heard coming from the forest that surrounds the cemetery. And some Worcester street gangs are said to use Spider Gates as part of their initiation rituals. New members must be tied to a tree in the cemetery and left overnight before they become full-fledged members of the gang.

How many of these rumors can we trust? And how much can we trust the denials of the cemetery's owners? Only time and further investigation will tell.

The Eighth Gate to Hell?

I investigated Spider Gates with a friend on November 17, 2001, a crisp, clear autumn morning. The cemetery is set back on its own private gated lane, Earle Street, about eight hundred feet from the main road, in the woods between the Worcester airport and the Leicester landfill. The graves range from the 1700s to March 2000. We thoroughly explored the cemetery for anything to substantiate its reputation as a magnet for unholy powers.

First, there is only one gate, not eight. Whether this gate, with its wrought-iron pattern truly is the eighth gate to hell, I can't say.

Immediately to the left upon entering is a large oak tree. Attached to a fork about fifteen feet up is a short length of thick weathered twine. I would speculate that this is the "hanging tree." There is no official record of a hanging here, so I would guess it is the twine that gave rise to the rumor. The twine does not seem bulky enough to facilitate a suicide, and I doubt it would have been left up there if such an event did indeed happen.

Some visitors report hearing a roaring from the woods. Others speak of leaves rustling when there is no wind, and still others claim to have heard voices. All I can say to this is that the cemetery is under the landing approach for the Worcester airport. Certainly there is the occasional roar, but from above.

I looked for the cave where the girl was said to have been killed. While I did not find any obvious caves, I did find a small overhang of rock on the southern slope behind the cemetery. Also, not far away, the old path of Earle Street crosses over a Shaker-style laid-stone culvert. The culvert was conceivably large enough to stuff a body into. But there is no official record of anyone being murdered in this area.

Is Spider Gates haunted? Is it a home of unholy powers, perhaps a gate of hell? My visit did not reveal anything to confirm this reputation. But perhaps the true test is a nighttime visit. And it has been noted that supernatural events tend to find those who aren't actually looking for them.–*Daniel V. Boudillion*

Demons Can Go to Hell at Spider Gates

Legend has it if you enter the clearing at night and attempt to walk back through the gates, you will be killed by some spirit. They say that a bunch of devil worshippers called up the wrong demon one night and were all killed. So now the demon protects the clearing and will kill anyone who enters it and tries to leave. I heard this is because the devil worshippers would sacrifice a person so the demon would be satisfied and go back to hell willingly.–*Nate*

Haunted Places, Ghostly Tales

*"I'm just a ghost in this house / I'm shadow upon these walls,
As quietly as a mouse / I haunt these halls."*

—**Allison Krauss,** *Ghost in This House*

There are many theories about ghosts and why they exist, if in fact they do exist. One popular thought is that ghosts are victims of untimely deaths, eternally trapped in a vortex between the here and now and the afterlife. Traditionally, it has been said that ghosts do not know they have passed on. They see us living in our plane of existence, yet cannot communicate with us. Think of the movie *Poltergeist.* Imagine looking out of a TV screen at a family going about their daily routine—seeing all but not being able to move out of a one-dimensional realm.

Some ghosts are said to endlessly repeat a single action or movement, as if they were caught in a tape loop. In this state they may be able to affect material objects, even communicate with humans. Humans are most receptive to communication when they are in a light trancelike state, as when falling asleep or just waking up, which is probably why most sightings occur during those times.

The legends of some spooks have become so familiar in certain places across the nation that the indigenous ghosts have been given names, such as Resurrection Mary and the Bell Witch. Other specters shun the notoriety of such famous apparitions and choose to make their presence known only to the owner of the house in which they dwell.

If you believe in ghosts or have seen one yourself, these stories may reinforce some of your beliefs. If you are a skeptic, you may dismiss these tales as the products of peoples' overactive imaginations. Either way, you may find yourself sleeping with the lights on tonight. So curl up, get settled in, and read on.

House Ghosts and Uninvited Guests

As a rule, we at *Weird U.S.* tend to take incredible stories with a grain of salt. A healthy dose of skepticism in such matters helps us to weed out the kooks who are just scared by their own shadows. Still, some cases are not so easily dismissed. Some stories have come to us from folks who we believe are being completely truthful and would have no apparent motive to fabricate a ghost story. The following tales are a culmination of letters we've received and correspondence via e-mail from people who wanted to share their own ghostly tales.

Harry Houdini's Haunted Hollywood Home

Jackie Post of Hoboken, New Jersey, sent us the picture at left, which she took at the abandoned Hollywood estate of world-renowned magician and escape artist the late Harry Houdini who died on Halloween 1926. Several ghostly images of peoples' faces seem to appear in the photo. See how many you can find. Here Jackie explains how the photo came to be:

"In June of 1993, I went out to Los Angeles to visit my best friend Barbara. We picked up a little tourist booklet entitled 'This is Hollywood—An Unusual Movieland Guide By Ken Schessler,' at a bookshop on the Sunset Strip.

"We hit the usual spots: where Marilyn died, her grave site, the Tate house where the Manson murders took place, where the Black Daliah's corpse was found—all good fun. On my ride back to the airport, I had one final request: to stop at the 'haunted' ruins of Harry Houdini's house. My ride reluctantly pulled over to an embankment below some old, crusty, stone ruins. I flew up a thirty-foot stone stairway surrounded by grottos and palm trees and overgrown foliage. There were rotting walkways, stone benches, and dead calm. Everywhere I turned, I felt like I just had to pop a shot. I had the film developed, and without thinking much of anything, I put the prints in a box.

"Two months later I had some friends over and showed them my vacation pictures. Someone looked at a photo and asked 'Who's that guy?' The negative has since been sent to Cal. State U. and is documented as an 'authentic paranormal phenomenon.' The negative has not been tampered with and is intact. I am happy to share this story with you guys. Maybe we don't have to wait for Halloween for Harry to come back after all.

"P.S.: In the mid-'90s the property was sold. All that was left standing was bulldozed, and a new house was constructed. I have heard that the new owners have since abandoned the property."

Harry H. Please Call Home

According to the Houdini Historical Center (www.houdinihistory.org) in Appleton, Wisconsin, "Houdini was known as a debunker of fake mediums and spiritualists. His interest began during his bereavement after the death of his mother, Cecilia Weiss. Because of his background as an illusionist, he recognized the techniques of mediums and became a crusader against these charlatans who bilked grieving families of their money. He frequently attended séances in disguise in order to expose the mediums.

"The Official Houdini Seance, held each year since the magician's death in 1926, originated from Houdini's efforts to expose fraudulent mediums. He claimed that if there were truly a way to contact the living after one's death, he would do so. He set up a code with his wife, Bess, who faithfully attended the annual séances and awaited his return for ten years, after which time she gave up. The séance, currently organized by Sidney H. Radner, is held each year in a location with a significant connection to Houdini's life."

Oxford House

When I was young, my church made an annual fall retreat to a place called Camp Quinipet on Shelter Island, New York, a little island between Long Island's two forks. Quinipet is a colony of old mansions bought by the Methodist Church for use by retreat groups, one of which, Oxford House, was believed to be haunted. When I was about seven, some teenagers told me the legend.

It was said that a rich family lived there back in the 1800s and had one child. One night the parents went out and left the kid with the babysitter, Mary Oxford. Late at night she suddenly heard the kid crying uncontrollably, and then . . . silence. Alarmed, she slowly climbed the stairs. When she got to the top, she discovered the child splattered all over the place. Before she could gasp, she saw the shadow of a man with a hatchet cast on the wall by the oil lamp. When the parents came home, they found the body and decapitated head of Mary Oxford hanging from an attic window.

A different source told me an alternate version in which there was a fire on that fateful night, and, trapped in the attic, Mary looked down and saw the devil, who offered to catch her if she would become his. They never said what her decision was, but . . .

One year when my dad and I went to look at the house, as heaven is my witness, there were hoofprints burned into the side porch, under the attic. There were three crescent-shaped prints leading up to the door. I know this sounds incredible, but I offer you this: You can take it from a twenty-four-year-old naval officer with a very good education and a pair of good eyes. I don't know what it was, and I'm open to other-than-supernatural explanations, but there you have it. Unfortunately, I can offer no photos of Oxford House, as it was torn down and carted off, every last piece of red-painted wood.—*A. M. Moir, Ensign, USNR*

He Sells His Soul to the Devil

General Jonathan Moulton was one of the wealthiest men in revolutionary-era New Hampshire. He was granted over eighty thousand acres in the Hampton area, where he built his house and fathered fifteen children. But neighbors whispered that to obtain his wealth Moulton had sold his soul to Satan.

They said the devil demanded that Moulton hang a boot in his fireplace each night. Satan would then fill it with gold. In exchange Satan would have Moulton's soul. Every night Moulton positioned a large riding boot in his chimney. Each morning he would find it filled to the top with gold pieces. But this was not enough for him— he cut out the bottom of the boot. At first the devil kept pouring gold, but then he realized he had been tricked and exacted his vengeance. He burned Moulton's house to the ground.

Worse things happened. When Moulton's wife died— some say under mysterious circumstances—he quickly married one of her friends. And he took the wedding ring from her body to do it. On their wedding night the new bride awoke in horror to the sight of Moulton's deceased wife removing the plundered jewelry from her finger.

Moulton House has long been referred to as the Haunted House. It was even written about by local poet John Greenleaf Whittier.

The Ghost Behind the Hidden Upstairs Door

From August 1982 until April 1995 I lived with my parents in an old farmhouse outside Arlington, Nebraska. When we moved in, the house was 110 years old, with a machine shed, a big barn, and garage about a hundred feet from the house.

Ever since the day we moved in, I remember being terrified to go upstairs alone. I swear I could just feel someone or something there. But my parents thought it was just my imagination. I knew it was more than that. Things would go missing from my parents' room, nowhere to be found, and of course I would get the blame for it. They'd always show up in the place where you had already looked like five hundred times. I would also hear unexplainable noises and feel presences. When my father died in the house when I was fourteen, it got worse. I always felt like I was being watched, and I even reached a point where I could not stay in the house by myself.

Ever since the day we moved in, I remember being terrified to go upstairs alone. I swear I could just feel someone or something there.

One day while cleaning, my mother and I decided to go ahead and open a hidden door in the upstairs hall to see what was in there. When we did, there was a cool rush of air. My chest got heavy, and I couldn't breathe too well. We got to looking, and there was a very old crib in there, along with wallpaper rolls, old toys, and some other stuff, but I was too scared to look any longer. It seemed like someone had lost their baby or something. I just had to get out of there. Even thinking about that house right now gives me the chills.

Then there was the hall closet. One day I unscrewed the hinges and peeked inside. There was an old rocking chair, some baskets, and really old newspapers. All of a sudden I felt like I was being watched. I turned around, but nobody was there. The heavy feeling didn't go away, so I went downstairs. Whatever it was stayed with me. I felt panicky and ran out the door to the barn to get one of the horses ready to go to a neighbor's house. As I was leaving, I glanced up to my bedroom window, and I swear it looked as if someone was turning away from the window and walking away. My mom was at work.

After that day, I could not sit anywhere in that house unless my back was against a wall. Maybe I was just paranoid . . . but maybe I wasn't!–*Tonja Baker*

Devil Baby of Hull House

In 1856 a prominent businessman named Charles Hull built a house in a fashionable Chicago neighborhood. The building has served as home for the Hull family, a temporary shelter for the less fortunate, and a university-run museum. But whatever its purpose, Hull House will always be best known for one of its smallest residents—an infant so monstrously deformed that it became known as the Devil Baby of Hull House.

A decade after Hull House was built, the neighborhood began to change considerably. As immigrants, factories, brothels, and tenement houses moved in, wealthy families moved out. In 1889 a social reformer named Jane Addams opened the house as a settlement house for women, the homeless, and recent immigrants. Addams provided education, food, and shelter for hundreds of people—work that would later earn her the 1931 Nobel Peace Prize.

In 1913 Jane Addams accepted a baby into the care of Hull House. This was not unusual, as unwed mothers and their children were frequent guests. Some versions of the story say the mother was an unwed immigrant, but most say the parents were married. Legend has it that while the devoutly Catholic wife was pregnant, her atheist husband tore down a religious picture his wife had put on their wall, saying he would rather have the devil in the house than any religious decorations. The child born from this couple was said to bear all the markings of the devil—pointed ears, cloven hooves, horns, scales, even a tail. Some sources say that this legend was the basis for Ira Levin's novel, *Rosemary's Baby*.

The couple begged Addams to take the child in, and she eventually agreed. But word of the Devil Baby quickly spread throughout the immigrant population of Chicago. Hull House became a local attraction and even drew tourists from several states away. Addams repeatedly denied the existence of such a child, frustrated at the spectacle-seeking crowds that hampered her charitable efforts. A sizable portion of Addams's autobiography is devoted to refuting the wild tales of a devil child.

Over the next fifty years people passing by Hull House continued to report seeing a frightening, devil-like face staring at them from the upstairs windows. Some said it was the Devil Baby itself, while others believed it was its ghost. In 1963 Hull House was purchased by the University of Illinois and opened to the public as a museum. Visitors occasionally claim they see the Devil Baby in the upstairs windows, and there have also been reports of strange mists and ghostly monklike figures on the staircase. Despite these stories, museum employees continue to deny that any ghostly activity has ever occurred there. –*James A. Willis*

The Blood Stays Inn

The Martha Washington Inn in Abingdon, Virginia, is more than just a ritzy hotel. It's the home of otherworldly presences. Guests at the hotel often hear the sound of violins from the upper floors. This is supposedly the ghost of a woman named Beth who lived at the hotel during the Civil War. A ghost horse also occasionally tramps around the grounds outside the hotel. Most famously, the hotel houses a bloodstain that cannot be removed. Whenever it is washed away, it mysteriously returns. Legend has it that this is the blood of a Confederate soldier who was sent out on a secret mission. Before he left, he wanted to say good-bye to his girlfriend, but as he was doing so, he was shot dead. The hotel now covers the stain with carpeting.

Spirit Still Hangs Around

The Old Gaol of York, Maine, was originally built in 1656, making it the oldest prison still standing in America. Despite its non-operational status, it seems that the gaol still holds one prisoner—the ghost of Patience Boston. This Native American was imprisoned here after killing the son of a local minister. She arrived in the jail pregnant and stayed for two years until her child was no longer dependent on her care. Then she was hanged. Her spirit, many say, is still hanging around today.

Anna Lumpkins's Ghost

My family and I moved to the small town of Utica in southern Indiana when I was in the fifth grade. Because everyone knows everyone in Utica, and it was quiet and safe, it seemed a good place for us. And this is where I lived when I met Anna Lumpkins.

Anna was an elderly woman who lived a little down the hill from me. She had a big white house that she lived in alone (except for her two dogs). On a few occasions Anna would invite me into her house and show me pictures of her husband, Bill, who had passed away sometime before her.

After a while Anna's health started to fail, and she couldn't remember things. Her family eventually put her in a nursing home, and she soon passed away. I was sad that she was gone, but when my dad said that we would be moving into her old house, I was overjoyed. I was fifteen years old at the time, and moving into Anna's house meant that I would have my own room.

A few months after moving in, I started to notice little things. The door that led to the basement was often standing open after it had been shut and locked. We could hear people walking up and down the staircase. Almost every time I came down the stairs, out of the corner of my eye I could see someone standing at the top of the staircase. At first I figured it was just a shadow, until my cousin Hollie noticed it.

It was right around this time that my younger sister, Amy, started to ask if she could sleep in my room. When I asked her why, she wouldn't tell me at first; then finally, after two weeks of this, she said that every night a man would come upstairs and stand at the foot of her bed, and he would watch her until she would fall asleep.

One day after school I came home to find the house empty. I was glad. I had been ill all day at school and wanted to just soak in a hot bath and take a nap. I went to

every door and window to make sure it was locked. I also locked the basement door. Once I was in the tub soaking, I began to drift off to sleep.

There was a knock at the bathroom door, and then I heard a woman say, "Mindi, honey, don't fall asleep in there! You'll drown! I want you to get out of there, okay?" I couldn't figure out who had knocked on the door. The only one with the key to the house was my mother, and the voice hadn't been hers. When I stepped out of the bathroom, the whole house was dead silent. I called out to my mother, but no one was in the house. I searched every floor. I checked all the doors, and they were still locked.

A lot more happened after that. I would have dreams about Anna, and she would sit in a rocking chair and watch me. I hope it was her way of saying she was keeping an eye on me. —*Mindi Weber*

The Spirit Music Never Stops

Many ghost hunters regard Bobby Mackey's Music World, in Wilder, Kentucky, as a truly haunted place. During the late nineteenth century, a satanic cult used a building on that site for many strange rituals, including human sacrifice. The perpetrators of the sacrifices were convicted and sent to their deaths, but not before they had vowed vengeance on the town.

A bar built on the same site saw both a shooting and a suicide. In the 1970s ownership changed hands, but the evil of this place continued—a series of murders occurred here.

Since the building became Bobby Mackey's, numerous sightings have been reported. Headless ghosts, strange sounds, and inexplicable lights have all been encountered.

Ethyl Work Is Never Done

Bradmar Tudor Manor is an elegant twenty-room mansion that sits on a quiet secluded road on the outskirts of Denver, Colorado. The home is haunted by the spirits of its former occupants, Ethyl and Hubert Work. After Ethyl Work passed away, the house fell into disrepair for many years. A local doctor bought it, restored it, and lived there with his family. Almost immediately they began experiencing inexplicable phenomena, which they chronicled in detail.

The lights go on and off by themselves, and often surge brightly or become dim with no explanation. Stories say that Ethyl enjoyed keeping all the lights off. Her ghost, they say, still fiddles with the lights because of this. Even the wiring was tampered with: During the restoration of the home, electricians experienced frequent setbacks when wires they had just laid were disturbed by people unknown.

Strange noises are also common. Bells go off without provocation, often in the dead of night. And doors, even those the family has specifically remembered locking, sometimes slam of their own volition.

Things at the manor seem to have a life of their own. Some items have been seen floating across rooms. One resident of the house once watched the piano briefly play by itself. Strange objects also sometimes appear—a set of grotesque statues that no one remembered purchasing was discovered in the attic of the home.

Ghost of Viola Haunts Theater

I used to work at the Lancaster Performing Arts Centre in the Antelope Valley in California. The theater, which opened in 1991, was so new you wouldn't expect it to have a ghost, but that's not the case. While the theater was under construction, several important people in the community were given a tour. An elderly lady named Viola lost her balance near the orchestra pit, which was still a huge, gaping hole, and went plummeting to the bottom. She was rushed to the hospital and died soon after. Viola is said to haunt the orchestra pit and the catwalks of the theater.

I have had a few personal experiences with Viola. I would come into the theater during the day and hear footsteps even though no one was there. Speakers that were not turned on would snap and crackle. Whenever I went to the galleries or the spot booth, I would always have the strangest feeling that I was being watched. Odd noises were everywhere.

Viola has never done anything malevolent, as the entire staff can verify. In fact, they are rather proud of their "resident spook," and whenever anything odd happens or something goes missing, people will shake their heads and say, "Well, there's Viola again!" *—Absinthe*

Curse of the Bell Witch

This story begins in 1804, when North Carolina planters John and Lucy Bell moved their family to Tennessee and settled in a log house near present-day Adams. Public records, church records, and eyewitness accounts tell of what occurred there in the Red River settlement.

One morning in 1817, John Bell was inspecting a cornfield when he encountered a strange-looking animal he took for a dog. He shot at it, and the creature vanished — but the incident marked the beginning of a reign of terror that would hold Bell's family in its grasp for years.

They began hearing raps on the walls, scratching on the floors, stones hitting the roof, and chains being pulled through the hallways. The children complained of rats gnawing at their bedposts and their bedcovers being slowly pulled away. If they resisted, they were slapped hard enough to get visible welts and handprints. The youngest daughter, twelve-year-old Betsy, became the prime target. Her hair was pulled, her face was slapped, and her body often bore bruises and claw marks. She fell into trances that culminated with her vomiting needles.

> **The incident marked the beginning of a reign of terror that would hold Bell's family in its grasp for years.**

The creature's malevolence increased. John Bell began experiencing choking episodes and sometimes complained of needles sticking him in the back. Drewry Bell's chair was kicked away when he sat to read, and John junior noticed unusual animals in the forest. The children began seeing a strange woman walking about the orchard each morning and, on one occasion, hanging lifeless from a tree. During the cold nights of winter, melancholy whispers filled the house, sometimes speaking in musical tones in reverse speech.

In early 1818 John Bell confided in his best friend, James Johnston, who agreed to spend the night. A deluge of disembodied voices disturbed him, and he sprang from his bed and exclaimed, "In the name of the Lord, who are you and why are you here?" He received no answer. The following morning Johnson told Bell it was "a spirit, just like in the Bible!" and said that clergymen should investigate.

Soon the farm became a haven for believers and skeptics alike. Some felt the events were staged for profit; others believed they were of supernatural origin. The entity soon began poking fun at preachers. It once imitated two preachers, reciting word-for-word two sermons that occurred simultaneously thirteen miles

No haunting in the American South resonates as strongly today as the one in rural Adams, Tennessee, where John Bell's farm once stood. This is one of the rare cases in which a ghost not only injured the residents of a haunted house but also caused one of them to die. Although the sensational events in the case took place in the early 1800s, they have not been forgotten — partly because the land where the Bell farm stood remains haunted to this day. This sinister tale involves spectral creatures, disembodied voices, poltergeists, and, of course, the infamous Bell Witch.

apart. Both preachers were present when this demonstration occurred, and each confirmed its correctness.

One asked the being about its origin, and it exclaimed, "I am Ol' Kate Batts's witch, here to torment Ol' John Bell to his grave and straight into hell!" Mrs. Batts was an eccentric woman who lived a mile from the Bells; she was often ridiculed about her spiteful disposition and was suspected of involvement in the occult. People began calling the entity Kate, a name to which it readily answered.

Four distinct characters emerged as Kate's "witch family," as she called them, brought new terror to the Bell home. "Blackdog" spoke in a raspy, feminine tone and left no question as to who was in charge. "Mathematics" and "Cypocryphy" spoke like young girls, and "Jerusalem" sounded like a little boy. The drunken witch family visited nightly, singing off-key, arguing with each other, and yelling obscenities at the Bells.

Kate developed a softer side for some people. She seemed fond of Lucy Bell, singing hymns and comforting her when she was sick. She spoke highly of both the Johnston family and a young bachelor named William Porter. Skeptics, on the other hand, were met with hostility. When Major General Andrew Jackson, who later became President, paid a visit to the Bell house, cries from deep in the forest spooked his horses and a feeble voice proclaimed, "You can go now, General. I will see you tonight." An invisible force slapped one of his entourage, kicked him in the posterior, and pulled him out the front door by his nose. Jackson later said, "I'd rather fight the British at New Orleans than deal with the Bell Witch."

John Bell's health declined further, to Kate's delight. One morning as he was out walking with his son, Kate tripped him and removed his shoes. As a whisper filled the air, saying, "Your place is in hell, Ol' John Bell," he experienced a violent seizure. Disembodied voices began reciting biblical passages and screaming the word "legion." He eventually made it home and took to his bed, never to leave again. He died on December 20, 1820.

After forcing Betsy Bell to call off her engagement to Joshua Gardner, Kate finally bade farewell to Lucy Bell and the children in late 1821. She returned to the family twice—once briefly in 1828, and then 107 years later when she visited Dr. Charles Bell, a Nashville physician.

The Red River area boasts much unexplained activity today. Strange voices have been heard, photographic anomalies are common, animals sometimes act strangely, and on cold nights strange "candles" can sometimes be seen dancing in the fog-laden fields and forests—just as they did in the days of John Bell, nearly two centuries ago.

—*Pat Fitzhugh*

Four distinct characters emerged as Katie's "witch family" brought new terror to the Bell house.

Cave of the Bell Witch

Near where the Bell Farm once stood, not far from the old family cemetery, on land that the Bell family once owned, lies a wide-mouthed cave. Many in Robertson County believe that this cave is the place to which the apparition that haunted the Bell family fled—so it is known as the Bell Witch Cave.

The cave is in the center of a large bluff that overlooks the river. It is accessible only through a fairly long tunnel that opens onto a large room. This in turn opens into another tunnel and an overhead passageway. There's another large room farther back, but from that point on, the tunnels become smaller, narrower, and much more dangerous.

The Bell Witch Cave became an attraction thanks to a man named Bill Eden, who owned the property for a number of years. Although he was mainly a farmer, Eden became a wealth of information about the place and added electrical light to the cave. Despite being pretty much undeveloped, the cave attracted hundreds of visitors every year. Bill always obliged by showing them around and telling stories of the witch and his own weird experiences at the place.

The main story goes that Betsy Bell and some of her friends were exploring the cave, using candles as a source of light. One of the boys came to a place where he had to get down on his belly and wriggle through.

When he got stuck, he twisted around trying to get free and dropped his candle. His friends could hear his cries for help but could not find him in the total blackness of the cave. Suddenly the boy heard the witch's voice coming out of the darkness behind him. "I'll get you out," Kate assured him, and sure enough, he was dragged through the muddy cave all the way back to the entrance and was left in a small pool of water.

But there were many other stories, some of which Bill Eden himself experienced. One time a group of fifteen people followed Eden down the treacherous path to the cave's entrance; then all at once the woman in charge of

the group abruptly sat down in the middle of the path. She claimed that a heavy weight, which felt like a ton of lead, was pressing her down to the ground and she couldn't get up. Several members of the group managed to get the lady to her feet and got her back up the hill to her car.

Bill Eden also tells of encounters of his own in the cave. "You can hear footsteps in there all the time," he told *Weird U.S.* "I saw one thing . . . it looked like a person with its back turned to you. Looked like it was built out of real white-looking heavy fog or snow, or something real solid white. You couldn't see through it. It wasn't touching the floor at all. It was just drifting . . . bouncing along."

On another occasion Eden was leading a man, his wife, and grown son on a tour of the cave when the woman looked up over some rock formations and began to scream. "Look at that woman!" she screamed. "She's not walking! She's floating through the air!"

The men looked to where she pointed, but none of them saw anything. The woman's knees buckled, and she fell to the floor of the cave, so they helped her up and started walking her toward the front of the cave. As they approached a limestone outcropping near the entrance, they heard loud and raspy breathing coming from the rock itself. Eden would later say that it was like the hard and labored breathing of a person, which became more labored until it was finally the struggling breath of someone dying.

In the early summer of 1977 several soldiers from Fort Campbell came over to visit the cave. Eden took the young men on a tour and ended up in the back room, where all of them sat around talking and Eden told his stories of the odd events on the farm. One of the men politely expressed some doubts about the validity of the story, and when they got up to leave, that soldier was unable to move. Eden assumed that he was joking, until he took a good look at the man. His face was drenched so badly with sweat that it looked like someone had poured a bucket of water over him. When Eden took hold of his hand to help him up, he could feel the man's hand was cold and clammy as if he were going into shock. The man claimed that he could feel strong arms wrapped around his chest, squeezing him tightly so he was unable to breathe. Eden and the others helped their friend to his feet. By the time they were ready to leave, the young man had completely recovered and was suffering no ill effects from his harrowing experience. But he never came back.

Bill Eden passed away, and the present-day owners of the Bell Witch Cave are Chris and Walter Kirby, who purchased the land in 1993. Walter is a tobacco farmer, and Chris manages the upkeep and summer tours of the cave. I first met Chris Kirby in the spring of 1997 on a visit to the cave. It's easy to reach the site by turning off Highway 41 right next to the Bell School. You can't miss the sign for the cave alongside the roadway. A right turn

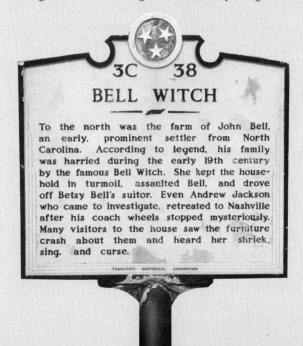

3C 38

BELL WITCH

To the north was the farm of John Bell, an early, prominent settler from North Carolina. According to legend, his family was harried during the early 19th century by the famous Bell Witch. She kept the household in turmoil, assaulted Bell, and drove off Betsy Bell's suitor. Even Andrew Jackson who came to investigate, retreated to Nashville after his coach wheels stopped mysteriously. Many visitors to the house saw the furniture crash about them and heard her shriek, sing, and curse.

TENNESSEE HISTORICAL COMMISSION

takes you onto a curving gravel road and up to a small brick house built by Bill Eden, with a sign that reads BELL CAVE PARKING.

Behind the house is the trail that leads down to the entrance of the cave, which is closed off by a locked, heavy steel gate. This gate stops unauthorized visitors from entering the cave, where curiosity-seekers attracted by unexplored caverns and ghost stories could put themselves in danger. The trespassing becomes so bad at certain times of year that the Kirbys have been forced to prosecute anyone caught inside the cave at night.

After taking us down to the cave, Chris told us about some of the strange incidents that have taken place there. She too has heard the raspy breathing sounds that Bill Eden heard near the entrance. And on one tour her dog suddenly reacted to something that no one else could see. The hair on the animal's back stood up, and she began showing her teeth and growling. Just when the dog began cowering against Chris's legs, the flashlight in her hand suddenly went out!

"I guessed that it was just the battery at first," she remembered, "but then a lady's video camera stopped working too. We were all standing there in the dark, and I'll tell you, I was ready to get out of there, and everyone else was too!"

Since that time, I have visited and have talked with the Kirbys often. I have walked the old Bell farm and stood next to John Bell's grave. I have been amazed at the beauty of the hollows and the woods of Robertson County, and I have thrilled to the thunder of the Red River after a summer rain. And I have walked into the gloom of the ominous Bell Witch Cave. That was enough to convince me that something strange is in the place. The darkness that lurks here is unlike anything else that I have ever encountered.—*Troy Taylor*

Rebecca Roams and Roams

She wanders around the elegant old lodge in Cloudcroft, New Mexico, nightly, her flaming-red curls tumbling over piercing sky-blue eyes as she glides through the hallways and staircases. The thing is, she's dead. Yes, the beautiful young woman that roams these halls is thought to be the flirtatious spirit of Rebecca, a chamber-maid who reputedly disappeared from the premises sometime in the 1920s. They claim her restless wraith has made her presence known here ever since.

The lodge was constructed in 1899 by the Alamogordo & Sacramento Mountain Railway. It was intended to be a resort for workers who were involved in the railway's search for timber. It was immediately successful—its breathtaking location in the lushly wooded Sacramento Mountains offered a welcome cool retreat to thousands of heat-punished Texans (New Mexico, Oklahoma, and Arizona were not yet states at this time). An article published in the *Albuquerque Journal-Democrat* near the completion of the lodge stated, "This beautiful building will be known as Cloudcroft Lodge and its interior will be furnished with a lavish hand, yet in keeping with the character of the place. Fireplaces, with wide, hungry mouths, will sparkle, crackle and dart forth welcome tongues of flame to hundreds of merry guests, who will find new pleasure in life during the long, sultry summer."

On June 13, 1909, a raging fire

blazed through the lodge, utterly destroying it. By 1911 the building had been rebuilt and reopened on its current site, and its appearance has remained virtually the same since then, a historic, timeless gem. Over the long, distinguished history of the lodge, it has played host to numerous famous folk, including Pancho Villa, Gilbert Roland, Judy Garland, and Clark Gable (in fact the last two carved their names into the wall of the lodge's tower, where they can still be seen to this day). But the most infamous guest of all is the specter of Rebecca.

Rebecca was said to be a gorgeous red-haired chambermaid who worked and lived at the lodge in the 1920s and '30s. She lived in the employees' rooms, which were located in the basement. She was by all accounts a very friendly and flirtatious young lady. There was a rumor that Rebecca moonlighted as a prostitute, although

no proof of this claim existed. Whatever the case, Rebecca's jealous lumberjack boyfriend caught her in the arms of another man at the lodge (possibly in room 101, the Governor's Suite) and became enraged. Shortly after, Rebecca disappeared, never to be seen again. Well, not alive, anyway. Because soon after her disappearance, people began to report having some very strange, even ghostly, experiences.

Over the years there have been many sightings of an auburn-haired apparition floating through the halls, a vision seen by both employees and guests alike. One guest heard scraping sounds in the hallway late one night and opened the door to see a red-haired woman in a '30s-style nightdress rearranging flowers in a vase on top of an antique chest. Another guest was shocked when he went to take a shower, only to find a "vaporous female" reclining in his bathtub. There have also been reports of objects such as watches, ashtrays, and silverware sliding across surfaces untouched, doors opening and closing on their own, lights and other appliances turning on and off by themselves, furniture moving inexplicably, and even faucets turning on and toilets flushing for no apparent reason.

But one of the strangest events happened one Halloween night when a man dressed in a tuxedo came into the lodge's dining room and sat alone at an intimate, two-chaired table. He ordered two dinners and two glasses of wine. Everyone in the room watched closely as the man ate his meal and carried on a conversation with someone who wasn't there. No one ever saw anyone sit with the man or even go near him, yet at the end of his meal, both wineglasses and both plates were empty.

Rebecca's manifestations are many. One of her favorite "hangouts" is the Red Dog Saloon—an Old West–style saloon with rough-hewn walls and southwest decorum, which is located in the basement, where the employees' showers used to be. This is a very active spot—lights go off and on untouched. Nineteen thirties–era poker chips have been mysteriously found in the middle of a floor that had been clear only minutes before. Lodge patrons have called the front desk to complain about the loud music coming from the saloon at times when the saloon was empty and wasn't even open. Reportedly, an apparition of a twirling woman has been seen on the dance floor, and a bartender claimed to have seen the reflection of a beautiful red-haired woman wearing a long dress in the mirror behind the bar—yet the woman wasn't there when the bartender turned around to look at her.

Another paranormal hot spot seems to be found in the tower, a three-story structure that stands tall above the lodge itself. The tower, which is kept locked, has two levels of small sitting rooms with windows that yield a panoramic view of the lush mountains. Some have reported feeling cold spots and a "presence" in the tower, and the third floor of the lodge, where the locked door leading to the tower can be found, apparently is also paranormally active. There is also said to be a lot of activity surrounding the Governor's Suite. Even when no one was in that room at the time,

the lodge staff has gotten calls from the Governor's Suite, and there was no one on the other end. Despite the fact that the lodge has a modern computerized phone system, the phone calls from room 101 persist. The light in the ceiling fan just outside the room is also said to turn off and on at will. A former housekeeper claimed that after making up a bed, she would come back only to find an indentation as if someone had just lain or sat there. She also said that guests' shoes would mysteriously move a few rooms down from where they were supposed to be. It would seem that Rebecca is a very fun-loving and mischievous spirit.

To this day employees and guests alike still report strange and mysterious encounters at the lodge. In fact, when we were there to shoot pictures, one of the clerks told us that the toilets in the ladies' room had been flushing by themselves earlier that day. Whether you believe in Rebecca or not, the lodge is still an amazing, unique place with a lot of fascinating history. There is even a fabulous restaurant called (what else?) Rebecca's.

The last time we were at the lodge, we photographed a carved wooden box set up on the beams in the dome of the tower. We asked someone about the box later, and nobody wanted to tell us anything or acknowledge it, as if it weren't up there. But it IS, and if you look at it, you'll see how deliberately it was placed there. Finally we talked to an employee who told us the story. It is a kind of a memorial to some of the lodge's most beloved patrons, who frequented the place for decades until they passed away. You could even say the mystery box, which has a glass front and is set up to "look" out the front window of the tower, is a "resting place." –*Shady*

Never-ending Curtain Call

Every respectable theater has a venerable ghost, and the National Theatre in Washington, DC, is no exception. John McCullough, a popular American actor of the 1800s, is said to roam its premises in the dark of night. No longer thirsting for an audience's applause, he has taken on the lonely role of ghostly custodian and spectral overseer, checking to be sure that all is in readiness for the next performance.

One legend has it that McCullough fell to arguing with another actor over an alluring actress in the touring company in which they were all then performing. In other versions of the story the two actors began fighting for a coveted stage role. Declamation led to shouting, and shouting led to worse: Shots rang out . . . and John McCullough fell dead beneath the stage. Reportedly, whether in order to avoid a public scandal or as a scheme to get rid of the incriminating evidence, McCullough's remains were consigned by lantern light to a grave dug hastily in the dingy, dirt-floored cellar under the stage.

The Washington Post, on Sunday, October 4, 1896, reported the eerie experience of Frederic Bond, a well-known comedy actor and close friend of John McCullough. Mr. Bond was sitting late one night at the prompter's table, which had been placed at the front of the stage for a rehearsal earlier that day. Going over his cues in the flickering gaslight, he heard a disturbing noise.

Looking into the wings and then out into the darkened auditorium, Bond saw no one. Thinking he had misheard, he returned to his memorization. But again he heard the frightening noise. Peering into the shadowy gloom once more, he wondered if the watchman or another actor had crossed behind the stage draperies or if someone was playing a trick on him.

Suddenly the hair rose on the back of Frederic Bond's neck as he felt the mysterious presence of some invisible being hovering near him. He was about to cry out when he saw a weird but human-looking apparition that glided across the stage, stopping a little distance in front of him. Recognizing the ghostly visage, Bond called out, "John McCullough! John!!" Whereupon the figure turned away from him, walked gravely toward the wings, and then suddenly disappeared.

—Donn B. Murphy, Ph.D. (Paraphrased with permission from the National Theatre website.)

> Shots rang out . . . and John McCullough fell dead beneath the stage.

Ghosts Along the Road

Perhaps it's apropos that in our fast moving, highly mobile nation, many of our most notable ghosts are seen hanging out at the side of the road, where it is said that they met their untimely end. These roadside apparitions have been witnessed by countless motorists over the course of several generations. Sometimes they'll even hitch a ride, only to disappear from their seat in the car right before the eyes of an incredulous driver. They seem to be content to just wander their own stretch of highway year in and year out, eternally reliving their final moments of life here on this earth.

The Legend of Resurrection Mary

Hundreds of people have seen her. Dozens have danced with her. A handful even claim they've kissed her. She walks along Archer Avenue on the outskirts of Chicago, Illinois, hitching rides. Sometimes she's seen lying in a heap along the border of a cemetery or dancing within its gates. Her name is Resurrection Mary, and her story has frightened, fascinated, and confounded local residents of Chicago and Justice, Illinois, for the past seventy years.

According to local lore, Mary was a girl of sixteen in 1934. She was fond of dancing and frequented the O'Henry Ballroom (now known as the Willow-brook) on Archer Avenue. One winter night Mary and her boyfriend got into an argument on the dance floor. Mary stormed out of the club and began walking home along a desolate stretch of Archer Avenue. As she passed Resurrection Cemetery, an automobile swerved out of control and struck poor Mary, killing her instantly. The driver left the scene and was never caught.

Mary's family and friends, who lived in a close-knit Polish community, mourned her passing and tried to move on. She was buried within the cemetery outside of which she had died. For five years she lay at rest, buried in the very gown and dancing shoes she had worn the night of her death.

Then, around 1939, people began reporting sightings of a young girl walking along Archer Avenue in the vicinity of Resurrection Cemetery late at night wearing a white ball gown. Several had stopped and offered the girl a ride, only to witness her disappear as they approached the gates of the graveyard.

As a young man in 1939, Jerry Palus frequently visited the O'Henry Ballroom. One night he approached a beautiful young girl with radiant blond hair who wore a flowing white gown. They danced all night, but Jerry was baffled that the girl hardly uttered a word. When the evening came to a close, Jerry offered to drive her home. As they drove up Archer Avenue, the girl wouldn't speak beyond instructing him where to drive. As they approached the gates of the cemetery, the girl suddenly said, "I must get out here. You cannot follow." He stopped the car, she got out, and, as she walked toward the gates, she disappeared.

The next day Jerry went to the address the girl had said was their final destination. The woman who answered the door told him that no one who matched the girl's description lived there. Jerry saw a picture hanging behind her on the wall and recognized it as the same girl whom he had courted the night before. When he pointed this out, the woman told him that the girl in the picture was her daughter, who had been dead for five years.

Since that night literally hundreds of people have seen Mary. She usually appears to men who are traveling alone, although women and groups have also sighted her. Most of the people who encounter Mary describe two telltale traits: She hardly speaks, and she is cold to the touch.

One of the most intriguing twists to the Mary tale occurred in 1977. A man driving by the cemetery saw a young girl who appeared to be trapped inside, clutching the bars of the cemetery's iron fence in fear. He traveled to the nearest police station and told them what he had seen.

Two of the iron bars of the fence were bent and twisted. Upon them were the very discernible handprints of a child; they appeared to be melted into the scorched metal.

When they all returned, there was no sign of the girl, but two of the iron bars of the fence were bent and twisted. Upon them were the very discernible handprints of a child; they appeared to be melted into the scorched metal.

Cemetery officials removed the bars and had them examined. It was determined that it would take an incredible amount of heat to twist them in that fashion. And although they reshaped and repainted the bars, they always return to a crooked state and continue to display a pattern resembling handprints.

The legend of Resurrection Mary has become nationally known. There are other states that boast tales remarkably reminiscent of that of Mary. New Jersey has two: The legend of Annie's Road in Totowa and the White Lady of Newark's Branch Brook Park. Pennsylvania also has two similar legends—Bristol, Pennsylvania, is home to Midnight Mary, and the White Lady of the Buckhorn haunts Altoona. Whether some of these stories are copycats of the other or they all sprang up from the same place in the collective unconscious, there seems to be something of an American fascination with this type of ghost legend.

Resurrection Mary still periodically appears in the area around Archer Avenue. Police constantly patrol the Resurrection Cemetery, but they have not managed to dissuade the flocks of curious who visit the area looking to dance a midnight dance with Mary.

Resurrection Mary Seen Out on the Town

It's said that in 1973 Mary showed up at least twice at a nightclub called Harlow's, on Cicero on the southwest. She danced alone in a faded white dress. Although bouncers checked the IDs of everyone who came through the door, no one ever saw the girl enter or leave. Later that same year an annoyed cab driver entered Chet's Melody Lounge, located across Archer from the gates to Resurrection Cemetery, looking for a fare that had skipped off without paying. The young blond woman that he reportedly picked up was nowhere to be seen. The manager explained that no blond woman had entered the bar.

During the middle 1970s, the number of Mary sightings began to increase. People from many different walks of life, from cab drivers to ministers, said they had picked her up and had given her rides. Resurrection Cemetery was undergoing some major renovations during this period, and perhaps this caused her restlessness.

On August 12, 1976, Cook County police officers investigated an emergency call about an apparent hit-and-run victim near the intersection of Seventy-sixth Street and Roberts Road. The officers found a young female motorist in tears at the scene, and they asked her where the body was that she had allegedly discovered beside the road. She pointed to a wet grass area, and the policemen could plainly see a depression in the grass that matched the shape of a human body. The girl said that just as the police car approached the scene, the body on the side of the road vanished!

In May 1978 a young couple was driving down Archer when a girl suddenly darted out into the road in front of their car. The driver swerved to avoid her but knew when he hit the brakes that it was too late. As the couple braced for the impact, the car passed right through the girl! She then turned and ran into Resurrection Cemetery, melting right past the bars in the gate. Another man was on his way to work in the early morning hours and spotted the body of a young girl lying directly in front of the cemetery gates. He stopped his truck and got out, quickly discovering that the woman was apparently badly injured, but still alive. He jumped into his truck and sped to the nearby police station, where he summoned an ambulance and then hurried back to the cemetery. When he came back, he found that the body was gone. However, the outline of her body was still visible on the dew-covered pavement.

On the last weekend in August 1980 Mary was seen by dozens of people, including the deacon of the Greek Church on Archer Avenue. Many of the witnesses contacted the Justice Police Department about their sightings. Squad cars were dispatched, and although the police could not explain the mass sightings of a young woman who was not present when they arrived, they did find the witnesses themselves. Many of them flagged down the officers to tell them what they had just seen.

On September 5 a young man was leaving a softball game and driving down Archer Avenue. As he passed the Red Barrel Restaurant, he spotted a young woman in a white dress standing on the side of the road. He stopped the car and offered her a ride, and she accepted, asking that he take her down Archer. He tried to draw her into conversation, even joking that she looked like Resurrection Mary, but she was not interested in talking. He tried several times to get her to stop for a drink, but she never replied. He was driving past the cemetery, never having stopped or even slowed down, when he looked over and saw that the girl was gone. She had simply vanished!

During the 1990s, reports of Mary slacked off, but they have never really stopped altogether. Many of the roadside encounters happened near a place called Chet's Melody Lounge, which is located across the road and a little south of the cemetery gates. Because it is open into the early morning hours, it often becomes the first place where late-night drivers look for the young girl who vanished before their eyes!

Another bizarre encounter took place in the summer of 1996 when the owner of the lounge, the late Chet Prusinski, was leaving the bar at around four in the morning. A man came running inside and told Chet that he needed to use the telephone. He excitedly explained that he had just run over a girl on Archer and now he couldn't find her body. Chet was skeptical about the man's story until a truck driver came in and confirmed the whole thing. He had also seen the girl but stated that she had vanished, "like a ghost." The police came to investigate, but, not surprisingly, they found no trace of her. –*Troy Taylor*

Emily's Bridge

Why do motorists passing over a quaint, quiet covered bridge in Stowe, Vermont, often report that their cars were shaken or scratched by unseen forces during their travels over it? Why do the town's residents avoid using this bridge after nightfall at all costs? Why does the ghost of a young woman haunt this bridge a hundred and fifty years after her death?

According to legend, the answers to all these questions lie in the fact that Emily's Bridge is the site of an infamous case of heartbreak, anger, and death. Even a century and a half later the woman who suffered here still haunts the spot of her demise.

The Gold Brook Bridge was erected in 1844 by John W. Smith as a service to the three villages of Stowe. Early in its history the bridge was simply used for safe passage for horse-drawn carriages traveling the country roads of the area. This all changed one night when the bridge was used not as passage, but as a meeting place between two forbidden lovers.

Emily, a resident of Stowe, was one of these young lovers. Her parents disapproved of her beau and ordered her never to see him again, which led to a major falling-out between Emily and her parents. After a vicious argument Emily decided to meet her man, elope with him, and run away forever.

When Emily got to the bridge, she waited patiently for her lover to whisk her away from her overbearing family. Unfortunately, he suffered from a case of cold feet and never arrived at their meeting spot. Emily reached a state of despair. She had severed ties with her family and left them, only to be jilted by the man for whom she had left.

Emily couldn't face her family again and couldn't handle the idea of not being with her lover. She tied a rope to the beam running down the middle of the covered bridge and hanged herself from it.

Since that day locals have said that strange supernatural occurrences take place at what is known unofficially as Emily's Bridge. A woman's voice is often heard, cars are shaken and scratched, and strange shadows, figures, and lights are often seen in the area.

Is the story of Emily's Bridge just a tall tale told among the locals of Stowe? Or does Emily's sad, lonely spirit still wait upon the bridge for the lover who's never going to arrive?

White Lady Lane

I read the story about Emily's Bridge in Vermont on your *Weird U.S.* website and got chills because there is a remarkably similar tale where I come from in North Dakota.

The story goes that there was a young girl, a local farmer's daughter, who got pregnant out of wedlock and, right after the baby was born, was forced into a shotgun wedding by her insanely religious parents, who made her marry this man that she didn't even love. On the day of the wedding the bride returned home after the ceremony only to find that the baby had died in its crib.

Distraught over the loss of the child and the thought of having to spend the rest of her life with a man she didn't want, she went to a lonely lane on the outskirts of town and hung herself from a bridge, still wearing the dress in which she'd been married. Many people claim that if you go to this bridge at night, you can still see the ghost of the grief-stricken girl hanging there in her white wedding dress. Some say that it is just the lights of Walhalla off in the distance, but I think that's just silly.

These days a trip to the bridge is a big part of many an evening's activities for me and my friends at North Dakota State University. The bridge is located down a narrow road off County 9. The road leads through the Tetrault Woods between the towns of Leroy and Walhalla. It's known locally as White Lady Lane, and I have to tell you, this trip is scary! The road gets smaller and smaller until it is barely wide enough for a car to get down. The woods are dark and eerie at night, and by the time you see the bridge, you are usually ready to turn back out of sheer terror.

The bridge is old and rickety-looking, and it would scare you at night even if there weren't a ghost there—but there is! Many people have seen the White Lady hanging there, including some of my friends who swear they saw her—wedding dress and all!

Though I have not yet seen her myself, I can tell you that there is a certain sensation I get every time I go to this place. It's an ominous and unsettling feeling, as though a heavy, melancholy presence is everywhere around me, yet nothing is there. This strange pall lifts as soon as we leave the spot. Others are not as lucky, though, and claim that the spirit, or whatever it is, has actually gotten into their cars with them when they've left or has followed them. They say the feeling of being followed always ends as soon as they turn off White Lady Lane.

Although the place scares the hell out of me, for some reason my friends and I continue to go there. Something, or someone, keeps drawing us back. Perhaps one day I'll see who or what it is.—*Mindy Reznik*

Children of the Tracks

I live in San Antonio, Texas, and just outside town sits a set of railroad tracks that have long been the focal point of a late-night local legend.

People come from far and wide to drive onto the tracks and place their cars in neutral in the dead of the night. After a short time the car will be miraculously pushed off the tracks without any explanation. Many years ago a gruesome event took place at the very crossing where this occurs, and people say that it is because of this that the phenomenon now exists.

A bus full of schoolchildren who were on their way home from a class outing had stalled on the tracks. It was late, and the kids had fallen asleep, so their teacher, a nun, was trying to restart the bus without waking them. Suddenly she heard a train coming. Its light was off, so she hadn't noticed it from a farther distance. She knew she didn't have time to wake the children to evacuate them, so she gave one last-ditch effort toward starting the bus. She failed.

The bus was ripped in half by the speeding train. The driver's area was thrown from the tracks, with only the nun inside. She was unhurt and witnessed the horror that followed. The train tore asunder the remaining section of the bus with the children entrusted to her care still inside. All of the kids died.

Weeks later, still wrought with immense grief, the nun decided to take her own life. She parked her car on the tracks where the accident had taken place. As a train approached in the distance, the nun began hearing the voices of children. The voices grew louder and louder, and then she felt her car begin to move. Just before the train struck, her car was pushed from the tracks and out of harm's way by some unseen force. She leaped out of the car in amazement, only to see children's handprints covering her vehicle. Her kids had returned and saved her.

Since that day the mysterious moving of cars has taken place. My friends and I have made more late-night trips out to these tracks than I can even count, always with similar results—our car gets pushed off the tracks. I've heard that if you sprinkle baby

powder on your car's bumper, after your car is pushed out of harm's way, you will see handprints appear on it, just as the nun did many years ago. (We've never tried this baby powder trick ourselves—it's not something we usually travel around with.)

The children who died on these tracks return time and again to make sure that no one suffers the same grisly fate they did at this very spot. Still, it's probably not the best idea to trust that these ghost kids will push your car from the tracks, especially if you happen to be staring down an oncoming locomotive!—*Travis T.*

Ghostly Images at the Haunted Railroad Trestle

About seven miles west of my home in Newnan, Georgia, there is a notorious haunted railroad trestle. The story is sad but true. A mother and her child were murdered on this railroad trestle in the 1930s. The police assumed at the time that the woman's lover and child's father was responsible. I never believed the story of the haunting until I experienced it myself.

One Friday night eighteen years ago, two friends and I visited the trestle; we pulled under it at ten p.m., turned off the car, and waited. Soon we could see the outline of a baby, a rope around its neck, on the trestle wall. One of my friends claims to have heard the anguished scream of a woman. I never heard that scream, but I believe my friend.

The murderer of the mother and child was never apprehended, for the liaison between the man and woman was well hidden. Perhaps he is still a free man today.—*Spookee*

She Walks Alone, at Night

Easton, Connecticut, is the home of Union Cemetery, regarded as an extremely haunted place. Many have reported supernatural encounters occurring within the borders of this burial ground. Most common are reports of the infamous White Lady.

The White Lady has been seen by hundreds of people; she is most often walking among the cemetery's graves in the dead of the night. She occasionally also walks the roads in the surrounding area. She wears a white nightgown and a bonnet.

Be wary while visiting the dead of Union Cemetery—they might decide to visit you right back.

It's Not Easy Being Green

Be alert while traveling through Burlington, Connecticut. Many travelers have encountered a strange green mist, which forms before their eyes into the shape of a beautiful woman. The apparition, fittingly enough, has come to be known as the Green Lady of Burlington. This gentle ghost will appear without warning, glow green for a while, smile at you, then just fade away.

Legends say that her grave is located in a small cemetery tucked away in the woods down a back road near her former home. In the Green Lady's time this area was rather remote, with not much around except a garbage dump. It is said that her life ended when she drowned in a nearby swamp. Some say that she glows green because she is covered in muck and slime as she rises from the swampy ground in which she is buried.

Curious locals still visit her grave in hopes of encountering the Green Lady. Those who believe that they have discovered her former residence report that they have seen a portrait of her through an open window. The picture hangs in a dimly lit room in the otherwise dark and spooky old house.

The Back-seat Mujer

In the little town of Heber, California, along one of the many picturesque canals, is a haunted highway. On certain nights a woman there will ask for a ride into town. If you do not stop, the woman—"the Mujer"—will hitch a ride from you nonetheless and appear in your back seat. The story goes that she was having an affair with a man in Calexico, about five miles from Heber, and she wanted to get home before her husband did. While speeding home, she came to a sharp curve, crashed through the guardrail, and drowned in the canal. Almost everyone in the little town knew the story. I know of several people that have given rides to the phantom, and they report that she is very beautiful and polite. Her widower left the Imperial Valley and moved to Bakersfield, California, and became a prominent citizen of that city.—*Thief of All*

Blank-faced Phantom

I live in Utah, not far from a town called Farmington. From time to time growing up, I would hear tales of a creature known as the Farmington Phantom, but I always brushed them off as the older kids just trying to spook us. In fact, by the time I had gotten a bit older, I had managed to forget about the old ghost story completely. I wish I had remembered it—then maybe I wouldn't have been so absolutely shocked by what I encountered for myself.

I was driving home and cut through the east side of Farmington on my way. My car, being little more than a hunk of rust on four wheels, broke down. I got out, cursing my luck, and went through my usual routine of banging on various things under the hood until it started up again.

As I leaned under the hood, I heard a very distinct noise—the galloping of a horse. It was rushing right toward me! I jumped up, nailed my head, and fell to the ground just in time to catch the fleeting image of a man on horseback rushing past me and disappearing.

Freakiest of all: The thing's face was blank. Needless to say, I shook off the hit to my noggin, fixed the car as fast as possible, and got the heck home.

Maybe I was just hearing and seeing things. Maybe I went a bit delusional after slamming my head. Or maybe, just maybe, the Farmington Phantom is more real than I ever believed.—*Tha Grimp*

Mountain Monk

A strange young man known as the Bulgarian Monk fascinated and terrified residents of Idaho in the late 1800s and still does so today.

He was actually no monk at all, but locals took to calling him that because of his odd choice in garb. He wore hooded burlap robes that he tied off at the waist.

Local youths told stories of the Bulgarian Monk and often dared each other to approach his cabin. He would routinely chase them away. During one of these incidents, he slipped off a rock and tumbled into the Salmon River, where he drowned. In death he didn't stop chasing the boys who had killed him. Around the Sawtooth Range stories are still told of the monk's ghost terrorizing adolescent boys.

The monk is most often seen at the Yankee Fork on the Salmon River, near the small town of Bayhorse.

Lights from Another World

In Ravenel, twenty miles south of Charleston, South Carolina, a quiet stretch of road was the site of a gruesome event and is still home to a legend relating to it.

Three teenage boys were struck and killed by a truck on the desolate street. They were buried in the cemetery of a nearby Baptist church.

Legend holds that if you go to the church at night, you can summon a strange phenomenon. Knock on the door three times and say, "Want to see the light?" Repeat these actions three times.

After the third time look back to the road. Supposedly, you will see three otherworldly lights. They appear in the exact locations where the boys died.

Pitcher Man

There are a lot of ghosts in this world, but not all of them know how to party.

In our years of researching local legends and strange folklore, we've come across a ton of specters, spirits, and spooks. Recently we've discovered our new favorite phantasm, the Pitcher Man of Rockport, Maine. He's a ghost who's really got a good head on his disembodied shoulders. Why scare people when you can get 'em drunk instead?

Rockport was once known as Goose River, named for the river that runs through it. During the Revolutionary War, Goose River really bore the brunt of British aggression. Redcoats tore through the town, destroying and stealing things on their way. Needless to say, local residents wound up having a real bitterness toward the imperial forces.

One of the angriest was William Richardson. In 1779 he had a bit of revenge against the hated Brits. It seems that a privateer, or glorified pirate, had commandeered a British ship and was fleeing a fleet of royal pursuers up the East Coast. He found his way up the Goose River, where he encountered Richardson, who saw his chance to spite the British by helping the man hide the ship from its pursuers. Richardson wanted to celebrate and threw a party for the entire town. The townspeople turned out in droves, happy to celebrate the small retribution their town helped to facilitate. Richardson himself was quite the wildman at this shindig and was

helping everyone else along in the debauchery as well. He made his way around the place with a pitcher in each hand, never letting anyone's glass get more than half empty.

Richardson left the party and wound up drunkenly stumbling through the town by himself. He made his way to the small bridge that crossed over the Goose River. While crossing it, he encountered three travelers on horseback. He immediately offered them drink and cheer, and told them that they all had something to celebrate in spiting the English.

What Richardson didn't realize was that these three men were British sympathizers, who had heard that the residents of Goose River were having a good laugh at the expense of the Brits. They struck Richardson down and trampled him with their horses, leaving him to die on that bridge.

Ever since those gruesome events of centuries ago, travelers have reported seeing a strange drunken man walking over the bridge. When they slow down to ask if he's all right, he thrusts a pitcher of beer into their car windows. Hundreds of people have reported being accosted by this unearthly booze-wielding being.

We can't help but hold a soft spot in our hearts for the so-called Pitcher Man. Too many ghosts are discontent about moving on, because they were jilted lovers, died young, or some other such melodramatic nonsense. The Pitcher Man is discontent because he just doesn't want the party to stop—and if there's any reason to refuse to move on, that's one we can wholeheartedly support!

Local Haunts

Sometimes whole areas appear to have an other-worldly aura surrounding them. Much like the settings of many H. P. Lovecraft novels, such places can be found in all corners of America. They may have been industrial villages whose productivity has faded or cemeteries that have been ravaged by time and the elements. Whatever it is, something about these locales has inspired tales of the supernatural. They all possess an unexplainable power over people that invites the local legends that have grown around them.

The Ghosts of Bachelor's Grove Cemetery

Located near the southwest suburb of Midlothian, Illinois, is the Rubio Woods Forest Preserve, an island of trees and shadows nestled in the urban sprawl of the Chicago area. On the edge of the forest is a small graveyard that many believe to be haunted. The cemetery is Bachelor's Grove, a ramshackle burial ground with more than one hundred documented reports of paranormal phenomena, from apparitions to glowing balls of light. The history of Bachelor's Grove is shadowy. Most historians agree that it opened in the early part of the 1800s. In August 1933 the famous Ripley's "Believe It or Not!" column featured a short piece stating that even though the cemetery had been set aside for bachelors, there were also women buried here. That statement was based on one of the misconceptions about the place—the name actually came from the Bachelor family who settled in the area.

According to the cemetery's last independent caretaker, Clarence Fulton, for many years Bachelor's Grove was like a park. People often came to fish and swim in the adjacent pond and picnic under the trees. Things have certainly changed since then! When the Midlothian Turnpike, in front of the cemetery, was closed in the 1960s, it became isolated and signs of vandalism and decay appeared. Gravestones were knocked over and destroyed, sprayed with paint, broken apart, and even stolen. Police reports later stated that markers from

Bachelor's Grove turned up in homes, yards, and other cemeteries. Worst of all, in 1964, 1975, and 1978, graves were opened and caskets removed. Bones were sometimes discovered strewn about the cemetery. Desecrated graves are still frequently found. Tombstones are scattered about, giving rise to legends that the stones move about under their own power. Many believe that these disturbances caused the hauntings. (Heavy stone grave markers were originally intended to keep the spirit of a dead person beneath the ground. Remove the weight, and the dead can roam the earth.) There is also evidence of occult rituals. Forest rangers and cemetery visitors have found inscriptions carved and painted on trees and grave markers, and the remains of chickens and other animals that were slaughtered and mutilated in a ritualistic fashion.

Just beyond the rear barrier of the cemetery is a small stagnant pond, visible to motorists on 143rd Street. One night in the late 1970s two Cook County forest rangers claimed they saw the apparition of a horse emerge from the water, pulling a plow steered by the ghost of an old man. The vision crossed the road in front of the rangers' vehicle, was framed for a moment in the glare of their headlights, and then vanished into the forest. Unbeknownst to them, this apparition was a part of an old local legend. In the 1870s a farmer plowing a nearby field was dragged into the pond when something startled his horse. Tangled in the reins and unable to free himself, he was pulled down into the murky water by the weight of the horse and the plow, and he drowned. The pond was also rumored to be a dumping spot for murder victims during the Prohibition era; their spirits haunt the water. The apparition of a two-headed man also has been seen in the area.

For decades people have sighted a phantom farmhouse along the deserted road leading to the

cemetery. Since the early 1960s the house has been seen in various locations along the road, in all weather conditions and even in the daylight hours. The descriptions rarely vary: It's described as an old two-story frame farmhouse, painted white, with wooden posts. A welcoming light burns in the window. As witnesses approach the building, the light gets smaller and smaller, until it finally just fades away. What makes these accounts credible is that many come from people who had no idea that the house shouldn't be there. Popular legend states that if you were to enter this house, you would never come back out again. But nobody has ever claimed to set foot on the front porch.

Author Dale Kaczmarek, who heads a paranormal

investigation group called the Ghost Research Society, has interviewed dozens of witnesses about the events at Bachelor's Grove, including the vanishing farmhouse. While all of their descriptions of the house are identical, the locations are not. Kaczmarek asked witnesses to place an X on the map of the area where they saw the house—and he now has a map of the Bachelor's Grove area with X's all over it!

Also along this road come reports of ghost lights, the most common being a red, beaconlike orb flying rapidly up and down. The light is so bright and moves so fast that it is impossible to tell what it really looks like. Most witnesses state that they have seen a "red streak" that is left in its wake. Others, like Jack Hermanski from Joliet, have reported balls of blue light in the woods and moving in and around the tombstones in the cemetery itself. Hermanski encountered the lights in the early 1970s and chased a number of them. All the lights managed to stay just out of his reach. However, a woman named Denise Travers did manage to catch up with one of the blue lights in December 1971. She claimed to have passed her hand completely through it but felt no heat or sensation.

In addition to these weird phenomena Bachelor's Grove Cemetery also has its share of ghosts and apparitions. The two most frequently reported figures are phantom monks and a young mother often called the Madonna of Bachelor's Grove. The monklike ghosts, clothed in the robes and cowls of a monastic order, have appeared in Bachelor's Grove and elsewhere in the Chicago area. But no records indicate that a monastery ever existed nearby. The story behind the Madonna of Bachelor's Grove—also called the White Lady and Mrs. Rogers—is more developed. Legend has it that she is buried next to the grave of her young child and wanders the cemetery under the full moon with an infant wrapped in her arms. She appears to walk aimlessly, completely unaware of the people who encounter her. There are lesser-known apparitions there, including a child who runs across the bridge, a glowing yellow man, and a black carriage that travels through the woods.

In August 1991 Ghost Research Society members mounted a full-fledged investigation of the cemetery. The group was armed with scientific equipment, cameras, tape recorders, and video cameras. They noted changes in electromagnetic readings and atmospheric fluctuations on their maps. After the maps were examined, a number of distinct areas were obviously out of the ordinary, so they photographed those areas using both standard and infrared film.

Nothing was seen at the time the photographs were taken, but the developed photographs told a different story. In a photo, left, taken by Mari Huff there appeared the semitransparent form of a woman who was seated on the remains of a tombstone. Was this one of the ghosts of Bachelor's Grove?

Whether Bachelor's Grove is haunted or not, it is still a burial ground and should be treated with respect. To protect it against the abuses of the past, the old road to the cemetery is now blocked with chains, concrete dividers, and a dented NO TRESPASSING sign. Thanks to the efforts of local preservation groups, it appears that the cemetery is not beyond restoration. And that's a good thing too: This is a piece of our haunted history that we cannot afford to lose.—*Troy Taylor*

The Ring of Children and the Banshee

The Texas county of Brazoria is home to more than a hundred eerie things. If you take County Road 218 past the Primitive Satanist Church (wait, it gets worse) and turn right just before Dead Man's Curve, you will find yourself on a small country road with no name. A swamp lines one side of the road, with alligators, snakes, and about a foot of fog covering the ground. To your right are Spanish oaks, with moss hanging down to the ground.

At the end of the road you have to get out and walk about another half mile. You can't see your feet due to the fog, and there are wild noises coming from the forest. You'll arrive at an abandoned seventeenth-century Gothic church, with gargoyles and the whole bit, built by Spanish missionaries who were later killed and eaten by the local Indian tribe. The tombstones in the cemetery in the back are scorched because the Indians tried to burn them to the ground.

Now for the scary part—two sets of ghosts haunt the area. The first is the Ring of Children. The story goes that during frontier days, a group of children were playing ring-around-the-rosy in the woods, when a black magic sect killed them. (Some say their descendants are still practicing at the Primitive Satanist Church up the road.) You can still see their ghosts if you and all your friends stand in the middle of the graveyard and play ring-around-the-rosy.

The second ghost, the Banshee, is rarely seen but often heard screaming in the woods. I have heard this—it sounds like a lady being strangled and screaming at the top of her lungs. My dad, who was with me, said it was a panther stalking us. Either way, we left immediately.—*Ran Scot*

Night Visitor

The most infamous story of South Carolina is about the Blue Lady of Hilton Head Island, who is said to haunt the island's original lighthouse. The story is that she waited for her lover to return from sea, but he never came home. She walked into the ocean and drowned herself and has haunted the island ever since.

Some fifteen years ago my brother and I hiked through the woods into Palmetto Dunes Plantation to find the lighthouse. Next to it was a small concrete temple with thousands of names written on its interior walls. The legend goes that if you etch your name, the Blue Lady will visit you. Needless to say my brother etched his name. That night we were visited.

It was terribly windy that night, and broken limbs knocked out power in Shipyard Plantation where we lived. My brother and I, home alone, went into the kitchen to find candles. Outside the window there was a blue glow and the figure of a woman. Our house was on stilts, so the window was at least twenty feet from the ground.

—Lindsay Coleman

Weeping Lady

Colfax, New Mexico, is one of the scariest places I've ever encountered. The only remnant of this once bustling town is a collapsed, dilapidated, evil-looking wooden church. It's falling apart, yet the steeple still stands atop it.

I went inside and found that the church had been a schoolhouse at one time—there were chalkboards on the walls and workshop books lying all over the ground. Any location like that is bound to have a story or two. Here's the one the locals tell.

A ten-year-old boy died around the turn of the century. A funeral was held at the church and schoolhouse. His mother couldn't bear the thought of her son's being dead. Each day she would become more and more hysterical. And each day she would go back to the church, where she would sit and cry. Simply put, she had given up on life.

This went on for weeks, until the woman simply died herself. She was buried next to her son in a nearby cemetery. People thought that would be the end of her mournful madness. They didn't realize how wrong they were. Every Sunday night her ghost would appear sitting in the back pews of the church. She would weep uncontrollably and make loud, sorrowful noises. Everyone in the area came to know this ghost as the Weeping Lady of Colfax.

Frightened families soon moved away. Even those who didn't know the story and who just happened upon the town were scared away. *—Letter via e-mail*

Grey Man

Before every major hurricane in the past century, people on South Carolina's Pawley's Island have reported encounters with the infamous Grey Man. He warns people of the impending danger and urges them to leave the island. If they heed his warnings, their homes survive unscathed. If they ignore him and stay on the island to weather the storm, great damage is inflicted upon them.

According to legend, the Grey Man is a former resident of the area who suffered an untimely death. He had been overseas for months and upon his return did not want to waste time before reuniting with his fiancée. So he took a shortcut through some marshland, where he rode his horse into a patch of quicksand and met his end.

A few days later, as the bereaved fiancée walked along the beach, a figure appeared before her. She recognized her fiancé and ran toward him, but instead of a happy reunion, the figure gave her a stern warning to leave the island at once to avoid grave danger. She and her family did so, and they were spared a raging hurricane.

Since that first warning so many decades ago, the Grey Man has continued to patrol Pawley's Island, warning the unsuspecting whenever danger approaches.

Misdeeds at the Bennington Triangle

In the late 1800s a stagecoach traveling along what is now Route 9 near Glastenbury, Vermont, encountered a strange creature. The occupants described a huge apelike monster that attacked and overturned the vehicle. This was the first reported incident in an area that would come to be known as the Bennington Triangle.

Glastenbury is some fifteen miles northeast of Bennington near Fayville, at the base of Glastenbury Mountain. Despite its seclusion and brutal winters, Glastenbury was a thriving town of nearly two hundred and fifty residents in the 1880s, with a dance hall, a casino, two schoolhouses, and a mill. But it wasn't to last. A flu epidemic and the promise of more fertile land elsewhere prompted an exodus that left Glastenbury's population at seven by 1930.

Today Glastenbury stands in 27,341 acres of wilderness with a population of nine, all members of the same family. Towering 3748 feet above the town is Glastenbury Mountain—one of Vermont's highest peaks—which local Indians considered cursed because the four winds converged on the peak. They refused to live near it and rarely ventured there, except to bury their dead. Throughout the years residents of Fayville and Glastenbury have told stories of mysterious lights and unusual sounds from the mountaintop, but these tales pale next to those of the Glastenbury Monster and mysterious disappearances on the mountain.

On November 12, 1945, seventy-five-year-old Middie Rivers, an experienced local outdoorsman, guided a party of hunters onto Glastenbury Mountain. While returning to camp, Rivers got ahead of the others and vanished. Police and volunteers launched an unsuccessful search for the hunter. The only clue was a single bullet found by a stream; searchers guessed it fell out of his belt when Rivers stopped for a drink of water.

On December 1, 1946, an eighteen-year-old Bennington College coed disappeared without a trace. Paula Welden, an avid hiker who was familiar with the area, decided to go for a day hike on Glastenbury. She got a ride to the trailhead, and several witnesses confirmed seeing her on the trail. When she failed to return to school, over a thousand volunteers scoured the area. Despite a $5000 reward and help from the FBI, Paula Welden was never seen again.

Three years to the day after Paula Welden's disappearance, James Tetford vanished from a bus bound for Bennington. He boarded it in St. Albans, Vermont, and although passengers confirmed his presence on the bus at the stop before Bennington, he was not on it when it reached that town. Neither the driver nor the passengers had any idea what happened to him.

On October 12, 1950, eight-year-old Paul Jepson became the next victim of the Bennington Triangle. His parents were caretakers of a local dump. His mother left Paul sitting in her truck unattended for a few minutes, only to find him missing when she returned. He had disappeared without a trace, never to be seen again. Bloodhounds followed his scent to a nearby road, then lost it.

Three weeks later Freida Langer was hiking on Glastenbury with her cousin Herbert Elsner when she fell into a stream. She told her cousin to wait while she ran a short distance back to their campsite to change her clothes. When she didn't return, Elsner went back to camp and discovered that Freida had never arrived there. Search teams made five attempts over the next week to find her, but came up with nothing. On November 11 and 12 the search party was three hundred members strong, consisting of national guardsmen, police, firemen, and other volunteers. But Langer's body did not turn up until the next spring. Badly mangled, it was found in an open area that had been searched repeatedly the previous fall.

The cause of death could not be determined.

Many people have tried to explain the strange disappearances in the Glastenbury area. Some say they were the victims of the Glastenbury Monster, the same creature that overturned the stagecoach many years earlier. Others believe the dead were victims of a mountain lion, although they are thought to be extinct in the area. Another theory is that a serial killer was responsible, though the only discernible pattern was that all disappearances occurred in either the month of October, November, or December.

James Crosier, a local outdoorsman who has roamed the Glastenbury wilderness his entire life, said, "Glastenbury is simply a wild and mysterious place. It's a place that wants to hold on to its privacy. It doesn't want to reveal its history. The ghost stories that come out are a reflection of this." That might be so—or perhaps the local Indians knew something we don't know.—*Brian Sniatkowski*

Coal Miners' Widow

In the 1930s Mamie Thurman was a local "black widow" here in Logan, West Virginia, in the southeastern part of the state. She married men for their money, and then they died under unusual circumstances. She and her husbands are buried in the local Boy Scout camp, which is named after her. The six husbands have a basic headstone, but she is buried under an obelisk. She was found dead—with eighteen bullet wounds and multiple stab wounds, practically decapitated by a deep cut to her throat—on a mountain known only for its coal mine, Holden 22. One theory is that she was killed by relatives of the men to whom she had been married, but it was more likely because she knew too much of the crime and corruption in Logan County and was in a position to blackmail influential members of a local swingers' club. Simply to close the case, her murder was pinned on a local black man who was not connected with Mamie at all.

People claim to see her ghost in the old coal company building on Holden 22, which is now long abandoned. The mountain has the dubious distinction of also being the site of a large coal-mine cave-in as well as the location of many lights seen in the woods at night. *.–PGJ*

A Very Creepy Place

There is an old abandoned homestead not far from Nemo, South Dakota, called the Dolquist place. When I was living out there, I heard many stories about this place. Back then a cabin and barn, both made of logs, were still there, as well as a few plank outbuildings. These are mostly gone now, but some of the ruins are still visible, along with old vehicles and equipment that sit on the hillside. The first thing one notices upon arriving there is that no matter how nice the day, it suddenly feels gloomy. There is a noticeable feeling of being watched from the trees on the hill.

Allegedly there are a few bodies buried at the place, remnants of the gold days, when an unsavory bunch living there would invite unsuspecting miners out to the ranch, torture them into telling where their gold was hidden, and rob them. They were killed and buried up on the hill somewhere. The other grim story of that old ranch is that one of the Dolquist family badly burned himself on the hip and was bedridden in a side room addition to the cabin. Gangrene developed and slowly killed him over the next six months. After his death the stench of the gangrene was so bad a team of horses dragged the addition to a caved-in root cellar, where it was burned.

In 1993 we attempted to verify this last part of the story by doing a little digging in the spot indicated to me to be where the building was burned. Our first shovelful of earth revealed charred wood and scraps of partially burned tarpaper roofing. Good enough for me—I'm no archaeologist, but I'm no dummy either.—*Jeepster*

Voices of the Dead

The settlement of Bara-Hack once existed in the woods outside what is now Pomfret, Connecticut. Founded by two Welsh families, the colony thrived for over a century until dying out in 1890. Now all that remains are stone foundations and an unkempt cemetery—as well as the voices of the dead. Visitors to the site often report hearing faint sounds, including that of laughing and singing. Others have seen apparitions in the area of the graveyard.

Bay City Specters

Bay City, Michigan, is said to have dozens of ghosts within its boundaries. Many dwell in Hell's Half Mile, a section of town that once housed close to a hundred and fifty bars.

One murder victim who haunts the Campbell house has a literary connection. Some believe that Joe Fournier was the basis of the character Paul Bunyan.

Old City Hall, now a restaurant, is home to a few bygone spirits. Some of them linger around the two jail cells that still remain in the basement. Others inhabit the restaurant proper. Workers often find chunks of coal on the ground and blame it on the specters.

Desolate Ruins

Foster, Rhode Island, was officially recognized as haunted in the state's 1885 census. More than a century later people still explore the ruins of this dreary factory town hoping to encounter spooks and specters.

The haunting of Foster began when a factory watchman named Peleg Walker was found hanging from the town's bell tower. After his burial in the local cemetery the bell was still heard ringing and people witnessed Peleg's ghost cavorting through the streets. The town was abandoned, and his ghost was listed as the official cause.

While largely destroyed and forgotten, some ruins of Foster can still be seen in the woods.

Cemetery Safari

What's on Your Tombstone?

Every tombstone tells a story, and each graveyard that we may whistle past offers reminders of life's triumphs and tragedies to anyone who takes the time to read the words inscribed there. Some cemeteries are spooked with legends of hauntings or curses, while others are of interest simply for their offbeat grave markers. Whichever the case, the way people are remembered after death is often a very revealing look at how they spent their time here on earth—or would have liked to. There are thousands of famous people buried in memorable monuments throughout our nation. But those folks have had their time in the sun. In this chapter we're placing the spotlight on those dearly departed who waited until after death for their turn to shine.

Memory Hill Cemetery

The cemetery in Milledgeville, Georgia, might just qualify as the weirdest graveyard in the whole nation. This twenty-acre resting place, known as Memory Hill, has three odd legends associated with it.

The Fish Family *mausoleum.*

Was Dixie Haygood Waybad?

Memory Hill is the final resting place of a woman who was known as dangerous and odd in life, and who continues to spread this reputation in death.

Dixie Haygood was a Milledgeville resident born just before the Civil War. Her legend quickly spread, as she was reported to be a witch with supernatural powers. She was known to go into violent, uncontrollable rages. She could lift up heavy wooden tables with full-grown men sitting on them. Local residents both respected and feared the strange, powerful young woman. The *Macon Telegraph* described her strange powers this way:

"It is said that Dixie Jarratt Haygood, whose stage name was Annie Abbott, had a strange 'power.' She could lift 4 men on a chair by simply touching the chair. She could stand upon one foot and resist the united efforts of four strong men to move her. She could lift men into mid-air by placing her open hands upon their heads. She is believed to have performed for the Prince of Wales, Queen Victoria, the Czar of Russia, and other royalty of Europe."

According to her obituary in the *Union Recorder,* "Mrs.

Photo shows *three men trying, unsuccessfully, to force a billiard cue down to the ground, while Dixie Haygood is able to prevent them from doing it by the mere touch of her hand.*

Haygood, also known as the Little Georgia Magnet, achieved a reputation as a spiritualist which not only made her well known in this country, but in many of the European nations. She appeared before the crown heads of Europe where she demonstrated her supernatural powers."

Just before her death Dixie Haygood reportedly placed a curse upon her own gravesite. She proclaimed that anyone who stood between the grave and the sun would be cursed forever. This legend seems to have unfairly affected the peace of the family buried next to her, the Yates family.

Each year, just before Christmas, a large hole inexplicably opens up just next to the Yates plots and swallows up a chunk of land. In some years the depression has actually consumed some of the Yates family's tombstones. Each year the hole is filled in—sometimes even with cement—and each year the same thing happens again. Stories say that this is the effect of the vindictiveness of Dixie Haygood and is her effort to prove her powers still work. Others claim that Dixie is so frightful that the Yates family is striving to escape being buried next to such an evil being.

Echoes of the Fish Family Mausoleum

In the last quarter of the nineteenth century a typhoid epidemic swept through Georgia. Many Milledgeville residents buried their loved ones at Memory Hill. One resident, William Fish, found himself depressed and lonely after burying his wife and child. Unable to cope with his grief, he entered the gates of Memory Hill one night, went into the small crypt that held the remains of his family, and blew his head off in a desperate bid to reunite his shattered family. It's said that this act not only reunited the family but set their spirits into a state of extreme restlessness. Legend has it that if one knocks on the door of the Fish mausoleum, a faint but distinct knock answers from the inside.

The Screaming Devil Faces of Memory Hill

One tombstone in Memory Hill features a tall spire surrounded by an iron fence. This fence is decorated with hundreds of small devilish faces. No one is sure who sculpted these faces or why they are there. On Halloween, they say, these faces let out bloodcurdling, high-pitched screams. People often visit the fence-demon grave in the dead of night around Halloween to hear the strange sounds for themselves.

The Legend of Midnight Mary

In downtown New Haven, Connecticut, in the vast Evergreen Cemetery, the massive headstone of Mary E. Hart carries a foreboding message:

AT HIGH NOON / JUST FROM, AND ABOUT TO RENEW HER DAILY WORK, IN HER FULL STRENGTH OF BODY AND MIND / MARY E. HART / HAVING FALLEN PROSTRATE / REMAINED UNCONSCIOUS, UNTIL SHE DIED AT MIDNIGHT, OCTOBER 15, 1872 / BORN DECEMBER 16, 1824

Then, in larger letters:

THE PEOPLE SHALL BE TROUBLED AT MIDNIGHT AND PASS AWAY

For generations the grave has been known as the final resting place of Midnight Mary. Though no one knows exactly who Mary Hart was, how she died, or why this mysterious marker was erected over her grave, locals tell stories of her and warn of the dangers of trifling with her grave.

Some say that Midnight Mary was a witch and the inscription is a curse against the people of New Haven who persecuted her in life. It is said that those who visit her grave late at night will be struck down dead at the stroke of midnight.

Stories tell of brave souls who have challenged this curse and entered the cemetery just before midnight to stand at Mary's grave. In the morning they were found dead—some apparently of fright, others impaled on the wrought-iron spikes of the fence that surrounds the graveyard.

Another legend says that Mary's stone is actually a warning to others to avoid the same horrible fate that she suffered. According to the tale, Mary had fallen unconscious and was presumed dead. She was then hastily buried. That same evening one of her relatives had a terrible nightmare in which she saw poor Mary writhing in agony and screaming for help in the dark. The next morning she demanded that Mary's grave be exhumed. When the coffin was dug up and opened, all present were horrified at what they saw. The lining of the casket was torn to shreds, and Mary's nails were bloody and ripped away from her fingertips. She had been buried alive and had died an excruciating death, struggling to free herself from her underground tomb.

Death Didn't Do Them Part

Love knows no bounds. For necrophiliacs this is particularly true. And for one Key West, Florida, necrophiliac there was no boundary that he couldn't overcome with a little ingenuity, a length of wire, and some wax.

At the beginning of the twentieth century the eccentric Count Carl van Cosel was living in a lavish castle in Weimar, Germany, with his wife and children. The count fancied himself an inventor and claimed to hold nine college degrees, but his eccentricities overwhelmed him. He began to dream of a deceased relative who was showing him the image of a woman he was supposed to marry. In 1926 van Cosel moved his family to a small town in Florida but left them and moved by himself to Key West, where he told his neighbors he was a former submarine captain. He worked as an X-ray technician, and one of his patients turned out to be the girl of his dreams—literally.

Elena Milagro Hoyos Mesa, a twenty-year-old Cuban immigrant suffering from tuberculosis, came to van Cosel for her X rays. He marveled at her resemblance to his dream girl and dedicated all of his time and effort to curing her. He also propositioned her, but since van Cosel was older than her own grandfather, Elena passed on the chance to date him.

When Elena died soon after, the count contacted her family and gained permission to place her above ground in a mausoleum. He outfitted her oversized coffin with a formaldehyde-spraying device to preserve her body and hooked up a telephone so they could have conversations.

In 1933 van Cosel took a wingless airplane he had built (basically, a tube on wheels) to Elena's tomb to take her body home with him. When he opened her coffin, he discovered to his horror that his attempts to preserve her body had failed. Her bones were in a pile, along with some decayed flesh and putrid green liquid. But Carl van Cosel was no quitter! He strung her bones together with wire and began using wax to reconstruct the young girl's body. Using hair he had collected during Elena's radiation treatments, he made a wig for her remains. He inserted glass eyes into her skull, placed her in a wedding gown, and laid her on a bed, where she remained as the count's companion for seven years.

Van Cosel's original plan was to fly Elena's corpse into the sky in the wingless airplane, where radiation from the sun would bring her back to life. Instead, he spent most of his time loudly playing an organ and disturbing his neighbors. Rumors spread about his bizarre nature and reached Elena's family. When her sister confronted the count, he calmly showed her Elena's reconstructed and defiled body. She demanded that he return Elena to her tomb, and when he refused, she had him prosecuted.

The count was imprisoned for a short time, and Elena Milagro Hoyos Mesa was buried in a secret location in the Key West Cemetery. When he was released, van Cosel returned to a hermit's life for twenty years. But when his neighbors found him dead on the floor of his shack in 1952, they discovered he was not completely alone. Next to him was a plaster image of Elena, his companion for more than two decades.

End of the World and the Crying Lady

In the suburbs around Williamsport, Pennsylvania, are two places of great interest. One is a road called the End of the World that appears to be the edge of the world when you drive along it in the middle of the night. It's a great place to catch the skyline of Williamsport.

Five miles from that is Wildwood Cemetery. The cemetery has a good side and a bad side. The good side is supposed to be filled with fairies on a clear night. The bad side includes a hill at the top of which is a banshee who sings sorrowful songs. Also on the bad side are many small mausoleums. Inside several of them you can hear knocking or voices, as if the entombed are having a conversation. From the road you can see a statue called Crying Lady that literally cries and changes position on her pedestal. The night I saw her, she had her arms open as if waiting for a child to hug her. –*Nicolle L. Brandle*

Horseback Horrors of Mililani Cemetery

In the Mililani Cemetery on Oahu, Hawaii, stands the statue of a man on horseback—but it doesn't always stand still. It is said that if you reverse your car around this statue three times at midnight, then stop before it with your high beams on, the statue moves and even dances. But beware: The sinister statue's stare is said to paralyze you and stall your car. If you're lucky enough to get your car started again, you should get the hell out of there. If you don't, the statue will actually come after you!

Moonshine Church

There is a legend about Fort Indian Town Gap, an army base in Pennsylvania near Harrisburg and Hershey. Inside the base is Moonshine Church. People have told me that if you look inside the windows, you can see ghosts of soldiers walking around. Across the road is a graveyard where the notorious Blue-Eyed Six are buried. The Blue-Eyed Six were put on trial and hanged for drowning a man in the Susquehanna River for his $1000 life insurance. They were buried in the church's graveyard. Sometimes you can see their eyes roaming in the graveyard or alongside the road. A warning though—never turn your car off when you arrive there; it may not start up again!–*James*

The Haunting Melody of Clifford Griffin

Perched on a mountain ridge above Silver Plume, Colorado, is a strange, sad memorial. The imposing obelisk is the rarely seen but often talked about grave of one Clifford Griffin.

Griffin was a man who discovered rich deposits of silver and gold in the Silver Plume area and began mining them in the early 1870s. Despite his wealth from these ventures, he was forever depressed due to the death of his fiancée the night before they were to be wed years earlier.

Griffin became known for playing his violin outside his remote cabin high atop the mountain at the end of each day. Locals would gather below and listen to the sad tunes. Every time he played, they would applaud him.

One evening in 1887, after the applause died down, a shot rang out. The miners rushed to his home and found Griffin dead in a grave he had dug for himself. He left a note behind saying that he wished to be left in the grave, and that was why he had shot himself standing over it. Shortly thereafter the miners erected the memorial over this sad man's final resting spot.

It is said that on still nights bittersweet strains of violin melodies can sometimes still be heard, echoing faintly through the mountains above Silver Plume. A haunting reminder that a man can find wealth, but still not gain happiness.

A KIND HEARTED MAN
SPREADING GOD'S WORD
IN A BIG WAY!
AN INSPIRATION AND A
SOURCE OF ENCOURAGE-
MENT FOR US ALL.
PHIL. 4:13

WORLD
RECORD
HOLDERS

A BIG MAN
WITH A BIG HEART.
LOVED AROUND THE
WORLD. WITH A
LEGEND AS BIG AS
THE MOUNTAINS
AROUND HIM.

BENNY
727

BILLY
747

McCRARY

THE WORLD'S LARGEST TWINS

The Titanic Twins' Tombstone

When twin brothers Billy and Benny McCrary of Hendersonville, North Carolina, suffered a childhood bout of measles, something weird happened. Their pituitary glands went haywire, and they began gaining weight at an extraordinary rate—about one hundred pounds a year. They finally leveled off at a massive seven hundred fifty to eight hundred pounds.

Their immense stature led them into the public eye—at first as linemen on their high school football team and then as entertainers in Las Vegas, where they performed stunts on miniature motorbikes. They even did a stint as professional wrestlers. And they were listed in *Guinness World Records* as the world's largest twins.

Sadly, a 1979 motorbike accident at Niagara Falls seriously injured Billy, who later died of complications. Benny erected a huge gravestone for his brother and left room in

the plot for himself. At more than thirteen feet wide, the three-ton memorial is reportedly the largest granite gravestone in the world. It even sports engravings of a pair of twin motorbikes. In March 2001 Benny died of heart failure at the age of fifty-four and joined his brother.

After *Weird U.S.* field scouts Chris Musto and Kim Childrey visited the graveyard, they met a bartender who said he had seen the twins perform at a local car dealership when he was a kid. "It was advertised for weeks that the twins would jump over two school buses on motorcycles," said Chris. "Sure enough, when the day came, the twins set up two toy school buses and easily cleared them on their bikes."

The grave, proudly proclaiming the pair as the World's Largest Twins, stands in the Crab Creek Cemetery off Kanuga Road, eight miles west of Hendersonville.

An Unfinished Mausoleum

John McMillan was one of the wealthiest men in Washington State during the late 1800s. He owned the biggest lime-producing operation west of the Mississippi, in Roche Harbor, as well as most of the buildings in the town. McMillan left many marks on the area, but the most obvious and the most intriguing is his family's unfinished mausoleum, which sits in the woods a mile outside town.

The mausoleum is ripe with Masonic imagery. Its pillars, unfinished columns, and arrangements of stairs are all symbols related to the ancient order of Freemasonry. A brochure explaining these strange inscriptions is available at the nearby Hotel de Haro.

No one is really sure why the burial site was never finished. The grand-iose structure was slated to include a bronze roof and to be surrounded by lush landscaping, but was instead inexplicably abandoned.

Graceland Cemetery

Visiting the Graceland Cemetery on North Clark Street in Chicago, Illinois, is like looking into the city's past. From early colonists to renowned residents of a century ago, its wealth of history is enough to make Graceland a fascinating place, but many memorials possess an added attraction—legends that push them beyond the normal into the realm of weird.

The most famous legend is that of Inez Clarke, a six-year-old girl who died in the late 1800s. Her parents commissioned a life-size statue of their girl and placed it in a glass box on top of her tombstone. People to this day leave toys, candy, and other gifts for the dead girl. But in life, thunderstorms always frightened Inez, and so the legend goes that during storms, you will find the glass case empty. Inez will be hiding. Stories abound about watchmen who quit after walking by the girl's grave on rainy nights when her ghost was roaming.

Inez's story, while macabre, deals with innocence and youth. The grave of Dexter Graves, located across the cemetery from Inez, is much more ominous.

Hotel owner Dexter Graves lived in Chicago from 1831 until his death in 1844. But despite his short stint in the Windy City, Graves managed to make a mark on it. Above his grave stands a landmark placed there in 1909, sixty-five years after his passing—a bronze statue by acclaimed artist

Lorado Taft of an ominous sentinel draped in cloaks and shielding his face from view. Officially known as Eternal Silence, the sculpture is known more popularly by its colloquial moniker—The Statue of Death.

The imposing, larger-than-life statue was once entirely black, but exposure to the harsh Chicago weather for nearly a century has given it an eerie green patina. Only the face retains its original obsidian cast, and this face is the focus of the foreboding figure's legend. If you believe the stories, you won't look directly into the statue's eyes. Doing so affords a glimpse of your own future, right up to the point of your death. It's said that many have challenged this tale by looking into those cursed eyes, only to see their ultimate demise.

Another interesting Graceland grave is that of William Hulber, who founded an early baseball league that eventually became part of major league baseball. Above his traditional headstone is an oversized baseball, engraved with the names of each city to which he helped bring the sport.

A single marble column in Graceland marks the resting place of George Pullman, the man who designed the railroad sleeper car. At the time of his death the Pullman family thought it wise to protect his body from angry factory workers who were in the midst of a strike. They covered his coffin in tar paper and asphalt, encased it in a block of concrete, then covered it over with railroad ties and more concrete!–*Troy Taylor*

The legend goes that during storms, you will find the glass case empty. Inez will be hiding.

The Devil's Chair

It sounds simple enough: come sit down in the chair, kick your feet back, and relax. It's okay if you want to bring a drink for yourself, just make sure you have enough to share with your buddy—he'll be along shortly, just after midnight. Like we said, simple enough, right? Well, no. Not simple at all. Not when the chair you're sitting in is the Devil's Chair and you're waiting for Satan himself.

It all happens in a strange town in Florida named Cassadaga, founded at the end of the nineteenth century by a medium from Iowa called George Colby. The town became a focal point for spiritualists who claim such supernatural abilities as clairvoyance and the ability to speak with the dead. To this day, when you visit the tiny burg, you'll invariably meet many spiritualists, some offering their services for hire. Small wonder, then, that Cassadaga has the perfect place to summon the dark prince.

The Devil's Chair is a graveside bench in the cemetery that borders Cassadaga and Lake Helen. The evil armchair comes with a few legends, but the most popular is that if you sit in it at midnight, the devil will appear, and you can have a conversation with him. Another rumor says that if you place an unopened can of beer on the Devil's Chair before midnight, the devil will drink it by the next morning and leave the beverage's container behind as proof.

Since the mid-'80s, Cassadaga has taken measures to keep people away from the Devil's Chair, especially around the Halloween season. Vandalism and underage drinking had gotten out of control in the cemetery, and because of Cassadaga's spiritualist traditions, the township felt it best to distance itself from rumors of dark practices. But recently Cassadaga has had a change of heart. Around Halloween it runs a haunted walk around

town that takes patrons through the graveyard and past the chair. Cassadaga has embraced its direct communication line to Satan—if you can't keep the kids from sitting in the Devil's Chair, you might as well charge them to do it!

Local police deny that the chair has any supernatural powers. The following is from the *Daytona Beach News-Journal*: "Lake Helen Police Chief Keith Chester has spent many a night on patrol in the cemetery, sometimes even seated in the Devil's Chair.

'I've been here 18 years and I've never seen [a devil],' he said. 'If there was one, I'd have been retired by now.'"

This makes us wonder whether it is really the devil who has been downing all those brews. Maybe it's been the Lake Helen police all these years.

Blood-Stained Mausoleum

Over the years Saint Luke's Episcopal Church has attracted curiosity-seekers to the southeastern Tennessee city of Cleveland. But it's the marble mausoleum at the rear of the 1870s-era chapel that draws the visitors. Its white surface is streaked with crimson stains that some locals believe are blood seeping from the stone. The cause lies inside the tomb, where four members of the Craigmiles family were placed after their tragic deaths.

John Henderson Craigmiles made his fortune in the shipping business. On December 18, 1860, John married Adelia Thompson, the daughter of a local doctor, who gave birth to the couple's first daughter, Nina, in August 1864. The family was absolutely devoted to the little girl, perhaps none more so than her grandfather, Dr. Thompson, who often took her on medical calls in his buggy.

It was during one of these outings that tragedy struck the Craigmiles family. On October 18, 1871, Dr. Thompson steered the carriage in front of an oncoming train, which threw him clear but instantly killed Nina. After the funeral services John built a church for the local Episcopal congregation in memory of his daughter. Saint Luke's was completed on the third anniversary of Nina's death.

Almost immediately the family began construction on a mausoleum for Nina at the rear of church. With walls four feet thick and a marble spire topped with a cross more than thirty-seven feet off the ground, the tomb contained six shelves in the walls and a marble sarcophagus for Nina's body.

As time passed, the other members of the family followed Nina to the grave. The first was an infant son born to John and Adelia, who lived only a few hours. John Craigmiles followed in January 1899, after death from blood poisoning following a fall on an icy downtown street. After an automobile killed Adelia in September 1928 as she crossed Cleveland Street, she was laid to rest with the other members of her family in the mausoleum.

The stories say that the bloody stains began to appear on the Craigmiles mausoleum after Nina was interred there. The stains grew darker and more noticeable with the death of each family member. What may have caused the bloody marks, and why they refuse to be washed away, remains a mystery.

Cleveland, Tennessee, is located in the southeastern corner of the state, a short distance north of Chattanooga.—*Troy Taylor*

Hope Cemetery

I come from New Hampshire, the Granite State, and had heard rumors of the famous monument carvers from Barre, Vermont. But I was unprepared for the astonishing tombstones of Hope Cemetery. Opened in 1895, this graveyard is an art gallery, celebrating life in the midst of death, with some of the most fascinating and quirky tombstones in the nation.

I arrived on an appropriately gray and threatening day in July and toured, first by car and then on foot, moving from stone to stone—touching and marveling. While the average New England tombstone speaks with a terse finality, these sculptures communicate volumes about both the deceased and the carver.

One final resting place is a stuffed armchair. In another a couple lie in their granite double bed, pajamas on, together as they were in life. No subject is too personal or too creative for the carvers of Barre, the Granite Capital of the World, from soccer balls and airplanes to cars and trucks. One carver evokes an image of the dead man's wife in the smoke of his cigar. In another stone, reminiscent of Michelangelo's *Pieta*, a woman clasps a turn-of-the-century workman. We from New Hampshire salute the stone carvers of Vermont who refuse to give death the final word. Bravo!–*J. Dennis Robinson*

Loon Lake Cemetery

Some distance south of Lakefield, Minnesota, lies an abandoned and forgotten graveyard called the Loon Lake Cemetery. Legend has it that this place has been haunted for many years by a variety of ghosts who have appeared since the last burial here, in 1926. These ghosts are not your average spirits either. They are strange, and they are many.

There is no longer a road that goes back to Loon Lake Cemetery, but those who seek the place can still find it, despite swampy and treacherous ground. The only people who still come here today are ghost hunters, curiosity-seekers, and the occasional visitor searching for some family history. The abandoned and remote setting serves to keep most people away, and those who do visit may actually be risking death!

The cemetery is said to be haunted by the spirits of three witches who were buried here many years ago. It is also said that anyone who violates their resting places will die an unnatural death. One of these three witches is remembered as Mary Jane, who allegedly died in 1881, when the townspeople of Petersburg cut off her head. Anyone who walks over the grave of this woman, the story goes, will also die — usually within seventy-two hours.

Trying to avoid crossing over Mary's grave is tricky, however, since her headstone was lost many years ago. Some say that it was removed to protect it from vandals, but others believe that the disappearance was the work of thieves, who died a gruesome death because of it. Regardless, the missing headstone of Mary Jane, as well as the vanished stones of most of the other inhabitants of the graveyard, add to the mystery of the place. At least sixty-seven tombstones once stood in Loon Lake Cemetery, but today only about eighteen remain.

While there are no records to say that anyone has ever really died from walking over the witch's grave, perhaps they have just been lucky. Or maybe they have simply not lived to tell the tale. —*Troy Taylor*

Tread Not on the Witches

Loon Lake Cemetery is just a few miles from my house here in Minnesota. It seems like everybody in this part of the state knows about it and goes there at least once while growing up. It's given me more sleepless nights than I care to admit. I've heard too many stories and been frightened personally too many times because of it. I will never go there again.

The stories about it are this: Apparently, a coven of witches used to live on the outskirts of the area. The townspeople were wary of the coven, but as long as they weren't bothered personally, they left the witches alone. But sure enough, these witches started causing trouble and really terrorizing the non-witch townsfolk. The people got together, hunted down the witches, and beheaded them. They buried them out in Loon Lake because it was desolate and used mainly to bury orphans. In other words, these witches would be out in the middle of nowhere, not buried with the God-fearing Christians.

The story goes that if you walk or jump over any of these witches' graves, you will die before the sun rises the next morning. There are so many stories of people taunting the witches and winding up in car crashes, or vandalizing the graves and having massive heart attacks right then and there.

I've been out there myself, and it is not hard to believe that something really eerie goes on. It's honestly in the middle of nowhere, surrounded by grass so tall that you can't even see where you're going. There are maybe thirty-five graves, although a bunch of those are toppled over or broken in half. Most of those that are standing are in fact the graves of very young kids, so maybe there is some truth to the orphan rumor.

I have never personally walked over the witches' graves, nor have I seen anyone do so. Someone always says they're going to, but when you're back there, it's the most incredibly unsettling feeling and we always chicken out. I have never been there without goose bumps springing up or the hair on the back of my neck standing out.

I will say this: Every time I go to Loon Lake, I wind up feeling sick to my stomach later that night. Maybe it's just nerves or my getting all worked up, or maybe the place really is cursed. I don't go there anymore, however. It's just too creepy for me. —*Sarah Lint*

The Buried Bomber

On Deer Mountain, near Wilson's Mills, Maine, is a very strange grave. It's not for a person. It's for an entire B-17 Flying Fortress bomber, which crashed in the woods during World War II. The bodies of the crew were removed, but the plane proved too difficult to move. So construction equipment was brought to the site, and the bomber was buried where it fell.

Witch's Footprint Grave

Jonathan Buck was quite the upstanding citizen. He was a hero of the Revolutionary War and one of Maine's most prominent residents. He even has a town, Bucksport, named in his honor. He is something of a legend in Maine, and one of the legends about him is odd, to say the least.

Buck, while serving in the military, ordered the execution of a woman purported to be a witch. Just before her death was carried out, she made the grim proclamation that his tombstone would forever bear her mark.

Buck died in 1795, and his family erected a large obelisk-shaped monument at his grave in Bucksport. Much to everyone's disbelief, within a short time the outline of a leg and foot appeared on the stone. The grave was scrubbed, and the mark disappeared, only to return almost immediately. Nothing over the centuries, not even replacing the stone itself, has managed to stop this strange imprint from appearing on Jonathan Buck's grave.

Going to Hell in a Hand Gesture

During the mid-1800s, many people had their gravestones carved to include images of hands with the fingers pointing up. The implication was that the deceased would be heading to heaven. The Methodist cemetery in Whitefield, New Hampshire, is home to either a very bad man or the world's biggest pessimist. The gravestone of Ira Bowles, who died in 1863, has a finger pointing down. No one is quite sure why this macabre yet expensive stone would be carved with such a grim message inscribed on it.

Blood Cemetery

No one refers to Pine Hill Cemetery in Hollis, New Hampshire, as Pine Hill. Instead, they refer to it by the name it has earned: Blood Cemetery. The cemetery got its name due to its most infamous resident, Able Blood. Legend has it that Able was involved in many strange activities, including occult practices. In death he is still participating in a ritual of sorts.

If one enters the cemetery during the day and visits Blood's tombstone, he will see an engraving of a hand with a finger pointing up, toward the sky. If the fearless visitor returns at night, the finger points straight down.

Some people report seeing strange fogs overtake the cemetery in the blink of an eye. Others claim to have seen a shady figure lurk about its grounds.

Stylish Ride to the Other Side

Located in the peaceful setting of the Linden Park Cemetery in Union County, New Jersey, is a monument to one young man's love of an automobile. The final resting place of Raymond Tse is an impressive enough mausoleum, adorned by marble pillars, urns, and sculptures of two oriental lions. But what really puts this tomb in a luxury class by itself is the full-sized granite replica of a Mercedes-Benz 240 Diesel that is parked right out back. The car, which is an exact scale model of the German four-door sedan, was chiseled from a single block of stone. There it sits, fully loaded, eternally ready to whisk the dear departed away to the hereafter. It even has personalized license plates bearing the name Ray Tse.

Legend has it that as a boy young Raymond had always dreamed of owning a Mercedes, but he was killed in a tragic auto accident at age sixteen, just before receiving his driver's license. Another story says that Ray's older brother David, a well-to-do Chinese American businessman, promised his younger brother a Mercedes when he earned his driver's license. This was never to be, though, as Ray is said to have taken ill and died before reaching the legal driving age.

Weird U.S. spoke with Richard T., one of the mourners present at Raymond's funeral.

"Ray lived in Hong Kong, but he visited his brother David in America often. When Ray died, his parents could not accept the loss and shipped the body over here for burial. They didn't even attend the funeral. At the service we were all given play money and fake gold bars to throw into a can of fire so that Ray would have wealth in the afterlife. They also gave out real money, which would have been disrespectful to refuse. I was given thirty dollars, which I threw in a drawer and did not touch for five years.

"Ray's mausoleum and the Mercedes take up forty cemetery plots and cost five hundred thousand dollars back in the '70s. David is said to still visit the grave every day."

The monument is a wonder of the modern stonecutter's craft. The car's grille, windshield wipers, treads in the tires, textured taillights, and even the exhaust pipe and muffler are rendered in painstaking detail. The only things missing are the two side mirrors, which might have protruded too much and been broken off. To carve the monument, expert stonecutters say, the craftsmen probably drove a real Mercedes into their shop to use as a model. The granite version could have taken over a year to chisel.

That would mean that by the time this car rolled off the assembly line it was already a late model, just like its owner.

Rock of Ages Carved for Thee

I'd like to share some facts about the stone Mercedes. First, the car is made of a single block of stone quarried at the Rock of Ages quarry in Graniteville, Vermont. It was transformed into the stone Mercedes at their craft center, and paid for by Ray Tse's older brother. There is a Chinese custom that if you promise something to someone and they die before the promise can be fulfilled, then you must do your best to keep the promise to the deceased person.—*Ray Makul*

A Special Way of Death

The cemeteries of New Orleans are much like the city itself; they mirror the opulence and decadence of a mysterious and enchanting place. They dance back and forth between beauty and ruin. Like New Orleans, the city cemeteries hide secrets . . . secrets that most people will never discover.

The way of death in New Orleans is a distinctive part of its culture. For more than two hundred years people here have housed their dead in small, aboveground tombs built along streets, in miniature cities of the deceased and the forgotten. These cities of the dead provide hours of discovery for the intrepid seeker and for the brave of heart. For not only ghosts lurk here, but the thief and the brigand as well.

To understand the strangeness of the New Orleans cemetery culture, we must return to the beginnings of the city itself. The original site of New Orleans, which is the French Quarter today, had a water table just beneath the surface of the soil. The land sloped back from the river toward Lake Pontchartrain, falling quickly below the level of the sea. The question soon arose: Where would the colonists bury their dead in such a waterlogged place?

The first site chosen for burials was along the high banks of the Mississippi, where over the years the river deposited soil, creating natural levees. During floods (which came often), though, the bodies of the dead would wash out of their muddy graves and come floating through the streets of town. Obviously, this was a problem.

A few years later a graveyard was created outside the city, reached only by a winding path. This was done not for aesthetic reasons, but for health. It was commonly believed that graveyards exuded a noxious odor that carried disease. The odor and the marshy soil of the area made the citizens regard cemeteries as unhealthful places.

During the years of 1787 and 1788 New Orleans was rocked with plague and disease. Hundreds died as malaria, smallpox, and influenza took their toll. The following year a fire broke out on Good Friday and swept through the city, destroying homes, commercial buildings, and churches. A few months later a hurricane wiped out another huge portion of the city; hundreds more lives were taken.

A new graveyard was desperately needed to cope with the victims of these tragedies, and the first of the now classic St. Louis cemeteries was officially opened in 1789. The new cemetery was a walled enclosure with its main entrance off Rampart Street. The poor were buried here in unmarked graves, and as available space filled, the level of the soil began to sink. Contracts for dirt were frequently bid upon, and city chain gangs shoveled it evenly throughout the graveyard, making room for more bodies. It is believed that there are layers of bones several feet thick beneath the grounds of the cemetery.

Aboveground tombs were the rule for all but the indigent. The reasons were obvious: In the wet ground of Louisiana, coffins would often float to the surface, despite gravediggers' placing heavy stones or bricks on the lids. Such conditions did not appeal to those with the wealth to be buried in style.

Most of the early tombs were simple but functional enclosures, and most of the doors were bricked over once the burial had taken place. Years later architects would design more elaborate tombs for the city's elite, but few of those can be seen in the older graveyards.

Perhaps one of the most famous residents of St. Louis

Marie Laveau II

This is said to be the grave of Marie Laveau II. Laveau I started out as a hairdresser to rich white women and became the Voodoo Queen of New Orleans. She had more than a dozen children but kept one daughter out of sight. As Marie I aged and then died, Marie II came out to take her place. People thought that she had transformed herself and become young again, and her authority became ever greater.

Cemetery No. 1 is Marie Laveau, the Voodoo Queen of New Orleans. Her tomb, the most frequently visited in the graveyard, looks like most others in the cluttered cemetery, until you notice the markings and crosses that have been drawn on the stone. Apart from these marks you will also see coins, pieces of herb, beans, bones, bags, flowers, tokens, and all manner of things left behind in an offering for the blessings of the queen. Legend has it that Marie's ghost sometimes walks here, and one man claims to have been slapped by her spirit one day, after making a disparaging remark at her tomb.

Another legend of the cemetery is the New Orleans version of the "Nail in the Tomb." This tale has crossed the country in many variations, but local folklorists swear that it had its start at St. Louis Cemetery No. 1. The story goes that three young men spent a night drinking and carousing in the French Quarter. Their talk soon turned to death, voodoo, and Marie Laveau. Before long one of the men was enticed into a wager. His friends bet him $30 that he would not climb the cemetery wall and drive a spike into the wall of Marie's resting place. He accepted the wager and a short time later entered the cemetery.

His friends waited for him to return, but minutes turned into hours. Dawn came and, with it, the opening of the cemetery gates. The worried young men hurried to the

tomb and there they found their friend . . . lying dead on the ground! In his drunken state he had hammered the spike through his coat while hammering it into the stone wall of the crypt. As he started to leave, what he believed to be an unseen force (actually the misguided nail) held him in place. Panic and fear overwhelmed him, and he literally died of fright.

By 1820 New Orleans was outgrowing its boundaries, reaching Rampart Street, and the old cemetery became overcrowded. The city chose another site, not too far away for the funeral processions, but far enough to avoid contagion, and called it St. Louis Cemetery No. 2.

The new cemetery was laid out in a perfect square with large houselike mausoleums on orderly streets. Over time the tombs here became much larger and grander than in St. Louis Cemetery No. 1.

As the city grew, more cemeteries were added, but only one other boasts a ghost story. It is called Metairie Cemetery and has always been known as the most fashionable in the city. This opulent, parklike resting place was organized by a group of local businessmen and promoters in 1873. It was the epitome of the classic Victorian graveyard, far removed from the jumbled chaos of St. Louis Cemetery No. 1.

One of the city's most fascinating tales comes from Metairie Cemetery and involves the ghost of Mrs. Josie Deubler, also known as Josie Arlington, the most colorful and infamous madam of New Orleans.

From 1897 to 1917 New Orleans was the site of America's largest district of prostitution. The city officials realized they could not get rid of prostitution, so they decided to segregate and control it instead. Based on a plan created by an alderman named Sidney Story, a district was created in which only licensed prostitutes could ply their trade. Much to the alderman's chagrin, it was dubbed Storyville in his honor.

It was here that Josie Arlington operated her house of ill repute and became very rich. The house, known as the finest bordello in the district, was stocked with beautiful women, fine liquor, wonderful food, and exotic drugs. The women were all dressed in expensive French lingerie and entertained the cream of New Orleans society. Josie had the friendship of some of the most influential men in the city, but was denied the one thing she really wanted: social acceptance. The men who were her willing companions at night shunned her in the daytime, especially if their families were nearby.

But what Josie could not have in life, she would have in death. She got her revenge on the society snobs by electing to be buried in the most fashionable cemetery in New Orleans—Metairie.

The notorious madam purchased a plot on a small hill and had erected a red marble tomb, topped by two blazing pillars. On the steps was a bronze statue showing Josie ascending the staircase with a bouquet of roses in the crook of her arm. The tomb, an amazing piece of funerary art designed by an eminent architect named Albert Weiblen, cost a small fortune. But Josie considered it well worth the money for the scandal it created. No sooner had work been finished, in 1911, than a strange story began making the rounds of the city. Some curiosity-seekers had gone out to see the grave one evening and were greeted with a sight that sent them running. The tomb seemed to burst into flames before their very eyes! The smooth red marble shimmered with fire, and the tendrils of flame appeared to snake over the surface like shiny phantoms. Word quickly spread, and people came in droves to witness the bizarre sight. The cemetery was overrun with people every evening, which shocked the cemetery caretakers and the families of those buried on the grounds. Scandal followed Josie even to the place she had chosen for her final resting.

Josie passed away in 1914 and was interred in the "flaming tomb," as it was often called. Soon an alarming number of sightseers began to report another weird event.

Many swore they had actually seen the statue on the front steps move. Even two of the cemetery gravediggers, a Mr. Todkins and a Mr. Anthony, swore they had witnessed the statue leaving her post and moving around the tombs. They claimed to follow her one night, only to see her suddenly disappear.

The tradition of the flaming tomb has been kept alive for many years, although most claim the phenomenon was created by a nearby streetlight that would sway in the wind. Regardless, no one has ever been able to provide an explanation for the eyewitness accounts of the "living" statue. Perhaps Josie was never accepted in life, but she is still on the minds of many in New Orleans long after her death.—*Troy Taylor. Picture captions by Tess Conrad*

Josie Arlington's Glowing Grave

Now the tomb of the Morales family, this mausoleum is actually a resale. If a family wants to, it can move its relatives' remains elsewhere and let somebody else take over their plot. The original occupant was Josie Arlington, who ran the swankiest bordello in New Orleans—or, actually, the next swankiest. Her common-law husband and state legislator Tom Anderson ran the top digs, there being a legalized district for prostitution at the time. After the navy had the district outlawed because it was prepping for WWI and too many of its boys were going AWOL there, Josie tried to turn herself into a lady of culture and class. She donated huge sums of money to good causes, but the New Orleans society ladies would not so much as speak to her. She therefore commissioned this tomb that shows her turning her back on the world that had rejected her and entering into the next.

Interestingly, Josie was still a scandal after she died. First, the pink of the stone was considered shocking. But it became a huge news story when reports came out that at night the whole tomb lit up red, a reflection of the fires of hell where Josie no doubt burned. Huge crowds gathered to see this phenomenon, and then someone noted that hell must be a really orderly place, because the lights came on at regular intervals. Finally people realized that a streetlight that had been put up on the other side of the street was reflecting the red light back on the tomb. Still, after several years the family had had enough and moved her body out west.

The Pyramid Tomb

is in Millionaire's Row in Lake Lawn Metairie. Not much is known about this one, including why this design was chosen.

Lake Lawn Metairie was originally a private racetrack. The story goes that when denied membership to the track, an enraged patron screamed that he'd get revenge; he'd turn the place into a graveyard. And so it happened, but it's still kept its uptown feel.

If you're going for a visit, you definitely need a car to get around; it's huge and arranged in an oval shape. You wouldn't be able to get through a tenth of it on foot before feeling disoriented, like you've been walking in circles, which, of course, you are!

The Weeping Angel

This weeping angel is from Lake Lawn Metairie Cemetery. The angel has dropped down in grief, the scroll of the dead falling from her hand to the floor.

St. Louis Cemeteries

The picture above was taken in St. Louis No. 2 and was literally a shot in the dark. The flash was turned on and stuck in a crack in the tomb, and this is the picture that came out. You can very clearly see a skull in the upper right-hand corner, a rib, backbone, and so on. The coffins were all wood; the only metal was the hinges and handles, which lie just where they fell after the wood coffin had rotted away.

St. Louis Cemeteries Nos. 1, 2, and 3, the oldest existing cemeteries in the city, are also the most interesting. When people speak about the decay of the dead, it's usually these cemeteries they're talking about. Restoration work has begun on these and other New Orleans cemeteries over the last decade, but thankfully, it's slow work. The broken tombs shown here, with their exposed bones, have been patched, and the worst of the tombs have been cleaned up.

A word of caution: While St. Louis No. 1 is usually fairly safe because tour groups are constantly going through, St. Louis No. 2 is another matter. It stretches over three blocks, with high walls and one road through the middle. It's easy to get turned around and disoriented in there, and there are perfect hiding places for those up to no good—lots of blind corners and blank holes to jump out of. Go with a group if possible.

Holt Cemetery

Holt Cemetery, below, is a sort of New Orleans' Potter's Field. Two hundred dollars gets you planted, though only two and a half feet down. At three feet you hit water, but in a storm you're coming back out anyway. I ran into the very colorful caretaker who's been there seventeen years and heard many a story. I've been there before, and each time found evidence of voodoo stuff going on. If you're going to try to pull a body out, I guess you go where they're easier to get, and I'm sure the poor folks don't have as much clout as the rich ones next door at Metairie. So the caretaker took me over to see this one grave, which he'd dug just a week before. You can see the hole where they pulled the body out, and the box to the side is the simple marker (the caretaker makes them on the side and sells them to the families) that was pulled up and tossed aside. It's amazing how people really put their heart into some of their tributes to their family members here. They're actually much more personal than many of the stone tombs.

Still Hawking His Wares in the Afterlife

Some salesmen are so addicted to their calling that they can't put down their wares even in the afterlife. J. S. Jacobs was a traveling salesman who passed away in 1891. His gravestone, in the Lincoln Cemetery of Lincoln, Kansas, is shaped like the suitcase from which he sold his products. Appropriately enough, the engraving on his stone reads HERE IS WHERE HE STOPED [*sic*] LAST.

Mirror Image Grave

In Maple Hill, Kansas, Sarah Ann Oliver's family was known to be a thrifty bunch. So when Sarah died in 1923, they decided that instead of spending hundreds of dollars on a gravestone for her, they would simply cast it themselves. If the family's common sense had only been equal to their desire to save a buck, everything would have worked out fine.

The problem was that whoever cast the stone didn't realize that when making a mold, the letters must be reversed for them to appear correctly in their final form. So the lettering on Sarah Ann Oliver's tombstone is all printed backward.

This unusual gravestone is located in Maple Hill Cemetery, on South Thirty-fourth Street.

Pulling Up Roots

Roger Williams, the founder of Rhode Island, died in 1683. But his story doesn't end there. He and his wife were originally interred beneath an apple tree on a private estate. Years later some local residents decided he deserved a more prominent burial site and attempted to move the graves. What they found was shocking, to say the least.

The corpses were missing, and in their place were wooden replicas of the couple's bodies. The apple tree had burrowed its roots into their coffins and filled in their bodies as they rotted away. The roots, which appear vaguely to resemble human bodies, are on display in the John Brown House Museum, in Providence.

Keeping a Bad Witch Down

The Old Burying Yard of York, Maine, is host to the remains of Mary Nasson, who lies in the infamous Witch's Grave. Her plot is actually made up of three stones: a headstone, a footstone, and a large slab placed over her body. The slab was placed there by her husband in an effort to keep the powerful witch from reemerging from her final (one hopes) resting place.

The stones of Mary's grave are said to be hot to the touch. There are also reports that crows often gather around the Witch's Grave. Supposedly, these creatures are emissaries of evil paying tribute to their comrade in wickedness.

Within the Pet Cemetery Circle

I was working on my degree in a small Kentucky college town called Morehead, when I began to hear stories about the Pet Cemetery. The story I heard from the locals was that there was a spot in the mountains where occult activity took place: Animals were killed to perform magic. I was curious but figured I would never be in a situation where I would be anywhere near the place.

Fast forward a couple of months, and my friends Pat and Cynthia had located the Pet Cemetery from a combination of driving through the mountains and talking to local people who knew the region pretty well. It is located on a mountain that had a reputation of being haunted and/or the site of a bloody Indian conflict. My friends and I decided to go there, but I must admit I was nervous, though intrigued.

We arrived at night under a full moon. The first thing I noticed was that it was a large circle, roughly the size of a football field, covered with gravel. It was near the top of the mountain and was surrounded by trees. In the center were large stones that rose to about eight feet. Even though it was a hot July evening, the air was windy and cool. My gut reaction was to jump back into the car and leave.

We explored the area, and the first disturbing and scary thing was the amount of animal skeletons that were littered throughout the circle. Every four or five feet there was a complete or partial skeleton. As we neared the stone structure in the center of the circle the sound of whip-poor-wills got louder and louder. We looked around for a couple of minutes and discovered something unnerving: The wind was moving the trees around the circle, giving the impression that things were moving in the shadows. This, combined with the frantic birdcalls, made us decide to leave the Pet Cemetery.

As we turned to go, I felt a tug in my mind to stay there in the circle and never leave. This feeling increased slowly and confused me for a moment. I felt torn for a second, but didn't voice what was going on to the others. My friends and I increased our pace to the car, and the birdcalls were getting louder and louder. Nervous conversation went on between us. I tried to joke in an attempt to break the considerable tension.

I turned to my friend Pat and joked that the birds were warning people about us. Right after I said that, all bird noises died suddenly and we were surrounded by silence. Pat's eyes widened at this, and we were stumbling over each other to get into the car. We drove off and said nothing until we left the mountain. When we did start talking, we realized that we all had had the same experience: All of us felt that mad urge to stay there and never leave.

Days later we came back to the Pet Cemetery with others to check out the experience, but the dark, tense atmosphere was gone. Someone had removed the animal skeletons and rearranged the center stones. For some reason it disturbs me much more that someone had tended the circle.–*Jerry R. Williams*

This strange event happened in Missouri in 1993, when all the major rivers that run through the state—the Missouri, the Meramec, and the mighty Mississippi—flooded to record levels. The deep, raging waters destroyed dozens of homes and businesses, and washed a few people away to their deaths.

The creepiest thing, though, was that an old cemetery in an outlying St. Louis area was completely flooded and stayed submerged for weeks. The water soaked into the ground so much that it loosened the earth, sending the unvaulted caskets below shooting out of the ground. Seven hundred and ninety-three caskets floated around flooded subdivisions like bobbing boats, and a few actually crashed through the first floor windows of some of the homes. However, it wasn't until after the water had receded that the real horror was exposed.

As area residents went back to their waterlogged, mud-caked homes to salvage whatever was left, they opened their doors to find caskets lying about their living rooms and kitchens. Some caskets had even burst open and spilled out corpses; bodies were found strewn about, lying on beds and countertops. Outside was just as horrific—bodies were everywhere, in fields and parking lots, on top of cars and tangled in chain-link fences. A guy I know told me that his uncle found the decayed head of an old lady hanging from the swing set in his backyard. Her long grey hair had tangled around the swing chain, and her body had ripped away with the flowing water, leaving the skull and hair behind.—*Stephen, Marina del Rey, CA*

Gravestone

When Hiram Smith of Chester, Massachusetts, saw his parents' graves upheaved by flooding, he resolved to never suffer the same fate. He located a huge boulder, ten feet high and thirty feet wide, and had it built into his tomb. When he died, his body was placed within the stone and the opening was sealed shut. Later someone lost to history named Sarah Toogood was placed in an adjacent opening. While his grave is unusual, Hiram can rest easy knowing no natural disaster is ever going to wash him away.

Highway to Heaven

The Pocasset Hill Cemetery in Tiverton, Rhode Island, is home to a sentimental and strange gravesite. Rose Martin died in 1998 and asked to be buried in her car. Her request was honored, and her casket was placed inside her modest 1962 Corvair, which was then lowered into the ground. The grave takes up four plots, and Rose's headstone is engraved with a picture of her beloved automobile.

Bigger Is Deader

I grew up in Worcester, Massachusetts, and have always had an affinity for graveyards. They're quiet, and especially in towns that date back hundreds of years, there are always interesting gravestones, tombs, and stories.

Sacred Heart Cemetery in Milford has a number of oddities. It is home to one of only two Irish round towers found outside of Ireland. It has several entire tombs on which no names can be discerned. And it has a section of graves and memorials that try to outdo one another because in death, as in life, some people are convinced that bigger is better. Huge plots with enormous spires, columns, globes, and other forms of decoration occupy one of the older fields. The most spectacular, however, is a human-size angel, wings spread, carved entirely out of black marble.

—Sylvia Bagaglio

Neither Heaven nor Hell

Do you know about Emo's Grave in Utah? I lived out there for a few years and always heard stories about it. It's supposed to be the grave of a vicious serial killer. They say that this man was so evil in life that he couldn't get into heaven, and hell was too scared to have him, so his soul just haunts his gravesite. If you go up to his grave and look into it, you can see his face smiling back at you. *—Carl Von Stricktenhousen*

A Grave that Glows

South Cemetery in Portsmouth, New Hampshire, contains a tombstone that has generated quite a bit of hubbub. It is known far and wide as the Glowing Grave.

At night the middle stone in a row of three identical gravestones lights up. Believers claim that the light is a supernatural occurrence and that the grave is of either a murderer or someone who was murdered. Detractors discount it as the reflection of streetlights or the moon.

Don't Dis the Black Angel

In Oakland Cemetery, on the north side of Iowa City, Iowa, stands a foreboding, mysterious statue. Locals tell tales of the powers and curses the memorial contains. Legions flock to the site to tempt their fates by testing the various legends surrounding it. She is the Black Angel, an eight-foot-tall bronze statue that stands over the graves of three members of the Feldevert family. Over time this mournful creature's bronze luster changed to a foreboding black hue, and all attempts to restore its original gleam have failed. Each year, the angel looks darker and more ominous.

Several legends explain the transformation. One says that Teresa Feldevert, the matriarch of the family buried beneath the angel, was a witch whose evil was so great that even in death it taints the monument above her. Another legend states that when Teresa's husband buried her, he swore to remain faithful to her forever. As time went by, he found a new sweetheart and slept with her; the angel turned black to condemn the breach of his graveside promise.

Whatever the origins of her dark patina, the angel bears some menacing legends, many of which involve kissing. It's said that if a virgin girl receives a kiss in front of the angel, the original golden color will be restored. But this is a risky venture, since another legend states that any woman kissed in front of the monument will die within six months. But nobody should pucker up to the Black Angel herself, since any man foolish enough to attempt this is said to die instantaneously. Even touching the angel or looking directly into her eyes brings the offender down with an unknown, incurable illness. Anyone trying to vandalize the monument will also be struck down swiftly. One story says that a group of men once urinated on the statue and were in a fatal car accident on their way home from the cemetery that very night.

Unlike most angelic grave markers, the Black Angel makes no effort to focus on heaven, but stares down at the ground with downcast wings. She holds her ground here on earth, reminding us of pain and death, and perhaps inflicting both upon those who disrespect her.

The Look That Kills

For those who grew up in the Iowa City area, a nighttime visit to the Black Angel is almost a rite of passage, a necessary part of growing up and facing your darkest fears. To many, dark tales of the angel are little more than local legend. However, the Black Angel does have a very real history . . . and, according to some, there is reason to be afraid of her!

Teresa Feldevert commissioned Daniel Chester French to build the bronze statue in 1911, as a monument for both her husband, Nicholas, and her teenage son, Eddie. The sculptor, who also created the famous statue of Abraham Lincoln at the memorial in Washington, made one of the greatest works of art in the area.

No one knows how the stories of death and curses got started, but the appearance of the statue itself may be the cause. The eyes of the figure are truly eerie, with swirled irises that seem to bulge from the blankness of the rest of the eye. They appear to stare at the visitor from beneath strangely drooping eyelids, an unnerving effect. The sheer size of the statue does little to convince the visitor of the angel's celestial goodwill either. Some claim that looking directly into her eyes at midnight will result in a fatal curse upon the gazer. Others maintain that the curse is transmitted only if a person actually touches the statue.

Is the Black Angel of Oakland Cemetery really cursed? I don't know, but I don't suggest waiting around the cemetery at midnight to find out!

—Troy Taylor

Whether Stuffed, Stone, or Spirit, Stiffy Green Is a Dead Man's Best Fiend

In Terre Haute, Indiana, there is a local legend of a man and his dog that dates back to the early 1900s. The man was named John Heinhl, and his eternal companion, a bulldog, would come to be known in local lore as Stiffy Green. In life Heinhl had the green-eyed statue of the dog as a decoration on the front porch of his home. After his death the statue was placed in his mausoleum to keep him company for all eternity.

As the years passed the reasons for this entombed dog were forgotten as his legend grew. Local lore told that Stiffy Green had actually been Mr. Heinhl's pet pooch and the two were inseparable in life. They went everywhere together, and people marveled at how much this dog truly was this man's best friend.

When Heinhl died in the 1920s, so the stories went, Stiffy sat right next to his casket for the entire funeral, crying. Anyone who tried to comfort or move the despondent dog was met with barking and biting. When the wake was over and the body was placed in a mausoleum at the Highland Lawn Cemetery, Stiffy refused to move from in front of the tomb's doors. The little pooch returned home a few times, but would only stay for a few hours before returning to his grim vigil. He even sat there during hurricanes! Stiffy Green eventually died as well, lying down in the cemetery. As the story goes, Heinhl's wife had the dog stuffed and placed inside the mausoleum with her husband, reuniting the inseparable pair.

As the decades passed the Heinhl mausoleum became a popular nighttime hangout for the local teenagers of the area, who would often bring flashlights to shine inside the tomb. Staring back at them would be the green glowing eyes of the faithful canine they had christened Stiffy Green, standing guard over his master's coffin. Visitors to the crypt would often tell ghost stories of a strange specter that patrolled the cemetery grounds, accompanied by another apparition that was in the form of a dog. The sound of barking and a dog's whining are said to be heard each night in stillness of the graveyard.

At one point some late-night callers to the Heinhl mausoleum actually shot bullets into the crypt, shattering one of Stiffy's green eyes. Because of this the Heinhl family decided to remove the dog from the crypt. Fortunately for the people of Terre Haute though, the legend of Stiffy Green has been given new life. The local Lion's Club convinced the family to donate the dog to the Vigo County Historical Society. Today Stiffy Green can be seen, still stoically standing guard over his master's remains, in a replica of the Heinhl mausoleum reconstructed as part of the "Haunted Legends" display in the Historical Museum of the Wabash Valley, located at 1411 S. Sixth St. in Terre Haute.

BRUCE P. BERMAN

APRIL 12, 1966
NOVEMBER 14, 1998

WWW.BERMANIMATION.COM

Star Wars Grave Site

On Mother's Day, I was visiting my mother and father's grave in Hazelwood Cemetery in Rahway, New Jersey. I noticed a long inscription on the back of a nearby stone. It told of a young man who had died after a long fight with a horrible disease.

As I walked around to the front, I noticed his website was inscribed into the bottom of the stone! Then I almost fell over when I looked at the entire front—there he was: His face and hands were cut into the marble, with his hands on either side of his head, palms out! It looked exactly like Han Solo when he was frozen in carbonite during The Empire Strikes Back.—*Chris Payne*

The Force Was Strong with This One

I designed the tombstone in Rahway that bears the web address. The sculpture of the face and hands pushing out from the granite is from a computer scan of the deceased, my friend Bruce Berman.

Before he passed away, he gave me the files and asked me to carry out the headstone if he died. Bruce had a twisted sense of humor and would have enjoyed being in your book.

—*Rob Dressel*

Haunts and Voodoo

The William Ganong Cemetery in Westland, Michigan, is considered one of the most haunted spots in the whole state. One of its ghosts notoriously takes pleasure in distracting drivers and causing automobile accidents. Another scatters flower petals. The cemetery stands only a few hundred yards away from another famous Michigan haunt, the abandoned Eloise Mental Hospital. Witchcraft is prevalent in the cemetery— evidence of voodoo ceremonies involving animal feathers and bones has been found on certain graves. In one instance, when some of these items were turned over to police, someone from the Wiccans contacted the police, demanding the return of his property.

Tomb with a View

Like many people, Timothy Clark Smith of New Haven, Vermont, was paranoid about his own death. Unlike many people, he went to very great and very creepy lengths to protect himself in his postmortem fate.

Smith died on Halloween in 1893 and was buried under some very unusual circumstances. Fearing that he would be accidentally buried alive, Smith had earlier instructed those who would be in charge of his funeral to bury him with a bell in his hand. This way, if he woke up, he could ring the bell and be removed from his grave. So Smith was buried beneath a mound of earth. At the top of this mound is a window that looks down through a cement tube placed right above his face. The dead man could be seen and could see out—in case he was in fact not really dead.

The good news for Smith was that he was not buried alive as he feared he would be. The bad news was that he never did get to ring his bell or peer out from his cemetery skylight. Smith's strange grave can be seen in the Evergreen Cemetery.

Quoth the Tombstone: Lenore

The tombstone of Truman F. Betts, MD, found in Trenton, New Jersey's Riverview Cemetery, is a tribute to Edgar Allan Poe's macabre masterpiece poem *The Raven.* After 130 years of weathering of the limestone tablet, its features are difficult, but not impossible, to decipher. First, it is carved in the shape of a door, complete with a jamb, molding, knob, and keyhole. The word Nevermore is almost undetectable, yet undeniably present, across the top of the stone door's frame. Above that there used to be a sculpted bust of Pallas with a raven perched atop his head. We learned that the statuette had been stolen four years ago.

Though not at first visible to the naked eye, after we gently rubbed away several years growth of dark green moss, the name Lenore became more pronounced on the door's nameplate. The name of the deceased appears below this, accompanied by his death date: Oct. 11, 1872. Aged 28 years, 3 months, and 28 days.

According to an 1872 obituary, Truman Betts died in Trenton by taking his own life after traveling to Florida and Europe to try to regain his health. The mystery is why the doctor's relatives had such a stone placed on his grave. Did Truman himself design the stone in anticipation of his death? If so, his morbid preoccupation with death and the hereafter would have undoubtedly impressed even Poe himself, the master of the macabre.

Trenton historian Charles Webster has his own thoughts about the Poe tombstone:

"The local legend around here is that Betts was obsessed with a woman who lived in New York and had asked for her hand in marriage, but she refused. Eventually she married another man, which is what probably drove Betts to suicide."

Abandoned in America

There are probably no places in the United States weirder than abandoned sites. Whether they are vacant houses, forgotten amusement parks, or decommissioned military installations, abandoned places possess an aura that is both foreboding and inspiring. A person wandering through these sites often has a melancholy sense of loss.

Some of our most thrilling adventures are those spent exploring these abandoned locations. Stepping into a strange world others once inhabited is a very weird sensation. Who lived here? Why did they leave, and where did they go? These are the questions that come to you while walking through these forsaken monuments of rotting wood and broken glass. There usually aren't many clues: maybe some furniture, perhaps some clothes in the closets, and, if you are really lucky, old books or family photographs. With these discards we try to piece together a puzzle and answer the riddles of the former inhabitants, much like an archaeologist trying to identify an unknown species of dinosaur using just a few fragments of bone.

If a place is left abandoned long enough, it will almost always become the subject of local mythology. Stories spring up about what might have taken place there to cause the occupants to flee. Abandoned houses inspire legends of gruesome murders that occurred there and the tormented souls that still linger behind. Such tales are all the more poignant if the abandoned site has a history as a site of human suffering, such as an insane asylum. There is no denying that people will conjure up all manner of fantastic stories and project them into places that have been left to rot. But have the stories sprung forth from our overactive imaginations, or is there really something weird going on behind some of America's forlorn façades?

This is the question we seek to answer each time we enter a darkened doorway to explore another mysterious abandoned location.

Towns with Tales to Tell

We all know about the ghost towns of the Old West—boomtowns of mining left to rot when their once rich veins of ore were bled dry. It is easy to understand why such places are now deserted; the thing that brought people to them in the first place has vanished. But in other ghost towns in America, the reasons for their abandonment are not so obvious. What could have caused a mass exodus from some of these places? While the true reasons might be just as logical as those behind the Old West ghost towns, they are not always so apparent to the out-of-towners who wander in. Whether the explanation is simple or hidden from us, there is one thing that cannot be denied: The experience of visiting one of these has-been hamlets can be a very weird one indeed.

Traveling to the End of the World

I have traveled to the End of the World. I speak of the scariest place I have ever visited, Hell Town. Formally known as Boston Township, Ohio, Hell Town is a little rural town, partially abandoned, and home to many mysteries. Hell Town is not truly abandoned. It does have residents, but they are a strange and frightening breed.

I have gone exploring the woods and cemetery there late at night, and have returned to find strange people dressed in black looking in my car windows. This has happened twice—once at two a.m. and once at four thirty a.m. Both times the people fled as soon as they saw me approaching the car, before I had a chance to speak to them. A part of me is glad that I didn't get to converse with them, because I have heard that Hell Town's residents are all satanists and worship at the town's two evil churches. I have been to both of these churches, and one, the Mother of Sorrows, has upside-down crosses hanging from it.

I have also been to the Boston Cemetery, where the graves date back to the early 1880s and a ghost has been seen sitting on a bench. I didn't see the ghost when I visited, but I did hear strange growls and howls from the depths of the graveyard, which convinced me to leave. The prospect of getting attacked by some strange boneyard-dwelling beast was not appealing, to say the least.

The End of the World is a road with a large hill and dip. I have never opted to test the fates by speeding on it. I have traveled it at normal speeds, but it is a dangerous-looking freaky road that always leaves me feeling very unsettled.

The scariest part of Hell Town is no longer there—town officials have removed it. Next to an abandoned house in the woods, an abandoned school bus sat for years. The story of how the bus got there still gives me chills. It was carrying a group of high school students to one of the ski resorts near Boston when an elderly woman flagged it down. She explained that there was a young boy in her house who was seriously hurt. The bus driver turned down her driveway and drove into the woods, but when the bus approached the house, Satan worshippers swarmed it and sacrificially murdered all those aboard. The bus sat back there for over thirty years, standing as a warning to all who decided to venture into Hell Town. *–Randall Chilesworth*

Welcome to Hell Town

My website, Ghosts of Ohio, had been in operation only a few months when we first began hearing rumors about Hell Town—a dark, foreboding place where ghosts, cults, and even a serial killer were said to lurk. Some told us that the entire town was cursed, warning us that it was dangerous to be in the area after dark. Needless to say, we were intrigued and wanted to learn more. In the summer of 2001, I made my first visit.

Hell Town is a nickname given to the northern part of Summit County. The areas most often associated with the Hell Town legends are Boston Township and Boston Village, along with portions of Sagamore Hills and Northfield Center townships. In most of the legends all of these areas are combined into one large region, which is referred to as Boston Mills.

First settled in 1806, Boston stands as the oldest village in Summit County. The first mill was built in the village in the early 1820s. Several years later the construction of the Ohio & Erie Canal brought more people to Boston, and over the next few decades mills began to flourish in the area. When a railroad station was constructed in the town in the early 1880s, the station was named Boston Mills, and the name stuck.

Over the years little changed in the small town. However, in 1974, in an effort to save the nation's forests, President Gerald Ford signed legislation that enabled the National Park Service to purchase land and use it to create national parks. As a result, on December 27th, 1974, hundreds of acres, including land within the township of Boston, were officially designated a National Recreation Area.

What many people did not realize until it was too late was that this legislation had a darker aspect to it. It gave the federal government jurisdiction to buy houses and land right out from under the current owners in order to clear the way for the national park. Almost immediately after the bill was passed, the government began acquiring houses throughout Boston Township and the surrounding area. Once the government had decided to buy a property, there was no negotiation involved—the owners were forced to relocate.

Residents began leaving in droves, and entire townships began to be swallowed up by the Cuyahoga Valley National Park. These tragic events were featured in the 1983 PBS documentary *For the Good of All.* The general feelings of the displaced homeowners were best summed up in a statement scrawled across the wall of a vacated home: "Now we know how the Indians felt."

Houses were boarded up, covered with government-issue NO TRESPASSING signs, and left vacant until the government could arrange to tear them down. Some houses were intentionally burned in training exercises for local fire departments. But with hundreds of homes being purchased in such a short period of time, the government quickly fell behind. It was not uncommon to drive down a street and find several boarded-up houses sitting next to the burned-out remains of other ones. To a passing motorist, it seemed as if an entire town had mysteriously disappeared into thin air. Undoubtedly, this is where the roots of the Hell Town legends lie.—*James Willis*

Fire Down Below

When the town officials of Centralia, Pennsylvania, ordered a small landfill cleared out in May of 1962, they had no idea what they were getting into. They chose to burn the rubbish, but there was one snag: Centralia was a coal-mining town built on an underground deposit of anthracite. The small fire spread to the coal, igniting a blaze that has burned now for more than forty years.

Initially this was not considered a major problem. Residents and government officials assumed that shoveling out the burning coal would stop the fire.

They were dreadfully wrong.

In the mid-1980s the United States government offered to buy property from the residents of the town, and most jumped at the chance. A handful of stragglers refused to budge, believing the government simply wanted to clear everyone out, put the fire out, and take the mine as government property. In 1991 the state actually purchased these peoples' homes, but they are still living there and paying property taxes.

Besides these hardliners, most people who visit the town are scientists or curious onlookers. A team of researchers from nearby Susquehanna University has set up camp at Centralia to study the phenomenon, with funding from the National Science Foundation's "Life in Extreme Environments" program.

The fire moves rapidly underground, threatening not only Centralia but, occasionally, the neighboring town of Byrnesville. While no one has died due to the fire, it nearly claimed the life of teenager Todd Domboski in 1981. It seems the lad was minding his own business when a fiery crater four feet wide opened up directly beneath him.

It was a hundred and fifty feet deep and filled with carbon monoxide and other noxious gases. Domboski clung to roots along the side of the fissure; his cousin managed to pull him to safety. The hellish situation brought national press coverage to the town's plight.

There are no plans by government agencies to further fight the blaze. In essence Centralia is being left to burn itself out. With 3700 acres of coal underneath the town, experts estimate that the fire has enough fuel to burn for nearly a thousand more years. With its numerous abandoned homes and businesses, it seems that Centralia's only hope of ever coming back to life is if the hell beneath it literally freezes over.

Centralia's One Thousand Years of Hell

When I visited the town of Centralia, I found detours and barricades closing off roads with huge fissures in them, spewing fire and brimstone. Throughout the area toxic fumes fill the air and the smoke rises off the ground like a Hadean fog. The surrounding towns are considering digging a trench five hundred feet deep around the mountain Centralia is built on, in hopes of saving nearby communities from the same hellish fate.

To help alleviate the pressure of the hot gases beneath the ground, the hills were speared with large venting pipes. But the heat underground became more and more apparent: Snow would not stick in winter, giant cracks appeared on Rte 61, basement and garage floors were hot to the touch. In 1979 one gas station owner found the temperature of his tanks to be 173 degrees. Just a dozen feet lower the thermometer read over 1000 degrees! It was as if the dark abyss itself was coming to claim Pennsylvania.

It's an amazing tragedy, and one that does not seem likely to be resolved by a happy ending. Go, if you dare, to see this modern ruin, a fiery tragedy that still has at least 960 years to go.–*Dr. Seymour O'Life*

Centralia: A Hard Place to Love

I used to drive through Centralia all the time. The place doesn't smoke all that often anymore, but there are only five houses left—and a place to buy auto parts on the corner. You can see the smoke rise up through the trees surrounding the town.

Signs going into Centralia warn everyone of the danger and ask people to beat a hasty path out of town. Some of the few people who still live there have a place on the corner with lawn chairs to sit in underneath a tree, with a big red, heart-shaped sign that says WE LOVE CENTRALIA.–*Nicolle L. Brandle*

Holy Abandonment!

Religious schools and convents are often rife with tales of evil deeds committed by their former inhabitants: priests and nuns. These legends only grow stronger when the places are abandoned. But why is our imagination so willing to cast upstanding citizens in the role of maniacal tormentors? Perhaps such stories appeal to our sense of irony or belie our suspicions toward people who position themselves as pillars of virtue. Whatever the reason may be, the mystique of an abandoned and crumbling convent is always enhanced by a good tale of the murder of innocents by a demonic holy man. Case in point: Maryland's Hell House.

Hell House

Five miles outside of downtown Ellicott City, Maryland, Hell House is located in the old mill town of Ilchester. It was built in the mid-1800s and was once known as St. Mary's College. And, supposedly, it was the scene of a grisly murder and suicide. The story goes that a priest hanged five students over a pentagram on the floor before doing himself in.

Hell House sits on a desolate site surrounded by woods on all sides. One of the first glimpses of the place is from River Road, a winding road lined by strange old gingerbread-style houses. The buildings are only four feet tall. They lie in ruins and look as though little people once lived in them. Right near the house itself is a mysterious factory and the Ilchester train bridge, part of the Baltimore & Ohio Railroad, which is also supposedly haunted.

One long, creepy set of stairs, overgrown with brambles and grass, leads up to Hell House. Many people have commented on a cold spot at the top. The crumbling façade of the building shows evidence of a fire, and another side looks as though it was destroyed by a wrecking ball. Over the entrance, on the marble above the columns, are the letters GE.

There is a strange pit in the foundation that looks like some sort of subterranean entrance or hiding place that leads to tunnels under the property. *–Betsy Earley*

The History of Hell House

Hell House was once a Redemptorist seminary named Mount Clement, which later became St. Mary's College. The Redemptorists provided services there for the Catholics in the communities of Thistle, Ilchester, and Gray's Mills. A group of Redemptorists came to the rural farming area of Ilchester in 1866 and met George Ellicott Jr., who owned 110 acres near the Baltimore & Ohio railroad station. On his land there was a stone house

that he had planned to turn into a tavern, but when the B&O selected Ellicott City for its train stop, Ilchester had no need for his tavern. So he sold his land to the Redemptorists, who paid $15,000 for it on July 21, 1866.

Ilchester was a perfect location for a seminary, since it was only a few miles by train to St. Alphonsus Church, which was the Redemptorist residence. The first Mass was held in the stone house on August 28, 1866, and the seminary opened in 1868. But a fire destroyed the lower house and former church and school in 1968. Four years later the Redemptorists closed St. Mary's College and put the property up for sale.

This lovely property now sits in ruins. In 1997 vandals threw a firebomb into a window and burned the school. The night watchman was inside and was able to escape. The buildings are now falling down and reportedly haunted. There is a legend about a priest who, in a fit of insanity, hanged five young girls facing one another around a pentagram, and then shot himself. People believe the building is haunted by the girls. Sometimes at night you can still hear their tortured screams, and there is a cold spot at the top of the huge stairs.

—Beverly Litsinger

When Visiting Hell House, Leave the Kids at Home

My boyfriend and I went up to Hell House last week with my younger brother and sister and their friend. It was real late at night, and it is dark as hell up in those hills. I swear, it was like something out of a movie, sitting there on top of the hill. My boyfriend didn't want to go up, because he said it was stupid (in other words, he was scared). So he stayed in the car as the rest of my group climbed over the rail and maneuvered up the steep, slippery hill. At twenty I was the oldest one there, so I was acting all brave and was like, "I'll take the lead! I'm not scared!" Lies, all lies.

    The whole time we were climbing, I felt like something was behind us. I kept looking back, but I didn't actually see anything head-on, just movements and stuff out the corner of my eye that I couldn't explain. The kids were scared (they're twelve and thirteen). I was feeling too many vibes, and my boyfriend kept honking the horn. So as a joke we all ran screaming to the car like we were being chased.–*Lauren L. Humphrey*

Hell House Dangers

My friends and I have been to Hell House many times. Every time we've come off Frederick Road, but you can come in through Ellicott City and other places as well. When you come to the infamous paper factory in front of Hell House, you just climb the hill and you will find the road that leads right up to the house. The house is in ruins now. You can walk through it, although I wouldn't recommend it—it's very dangerous. We've done it plenty of times, and someone always manages to get hurt.–*Matthew Boyd*

Hell House Cold Spots

One time when we went, something kind of weird happened. We found this cool spot under the stairs. We didn't say anything to each other about it, but my girlfriend started crying uncontrollably for no reason. When I put my arms around her, she was really freezing cold. As we looked around a little more, I began to feel these cool spots going through me and I began to feel anxious. We went back to the car and talked about what happened. I told my friends about the cold spots, and they all felt them too. My friend told me that when we started searching the school again, he felt really dizzy and cold.

    Sadly, Hell House is falling apart. Large sections of the wall are down. The basement is now caved in. The toolshed looks as if part of the wall fell on it. And the pavilion is collapsed. The old watchman and dogs are long gone, so it's as "safe" as a hundred-year-old crumbling, collapsing building can be.–*Steve Hart*

Monastery on the Hill

St. Augustinian Academy in the Grymes Hill section of Staten Island, New York, was once a boys' high school. It closed in the mid-1960s and later became a religious retreat, which was abandoned in 1985. It is now owned by nearby Wagner College, and there are plans to use it for student housing. Local legends, however, paint a much different picture of what once went on at—and under—this deserted old parochial school.

The monastery, as it's known locally, was the inspiration for countless chilling tales, making it the chosen destination of a generation of late-night thrill-seekers. Now surrounded by neighborhoods of suburban houses with manicured lawns, the all-but-forgotten fortress is shrouded with overgrown weeds, vines, and gnarly trees. Turkey vultures circle lazily overhead, occasionally landing to roost on the monastery's crumbling bell tower, where they keep a watchful eye over the long-dead institution.

Spooky Staten Island Monastery

In Staten Island, New York, is an abandoned monastery in a dark forest. It's so scary and big! There are three floors, and the basement goes down at least ten floors underground. There are rumors of dead bodies to be found down there, and it's probably true because it has the worst smell in the world. But no one dares to go down to the levels below the basement. When you're there you hear footsteps behind you, people talking. . . some people even see ghosts. It's really spooky!—*T.*

Signs of Satan

We drove up a winding road through the quaint neighborhood in Staten Island, to a secluded hill surrounded by trees, where a huge churchlike building stood. When we walked up in front of the monastery, the door was wide open. There were long staircases and many basement and sublevels. Up the main staircase we saw lots of graffiti and Satan signs. The building also has no roof, and in the back is a fountain shaped like a cross. There are many stories of Satan worshippers gathering there.

—DAVEJKLIM

Ten Stories Beneath the Old Monastery

The story of the monastery goes like this: About sixty years ago a bunch of monks lived there in solitude and silence. But one monk went on a killing spree, massacring all the other monks and dragging their bodies down to a secret sublevel. (The monks slept underground—people say the sublevels go down thirty floors.) There, he mutilated their bodies. People say if you want to see the monks' ghosts you have to go down to the last sublevel at night.

One summer night we went there. It was so dark inside that if we shut our lights off we couldn't see our hands in front of our faces. The building consists of three stories, two wings, and whatever is below. We went upstairs first. It was dark and creepy, and there had to be at least thirty rooms on each floor. The roof had caved in, and there were holes in the floor that dropped down two stories. Hanging from the ceiling were bloody animals wrapped in cloth. We really didn't want to go on. . . every now and then we heard the sounds of chains dragging and banging and the opening of a door behind us. But a kid with us kept pushing us to go on farther. So we followed him down three flights of stairs to the sublevels. The stairs were wooden and shook as we were walking down. At about the third sublevel we found the monks' quarters. They were very small and cramped. The walls had scratch marks down them that looked like fingernails were imbedded in them.

Then we came to a room blocked by wood. Behind the door were small stairs that looked like they went on forever. We followed these shaky stairs down about ten floors and entered a room with what looked like jail cells. It was getting a little too scary, so we left.*—CP11 2*

Getting Subterranean

The abandoned building in Staten Island has tons of graffiti on the higher levels, but as you travel lower and lower underground, signs of life become less and less evident. The underground hallways are a maze that travels to God-only-knows how low beneath the surface. On one trip to the flooded seventh level below the surface, we found a giant stone in the middle of a room where the ceiling was not at all caved in and neither were the walls. In the same room we found candles and something that made the hairs stand on the back of my neck: marks on one of the ancient wooden doors as if it had been locked from the outside and someone had tried to claw their way out of the room.

What happened in the ancient abandoned monastery? I have heard many stories, but I only know one thing for sure. If you make your way to the last underground chamber, all your questions will be answered.—*Dale Newton*

Getting Educated at the Monastery

I attended Wagner College on Staten Island in the late 1980s, and since the monastery was only a short walk up the road from our campus, the huge abandoned grounds were irresistible. Prowling around there was always an adventure, due mostly to the decrepitude of the building itself and the debris surrounding it. The place looked as if demolition had been halted before the job was even halfway done. Many of the rooms inside had been gutted, but occasionally we'd come across one that still had a desk or chair in it, as if the occupants had just left one day and never returned. I especially remember how creepy the abandoned chapel and its choir loft looked. The Stations of the Cross sculptures set into the walls all around the room had been heavily vandalized. There was at one time an elaborate mural painting of Saint Augustine on one wall facing the front door of the building. Unfortunately, it was later defaced with satanic graffiti. Around the back of the building were numerous abandoned cars—some upside down—nearly hidden in the tall weeds and grass that choked the entire property. Rumor had it that if you popped the trunks on some of these cars, you'd find the remains of Mafia hit victims. I never felt brave enough to investigate this for myself.

I tried to explore the basement areas, but we could only go so far before being blocked by water. Maybe down there in the depths is where the mythical "mad monk" hid the bodies of his slaughtered comrades. . . .—*Roadkill*

Possessed by the Monastery

I was a postulant at Augustinian Academy from fall of 1964 through spring 1965. This is the same building that's known as the Staten Island Monastery. In 1966, the postulants were moved to Malvern Prep in Pennsylvania and the school was shut down.

The monastery was indeed a strange place. I felt I was being taken over by evil spirits before I ever heard the word "possession." I was fifteen years old at the time, and I kept asking the Father Prior if I could leave, but he would not notify my family. Incoming and outgoing mail was censored, and it was hard to get a message home that was not intercepted. Many of the fathers and brothers laughed at my strange behavior, as I was well into a mental breakdown—and to this day I have not completely recovered.—*Ted B.*

Sacrificed Cats and Axe Attacks

I grew up and still live down the hill from the St. Augustinian Academy on Staten Island. I'm twenty-four years old now, but when I was fourteen, I practically lived there. About fifteen of us played manhunt in the monastery almost every day for about a year. We knew the place like the back of our hands. On the second floor we used to climb up a ladder to get into the bell tower. That was scary because there were always crows in the tower, and they used to fly out when we were coming up the ladder, and if you fell back you'd land on the first floor. The second floor was really kind of empty. . . it just had a lot of broken windows and holes in the floor.

The basement floors were filled with crawl spaces that we went through, but they never seemed to have an end. We once went in a room in the basement and saw a baby carriage surrounded by candles. Inside the carriage was a crucifix with Jesus' head cut off. Another time we saw a sacrificed animal. There were bones, cups filled with blood, hanged cats, and crazy-looking writing on the walls.

The last time I went, I was with a couple of friends and it was at night. While walking up through the woods to the back of the monastery, we saw something move by the entrance. The next thing I remember is a man chasing us with an axe! It was hard to run because the grass was so high, but we managed to get out. That stopped me from going back there.—*B. Hirsch*

Get Ye to an Abandoned Nunnery!

In the early 1920s the Catholic Church owned a retreat known as Saint Anne's in Logan Canyon, Utah. Remnants of this place still stand today, and it is one of the most chilling places I have ever visited. Hearing the story of the place only makes it worse.

This retreat was not for rest or relaxation. It was actually the place where the church sent nuns who had committed terrible wrongs. In many instances this meant pregnant nuns would live there in seclusion, have their children, and the children would be discreetly given up for adoption.

One nun decided that she wanted to keep her baby. She tried to steal away in the dead of the night, but the head nun caught wind of her plan and followed after her into the woods. The head nun began yelling that she would kill the nun and the baby when she caught them. Knowing she might not escape, the nun hid her newborn child in the underbrush and took off. She soon lost the head nun and waited in the wilderness, scared and alone, for a few hours. Then she made her way back to retrieve the baby from its hiding spot.

When she got there, her baby was gone.

Fearing the worst—that the head nun must have discovered the child and taken it—she sprinted back to the nunnery. There, her worst fears were confirmed. As she sneaked around the grounds, she came to the pool outside the main buildings and there, floating face down, was her child. Overwhelmed by guilt,

shame, and anger, the nun committed suicide right there at the edge of the pool.

Life went on at the nunnery. The nun who died was cast as the villain who got what she deserved. For years Saint Anne's continued to function and no one ever spoke of the awful atrocity inflicted on the nun and the baby. Nowadays the spot is abandoned. You can visit it and see the buildings, the woods through which the women chased each other, and the pool where the baby drowned. They say that on certain nights you can even hear desperate screams and cries of babies off in the distance. —*Alicia McKetrick*

The Good Friday Earthquake

The Jesse Lee Home in Seward had served the disadvantaged youth of Alaska for almost forty years by 1964. It was originally constructed as a home for children who had lost their parents to epidemics of tuberculosis and influenza. At any given time, it housed more than one hundred children, but in 1964 this heartwarming tale became horrifying as the youthful residents of Jesse Lee Home met with a terrifying fate.

On Good Friday, 1964, the second-largest earthquake in recorded history struck Alaska. The ground shook for nearly five minutes, tossing buildings into the air, splitting streets, and causing fires to erupt. Things got worse. The sand and dirt beneath Alaskan cities began to liquefy, causing an underwater mudslide to slip into the ocean. The displacement of earth destroyed more buildings and set off a ninety-foot-high tsunami that hurled itself onto the shores of the state.

The devastation reached the Jesse Lee Home, destroying part of it and killing many of its orphans. The orphanage was abandoned completely, and a new one was constructed. Many adventurers find their way to the old

Disappearances at the Ellerbe Road School

I have spent my whole life in the very haunted town of Shreveport, Louisiana, where there's a burned-up abandoned school on Ellerbe Road. The Old Ellerbe Road School is huge, with four wings and a gymnasium, but it closed down because of a janitor who vanished one day. His car was still in the parking lot, but he was nowhere to be found. Rumors started swirling, and a few kids in the school decided they would find the janitor and rescue him. They arranged a sleepover, sneaked out of the house, and made their way to the school. No one knows what happened next, because they too were never seen again. Hysteria sprung up around town—children were petrified, and parents were frenzied—and so the school closed down. It never opened again.

Nowadays if you go in there at night, you can hear the sounds of children playing in the distance. No matter where you go, it sounds far away. If you run to the sound, it seems to move and be in a different spot by the time you get to where you thought it was. A school bell sounds, even though the school doesn't even have electricity anymore. And people tell me they've seen strange lights coming from the windows of the school at night.

I have been inside and seen pentagrams and other strange symbols painted on the walls of the school. Be careful of those Satan worshippers—I have heard that they are a vicious bunch who have performed human sacrifices inside the building.

Though I have not been able to locate it myself, they say that in one of the wings all the lockers have been removed. In their place someone has painted a huge mural of the Grim Reaper. While I do want to see it for myself, I'm also frightened to find it.—*Tex LaRone*

Jesse Lee Home, and many report hearing strange sounds emanate from within it. Most often, the sound of a group of children giggling is heard. Others have reported hearing children playing outside, even though no children are there.

In life, the children of the Jesse Lee Home had it rough. In death, they witnessed destruction that must have looked like the entire world ending. It's hardly surprising that this abandoned building now serves as home to their lost souls, since they had no other home to turn to. But it's also comforting to know that when they're heard among the ruins, they are usually heard laughing and playing.

Insane Adventures

Say the words "lunatic asylum" and many people get a mental image of the raving madman Renfield from *Dracula*, straitjacketed in a damp stone cell, eating flies and spiders. Sadly, at times in the not-so-distant past, this image was not too far from accurate.

Though they started out with the best intentions—and what were then state-of-the-art medical practices—many mental hospitals were reduced by overcrowding and understaffing to little more than gargantuan warehouses in which to lock away the mentally ill.

Advances in medicine and more humane treatment methods made many of these institutions obsolete, so now they lie abandoned, languishing in silence and solitude, hollow husks of their former selves. Like decomposing carcasses of hulking prehistoric behemoths, they deteriorate on the outskirts of towns throughout the nation, slowly being reclaimed by nature.

The powerful presence of these magnificent monuments to mental illness has not diminished. In fact, in their abandoned state, ancient asylums evoke even more inspiration and personal reflection. They radiate an almost supernatural aura, dark and somber, melancholy and mournful. These days, there seem to be abandoned—or partially abandoned—mental institutions wherever we go in our travels. Perhaps the most magnificent and awe-inspiring of all these is Danvers State Hospital in Massachusetts—the dark castle on the hill.

Danvers State Hospital: The Castle of Lost Souls

For the past seventeen years I have been obsessed with an abandoned lunatic hospital. Perched on a hill north of Danvers, Massachusetts, on Interstate 95, stands the foreboding tree-shrouded silhouette of Danvers State Hospital, its distinctive Gothic architecture now far along the road of decay.

Parents used to threaten disobedient children with a corrective trip to the "Witches' Castle," probably unaware of the connection between Danvers and witches. The Salem witch hysteria and trials did not occur in Salem, but in Salem Village, which is present-day Danvers. The most fanatical judge of the witch trials, Johnathan Hathorne, lived exactly where the hospital was later constructed.

I first encountered Danvers State Hospital on a hot and

hospital's labyrinthine depths, pored over its records, and interviewed former employees and patients. This is a very brief look at its story.

Danvers Lunatic Hospital was built during the 1870s—a time of deep social commitment to the mentally ill. The noted Boston architect Nathaniel Bradlee designed the massive domestic Gothic structure, drawing inspiration from the "guiding spirit of the model-hospital building," Thomas Story Kirkbride. The superintendent of the Pennsylvania Hospital for the Insane, Kirkbride pioneered an institutional design that he believed would help cure eighty percent of its patients. Lighting and ventilation were essential elements of the Kirkbride plan. Hospitals featured wings radiating off a center section, so that each ward had proper ventilation and an unobstructed view of the grounds. By leaving open spaces at the end of each wing, Kirkbride believed "the darkest, most cheerless and worst ventilated parts" could be eliminated.

At Danvers this complex design featured a mile-long foundation wall made of fifteen hundred tons of stone, arranged into more than 240 angles. The floor area totaled 700,000 square feet, and the roof surface topped 325,000 square feet. And the exorbitant construction cost of just under $1.5 million drew public criticism. People in the town called it "the Castle" not just because of its architecture, but out of envy and bitterness. The conditions in the hospital seemed vastly superior to the almshouses and prisons—and the town itself.

When it opened in 1876, Danvers was considered a leader in humane treatment. The patients' regimen involved exercise and the creation of elaborate gardens. The patient-run farm produced large harvests that kept the institution's kitchen busy. But some difficult patient populations brought problems with them. A large and unwanted influx of criminals stirred things up, though

sultry evening in the summer of 1986. I was a residential counselor in a nearby group home, returning a resident who had been out on a pass. I sat in the van at "the Castle," and the main hospital building, which had been shut down for four years, cast its dark shadow across the curving brick driveways and the burned-grass campus. My imagination fed on the texture and pattern of Danvers—its time-stained brick, rusted mesh screens, decaying vents and turrets; its tar-stained roofs with their green copper valleys and their elaborately designed brick eaves. As I sat transfixed, a man's head suddenly appeared in the car's passenger window. His face taut with anxiety, he repeatedly asked, "I'm not going to die, am I?" I told him no, and apparently that was good enough for him, because he then wandered off.

Since that first encounter I have tramped the grounds, drawn the buildings from every angle, explored the

the 1886 construction of a hospital for the criminally insane in Bridgewater, Massachusetts, helped stem this tide. Another difficult group to treat were those suffering from intemperance and dipsomania—the nineteenth-century terms for substance abuse, or "the ancient enemy," as administrators called it. In addition, mentally retarded patients mixed in with the general psychiatric population—it was not until around 1980 that they were moved to their own unit.

By the 1920s the hospital's overcrowded wards and the prevailing psychiatric "faith-cure artists" took their toll. Around 1930 the hospital's formerly expressive annual reports became statistical repositories supporting the clinical triad of psychotherapy, hydrotherapy, and occupational therapy. These reports hid a sad fact: The hospital's founding tenet of moral treatment had completely dissolved. Danvers was becoming just another "snake pit." Its superintendents had seen this sad state of affairs well in advance, but their warnings of "the evils of overcrowding" and requests for state funding went unheeded.

The hospital had been designed for 450 patients, 600 if the attics were full. By the 1940s and 1950s it held up to 2600 patients. Danvers had become overcrowded and understaffed. To keep its burgeoning census under control, the staff used shock treatment, hydrotherapy (including continuous baths), insulin-shock therapy, psychosurgery, and industrial therapy. Crumbling plaster, wall stains, and holes created a general sense of physical decay. Poorly clothed and sometimes naked, legions of lost souls paced aimlessly on the wards, lying on the filthy cement floors, or sitting head in hand against the pockmarked walls.

Danvers continued its downward spiral until it was shut down in the summer of 1992.

I've had several opportunities to study this gargantuan wreck after the hospital closed. Wing "A," on the eastern side, continually drew my attention. It was a ghostly section of the Castle, located next to a beautiful field of colorful flowers, majestic gnarled trees, and high grass (which, according to my interviewees, used to supply cover for patients having sex). Out of the bucolic splendor rose dark and stained turrets with forlorn barred windows. On a late afternoon visit I watched the sun's rays reflect from an arched attic window in a ravaged section of the slate roof. Sinewy tendrils of ivy crept inside the window, disappearing into the inky depths. I wondered, What energy dwelled in that forgotten part of the world? Who once inhabited that remote room?

On another visit the snow was piled several feet deep on the ground and clung to the dilapidated slate roofs, so that their white shapes stood out starkly against the leaden-gray winter sky. I was struck by the sight of one particular window. It rose as a small point directly behind a rectangular addition built in 1920. It was not a prominent window—it was small, not high off the ground—and the frozen snow provided me with a base on which to stand and look inside. I felt as if I were peering into the soul of Danvers, contemplating the myriad tragedies, fears, hopes, and dreams contained within.

In an effort to understand the bedlam, I interviewed a number of ex-employees and ex-patients. The one irrefutable conclusion is that people either loved or despised the place. Both points of view were held with

equal passion. One person would tell me, "Danvers was a beautiful place, so peaceful, and what a view!" Another would say, "That place is the Witch's Castle—right out of Edgar Allan Poe. There were maggots in the food there!"

In an article titled "Too Many Patients to Treat, Human Flood Turned Hospital into Madhouse," which appeared in the September 6, 1987, *Lynn Sunday Post,* reporter David Marrs wrote: "Stories like the tale of a boy whose mother could not discipline him anymore and decided to place him at Danvers State for 'treatment' are not unusual. Forty years later, when asked to sign his name, he held the pad and pencil, and in a rough free-hand sketch, drew a picture of the hospital."

After the hospital's closure an organization of ex-patients and their allies formed to close a final chapter on the hospital. For more than thirty years graveyards stood untended on the grounds, marked with numbered stones and no names—and the state had lost records of which name went with which grave number. The Danvers Memorial Committee dedicated itself to remembering those former residents interred there. They researched the death certificates at the respective town halls in order to identify the buried. And in November of 1998 they held a service to commemorate the grave sites. The day was cold and blustery as some sixty members of the committee, a state representative, and several members of the media convened to witness the blessing. At one point they released balloons to symbolize "the letting go of the stigma of the past and the beginning of a new age of respect and dignity for people with mental illness," according to a pamphlet published by the Danvers State Memorial Committee.

A tour of the two graveyards followed the ceremony. It was an unforgettable experience, walking through the recently cleared site, looking at the rows of circular stone markers, each with a number on top. I found myself reading the numbers as we walked past the remains of more than seven hundred people. Each had been a unique individual in life, yet here they were unnamed and unacknowledged in death. Like many of the complex issues at Danvers, it went far beyond my ability to convey. My obsession with the place continues.—*Michael Ramseur*

Asylums of Connecticut: Remnants of Permanence

High on a hill overlooking Middletown, Connecticut, is a mental institution constructed in 1868 called the Connecticut Valley Hospital. The facility's buildings range in age from forty to one hundred and thirty years old. Some of the older buildings are slated for renovation and others for demolition. I was invited to document these places before they were lost.

Before I started this project, I thought it would be a great adventure to explore old and eerie abandoned mental hospitals in the state. After I had spent several days photographing these places, I began to feel that they had a lot to teach me.

When I am in these buildings, I have learned to quiet my mind and see as clearly and compassionately as possible what they have to say. This project has opened my life to a topic that I assumed I understood—mental illness. My reeducation led me to feel and see the legacy of ignorance and presumption that caused further suffering for those seeking refuge from their already difficult lives.

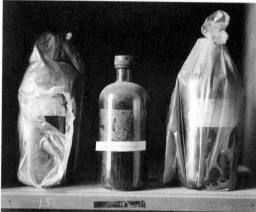

Norwich Hospital for the Insane

The Norwich Hospital for the Insane opened its doors in 1904. Originally designed to hold just a few hundred patients at most, the hospital quickly grew into one of the most infamous in all of New England.

During its operation, Norwich adapted to the shifting attitudes of the public toward mental health. Some years saw dozens of patients pass through, while others saw thousands. As patients flooded into the facility, the hospital grew from a single patient building on less than one hundred acres to dozens of buildings on over nine hundred acres. The complex included over twenty patient buildings, an administration building, a greenhouse, industrial buildings, and an employee clubhouse.

The peak of the hospital's use was in 1955, when 3186 patients were living on the premises. During the '70s, the hospital's usefulness was brought into question. Those confined there were staying for shorter and shorter stints, as public opinion shifted away from hospital care to treatment by families and communities. Norwich saw a sharp decline in the number of patients, until it was finally abandoned. Nowadays it stands in ruins as a reminder of the past.

Fairfield State Hospital

The Fairfield State Hospital, more recently called Fairfield Hills, was established in 1932 as an institution for mental patients. The campus sits on eight hundred acres on the outskirts of Newtown, in the greater Danbury area. Facilities included a dozen major buildings as well as staff housing, a sewage treatment plant, and a large farm. In 1998 Fairfield Hills consisted of one hundred buildings on a 185-acre campus. The institution is now closed, and the Newtown community is currently considering options for new uses for the complex.—*Chad Kleitsch*

Going Mental

In my town of Newtown, Connecticut, there is an abandoned mental institution called Fairfield Hills Hospital. A few of the buildings are still occupied by the parks and recreation department and the department of transportation, but most of the complex is abandoned and in disrepair. A few years ago it was used for scenes in the movie *Sleepers,* with Robert De Niro, Brad Pitt, and Kevin Bacon, where it was transformed into the Wilkinson Home for Boys.

Rumor has it that the entire hospital is connected by underground tunnels. In my senior year of high school my friends and I decided to check it out. We parked our cars by one of the baseball fields and walked to a building called the Cochran House. We went in through a broken window on the first floor. It was damp and dark. We made our way to the basement and found the entrance to a tunnel. We kept walking and came upon a door to what appeared to be an old movie theater. The screen had a huge rip down the middle of it, and it was eerie as hell. We continued down the tunnels for a while, but we didn't stick around too long, because we were afraid of getting arrested.

A kid I worked with somehow obtained a map of the entire hospital. He told me that he and some friends had found the morgue. There is also supposed to be a bowling alley somewhere. There is a lot that I haven't explored yet that I plan to see this summer.—*Randy Calderone*

An Asylum Called Eloise

The asylum in which this story takes place is in the Westland area of Michigan. The whole of Westland was once a city for the insane and the terminally ill poor who couldn't afford the care they needed. The place was named Eloise after the founding physician's daughter, and it lasted until 1981, when all but three buildings were closed and left to deteriorate.

When I was in my teenage I-want-to-be-scared stage, only the three dilapidated buildings remained on the hospital side of Michigan Avenue, and on the farm side stood the piggery, the cannery, and the train depot. My friends and I were very taken with the buildings and toured them many a late night. Though we often saw cops patrolling the area, they never saw us.

Upon entering the first of the old hospital's many steel back doors, we chose to go downstairs first. In the ruined basement our flashlights played upon five-foot-tall metal criblike enclosures and a metal straight-backed chair with leather straps on the armrests and legs. Immediately on the right was the morgue, complete with pull-out drawers and a metal table with leather padding. Also in the basement was a disturbing room only eight by six feet across. Along the left side was a cell with a swinging door that contained a metal cot bolted to the wall and a place where the toilet had once been.

My friends and I also searched the farm side of the area and first entered the piggery, complete with ton scale, meat hooks, and ten-by-ten-foot coolers. The cannery looked as if it had most recently been a file storage area.

Now all but two of the buildings are gone. The place still gives off an eerie feeling as you drive past the lone sentry of many generations of abuse: the smokestack, on which is clearly printed ELOISE. But despite the many ghost stories, the thing I remember most is the feeling of sadness and sorrow mixed with the feeling of safety and protection as we walked through the broken halls where so many were tortured and died.–*Nite Wolfe*

Waverly Hills Sanatorium Is a Real Haunt

After three years in Louisville, I'm starting to learn a few things about "Weird Kentucky." One of the famous local sites is Waverly Hills Sanatorium. It was a tuberculosis hospital at the beginning of the twentieth century and later a mental hospital. The building has been abandoned since 1980 or so. During the Halloween season they hold haunted tours there, and I have heard many media people tell stories of how their equipment stops working or they have other strange experiences. They say things like, "I'm going to the other Halloween haunted houses. You know they are just theater—this one is for real!"–*Judi Schneider*

The Hell That Is Byberry

As you walk down a dark hallway, the smell of death and decay ambushes your senses. Faint screams in the background set your heart racing. Satanic markings cover the halls like demonic wallpaper. You notice bloodstains on the floor and wonder, Where the HELL am I? You're not in hell, but you're close. You're in Byberry Mental Hospital.

In 1732 the insane of Philadelphia, along with orphans and the elderly, were housed in the Philadelphia Almhouse. It expanded and changed locations several times before tragedy struck on February 12, 1885, only two years after it relocated to the Blockley section of West Philadelphia. One of the Blockley buildings caught fire, and because all the patients were shackled together, many burned to death.

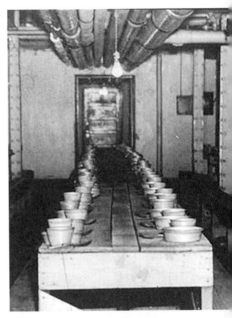

After the fire the city started to look for a new location to house the insane. More than twenty years later the city council bought 874 acres of farmland in the suburb of Byberry. Byberry was the former home of Benjamin Rush, the eighteenth-century doctor who made major advances in the field of psychology. Rush believed that insanity was a disease rather than a spiritual symptom, and although he died almost a century earlier, his influence lived on. The new facility near his former home would be known as Byberry City Farms.

On July 3, 1907, six patients were moved there from Blockley. Their relatives were excited about the new and improved facilities, but it would not be long before their minds would be changed.

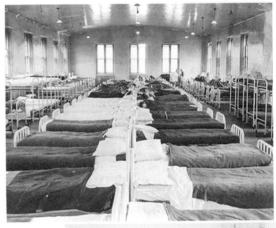

Over the years the city of Philadelphia added more buildings and changed the name of the facility to the Philadelphia State Hospital. The asylum soon became overcrowded and under-staffed. Reports of patients being abused and killed were not uncommon. Patients would sleep naked on floors, in hallways, and in the basements. Some became extremely violent and started to kill each other or commit suicide.

In his book *Great and Desperate Cures* (Basic Books, 1986), Elliott S. Valenstein described the state of mental care in the United States at the time:

It was a hopeless, depressing atmosphere; staff psychiatrists themselves had to struggle not to be engulfed by it. A series of exposés in the 1930s and 1940s describing the "ugly," "crowded," "incompetent," "perverse," "neglectful," "callous," "abusive," and "oppressive" conditions in state mental hospitals effected little change.

Patients were beaten, choked, and spat on by attendants. They were put in dark, damp, padded cells and often restrained in straitjackets at night for weeks at a time. *LIFE* magazine's article, "Bedlam 1946," vividly described the deplorable conditions that existed in most of the 180 state mental institutions, which were said to have degenerated "into little more than concentration camps on the Belsen pattern." A photograph taken at Philadelphia's Byberry Hospital showed nude male patients on concrete floors. They were given "no clothes to wear and live in filth," with neither exercise nor any other activity or therapy to relieve them.

The federal government decided to take over Byberry, but the abuse and torture continued. After much legislation the decision was made to shut Byberry down in the 1980s. About thirty buildings were abandoned at that time, and before long people began looting the buildings.

Numerous bodies have been found in or around Byberry, and the police have stated that they think the murders/suicides had something to do with the abandoned hospital. Some people even claim that Byberry is possessed. Allegedly a satanic cult took over the institution and desecrated the hallways with their evil markings. You can still see remains of animals sacrificed for their rituals. Dogs hang from ceilings, chickens with their heads cut off lie on the floor, and bloodstains serve as a testament to the horror of this cult. The police have found bodies around Byberry that were all cut up.

My neighborhood organized a meeting with the Philadelphia police to get rid of the devil worshippers. The big field in front of my house and behind Byberry was filled with cop cars, and my neighbors were right behind them. I think that the raid must have worked, but who knows? The cult could have just moved deeper into the darker recesses of the forlorn buildings.–*Mark Werner*

Spirit Boy and the Burnt Room

I have been in Byberry three times. The first time nothing special happened—it was basically a feeling-out process. A group of seven of us wanted to see where we could park, how long we could stay, and what we should expect. The second time, we parked by a corner store about a quarter of a mile from the entrance. We were in there about four hours, and we covered a lot of ground in one of the buildings north of Byberry Road and west of Roosevelt Blvd. The place is destroyed, and there is graffiti all over the place. All the windows inside and out are busted—the outside ones are boarded up.

This was the trip that freaked me out. On the third floor one room was blocked by a huge steel door. We wanted to see inside—and when I opened the door, the room was burnt to a crisp. I didn't see anything much, but a couple of friends and I felt something . . . this presence that didn't want us there. It was like pure hatred.

The next night I had a really weird dream. I was lying in my bed, and, in the dream, I woke up. This little boy was standing in my room. He looked like a normal nine- or ten-year-old child, with black pants, red T-shirt, and dirty blond hair that looked messed up. I couldn't move or talk. He just looked at me and said, "I don't come into your house, don't come into mine." All I could do was nod, and he turned around and walked away. I woke up in a cold sweat. Although it freaked me out, it didn't stop me from going back to Byberry.–*Dennis*

Hanging on for Dear Life

One Byberry story has stuck with me over the years. In one of the buildings there is a hole through the floorboards. The story says that gangs would tie a new joiner to a rope and lower them into the hole. The next morning, if the new guy was still on the other end of the rope, he was welcomed into the gang. I've heard that many guys were never pulled back out. —*Jill*

Explorations

Abandoned and decaying, the ivy-covered brick structures of the Philadelphia State Hospital or Byberry, as it is more commonly called, were built in the early 1900s. There are more than ten massive buildings, connected by tunnels through which the patients were transported. There are the cells where they slept, the cafeterias where they ate, and—most terrifying of all—there is the morgue, their final exit from the petrifying lives they lived.

When you walk in, you see piles of rubble from the slowly cracking ceilings and desiccated walls. The floor is covered with broken glass. When you look down the long, dark hallways, every door is open—or broken off and lying on the floor. Some rooms have windows that once let in light, but these are now boarded up, keeping light out forever.

In the patients' rooms, there are scraps of wallpaper glued to pieces of wood, providing a bizarre and depressing ambience. What once was a cot where a patient slept is now just a rusted frame. The ceilings are mostly gone, and the lights are scattered on the floors.

Beneath the ground are tunnels linking the buildings, which people call "the Catacombs." They say it's the best way to explore Byberry, but many homeless people live there, and you take a risk in entering these places

Straight down the tunnels is a place they call "the Echo Hallway" for obvious reasons. After you pass that hallway, the refrigeration building is straight ahead, and to the right of it stands the morgue building. "The Black Hallway" connects the refrigeration and the morgue buildings. The morgue contains ten freezers that once held the bodies of dead patients.

When you visit, be prepared with flashlights and extra batteries. Because once your lights go out, you, like so many others who have stayed at that hospital, will be left confused, frightened, and worst of all, in the dark. —*Sarah G.*

The Graveyard Elm

If spirits truly are the personalities of those who once lived, then surely these spirits reflect whatever turmoil plagued them in life. As proof, you need look no farther than the strange events at the old state mental hospital in Bartonville, Illinois, a small town near Peoria.

In its final years, after the last patients had departed, staff members started to report some odd occurrences in the now empty wards and cells. In more recent years many vandals, trespassers, and curiosity-seekers claim to have had their own weird encounters in the place.

The first ghost story about the hospital came from its founder, Dr. George A. Zeller, who was one of the most influential mental health care providers in Illinois history. Shortly after the hospital opened in 1902, Dr. Zeller supervised the creation of cemeteries for the facility and a burial corps to deal with interment. Dr. Zeller's burial corps always consisted of a staff member and several patients competent enough to take part in the digging of graves. Of all the gravediggers, the most unusual man was a fellow called A. Bookbinder. Old Book, as he was affectionately known, had come to the hospital from a county poorhouse. He had suffered a mental breakdown and lost the power of coherent speech while working in a printing house in Chicago. The officer who had taken him into custody had noted in his report that the man had been employed as a bookbinder, and a court clerk inadvertently listed this as the man's name. After Old Book was attached to the burial corps, attendants soon realized that he was especially suited to the work. During Old Book's first interment he removed his cap and began to weep loudly for the dead man.

"His emotion became contagious and there were many moist eyes at the graveside," Dr. Zeller wrote.

Old Book would do the same thing at each service. As his grief reached its peak, he would lean against an old elm tree in the center of the cemetery and sob loudly. Eventually Old Book died. More than one hundred nurses attended his funeral, along with male staff members and several hundred patients. As the last hymn was sung, four men grabbed the ropes holding the casket above the empty grave.

"At a given signal," Dr. Zeller wrote, "they heaved away the ropes and the next instant, all four lay on their backs. For the coffin, instead of offering resistance, bounded into the air like an eggshell, as if it were empty!"

"In the midst of the commotion," Dr. Zeller continued, "a wailing voice was heard and every eye turned toward the Graveyard Elm from whence it emanated. . . . There stood Old Book, weeping and moaning with an earnestness that outrivaled anything he had ever shown before. . . . It was broad daylight and there could be no deception."

After a few moments the doctor summoned some men to remove the lid of the coffin. As soon as the lid was lifted, the wailing sound came to an end. Inside the casket lay the body of Old Book, unquestionably dead. Everybody looked over to the elm tree. The specter had vanished!

"It was awful, but it was real," Dr. Zeller concluded. "I saw it, 100 nurses saw it and 300 spectators saw it." If it was anything other than the ghost of Old Book, Dr. Zeller had no idea what it could have been.

A few days after the funeral the Graveyard Elm began to wither, and within the year it died. Later workmen tried to cut down the tree but stopped after the first cut of the axe caused the tree to emit what was said to be "an agonized, despairing cry of pain." After that Dr. Zeller suggested that the tree be burned, but as soon as the fire started around its base, the workers, hearing a crying sound coming from the tree, quickly put out the flames.

The hospital was finally closed down in 1972 and remained empty for a number of years before being sold at auction in 1980.

Even though the site is private property and trespassing is forbidden, vandals and would-be ghost hunters still enter the place. Many claim to have encountered some pretty frightening things, from unexplained sounds to full-blown apparitions. Some might even say that many of the former patients are still around!

"The place is full of spirits" has been said on more than one occasion. I wouldn't be surprised if this proclamation is right.–*Troy Taylor*

The Gravedigger's Ghost

The Bartonville asylum is haunted. There are four different buildings and a lot of hidden passageways. One part that is boarded up used to be the shower room and was thought to be a torture chamber. We went into one of the buildings last summer, and it was freaky. It was ninety-five degrees out, but as soon as we went into the building, the temperature dropped to below thirty. There was a downstairs, and we were going to go down into it, but we heard a lot of stuff, then left in a hurry.

I have been back since, but never went in. I just went to the graveyard. That place is very haunted. There is a ghost of a gravedigger that we have seen under a weeping willow.–*Chris B.*

Played by the Piano

As you walk up to it, the Lakeland asylum building in Blackwood, New Jersey, looms ominously. Its windows are boarded up, and the doors are chained. In one of the hallways there are bloodstains. There are medical files everywhere, and old hospital beds line the hallways. The place is said to be haunted, and there is definitely a force that wants all outsiders to stay out. The sixth floor is the weirdest. Every floor has a recreation room with a piano, but the one on the sixth floor works, and as you walk through the halls on that floor, you can hear keystrokes.–*XOpRiNcEsS331*

Squeals in the Night

What could be spookier than an abandoned slaughterhouse on the grounds of an abandoned asylum? In the town of Marlboro, New Jersey, stands an old piggery that once fed the inmates of the Marlboro Psychiatric Hospital. It sits all alone in the middle of a vast fallow, unattended farm field. Some say on quiet nights you can still hear the high-pitched death squeals of livestock being butchered there.

Slaughterhouse Rules

The Marlboro slaughterhouse terrified me as a child. It is by far the creepiest place I have ever seen and has haunted my dreams since before I even first laid eyes on it. And spending my formative years in the shadow of the Marlboro Psychiatric Hospital weighed heavily on my mind. Lying in bed at night knowing that hundreds of demented souls lay just a stone's throw away was none too comforting for a young boy with an overactive imagination.

More terrifying, though, were the stories that the older kids told of the slaughterhouse. I heard that sometimes people who live close to the old farm still hear the faint sounds of animals in their death throes emanating from the building's ruins.

Around the time I was sixteen, I decided to face my fears and finally visit the place. To get to the slaughterhouse today you have to walk across vast overgrown fields into the woods. The pavement is old and cracked, with weeds poking up through it. Near the end of the road you see this huge white wooden building rising up out of a tangle of vines and thorn bushes. Outside, there are animal cages, pens, and mangerlike structures.

I rallied my courage enough to enter the building. I saw a long dark room with pens and cages for the pigs that would be the next to die. On the floor of this room were painted the words DEATH ROW. I turned a corner out of the paddock area and found myself standing right in front of an enormous walk-in freezer, with a huge steel door and an overhead track from which the butchered livestock once hung. On the walls of this room the words I SEE YOU and ALL WILL DIE TONIGHT were sprayed on the walls in blood-red paint.

This made everything that I had heard about this place seem suddenly all too real to me. As I inched my way into the freezer, I felt a sudden chill run through my entire body, so I rushed out into the next room. This didn't do much to calm my jangled nerves, though, as I realized I had just entered the killing room itself! There were iron rings affixed to the walls where they would tie up the animals to prepare them for the knife. The floor was graded slightly downward toward a large drain in the middle, where the spilled blood of the butchered beasts could be neatly hosed away.

I don't believe that a bat out of hell could have beaten a hastier retreat than I made from the slaughterhouse that evening.

–Shaggy Doo

The time for exploring these massive abandoned asylums may soon come to an end. But surely some of these awe-inspiring structures will survive demolition and redevelopment so that future generations will have a place to point to, telling tales of what may be found beyond their darkened thresholds. We all need mystery and wonder in our lives, and there may be no better way to fire the imagination than to let your mind go wandering into places where your feet dare not tread.

THE END?

*"Take a right at the light, keep going straight until night,
and then boys you're on your own."*
–*Bruce Springsteen,* Blinded by the Light

I n the end, whether all these stories of ghosts, satanists, strange
creatures and otherworldly encounters are true or not doesn't
really matter. All that really matters is that the stories are still
alive and being told and retold, and enjoyed by people of all
ages throughout the country. These tales are an important part of
our collective history and shared modern folklore. They speak
volumes about who we are, and reveal our innermost curiosities
and fears. They open our minds to the possibility that there is
something out there that is beyond our realm of knowledge and
comprehension—something mysterious and powerful. These
stories challenge us to define the boundaries of our own beliefs
and reexamine our ideas of what is real and what is imagined.
Based on these determinations each of us must decide which
road in life to take—the safe and well-traveled one or the weird
one leading off to parts unknown.

We're sure by now you can guess which one you'll find us
riding on.

INDEX

Page numbers in **bold** refer to photos and illustrations.

WEIRD U.S.

by
Mark Moran and Mark Sceurman

Co-Authors:
Troy Taylor
Chris Gethard

Contributing Authors:
Jeff Bahr
Jeff Belanger
Daniel V. Boudillion
Charlie Carlson
Loren Coleman
Pat Fitzhugh
Linda Godfrey
Larry Harris
Rick Hendricks
Matt Lake
Jim Miles
Dr. Seymour O'Life
Ryan Orvis
Michael Ramseur
Timothy Renner
Shady
James Willis

Publisher: Barbara J. Morgan
Assoc. Managing Editor: Emily Seese
Editor: Matt Lake
Production: Della R. Mancuso
Mancuso Associates, Inc., North Salem, NY

PICTURE CREDITS

EDITORIAL CREDITS

SHOW US YOUR WEIRD!

Do you know of a weird site found somewhere in the United States, or can you tell us about a strange experience you've had? If so, we'd like to hear about it! We believe that every town has at least one great tale to tell, and we're listening. It could be a cursed road, haunted abandoned site, odd local character, or bizarre historic event. In most cases these tales are told only in the towns in which they originated. But why keep them to yourself when you could share them with all of America? So come on and fill us in on all the weirdness that's lurking in your backyard!

You can e-mail us at: Editor@WeirdUS.com,
or write to us at:
Weird U.S., P.O. Box 1346, Bloomfield, NJ 07003.

www.weirdus.com